"Anthony Trotta has significantly elevated the discourse on a core tension in American public policy: expert knowledge vs. participatory democracy. Technological determinism—rational, unbiased, efficient—is widely assumed to be the overarching architecture of American progress. Trotta, however, broadens and deepens our understanding of public policy tensions via a deep analysis of deliberative democracy—politically oriented, participatory, discursive—that is grounded in an inherent and growing mistrust of government. As such, he presents a valuable framework for understanding the critical and enduring tensions that are enduring threats to American society along political fault lines such as: technological remediation of global warming vs. public resistance to lifestyle disruptions, public health interventions to confront pandemics vs. discomfort with vaccines and stringent shutdowns, and the value of government-issued money vs. cryptocurrencies. Trotta's *Technology and American Democracy* is a welcome addition to university studies and policy debates across economics, technology, political science, cultural studies and beyond."

Marc Holzer, *Distinguished Research Professor at Suffolk University-Boston; Founding Dean of the School of Public Affairs and Administration at Rutgers University; Elected Fellow of the National Academy of Public Administration; Past-President of the American Society for Public Administration*

TECHNOLOGY AND AMERICAN DEMOCRACY

The growth and proliferation of technology in American society places new demands on the U.S. government and the health of its democracy, affecting both policymaking and public administration. *Technology and American Democracy* explores the underpinning democratic theories, including constitutional justifications, that guide decision makers during the application of Information Technology (IT) in governance to promote democratic principles such as transparency and accountability. The book examines the capacity of IT to facilitate deliberative democracy, alter modern bureaucratic structures and functions, and affect areas of public policy including public budgeting and performance measurement.

Author Anthony Trotta demonstrates the ways in which technology creates new problems for contemporary government, including a discussion of virtual currency and its possible issues that must be addressed by the public sector. The discussion avoids highly technical language and confusing industry jargon, focusing instead on explaining important concepts in an accessible fashion, applicable to a broad spectrum of readers. *Technology and American Democracy* is required reading for students enrolled in courses on politics, public administration, and public policy.

Anthony Trotta holds a Ph.D. in Public Administration from the School of Public Affairs and Administration at Rutgers University-Newark and has extensive university-level teaching and course development experience in political science, public administration, and public policy (both in the traditional and virtual classroom) at the undergraduate and graduate levels. Dr. Trotta is also the author of *Advances in E-Governance* (Routledge, 2018).

TECHNOLOGY AND AMERICAN DEMOCRACY

Anthony Trotta

NEW YORK AND LONDON

First published 2024
by Routledge
605 Third Avenue, New York, NY 10158

and by Routledge
4 Park Square, Milton Park, Abingdon, Oxon, OX14 4RN

Routledge is an imprint of the Taylor & Francis Group, an informa business

© 2024 Taylor & Francis

The right of Anthony Trotta to be identified as author of this work has been asserted in accordance with sections 77 and 78 of the Copyright, Designs and Patents Act 1988.

All rights reserved. No part of this book may be reprinted or reproduced or utilised in any form or by any electronic, mechanical, or other means, now known or hereafter invented, including photocopying and recording, or in any information storage or retrieval system, without permission in writing from the publishers.

Trademark notice: Product or corporate names may be trademarks or registered trademarks, and are used only for identification and explanation without intent to infringe.

Library of Congress Cataloging-in-Publication Data
Names: Trotta, Anthony M., 1974– author.
Title: Technology and American democracy / Anthony Trotta.
Description: First edition. | New York : Routledge, 2024. |
Includes bibliographical references and index.
Identifiers: LCCN 2023019675 (print) | LCCN 2023019676 (ebook) |
ISBN 9781032579641 (hbk) | ISBN 9781032579627 (pbk) |
ISBN 9781003441830 (ebk)
Subjects: LCSH: Deliberative democracy—Technological innovations. |
Internet in public administration—United States. | Social media—Political aspects—United States. | Information technology—Political aspects—United States. | Political participation—Technological innovations—United States.
Classification: LCC JC423 .T714 2024 (print) | LCC JC423 (ebook) |
DDC 351.0285/4678—dc23/eng/20230725
LC record available at https://lccn.loc.gov/2023019675
LC ebook record available at https://lccn.loc.gov/2023019676

ISBN: 978-1-032-57964-1 (hbk)
ISBN: 978-1-032-57962-7 (pbk)
ISBN: 978-1-003-44183-0 (ebk)

DOI: 10.4324/9781003441830

Typeset in Sabon
by codeMantra

In Loving Memory of My Grandparents
Josephine and James Bucchio
Mary and Anthony Trotta

CONTENTS

1	Technocracy and Deliberative Democracy	1
2	E-Government and E-Governance	36
3	Technological Determinism: A Technocratic Rationale and American Democracy	86
4	Permissionless Innovation and the Precautionary Principle	113
5	The Concept of Money	141
6	Cryptocurrency, Bitcoin, and the Concept of Money	166
7	Government Regulatory Efforts of the Cryptocurrency Industry in the U.S. Federal System	203
Index		*275*

1

TECHNOCRACY AND DELIBERATIVE DEMOCRACY

Technocracy

Technocracy is among the many politically oriented rationales that have enjoyed some measure of success in achieving a significant enough influential role to allow for its foundational tenants to affect policymaking in the U.S. political system. When the technocratic approach is applied in government this chosen policy path forward will correspondingly dictate a wide range of behavioral dynamics between system actors participating within the U.S. political system. Simply put, the idea of technocracy is one that places expert knowledge at the forefront of public-sector decision making. To advocates of technocracy, there is a preference for those within a governmental entity that possess specialized, technically oriented knowledge in a field to take a primary role in decision making. Centeno (1993, p. 314) defines technocracy as "the administrative and political domination of a society by a state elite and allied institutions that seek to impose a single, exclusive policy paradigm based on the application of instrumentally rational techniques." As an example of modern elitism, the technocrat is a topical specialist who is required to have some measure of "technical expertise" derived in part from real-world training in a given field and, perhaps most importantly to this ideal, through the act of receiving formal university instruction that yields "advanced educational credentials" (Putnam, 1977, p. 384). Once established, the knowledge held by technocrats is viewed as being able to place the experts in a unique position that allows its practitioners to be better able to assess the circumstances associated with problem identification and in generating policy solutions capable

DOI: 10.4324/9781003441830-1

of addressing such. In this, technocracy is an elitist approach that seeks to utilize expert knowledge to determine ultimate "truths" about society that, once discovered, are believed to be able to better guide decision making in a democratic government (Gaus, Landwehr, and Schmalz-Burns, 2020). The absolute faith in the ability of the technocrat to obtain specialized knowledge, which provides experts an unquestionable advantage in policy-making processes, also corresponds with advocating for other system actors to willingly grant primacy to those practicing this approach during government decision-making endeavors. In this sense, technocracy is often viewed in the context of degrees of control, in that government either comes to purely rely directly on "scientists, technicians, or engineers" or, at minimum, those serving within government base decision making that affects a wide range of official activities by relying on guidance stemming from the "virtue of technical competence and expertise in the application of knowledge" (Gunnel, 1982, p. 392). In addition to investing in the idea that specialized knowledge held by experts provides unique insight better suited to policymaking, the technocratic approach also touts the ability of its practitioners to avoid the politically oriented pitfalls otherwise oft associated with decision making in government. Fischer (1995, p. 11) explains that a "technocratic world view" is one that reflects "a pattern of thought which emphasizes technical solutions to social and political problems." Fischer adds that advocates of the technocratic perspective posit that this approach is capable of providing an important "value free" and "rational" analysis that contributes to policy development by "viewing society and its problems in technical terms." Wickman (2011, paragraph 2) expands on this perspective by noting that a technocrat is "an expert, not a politician. Technocrats make decisions based on specialized information rather than public opinion." Wickman (2011, paragraph 3) adds that, "the word technocrat can also refer to an advocate of a form of government in which experts preside." In sum, technocracy advocates prefer placing experts that have obtained specialized knowledge at the forefront of public-sector decision making. Here, expert knowledge held by technocrats is used to identify and disclose singular, indisputable societal truths and the application of such is deemed a rational means by which to guide decision making that avoids becoming bogged down in biased, irrational debates from among a wide array of policy actors attempting to advance their own politically driven agendas. Inherent within technocracy is a preference for expert, specialized knowledge to be used as the standard by which government decision making is predicated upon which by extension calls for a diminished role for non-experts from both within government and from among the public at large. For the technocrat, government actions based on specialized knowledge held by experts is viewed as being preferable to traditional decision making in a democracy that includes system actors engaged in biased, politically oriented maneuverings attempting to achieve official outcomes that serve to advance individualized preferences and pander to public sentiment instead of opting for the pursuit of a technically focused policy path.

In the U.S. political system, the emergence of technocracy is the result of less than favorable perceptions of government's capacity to fulfill its duties that is held by significant levels of system actors clamoring for change. Understandably, a diminishing faith in the public sector would cause the policy pendulum to swing in favor of those supporting a growing need for expertise to play a more influential role in public-sector decision making because of circumstances that may have called into question the ability of government to perform as expected at that time. The role of a vast cavalcade of self-interested and biased system actors engaging in endless episodes of political maneuvering in the hopes of affecting government actions is viewed by technocrats as creating a systemic issue affecting the government's ability to fulfill its duties efficiently and effectively as required. In general, a technocratic approach may be given more opportunity for wide-scale government expansion in circumstances in which there has been significantly diminished levels of "trust in pre-existing political-administrative systems" (Campbell, 2019, p. 5). Here, system actors' trust in government performance becomes diminished to the point where an opportunity for a different approach to public-sector decision making would become manifest, in that the influence of politics was preferred to be secondary to specialized knowledge held by experts. Technocrats, "whose separateness from (and perhaps ignorance of) the local political context" is viewed as an asset because it allows for impartial decision making predicated on technical proficiency to supersede the influence of political bias on the processes affecting government outcomes (Campbell, 2019, p. 5). In circumstances where levels of accountability throughout "democratic institutions" are thought to have decreased significantly, there may be a call to increase technocratic actions to serve as a corrective, counter-balancing measure to compensate for diminished levels of responsibility in government (Campbell, 2019, p. 6). Fischer (1995, pp. 11–12) observed that "technocratic policy analysis is thus a matter of uniformly applying empirically based technical methodologies, such as cost-benefit analysis and risk assessment, to the technical aspects of all policy problems." In relation, technocrats often validate any failures to strictly adhere to the expectations of a democratic system as being a necessary and justifiable sacrifice that was made in pursuit of efficient government (Meynaud, 1964, p. 154). In all, technocrats having lost some measure of faith in government actions derived from politicized discourse between system actors then advocate for

4 Technocracy and Deliberative Democracy

a more rationally oriented approach that relies heavily on expert knowledge. In this way, technocrats wield expert knowledge to defend against decision-making processes from traditionally facilitated discourse among biased system actors collectively seeking to generate government outcomes that represent politically charged preferences at the expense of an efficient and effective public sector.

Advocates of technocracy posit that there is great merit in efforts to reduce the opportunity for system actors to engage in democratically oriented debates where those competing for political influence craft value-based arguments in order to gain the support of other system actors. In this scenario, success in argumentative discourse is an endeavor that results in being able to dictate the direction of government in some way. Instead, the technocratic approach to policymaking denotes an authoritarian process that generally is unfavorable to the primary influence of dialogue between interested parties seeking to reach agreement regarding "values or ends" (Centeno, 1993, p. 327). The arguable assertion that technocracy's usage in governance inherently reflects "methodological objectivity" that should be beyond reproach also portrays those that choose to dispute its application as being "irrational" or "self-interested" in order to frame opponents as having no legitimate claim to the appeals against its wide-scale application (Centeno, 1993, p. 327). Here, technocrats attempt to portray those in opposition to the unchallenged application of this approach as being negligently self-serving in which the very act of contending the validity of technocracy renders the dispute, and the disputer, as lacking the requisite levels of rationality needed to reasonably offer a responsible or convincing response. Furthermore, advocates defend technocracy as being an indisputably exceptional means by which to guide decision making by further critiquing traditional democratic processes that, in their eyes, most often yields less than adequate policy choices. The application of technocracy in policymaking is grounded in part on the perceived benefits of utilizing decision making based on "logic, rationality and evidence" as opposed to the democratic approach that could conceivably thoughtlessly follow the public will wherever it may lead (Gilley, 2017, p. 15). Relatedly, such critiques of the democratic approach include the observation that public-policy development that bypassed technocracy simply to ensure that the participatory procedures are observed during decision making does not mean that the end result will suitably address the issue(s) at hand (Gilley, 2017, p. 16). Also, technocrats assert that the claim that public policy derived from democratic debates involving system actors is more likely "to generate ideal policies" may often be something of a fallacy (Gilley, 2017, p. 16). In general, the technocrat posits that public policy solely derived from participatory procedures fails to guarantee that the chosen path by government will be able to affect the political system as intended simply because popular support was ultimately used to help guide the decision. Although it may be politically prudent for democratic actions to reflect popular sentiment to some degree, it is uncertain that the resulting public policy that is crafted based on this lone premise will be effective in addressing the needs of the system. For the technocrat, government decision making based on an assessment of what constitutes the public will that is determined by interested parties engaged in deliberations is not a foolproof means to solve all manner of problems in all areas of public policy. This is especially relevant in cases where technocracy would have been useful to provide expert guidance capable of crafting and refining a public policy to potentially make it capable of achieving desired ends. The technocratic argument is based partly on the assessment that simply providing opportunities for system actors to engage in discursive events fails to guarantee that resulting policy actions will be best for society. To the technocrat, there is great merit in this argument as evidenced by the fact that democratic government processes often yield ineffective and inefficient policies. Relatedly, power dynamics inherent within the political system may in some cases result in a policy path that is neither wholly useful nor broadly appealing, which may have been avoided if technocracy had been used to guide decision making.

Ultimately, technocracy is promoted as a means by which technically oriented, unbiased government actions will be capable of restoring the trust lost by citizens in the capacity of the public sector to perform as expected. This trust was ultimately diminished by citizens bearing witness to unnumerable acts of perceived failed governance that were the result of traditional democratic processes. In this context, a technocratic attempt to repair citizens' trust occurs when traditional democratic processes by which participants would deliberate over various societal values in order to reach agreement on official actions (i.e. passing legislation, developing internal policy actions for an agency, allocating fiscal resources associated with the public budget, etc.) is supplanted by experts applying specialized knowledge as the default means by which to guide decision making. In the technocratic scenario, deferring to experts with specialized knowledge is thought to provide government with the opportunity to develop public policy that is more capable of achieving system goals associated with effective and efficient actions. Adoption of technocracy would provide a means for government to avoid becoming the exclusive domain of politically motivated participants reflecting irrational, biased preferences that most often led the way in public-sector decision making with a democracy. The technocrat posits that deliberative dynamics in action largely served to diminish the ability of the public sector to maintain proficiency in serving

6 Technocracy and Deliberative Democracy

its citizens and, if left unchecked, would continue to contribute to citizens gradually losing faith in government's capacity to fulfill its expected duties as needed. For those advocating for the adoption of this approach, the practice of technocratically derived actions taking precedence over traditional democratic decision making is viewed as a positive act and even a necessary corrective measure that will improve government's ability fulfill its vast duties while correspondingly augmenting trust held by citizens in the public sector's ability to consistently do so. In relation, the specialized knowledge held by experts is considered by technocrats as being beyond reproach in which it is perceived that factual, unbiased, and rationally achieved decisions are more adroitly applied to guide governance than public policy derived from deliberations between a wide array of system actors competing to impact the system by attempting to advance value-laden arguments promoting personalized agendas steeped in partiality.

Critiques of Technocracy

Despite technocrats' unfettered and unwavering faith in the argument that experts with specialized knowledge are best suited to guide government decision making, there are several critiques associated with this rationale that are deserved of consideration. Among the most significant of these critiques is the fact that technocracy prefers to circumvent the important role that meaningful deliberation plays in guiding the direction of government in the U.S. democratic system. In general, it is far from uncommon that a surplus of technocrats misunderstands and undervalues the intricately nuanced role that politics plays in a modern democratic government (Meynaud, 1964, p. 147–148). As such, the technocrat is adamant that only they can solve the "problems that concern the national interest," which indicates those individuals hold a lack of faith in legislative actors or party politics on this account (Meynaud, 1964, p. 154). The decision to support "technocratic control" as the primary means by which to guide a wide range of government activities, such as policymaking, may to some degree create an environment that is hostile to traditional practices associated with democratic governance (Centeno, 1993, p. 326). Furthermore, this approach officially gaining wide-scale support within government would permit experts to utilize specialized knowledge to guide policymaking in a largely unchallenged capacity and those advocating for the permanence of a technocratic status quo in decision making could seek to suspend traditional participatory actions associated with democracy until a later date when deemed appropriate by them (Centeno, 1993, p. 326). The promotion of technocracy being elevated to primacy as the rationale guiding public-sector decision making is one that mistakenly attempts to cede control to experts in lieu of government actions derived from a wide range of interested parties competing in discursive events as intended in the U.S. deliberative democracy. To unequivocally cede control of the political system to technocrats would systemically create a policy environment that runs counter to expectations associated with deliberative democracy, which promotes the importance of discourse in determining government actions. As such, a key critique of technocracy is predicated on raising concerns for an approach that is singularly focused on maintaining a system that caters to values held by experts rather than dialectic processes focused on identifying and responding to the policy preferences held by system actors. In this way, a key fundamental flaw associated with technocracy is that its standard for guiding government action, which is steeped in expertise and assumed rationality, may lack the requisite applicability expected in a democratic policymaking that requires official choices to be determined by interested parties participating in established deliberative procedures (Gilley, 2017, p. 15). When continued broadscale institutionalization allows for technocracy to become further entrenched in government, this process may further empower the elites supporting and directly practicing this approach to influence a wide range of public sector activities including policymaking (Centeno, 1993, p. 326). Technocracy is a uniquely elite approach that favors expert knowledge playing a primary role in government decision making in which the growing popularity of its functional position may become something of self-fulfilling prophecy in a policymaking sense. Those achieving preferred status in any aspect of decision making may in turn take actions that are geared toward supporting and protecting the continued permeance and permanence of such. In this, technocracy may be revealed as falsely being capable of promoting government actions that are unbiased, as technocrats reflect preferences for the continued usage of this approach that grants its practitioners an unchallenged, elevated role in public-sector decision making.

In the contemporary American democracy, technocracy has found some measure of success in public-sector decision making as responsible governance may require a measured application of technical advice in order to help diagnose and solve complex issues facing society. In this context, technocracy can serve as a valuable supplemental tool used by decision makers in which expertise can be a welcome contributing factor in modern-era governance. There are dangers to consider in becoming too heavily invested in the technocratic approach to the point that ceding decision-making authority to experts becomes an accepted status quo simply because the modern era is fraught with a plethora of complex, technically oriented problems that require the attention of the public sector. If this deference to technocracy is viewed as customary instead of a situational

8 Technocracy and Deliberative Democracy

practice, then there is a wide array of system actors whose comparative lack of expertise topically would serve as a natural barrier to participation in decision-making processes. Anderson (2006, p. 309) notes that in the modern era there is some measure of "technocratization of the policy process," which is caused in part by "the shift in power from congressional committees to subcommittees, increased staff assistance for members of Congress, and the fact that policy problems and issues are becoming more complex and technical." Anderson (2006, p. 309) adds that in some circumstances technocracy being integrated into public-policy dynamics has made it increasingly problematic for "ordinary persons or average citizens" to be engaged in "meaningful participation" due to the necessary threshold of expertise required to contribute to such processes. With the understanding that technocrats are generally averse to the political aspects typically attributed to democratic decision making, advocates of this approach would expect that participants hold some measure of applicable expert knowledge should discussions on the policy path of governance be required. This expectation for expert knowledge serving as a threshold of qualifying for participation in government decision making is problematic in the context of the deliberative system that is inherent in the American democracy. Fischer (2000, p. 23) explains that "it becomes increasingly clear that in many policy domains, politics more and more becomes a struggle between those who have expertise and those who do not." In many areas of public policy, such as those concerning the environment, it is often of great importance for participants to obtain relevant levels of technical knowledge in order to be able to meaningfully participate in political decision-making processes (Fischer, 2000, p. 23). Fischer (2000, p. 23) adds that this dynamic can affect the general public in that "the lack of access to such knowledge hinders the possibility of an active and meaningful involvement." Government mandates that are technocratic in nature may "unduly diminish democratic participation" when the resulting policy is predicated on a deferment to those perceived to be experts in a field without allowing for legitimate deliberations by interested parties over alternative values (Sadowski and Selinger, 2014, p. 3). This deferral to technocracy without allowance for challenge as a standard operating procedure (SOP) during the creation of public policy can cause harm in the political sense, as this tactic "disfranchises citizens and deprives them of appropriate political power" (Sadowski and Selinger, 2014, p. 3). The capacity of technocracy to disenfranchise non-experts should serve as a warning sign that reminds system actors that this option is best reserved as a supplemental tool in American democracy. To automatically accept technocracy as the status quo in government decision making clearly has the potential to disenfranchise a majority of the populous likely lacking the requisite levels of expert knowledge regarding a plethora of highly complex social problems. Pursuit of this policy path also provides tacit acceptance that technocratic preferences for the primacy of expert knowledge in decision making is acceptable and that information-based elitism will triumph over the expectations associated with participation in the U.S. deliberative democracy. On this account, Craig (2014, p. 32) claims that "technocracy is dangerous and ugly, anathema to democratic self-government." Among the many threats that technocracy poses to democracy is that systematic acceptance of this approach can correspondingly result in policy actors habitually "delegating ever more decision-making authority to this technocratic elite," which may promote "apathy and depoliticization in the citizenry" (Craig, 2014, p. 32). As the technocratic approach becomes further embedded in government decision making those once staunchly vested in the importance of being a "self-governing citizen, vigilant and prickly" that actively defend the importance of self-determination becomes transformed into a "timid and deferential client of an ever-growing state, dominated by a small cadre of elites armed with special knowledge" (Craig, 2014, p. 32). Here, technocracy, if left unchecked, could supplant the traditional means by which government decision making is expected to be facilitated in the context of American democracy. Instead of a civically minded public consistently interested and actively engaged in the democratic processes by which government decision making is facilitated, technocracy as common practice would relegate citizens to the role of disinterested spectator.

There may also be functionally oriented issues associated with the pursuit of a technocratic path regarding the absence of the requisite political ability and authority of the technocrat to clear the proverbial political path to allow for this change in decision making to take place. In this sense, technocrats may lack a requisite "sense of authority" as it relates to the ability to utilize influence to ensure compliance among system actors and the aptitude to persuade others to acquiesce to preferences as is commonplace by a wide range of key participants within the political arena (Meynaud, 1964, p. 148). Technocrats being averse, or worse unable, to engage in political dynamics associated with policymaking serves as one of the natural system checks keeping this approach from being integrated systematically with any degree of long-running permanence (Putnam, 1977, p. 409). In essence, technocrats may be lacking in the positional authority or political ability that would empower them to establish this perspective as primary in guiding public-sector decision making. Without sufficient representation within the hierarchy of government, technocrats may lack requisite support of those willing to serve as champions of the cause working to institutionalize this approach. Relatedly, technocrats being averse to and lacking faith in the important role that politics plays in American democracy may

10 Technocracy and Deliberative Democracy

limit the reach of technocracy within the political arena, which is largely predicated on dialectic processes that affect outcomes. Ironically, the technocrat's general distaste for decision making that is derived from political maneuvering, as expected in the U.S. deliberative democracy, may work against the ability of technocracy to become entrenched in policymaking to the extent preferred by its practitioners.

In addition to the preference to reduce political deliberations to the periphery of public-sector decision making, the advocates of technocracy also argue that because expert knowledge is believed to be undisputable in nature that this approach should become the institutionalized standard by which all policymaking is based upon from a governmental standpoint. Dahl highlights several weaknesses attributed to the attempt to pursue purely technocratic decision making in government that can be summarized as followed:

> Technocratic decisions may be unsuitable in which there is a question of morality because applying technical knowledge to reach a policy solution is neither applicable nor appropriate in such cases.
>
> Achieving the status of an expert in the modern era requires an individual being entirely focused on the accumulation of knowledge in a single area and this process limits the usefulness of the expert in decision making to that one topic of interest.
>
> The strict adherence to expert knowledge may be unable to address all situations as there are cases in which policy solutions require some measure of instrumental understanding of the real world in which applicable knowledge is individually experiential and observational in nature.
>
> Technocracy is unable to bridge the gap between moral and instrumental aspects that are often required when conducting judicious policymaking capable of satisfying system expectations regarding a public sector that behaves in a responsible manner.
>
> *Source: Dahl (1989, p. 69)*

In addition, there may be some measure of concern associated with the incongruent nature of underlying values represented by technocrats that can call into question unwavering support for this approach. There is often an absence of "cohesiveness of technocrats" as it relates agreeance on the importance of recognizing the role of politics in governance and as it relates to what constitutes how exactly to define "rationality" expected to be used to guide decision making (Putnam, 1977, p. 409). Although agreeing that rationality should take precedence over the political during policymaking, the lack of consensus regarding what constitutes rationality creates a dilemma regarding how this conceptualization will be implemented in practice. In addition, education and training does not guarantee that consensus will be reached—within a given field or between fields—regarding what areas should be the focal point regarding the "substance of policy" and solutions that should be adopted to address any problems (Putnam, 1977, p. 409). The rise of "technically skilled counter-elites" provides further evidence of the important role that "conflict" plays in a modern democracy even between experts deliberating among themselves regarding items of importance within a given field (Putnam, 1977, p. 409). Here, the nature of specialized knowledge indicates that even within a given field there may be some measure of topical disagreements regarding those considered to be experts, which may cause tension among practitioners when consulted for advice regarding policymaking. Relatedly, should the tension among experts be made public this may have a negative effect on how the other system actors view specialized knowledge and those that are responsible for furnishing such. Baber and Bartless (2014, p. 89) observe that deliberations regarding matters of public policy can be affected by expert involvement that impact outcomes in a similar way as matters of law in that "expert testimony can be offered in an adversarial manner by representatives of civil society organizations standing on opposing sides of a regulatory problem." In some cases, there may be some measure of discord from among the ranks of the technocrats regarding knowledge and this informational disharmony may be strategically wielded by parties representing opposite sides of an issue during politically charged debates in the policy arena. The possibility that conceptual cacophony among experts may be leveraged by system actors who integrate information into competing value-laden arguments while being actively engaged in discursive events may call into question the degree to which technocrats should be deferred to during government decision-making processes. In this sense, technocratic elites within the same field may be constantly challenging industry notions in which such specifics are used to help to guide the discipline forward. Those experts may disagree regarding if a circumstance should be termed a problem, exactly how to define a given problem, and how to go out developing solutions capable of mitigating negative societal effects attributed to said problem. The debates from among experts within a given field can serve as a natural barrier to a single technocratic viewpoint from becoming wholly entrenched within government. In that, internal deliberations among experts in an area of public policy can serve as a natural check on technocracy and ensure that various elements associated with this approach are not accepted within government unchallenged. If there is some measure of discord in a field of expertise as to what constitutes factual evidence or a rational choice, then this would complicate

12 Technocracy and Deliberative Democracy

deferring to technocrats during policymaking endeavors. Furthermore, the modern era often finds those standing on opposing sides of a given issue attempting to bolster a given policy preference by employing experts with specialized knowledge that supports said claims. In this scenario, various experts promoting conflicting evidence can cause system actors to develop some measure of skepticism as to viability of the information being used to guide decision making. Therefore, an abundance of conflicting data that supports the claims being made by those taking opposing stances on a given topic may call into question the credibility of allowing technocratic expertise to be used in government decision making without question.

A Potential Role for Technocracy in American Democracy

In the modern era, the increasing complexity associated with a vast array of technical issues facing society has most assuredly provided an opportunity for technocracy to be applied in that expert knowledge can be a helpful resource in guiding government decision making regarding the development of public policy (Yankelovich, 1991; Fischer, 1993; Fischer, 1995; Anderson, 2006; Fischer, 2000; Craig, 2014; McDonnell and Valbruzzi, 2014). Instead of being viewed in absolute terms capable of serving as an end, technocracy should be considered to be one of many means available to decision makers in government and a conceptual tool that should be used to "complement rather than side-line party politics and impartial administration" (Campbell, 2019, p. 9). Therefore, the role of expert knowledge in democratic decision making renders technocracy to a far lesser role than is preferred by staunch advocates of this approach. In a modern democracy such as the United States, it is important that government efforts are consistently made to institute "safeguards against undue influence" by those advancing a singular value in society such as technocracy (Sadowski and Selinger, 2014, p. 3). This can be accomplished in part by government ensuring that all interested parties are provided sufficient means and opportunity during various stages of the public-policy process that legitimately allows for the deliberation of multiple values so that agreement may eventually be reached guiding official actions that more accurately reflects societal preferences. In this sense, official actions based on technocracy by its very nature lacks the necessary levels of dialogue and discovery associated with crafting public policy that is expected in the U.S. deliberative democracy. Ultimately, technocracy can be very useful as *one* of many rationales (as opposed to being accepted as *the* sole rationale) that help to provide some measure of clarity on topics being deliberated within the U.S. political system.

The potential usage of technocracy in any capacity has an undeniably important relationship with any perceived failures of this approach in practice on behalf of system participants, which can directly affect its conceptual stature and overall usage rates. In relation, there are contextually systemic and in-the-moment situational factors that can contribute to the perceived role that technocracy should play in governmental decision-making processes. As the political system in place may affect perceptions held by society regarding accepted government practices, expectations associated with American deliberative democracy can most assuredly affect how the application of technocracy is viewed despite the preferences held by even the staunchest advocates of this approach. In addition, there is some room conceptually for the usage of technocracy to assist in guiding decision making within the U.S. political system and this is due in part to the possible circumstances-based usefulness associated with expert knowledge. In this, the perception of the usefulness of expert knowledge is derived in part from the need for government to pursue a more technically oriented policy path forward that will reduce inefficiency and ineffectiveness in public-sector actions. Relatedly, the perception of usefulness attributed to technocracy is conceived by system actors whose confidence in government has been diminished due to the perception that biased argumentation over policy choices has led to inefficient and ineffective public-sector outcomes. In circumstances such as this, there may be an opportunity for technocracy to warrant some measure of consideration as it relates to contributing to decisions that will dictate the direction of government.

Because of the intricate nature of the previously stated critiques and potential allowances derived from conditional dynamics associated with this approach, it makes it increasingly difficult to achieve, and then maintain, sufficient levels of universal support allowing for technocracy to be perpetuated for an extended period in the American democracy. Broadly speaking, the requisite levels of support for technocracy by key system participants—elected officials, the public, and bureaucrats—is inexorably linked to the base perception that this approach is adequately suited to provide the government with the ability to best address a wide variety of stated goals at a given point in time. Relatedly, support of technocracy on behalf of system actors is tied directly to perceptions regarding this approach's functionality in governance in relation to failures associated with traditional democratic decision making. To be sure, the initial support granted to technocracy may be just as easily revoked should those system actors believe that this approach would no longer allow government to achieve stated goals. Ultimately, a whole-of-government approach to decision making that grants permanent exclusivity to technocracy is a highly unlikely, if not impossible, scenario in the American democracy

14 Technocracy and Deliberative Democracy

given the expectations associated with participatory and responsive governance. Here, technocracy may be deemed more acceptable for use on a case-by-case basis rather than as a whole-of-government approach on a longitudinal basis in order to meet such expectations inherent within the U.S. political system. Should enough support be generated from system actors endorsing the usage of technocracy on a more limited basis in government, then this rationale may serve to provide invaluable guidance in shaping decisions that are programmatic, or agency oriented, on a case-by-case basis. Instead of granting technocracy primacy over discourse in all matters of governance, the use of expert knowledge in the deliberative democracy is more appropriate serving a supplementary role in government decision making. In relation, the degree of influence of technocrats is variable to some degree based on assessments of the political environment in which demand for more efficient and effective government may provide situational support to the perceived usefulness of expert knowledge in decision making. In sum, the possibility, and extent, of applying technocracy is based to some degree on a fluid assessment of situational dynamics and its limited usage is intentionally retractable partly based on preferences held by system actors regarding its relevance to democratic decision making.

Despite the technocrat's general preference to avoid political deliberations in favor of public-sector decision making that reflects deference to expert knowledge, any level of permeance and permanence of this approach is ironically dependent on discourse from within the political environment to some degree. In general, the relative permanence of technocracy in serving as an influential means to guide official activities in government is at least partially linked to how the act of providing support for this approach translates into opportunity for a wide array of key system actors. In relation, in some cases supporting technocracy may be the result of a self-serving relationship between the public and elected officials that is reflective of aspects associated with public choice theory. In this context, public choice theory posits that rational maximizing voters place those in public office who will best represent the electorates' interests and that are believed to be most capable to deliver benefits that are expected from government. The public's support for candidates during an election and correspondingly the conceptual means by which those running for office advocate for use during government decision making processes is granted conditionally dependent upon the perception of the success of both in achieving the interests of the voter. In turn, government officials in the U.S. are inclined to endeavor to support the interests of those that elected them to office. As it relates to technocracy, an incumbent serving in office or a new candidate intent on winning a contested seat for the first time may also act as rational maximizers of their own self-interests to some degree by actively advocating for this approach if there is considerable support for such among the constituency base. As such, those seeking public office that are supportive of technocracy may see their opportunity to be elected reduced significantly if the voting public is no longer convinced of the merits of this approach. Relatedly, the public may cease being supportive of the application of technocracy in government if they believe that backing this approach will result in negatively affecting services that are of direct interest to them. Over time, the levels and numbers of services adversely affected by technocracy in use may result in the public being increasingly less supportive of government actions rooted in this approach. This idea is also applicable should technocratic decisions lead to outright cancellation of the delivery of public services that are deemed too inefficient to warrant continuation. Relatedly, the public's views of technocracy may become increasingly negative if it is believed that technocratically derived policy consistently exposes citizenry to some measure of preventable harm. Should technocracy also be perceived to yield policy actions that are functionally inadequate or wanting from a morality standpoint, then the support by all parties for its usage in government decision making will most assuredly wane. Ultimately, there must be wide-scale societal support of technocracy's use and belief in this approach being able to empower government to fulfill its mandated duties in a fashion approved of by the populace whom the public sector is responsible to serve. If the public no longer believes in the promise of technocracy to empower government to better perform various activities that will directly benefit them, then support for this approach will be difficult to maintain for sustained periods of time. Lacking significant levels of public support for technocracy, officials serving in government will be reticent to pursue a path that is accommodating to this approach. Knowing this electoral dynamic is in play can understandably affect the levels of support for technocracy provided by those seeking to be voted into public office and reinforces the relationship dynamics that exists between key actors as it relates to the efforts to institutionalize technocracy.

Within the U.S. political system, elected officials and the public represent key actors that can affect the usage of technocracy in government with the understanding that those serving in the bureaucracy are also capable of influencing internal decision making in this dynamic. Without the necessary levels of support by both the public and elected officials, technocratic means applied by bureaucrats to guide government actions during the fulfillment of mandated duties may likely be far less prevalent on a wide scale. In that, the levels of consistent support provided by elected officials and the public will affect whether technocrats serving with the bureaucracy may continue to hold sway during internal decision-making processes that determine how public-sector entities implement the mandate that Congress

16 Technocracy and Deliberative Democracy

has legislated a given agency is responsible to fulfill. Should elected officials and the public alike lose faith in technocracy, the technocrats populating bureaucratic positions throughout government will correspondingly find themselves lacking in allies willing to allow for this approach to remain as the primary focus guiding internally generated agency activities. In this scenario, the support on behalf of elected officials and the public serves as the linchpin that can empower technocrats to remain protected to the point where this approach is permitted to broadly flourish in government. Without such, the influence of technocrats will be reduced throughout government and the application of technocracy will be relegated to a more supplementary role largely considered for use only on a case-by-case basis. Having said that, it is important to recognize the possibility that localized, incremental successes in applying technocracy to guide bureaucratic actions may be capable of creating a trickle-up effect first within a single entity and then perhaps throughout government. At the bureaucratic level, small-scale successes in applying technocratic decision making that is perceived to enhance governmental capacity to perform goals may garner the attention of other internal and external system actors. The expansion of technocracy in this scenario would be predicated on its programmatic success within an agency potentially allowing for this approach to experience an increased rate of proliferation in a trickle-up manner throughout the broader government structure. Here, evidence of technocratic success may correspondingly convince the public and elected officials as to the merits of this approach. In this regard, there is a certain level of locus interchangeability indicating a fluid origin point that would provide evidence for the acceptance of technocracy, allowing for this approach to become more widely accepted as a means by which to help guide governmental decision making.

Regarding policymaking in the American political system, it is important to recognize that applying technocracy in government without providing the legitimate opportunity for those representing alternate viewpoints to challenge this approach would cause harm from a democratic standpoint. By restricting the decision-making processes to favor those participants supportive of or practiced in technocracy, the range of possible policymaking outcomes may be limited by the narrow range of options made available through this approach. In addition, opting to automatically pursue technocracy as the conceptual means by which to guide decision making may yield an inability to properly address all circumstances from a functional standpoint. In that, not all government activities will necessarily benefit from sole deference to expert knowledge that is only focused on societal values such as efficiency and effectiveness, especially in the absence of wide-scale considerations regarding context that may be applicable.

In relation, a technocratically efficient response to an identified problem in society may not properly consider other important social values that could conceivably impact the ability of government to fulfill the expectations associated with the provision of public services. Although the promise of efficiency reflects one (of many) important core values associated with U.S. governance, other values such as equity are also of great significance. Here, the pursuit of efficiency at the expense of equity may render government actions unable to properly address the expectations of service held by society at a given time. This is especially true in the modern U.S. democracy in which the delivery of a wide range of public services would otherwise be discontinued if decision making was based entirely on the value efficiency so closely tied with technocracy. Preventing the facilitation of a rich, diverse dialogue between decision makers in government who may represent various, and often competing, societal values may yield policymaking whose capacity is somewhat limited functionally. Technocratic solutions to non-technocratic problems may unintentionally diminish the capacity of a democratic government to perform its duties by limiting the public sector's freedom to implement dynamically determined solutions in response to identified system concerns at a given point in time.

The entrenchment of technocracy denotes a decision-making environment that is accepting of placing limits on policy creativity and in constricting system malleability that is traditionally expected in American democracy. In doing so, the processes associated with the assessment of societal circumstances to identify problems and to develop solutions that may be best suited to address such is reduced to something of a mirage in the democratic sense, lacking in the opportunity for system actors to engage in meaningful deliberations. By automatically accepting technocracy as the primary means to guide decision making, those advocating for alternate methods to achieve government goals are prevented from functionally impacting the system as intended in a deliberative democracy. In this sense, the promise of technocracy supplants decision makers' responsibility to actively consider a wide scope of potential alternatives in pursuit of ascertaining the most applicable means by which to guide government activities. In the United States, the decision to apply a technocratic approach on a case-by-case basis (micro level) or a whole-of-government basis (macro level) is based in part by comparing the validity of existing means in use to achieve whatever goals are being targeted at a given point in time (i.e. increase government accountability, enhance citizens' trust in government, etc.) within the context of democracy. To be sure, the selection process is often cyclical in nature, in which circumstances at a given time can result in various ideological perspectives falling from, or being placed at, the forefront of decision making in order to affect government processes

18 Technocracy and Deliberative Democracy

and outcomes. The support of technocracy, and the extent of the potency of that support to some degree, is subject to situational circumstances in which there may be a perceived need by necessary levels of system actors to pursue this policymaking tactic instead of accepting traditionally oriented deliberations expected in American democracy.

Overall, attempts to subscribe to technocratic decision making broadly and consistently in government in an uncontested fashion would be grossly insufficient as it relates to meeting system expectations associated with participation in the U.S. deliberative democracy. Inconsistencies from among system actors to reach consensus on what constitutes rational courses of action in all cases, acceptance of standards such as efficiency and effectiveness over other societal values of importance during policymaking, and a failure to recognize the important role that participation in debates among interested parties plays in American democracy all serve as natural barriers to technocracy becoming embedded in a whole-of-government approach on a permanent basis. As it relates to the politics involved in democratically oriented decision making, technocrats are skeptical toward, or worse yet entirely averse to, the dialectic component that is integral to decision-making processes in the U.S. system. Whereas specialized knowledge held by experts can play an important role in contributing to decision making, the advocates of the technocratic idea of governance would prefer to utilize this approach to replace policymaking derived from broadscale participation that is a foundational expectation of American democracy. The technocratic approach would be incongruent with the political nature that is weaved into the governmental fabric of American democracy and this fact should therefore provide some measure of hesitancy in the idea of institutionalizing broadscale application of this approach. Ultimately, to promote technocracy over discourse in government decision making would result in processes that fail to conform to the expectations associated with participation in the U.S. deliberative democracy. With technocracy serving as an acceptable tool for usage by decision makers in government, the U.S. political system requires a policy path to be determined by a richer, deeper discursive exchange among interested parties that is expected in the U.S. deliberative democracy. As such, it is important to further expand the scope of the discussion by focusing on expectations for participation and communicative structural opportunities associated with responsive decision making in the U.S. deliberative democracy.

Deliberative Democracy

Technocracy represents a preference for government decision making to be guided by experts whose application of specialized knowledge will provide what advocates of this approach believe to be rational, unbiased means by which to base public policy upon. For the technocrat, experts with specialized knowledge are more capable of crafting efficient and effective government actions than public-policy endeavors that allow for the chorus of individualized interests engaged in discourse to guide the direction of government. Advocates of this rationale have the utmost faith in basing public policy on the ability of experts to apply what is believed to be discoverable and undisputable truths derived from specialized knowledge in a rational and unbiased fashion. For the technocrat, meaningful discourse facilitated among system actors used to determine the direction of government is viewed as an unnecessary burden on decision making in which political opportunists, savvy in argumentation, may gain sufficient levels of support in the political arena resulting in actions that are inefficient and ineffective. Here, technocracy is argued to be able to overcome outcomes-based deficiencies resulting from traditional decision making in the U.S. deliberative democracy, which utilizes collective intelligence generated through discourse between system actors engaged in participatory opportunities via multiple points of contact in the communicative structure. However, it cannot be understated that sole reliance on a technocratic policy path fails to reflect the expectations associated with how participatory endeavors involving system actors are expected to affect official actions in the U.S. deliberative democracy. As such, it will be helpful to expand on several pertinent aspects that are expected to guide decision making in the U.S. deliberative democracy.

The U.S. deliberative democracy includes a wide range of participatory expectations that are intended to shape the decision-making environment, which in turn affects public-policy outcomes and public administration responsibilities during implementation. At its conceptual core is the idea that the U.S. democracy should provide a plethora of opportunities, along many points of contact, within the communicative structure for interested parties to engage in deliberations over the direction of government. The idea of deliberation on the most basic level is focused on the act of discourse that occurs between interested parties in circumstances in which each is seeking to advance a particular viewpoint. Roberts (1997, p. 131) observes that the process of deliberation "is a sophisticated form of social interaction. Success may depend on the developmental mix of participants in the process." In the context of U.S. deliberative democracy, this process is expected to include a multitude of interested parties each crafting value-laden arguments that reflect different, and often competing, preferences for the direction of government. In that, deliberations in the truest sense must be conducted in an open system that avoids conversations regarding preferences held by only those that represents value homogeneity. Although

20 Technocracy and Deliberative Democracy

the U.S. is representative of a large, heterogenous society, making it logistically implausible to utilize direct democracy as a means by which to identify problems and solutions in modern-era governance, the communicative structure still requires openness so that those interested in participating in discursive events will have the opportunity to do so. In this sense, it is important to recognize the role that discursive events play in the U.S. political environment in which value-based deliberations are both heterogeneous and contentious. In relation, the circumstances attributed to discourse over policymaking in the contemporary era must account for a mounting array of complicated problems that are now associated with an increasingly modernized society. The rising levels of societal "complexity" can be directly linked to a corresponding increase in "problems in need of political regulation," which raises the degree of difficulty in the democratic sense in ensuring that those being affected by policy have some opportunity to be directly involved in its design (Habermas, 2015, p. 46). Despite preferences held by technocrats regarding limiting participatory discourse in favor of expert-led decision making, the complexity of contemporary problems and the corresponding development of potential solutions required of government within the modern era is not an indication that an opportunity to engage in meaningful deliberations should be absent from the U.S. political system. As such, advancing a "discourse-theoretical" methodology may provide a broad spectrum of means by which to contribute to maintaining a system more capable of fulfilling the "democratic promise of inclusion" so that interested parties may be increasingly more engaged in procedures involving the politics of government change (Habermas, 2015, p. 46). Although elections provide an important occasion for citizens to impact the political system, it is also important that the opportunity to engage in discussions contributes to a "vital public sphere" making it possible to share "free-floating opinions, arguments and positions" (Habermas, 2015, p. 47). Relatedly, the perceived legitimacy of U.S. governance is based at least partly on whether genuine opportunities are provided for system actors to engage in meaningful dialogue in which participation can provide evidence that support for preferred government actions is able to explicitly impact a given field of public policy. Cohen (1998, pp. 185) notes that "the fundamental idea of democratic, political legitimacy is that the authorization to exercise state power must arise from the collective decisions of the equal members of a society who are governed by that power." Here, all interested parties are provided the opportunity to engage in discursive events that are widely inclusive, as is expected in a deliberative democracy. In doing so, the resulting discourse is expected to play a role in authorizing actions taken on behalf of the state. Trotta (2006, p. 14) adds that "effective deliberation of values results from the government's efforts to promote the inclusion of multiple ideologies competing in the political arena (i.e. keeping the deliberative process open to all interested parties)." In this sense, deliberative processes are required to remain open to those representing various, and often competing, preferences for the direction of government. Therefore, system actors that are interested in engaging in discursive events will craft value-laden arguments and attempt to garner sufficient levels of political support that will authorize government to develop policy means that are reflective of such. In this context, the two-fold function of deliberations is that 1) participants seek to negotiate policy outcomes that support a specific perspective regarding societal problems, and 2) that the process itself is capable of affecting the system by creating new "institutional rules," "norms of appropriate behavior," and "conceptions of legitimate political intervention" (Hajer, 2003, pp. 175–176). With that said, the role of discursive events in the U.S. political system remains a highly important element in ensuring that government outcomes are viewed as legitimate responses to the societal preferences for public-sector action. Here, providing opportunities for system actors to engage in argumentation-based discourse is insufficient in the context of deliberative democracy, as there is also a requirement that participation in such events can create agreement on changes to the political system that are consistently identifiable.

On the matter of providing public-sector-generated discursive events, whose outcomes have some measure of influence on legitimizing government actions, there is a need to expand on additional qualities that are expected of the system by which deliberations between participants are facilitated. In this context, the perception of the legitimacy of government is partly based on the ability of citizens to formally engage in a deliberative democracy that is representative of specific system qualities, summarized as followed:

Established cyclical nature of opportunities in which citizens may choose to engage in discursive events on a longitudinal basis.

All parties accept the framework by which discursive events are facilitated and vest in the means available within the communicative structure.

Understanding that the deliberations are pluralistic in nature in which a vast array of parties representing competing interests participate in argumentation in the hopes of reaching agreement that will result in affecting the political system.

The outcomes of participating in discursive events consistently yields clearly evident results that deliberations directly affected the path of government.

22 Technocracy and Deliberative Democracy

All system actors that enter into the discursive events are cognizant of both the deliberative capacity of participation and shared goal to impact the political system held by all other participants.

Source: Cohen (1997, pgs. 72–73)

Trotta (2006, p. 19) adds that:

...in order for the deliberative process to be effective it must have the following characteristics: government actions are viewed as legitimate if perceived to be the end result of collective action, the deliberative system must be open to all interested parties (regardless of ideological viewpoints and different levels of group resources) and the deliberative process is continual (which enables "losers" in the deliberative process infinite opportunities to influence policy).

In a modern democratic society, it is of the utmost importance that "feedback loops" are in place that provide a legitimizing link between citizens voicing policy preferences through "democratic processes" and a wide assortment of government outcomes that result from said participation (Habermas, 2015, p. 50). Here, deliberative democracy is viewed as legitimate in part because system actors invest in the open and cyclical nature of participatory opportunities. In relation, the ability of citizens to participate in discursive events includes the expectation that such argumentation endeavors will result in achieving agreement among system actors that can affect some measure of change(s) to the political system. Therefore, system actors can engage in discursive events in the hopes of affecting changes to the political system with the understanding that success or failure to do so may be temporary because there are constant opportunities for interested parties to re-engage in the process on a longitudinal basis. The openness of the system provides all those interested in participating with cyclical opportunities to engage in meaningful deliberations that are capable of influencing government outcomes. The availability of participatory means is an important function of U.S. deliberative democracy with the understanding that opportunity to engage in discursive events is only one of many factors that contributes to whether citizens perceive government to be legitimate. The establishment of discursive events also requires that there is some measure of opportunity for system actors that participate to be able to affect change(s) to the policy path of government. In this way, deliberative democracy requires that meaningful discursive events are included in the communicative structures linking participation with the opportunity to realistically influence government outcomes. Ultimately, the deliberative system is expected to be open to those interested in participating and to include continuous opportunities for interested parties to engage in discourse in the hopes of affecting actual changes to the governmental system. The system openness is of import in that it recognizes that the U.S. is a heterogeneous society in which a vast array of participants hold different and often competing preferences regarding the policy path that should guide governmental actions. However, an open and cyclical system that provides access to discursive events to all interested parties regardless of values held does not necessarily imply that potential participants will achieve equality in outcomes as variances exist regarding resources available (i.e. time, information, money, etc.) that may impact that dynamic nature of deliberative events. Here, the ideal of deliberative opportunities is more focused on the communicative structure being open to those interested in attempting to influence government actions by participating in value-laden argumentation representative of a wide array preferences associated with pluralism that is present in the American democracy.

In the American democracy, the provision of formalized discursive events creates interactive opportunities for system actors to longitudinally engage in debates over preferences for government action along a multitude of points of contact within a seemingly ever-expanding communitive framework. In relation, meaningful deliberations require that those participating in discursive events are provided a genuine opportunity to impact the direction of government in some way. Without linking the opportunity to deliberate with the potential to affect the policy path of government, the discursive events being viewed as a viable means by which to engage with government will likely be questioned in terms of process legitimacy. As it relates to perceptions of the legitimacy of outcomes achieved in such questionable circumstances, the resulting government actions can be broadly perceived as being insensitive to the public will in which choices made ultimately result in creating a disjoint between actual system preferences and government policy initiatives. In the American democracy, a perceived input–output deficiency can be especially damaging to perceptions of legitimacy in instances in which citizen participation is viewed to be lacking in the expected levels of meaningful deliberation that is geared toward facilitating actual changes in government. There are dangers posed to the legitimacy of deliberative democracy should participatory events be perceived as being "hollow exercises" (Yang and Callahan, 2007) or examples of "tokenism" associated with several of the rungs on Arstein's (1969) "ladder of citizen participation," in which substantive opportunity to impact government outcomes is believed to be missing. In a deliberative democracy, making known the rationale used to guide decision making can allow participants to better understand why a specific path forward was chosen and can simultaneously substantively address any known concerns held by those originally in opposition to a given viewpoint that came to light during discussions for the purpose of persuasion (Gaus, Landwehr, and Schmalz-Burns, 2020, p. 342). In this sense, publicizing the rationale behind government decisions can functionally serve to make it known why a choice was made or, in more extreme circumstances, can persuade participants that had originally been opposed to a specific action of the merits associated with this choice in policymaking. If the goal of sharing in this context is for informative and persuasive purposes, then decision makers announcing why a policy was chosen may serve to address misgivings held by opposition groups, which can further work to legitimize public-sector outcomes in a deliberative democracy. Relatedly, once the government moves forward regarding a specific policy path it is of import for the public sector to publicize said choices and provide some measure of explanation as to the merits of pursuing such. The provision of a substantive explanation regarding the rationale used and the expected benefits of a given policy choice can be educational while also potentially having the capacity to assuage the misgivings of those who had reservations about supporting a specific government action. The advertising of selected policy choices is a means by which system actors may assess the legitimacy of government actions that were taken and may provide greater insight as to how to engage in discourse in impending participatory opportunities. In that, the winning arguments that were successful in impacting the policy path of government can provide a linguistic template for use in later discursive events, while also highlighting the values held by participants that were agreed upon as being important enough to warrant public-sector action. Additionally, routinely publicizing the outcomes that resulted from dialectic participation are capable of further promoting the expectations associated with deliberative democracy regarding transparency, accountability, and cyclicity.

The provision of the opportunity for system actors to meaningfully engage in discursive events—in which those successful in expressing values shared through argumentation can affect changes to the direction of government—is a key foundational element associated with U.S. deliberative democracy. If participatory events fail to create an opportunity for interested parties to engage in meaningful deliberations that can affect changes to the political system, then perceptions of the legitimacy of government processes, and outcomes may be irreparably harmed. The modern era has created a unique opportunity for the public sector to integrate a wide array of continuously emerging innovative technologies into the communicative framework, which can serve to broaden the participatory means available for system actors to engage in meaningful deliberations. The continuous technological advancements in the modern era associated with "the digital revolution" has a direct effect on both modern communications network structures and consequently the ability of societal actors to mobilize (Habermas, 2015, p. 47). The technology available in the modern era directly influences elements associated with network participation indicating that it is prudent to vacate the traditionally held "institutionally frozen picture of the constitutional state" (Habermas, 2015, p. 47). The structure of modern networks by which participants communicate are expected to remain dynamic, in which the public sector is responsible for efforts to apply emergent technologies capable of keeping current the means available used to facilitate discursive events. It is important to consider that "deliberative politics" can be facilitated through traditional communication networks that are now able to be augmented by technology, allowing for broader levels of discussions capable of affecting the development of public sentiments and contributing to determining the "collective will" (Habermas, 2015, p. 47). Trotta (2018, p. 92) notes that "a deliberative democracy framework is intended to reflect system openness allowing for interested parties to utilize a full range of activities such as directly participating in dialogue with government in a cyclical fashion over an indefinite period of time." Trotta (2018, p. 92) continues by explaining that "therefore, opportunities are provided that are able to sustain dialogue through a broad range of diverse means to increase points of access linking citizens and government." In that, the diversity of means in the contemporary era are now expected to also include modern communications technologies being added to the existing participatory framework to enhance the capacity in facilitating deliberations between network actors. Trotta (2018, p. 92) adds that "the advancements in technology have opened up deliberative democracy to the possibility of a dual approach capable of simultaneously utilizing traditional and digital means to facilitate civic engagement." Trotta (2018, p. 78) provides the following assessment of the role(s) that deliberative democracy plays in the context of participatory expectations in the modern U.S. system by including the digital means within the available communicative structure:

Citizen participation in the U.S. political system that is conducted through available deliberative means can greatly contribute to reinforcing the perpetuation of any number of important democratic principles including accountability, flexibility and transparency. These principles can be further institutionalized by creating digital means in which citizen–government interactions can be facilitated within a network structure that accommodates accountable, flexible and transparent participative endeavors associated with deliberative democracy. In relation, the means in which citizens interact in dialogue events with government occurs within and contributes to the strengthening of the overall deliberative democracy framework.

Source: Trotta (2018, p. 78)

In the U.S. deliberative democracy, the contemporary communicative structures by which network actors engage in discourse are expected to reflect an ability to transform in response to perceived system needs so that a dynamic expansion of means to facilitate participation more adequately is consistently maintained. In the modern era, the circumstances regarding the environment in which public policy is created has shifted, which indicates that addressing specific societal concerns solely through "established institutional arrangements" may prove ineffective in achieving desired goals (Hajer, 2003, p. 175). Therefore, it is important to recognize the influence of "polycentric networks of government" in which non-traditional sources of influence are playing an expanding role in public-policy development (Hajer, 2003, p. 175). In this sense, the communicative structure by which modern deliberations occurs should avoid becoming too rigidly stagnant but instead provide allowance for the continuously malleable integration of combined means—old and new—by which network actors have choices available to them to engage in discourse. Although the role of formalized interactions plays a primary role in facilitating discursive events that can be used to generate collective intelligence capable of guiding the direction of government, it is important to recognize that there are also informal communication dynamics that can affect the shaping of the public will regarding preferences for public-sector action. In the modern era, technology can further integrate informal means into the broader communication network, by which system actors may engage one another, in the effort to craft value-laden arguments in the hopes of generating agreement that will be capable of impacting government actions that reflect a given viewpoint. In this sense, the modern networks by which communications occur regarding policy preferences are reflective of informal and formal components, although there may be some measure of variance in the ability of each type to generate an impact on government. Similarly, modern communication networks have expanded in that participation can be facilitated in the traditional sense and through an increasing array of digital means that can further link system actors interested in deliberating preferences for the direction of government. In doing so, the public sector is able to fulfill its expected role to remain flexible and dynamic, in which integrating digital participatory events into the broader communicative structure create greater opportunities for citizens to engage in meaningful deliberations. Here, such efforts are evolutionary in nature, in which the public sector is expected to continuously be capable of and willing to adjust in order to be better be able to fulfill participatory responsibilities associated with institutionalizing a transparent, accountable, and cyclical political system as expected in the U.S. deliberative democracy. The communicative structure in the modern era is expected to include a vast array of participatory means that integrate both traditional and digital designs in order to create enhanced levels of opportunity for citizens to engage in discursive events capable of affecting changes in government. The decision makers in the modern era must consider whether the process of integrating emergent technological means into the communicative structure—to allow for system actors to engage in discourse—should be facilitated and to what degree that should be pursued. In relation, decision makers' choices can influence the practices of government regarding more basic activities, such as information dissemination and the delivery of public services, and more complex dynamics associated with establishing substantive, or meaningful, means by which interested parties may engage in value-based argumentation regarding preferences for the direction of government. In this way, the public-sector choices regarding maintenance of the structural communication network dictates how participation is conducted in the modern era, which can ultimately affect decision making regarding how government will go about performing a wide range of expected duties.

Closing Remarks

Although technocracy as a rationale may serve as a useful tool capable of contributing to decision making in government, there are a wide array of concerns associated with pursuit of this approach as a primary means by which to shape public policy in the American political system. In the context of government decision making in the U.S, there are several concerns associated with investing too extensively and rapidly in the advice of technocrats as it relates to issues regarding expert knowledge. Broadly speaking, any given field of research is generally considered to be dynamic in that the understanding of many aspects of relevant information is in a constant state of flux and obtaining absolute knowledge is a noble yet largely unrealistic goal. Whereas there are often foundational components by which a field is based upon, there is also a measure of flexibility in understanding, which is continuously added to said base of knowledge, longitudinally contributing to the continued development of the field. In reality, the expert knowledge in any field is both imperfect and incomplete in part because learning is a dynamic process in which information is continuously revealed over time. Relatedly, a technocrat is unable to develop a full understanding of available knowledge in any field due to the natural limits of the individual and the complex, broadly dynamic processes associated with the accumulation of expert knowledge. This somewhat benign observation is not intended to be some critique of expert knowledge or the usefulness of pursuing such to the betterment of the world including its potential contribution to enhancing government's ability to improve society.

28 Technocracy and Deliberative Democracy

Instead, it is a simple, yet often resisted, acknowledgment that there are very few, if any, absolutes in any field as it relates to the accumulation of expert knowledge. Whether it concerns the hard or social sciences, accumulated knowledge in any given field is often incomplete or, in some cases, even once-accepted standards may eventually be proven inaccurate. Therefore, unquestioned allegiance to any given idea as being irrefutable and beyond reproach may be ill-advised as it relates to the application of technocratic knowledge when applied to democratic governance. Although the technically oriented knowledge that is held by the individual and within a given field is to be respected, it would be imprudent to assume this to be the end of the journey in the informational sense. In recognizing the continuous nature of accumulating knowledge in any given field over time, and the possibility that any lone individual may possess various degrees of understanding regarding available knowledge that may exist in an area of expertise in which they are practiced, it can be concluded that unchallenged acceptance on either account by decision makers in government should be avoided during policymaking endeavors. If the array of knowledge available in a field and the ability of the individual to understand accumulated knowledge is fallible, unwavering loyalty to expert knowledge on behalf of government decision makers may yield equally imperfect policy.

Those advocating that expert knowledge is accumulated, assessed, and applied in an environment entirely free of bias may be somewhat naïve as to the political dynamics at play regarding those activities. This is evidenced in part by the fact that the individual is subject to personal biases regarding the decision of what to study, how to study the chosen topic, and even regarding the interpretation of the data that is accumulated during the study. In relation, the supposition that a technocratic decision is unequivocally preferable, partly because of the approach's assumed rational nature, fails to address the subjectivity associated with the concept of rationally. In that, there is often very little, if any, consensus as to what constitutes rationality, which indicates that a subscription to technocracy on this account would be somewhat misguided conceptually. Also, the mere fact that a technocrat may advocate for a government environment that is accommodating to the technocratic way is itself indicative of an obvious, and self-serving, bias. Relatedly, public choice theory indicates that, as rational maximizers of their own self-interests, those in government that seek out experts in a given field may do so in a fashion that supports whatever stance they may hold politically. The fact that those standing on opposing sides of a public-policy debate both employ experts that furnish evidence supporting their respective stances raises questions regarding the reliability of the process in general. Ultimately, the vast array of participants' biases directly attributed to various aspects of the technocratic approach is a cause for some measure of concern should decision makers in government willingly and uncompromisingly cede influence over policymaking to technocracy. Relatedly, this act runs counter to the expectations associated with the role that discourse is intended to play in the U.S. democratic system.

In purest form, the application of the technocratic approach in government decision making would wholly discount the usefulness of participatory dynamics expected in the U.S. deliberative system. A question that is naturally raised on this matter is to what degree should expert knowledge be sought out, be trusted enough to be considered for application, and be adhered to by decision makers within governance. The answer to this question is far from simple, which is to be expected given the complexities associated with expert knowledge and the dynamics regarding deliberative democracy in action within modern U.S. government. Those advocating for the technocratic approach are supportive of experts' specialized knowledge being used as the primary determining factor in guiding policymaking decisions. Here, those supportive of this supposed rationally oriented approach have the utmost belief in expert knowledge being used to guide government decision making because technocrats are assumed to be unbiased, and the specialized knowledge held should be indisputably beyond reproach by other system actors. For the technocrat, deliberative events create unnecessarily complex layers to decision making that degrades the expediency that would be present if expert knowledge was applied over outcomes derived from interested parties engaged in participatory events. Additionally, the ability of technocratic decision making to create more efficient and effective government action is viewed by those supportive of this approach as being of great importance even at the expense of expectations associated with participatory events in a U.S. deliberative democracy. However, the U.S. deliberative democracy requires that network actors are continuously provided the opportunity to engage in meaningful deliberations capable of affecting government outcomes. In this sense, the application of technocracy over discourse in government decision making is conceptually the antithesis of the expectations associated with participation in the U.S. deliberative democracy. Technocracy as an approach that moves government decision making forward may provide efficient and effective policy in some cases, but the act of doing so would potentially fail to address the societal value associated with equity. Here, technocracy in practice may promote official actions that fail to consider the important role that aspects of equity is intended to play in government decision making regarding public policy. Ultimately, the technocratic approach can find relevance in a more limited fashion, as expert knowledge is most assuredly a useful tool in contributing to government decision making.

30 Technocracy and Deliberative Democracy

The extent and scope of the usefulness may vary to some degree based on an assessment of situational and contextual circumstance inherent within the political environment, in which system actors may be supportive of the technocratic approach being used to help guide government decision making. However, those involved in the process of determining what capacity is appropriate for the role of technocracy at a given point in time should avoid considering applying this approach as wholesale replacement for decision making derived from discourse that is expected in the U.S deliberative democracy. Although expert knowledge plays a key contributing role in U.S. policymaking, a complete ceding of decision-making authority to technocracy would cause great harm to the perceptions that government actions are legitimate in the context of expectations inherent with a deliberative democracy. The absolute and unquestioned usage of expert knowledge to guide government decision making would be a direct violation of many of the expectations inherent within a modern, heterogenous deliberative democracy such as the United States.

Establishing and maintaining technocratic control over decision making in any significant capacity can be an uneasy prospect within the context of the modern American democracy, in part because doing would require government actions to consistently be based on deferring to the ideals of technical rationality inherent with this approach. If technocracy becomes widely embedded in government, and largely supported by system actors within the public sector, then the institutional ensconcing of this approach may naturally cause those intent on protecting this status quo to have some measure of opposition toward those others preferring to determine policymaking by engaging via traditional democratic processes. Doing so would serve to promote technocracy as the de facto means guiding government activities, thereby weakening the traditional expectations of a deliberative democracy in which interested parties are intended to have the opportunity to engage in discourse over competing social values. An environment overly protective of technocracy could challenge traditional expectations associated with democratic participation by functionally limiting the opportunity to deliberate by those representing values contradictory to the preferred status quo held by technocratic advocates. Supplanting the processes that would allow for interested parties to engage in meaningful discourse, in the hopes of affecting changes in government with an unchallenged deferment to all things technocratic, deeply diminishes opportunities that are expected for participation within a deliberative democracy. Government decision making regarding policy that is facilitated in a fashion that supports only those advocating for technocracy runs counter to many of the key expectations associated with deliberative democracy in which the system should be open (i.e. all interested parties have the opportunity to become engaged in debates regarding policymaking outcomes), accountable (i.e. the processes that leads to policy decisions is transparent at all stages and there is flexibility to shift the focus of policymaking if such a need is determined by actors participating in discourse), and cyclical (i.e. consistent opportunities at multiple points of contact are provided that will allow interested parties to affect changes to the system on a longitudinal basis). Here, allegiance to technocracy to the point where wide-scale institutional influence of this approach becomes increasingly unchallenged in the ability to affect government activities associated with policymaking would result in diminishing the integrity of a deliberative democracy. Technocracy used as the default setting to guide government actions largely caters to a specifically limited value system, in essence trading stability, uniformity, and rapidity in decision making for the participative processes and dynamic responsiveness traditionally expected in the U.S. deliberative democracy. In relation, government decision makers automatically accepting technocracy as the de facto approach to identify and solve all societal problems would result in one-dimensional outcomes reflective of singular, as opposed to pluralistic, values. In that, technocracy and democracy may be at odds with each other to some degree, should the allegiance to the former come at the expense of the expectations for participation associated with the latter. To protect the integrity of deliberative democracy, technocracy should functionally be considered one of many means available to help guide the decision-making processes associated with government activities such as policymaking. In this way, technocracy would be considered a welcome tool that can contribute to the goal of efficient and effective government without allowing for this approach to dominate decision making, which would degrade the capacity of interested parties to engage in meaningful deliberations as expected within the U.S. political arena.

Unlike the technocratic approach to policymaking, in which its advocates believe that this methodology should be unchallenged as the default rationale for decisions affecting the direction of government, a deliberative democracy in practice reflects expectations for system participants to recognize and actively address alternate viewpoints through discourse in the attempt to persuade opponents as to the benefits of suggested actions(s). In doing so, those advocating for a specific government activity will craft value-laden arguments designed to persuade other system actors as to the merits of such. The modern era deliberative means used to promote the preferences held by a wide range of interested parties regarding government actions occur simultaneously within, and between, traditional spaces and novel spaces that together comprise the established broad communicative structure in society. In the modern era, the traditional spaces remain a viable and stable venue capable of accommodating discursive events,

32 Technocracy and Deliberative Democracy

providing opportunity for interested parties to promote value-laden arguments for the purposes of affecting government outcomes. However, the dynamic and flexible nature of the U.S. government requires that the public sector applies emergent technologies to facilitate discursive events, which creates novel spaces by which interested parties can engage in meaningful deliberations. The usage of technology to create novel spaces is partly the result of shifting expectations derived from the waning belief in the primacy of participation in deliberations exclusively through the customary dialectic frameworks associated with traditional U.S. governance. Here, novel spaces are digital constructs that leverage technology to bolster the communication structural capacity, which increases the availability of means by which system actors can engage in meaningful deliberations as expected in American democracy. The addition of novel spaces does not suggest that a wholesale elimination of traditional spaces is now underway or should be considered anytime in the future. Instead, the usage of traditional spaces and novel spaces together have the potential to augment the deliberative capacity of the network that supports interested parties engaging in discourse, with the intention of affecting a wide range of government outcomes. In relation, traditional spaces and novel spaces may create an opportunity for overlap regarding the interactions that occur between system actors operating within events associated with each respective participatory venue. For example, interested parties may engage in debates in a traditional space provided within the apparatus of government such as a public meeting. In addition, many, or all, of those same interested parties could engage in dialogue through novel digital spaces such as those associated with social media. In this, there may be some measure of overlap between the dialogue facilitated separately via traditional spaces and novel spaces allowing for preferential ideas raised in each respective participatory venue to traverse the void between the two conceptual events within the broader communicative structure. It is important to consider that to some degree this dynamic may support topical permeability, allowing stated political preferences inherent within value-laden arguments, shared during meaningful deliberations, to freely migrate between traditional and novel venues.

With the understanding that informal dynamics at play in the modern era play a role in determining widely held policy preferences in the American democracy, this discussion is largely focused on the fact that the U.S. government is expected to effort to accommodate system actors by including formal discursive events that can be facilitated both traditionally and digitally. In doing so, the communicative structure present in the American system is focused on being maintained in a manner that continues to be reflective of key expectations associated with deliberative democracy.

This includes the importance that the communicative structure includes meaningful deliberations, capable of allowing participants to have the opportunity to affect changes to the policy path of government, required for participants to view processes and outcomes as legitimate. In addition, meaningful deliberations are expected to be available on a longitudinal and cyclical basis in which interested parties can continuously engage in discursive events over time along many points of contact within the communication framework. If outcomes of a discursive event fail to reflect a preferred conclusion for participants, then those system actors are free to re-engage in deliberations at a later date in the hopes of achieving a more favorable result. Lastly, the presence of meaningful deliberations further reinforces the expectations associated with transparency and accountability that are essential components associated with the U.S. democratic system. In all, in an effort to further institutionalize expectations associated with a deliberative democracy, the communicative structure in the contemporary U.S. is expected to apply traditional and digital means by which to facilitate a wide range of interactions between interested parties engaged in discourse. Therefore, the flexible and dynamic nature of the American democracy is extended to include efforts to apply technology to create means capable of facilitating discourse between system actors seeking to affect the policy path of government regarding a specific area(s) of public policy. Relatedly, doing so represents an actively concerted effort on behalf of government to create, maintain, and utilize broadly diverse means to facilitate meaningful deliberations between interested parties, in which results stemming from participation are capable of playing a role in determining the official direction of the public sector on a vast array of societal topics, including those related to emerging technical innovations manifesting in the modern era. In this, the ability to pursue dynamically flexible government responses remains an important hallmark associated with decision making in the U.S. deliberative democracy, further reinforcing the importance of avoiding becoming overly invested in technocracy during policymaking endeavors.

Broadly speaking, the two frames of reference introduced in this chapter—technocracy and deliberative democracy—provide vastly different perspectives on how government should go about making decisions that will correspondingly dictate public-sector actions in the U.S. political system. In general, decision-making processes in American democracy are likely better served by avoiding over committing to technocracy and disallowing the technocratic rationale to become the primary means by which to automatically guide all policymaking processes as part of a whole-of-government approach. Instead, technocracy is generally more appropriate serving an important supplemental role that is helpful in providing clarity to system actors regarding complex issues that are increasingly more commonplace in the modern era. Relatedly, it is of great importance that decision-making processes are conducted in a manner that ensures participatory opportunities are provided in accordance with expectations associated with the U.S. deliberative democracy. Here, the modern communicative structure is expected to include traditional means and novel means that conceptually expand the participatory opportunities available to interested parties, in which efforts to do so also reflects the dynamism expected of a flexible deliberative democracy. Ultimately, the legitimacy of processes and outcomes in this scenario is based in part on the perception that discursive events provide participants with the opportunity to engage in meaningful deliberations capable of affecting the policy path of the public sector in some way. The foundational components inherent in both technocracy and deliberative democracy reflect variances in preferences for system interactions and values of import that if subscribed to can influence government decision making. The essential tension derived from these competing preferences should serve as the conceptual anchor for the impending analysis of topics in the remaining chapters and should be routinely considered while advancing through each discussion, which are focused on various dynamics involving technology and American democracy.

References

Anderson, J. E. (2006). *Public Policy Making: Sixth Edition*. Houghton Mifflin Company.

Arnstein, S. R. (1969). A Ladder of Citizen Participation. *American Institution of Planners Journal*, 35(7): 216–224.

Baber, W. F. & Bartless, R. V. (2014). The Challenge of Slow-Motion Democracy. In A. S. Campos and J. G. André (Eds.), *Challenges to Democratic Participation: Antipolitics, Deliberative Democracy, and Pluralism*. Lexington Books, 2014. http://ebookcentral.proquest.com/lib/troy/detail.action?docID=1664776.

Campbell, A. (2019). In Praise of Technocracy. *Regional Innovations*, 2: 5–11.

Centeno, M. A. (1993). The New Leviathan: The Dynamics and Limits of Technocracy. *Theory and Society*, 22(3), 307–335.

Cohen, J. (1997). Deliberation and Democratic Legitimacy. In J. Bohman and W. Rehg (Eds.), *Deliberative Democracy: Essays on Reason and Politics*. MIT Press. https://public.ebookcentral.proquest.com/choice/publicfullrecord. aspx?p=3338820.

Cohen, J. (1998). Democracy and Liberty. In J. Elster (Ed.), *Deliberative Democracy* (Cambridge Studies in the Theory of Democracy, pp. 185–231). Cambridge University Press. doi:10.1017/CBO9781139175005.010.

Craig, T. (2014). Citizen Forums against Technocracy? The Challenge of Science to Democratic Decision Making. *Perspectives on Political Science*, 43(1), 31–40. https://doi.org/10.1080/10457097.2012.720836

Dahl, R. (1989). *Democracy and Its Critics*. Yale University Press.

Fischer, F. (1993). Citizen participation and the democratization of policy expertise: From theoretical inquiry to practical cases. *Policy Sciences*, 26(3), 165–187.

Fischer, F. (1995). *Evaluating Public Policy*. Wadsworth Thomson Learning.

Fischer, F. (2000). *Citizens, Experts and the Environment: The Politics of Local Knowledge*. Duke University Press.

Gaus, D., Landwehr, C., & Schmalz-Burns, R. (2020). Defending democracy against technocracy and populism: Deliberative democracy's strengths and challenges. *Constellations: An International Journal of Critical & Democratic Theory*, 27(3), 335–347. https://doi-org.libproxy.troy.edu/10.1111/1467-8675.12529

Gilley, B. (2017). Technocracy and democracy as spheres of justice in public policy. *Policy Sciences*, 50(1), 9–22. https://doi-org.libproxy.troy.edu/10.1007/s11077-016-9260-2

Gunnell, J. G. (1982). The Technocratic Image and the Theory of Technocracy. *Technology and Culture*, 23(3), 392–416. https://doi-org.libproxy.troy.edu/10.2307/3104485

Habermas, J. (2015). *The Lure of Technocracy*. Polity Press. Translated by Ciaran Cronin.

Hajer, M. (2003). Policy without polity? Policy analysis and the institutional void. *Policy Sciences*, 36(2), 175–195. doi:10.1023/a:1024834510939.

McDonnell, D. & Valbruzzi, M. (2014). Defining and classifying technocrat-led and technocratic governments. *European Journal Of Political Research*, 53(4), 654–671. doi:10.1111/1475–6765.12054

Meynaud, J. (1964). *Technocracy*. The Free Press. Translated by Paul Barnes.

Putnam, R.D. (1977). Elite transformation in advanced industrial societies: An empirical assessment of the theory of technocracy. *Comparative Political Studies*, 10(3): 383–412.

Roberts, N. (1997). Public Deliberation: An Alternative Approach to Crafting Policy and Setting Direction. *Public Administration Review*, 57(2), 124–132. https://doi-org.libproxy.troy.edu/10.2307/977060

Sadowski, J. & Selinger, E. (2014). Creating a Taxonomic Tool for Technocracy and Applying it to Silicon Valley. *Technology in Society 38*: 161–168.

Trotta, A. (2006). Budget arguments and military spending in the immediate post-World War Two era. PhD thesis, University of Michigan, Anne Arbor. UMI No. 3234425.

Trotta, A. (2018). *Advances in E-Governance. Theory and Application of Technological Initiatives*. Routledge/Taylor & Francis Group.

Wickman, F. (2011). What's a Technocrat? Have they ever really been in charge? *Slate*. http://www.slate.com/articles/news_and_politics/explainer/2011/11/technocrats_and_the_european_debt_crisis_what_s_a_technocrat_.html

Yang, K. & Callahan, K. (2007). Citizen involvement efforts and bureaucratic responsiveness: participatory values, stakeholder pressures, and administrative practicality. *Public Administration Review*, 67(2): 249–264.

Yankelovich, D. (1991). *Coming to Public Judgement: Making Democracy Work in a Complex World*. Syracuse University Press.

2

E-GOVERNMENT AND E-GOVERNANCE

E-Government and E-Governance: Interrelated Concepts Yet Distinctly Different Contributions to Deliberative Democracy

The creation of the World Wide Web in 1989 soon led to the development of the modern Internet, which correspondingly would result in the field of information and communication technologies (ICTs) experiencing continuous and rapid growth. In relation, the progression and ascension of ICTs would correspondingly create an increasingly wider scope of available innovative means at the disposal of the public sector by which to fulfill functions associated with E-Government. The focus of E-Government within the context of the American democracy is deserved of further explanation as the tasks to be fulfilled in pursuit of such plays a pivotal role in public administration. The first step in the process will be to provide some helpful definitions and an explanation as to the role of technology that can help to establish parameters regarding actions associated with E-Government. Sánchez-Torres and Miles (2017, p. 14) note that since the 1990s, when the modern Internet was created, it is increasingly common that governments have "incorporated Information and Communication Technologies in their internal and external processes, a phenomenon widely known as electronic government (e-Government)." Sprecher (2000, paragraph 6) defines E-Government as "any way technology is used to help simplify and automate transactions between governments and constituents, businesses, or other governments." Bannister and Connolly (2012, p. 1) explain that the origin of E-Government is the result of a broad technological metamorphosis in

DOI: 10.4324/9781003441830-2

society, which led to "the use of ICT in and by governments and public administrations over the period since the adoption by governments of the Internet and the World-Wide-Web in the 1990s." E-Government applies technology to allow the public sector to engage with a wide range of system actors and the application of innovative means prevalent in the modern era expands the capacity of government to perform specific functions. Trotta (2018 pp. 3–4) notes that "generally, E-Government is considered to include efforts on behalf of the public sector to apply ICTs for the purposes of delivering services and disseminating information to the public." Haque and Pathrannarakul (2013, p. 25) similarly explains that the practice of E-Government is represented by a "systemic use of ICTs to support the functions that a government performs for its constituents, typically the provision of information and services." For Marche and McNiven (2003, p. 75) E-Government is viewed as "the provision of routine government information and transactions using electronic means, most notably those using Internet technologies" in which, due to innovations in use, participants may be in receipt of such through a variety of venues, including "at home, at work or through public kiosks." Norris and Reddick (2013, p. 174) add that "e-government remains almost primarily about delivering services and information along with some transactions and interactions." Although the public sector is responsible for the fulfillment of a wide range of duties, E-Government applies modern-era technologies exclusively for the purposes of disseminating information and providing services. The nature of these two specific functions is clearly limited in scope and this correspondingly establishes similar limits regarding the general nature of the exchanges themselves. E-Government offers "governmental services electronically" through Internet-based technology, which reduces the need for citizens to interact with government in a traditional in-person fashion (Calista and Melitski, 2007, p. 101). Norris and Reddick (2013, p. 174) expands on this notion by observing that "E-government remains also a mostly one-way activity from governments outward." Here, E-Government's usage of ICTs largely establishes one-way communication dynamics in which citizens can go online to accomplish specific tasks, such as locating information published at a public-sector website. Similarly, citizens connected to the Internet may complete functions online associated with public services delivery, such as requesting benefits or paying fines. In either example of this dynamic in practice, the communicative structure utilized to facilitate E-Government-related activities is limited in both scope and function. Whereas E-Government plays an important role in helping to facilitate key public-sector functions, the interactive capacity associated with this process is intentionally somewhat limited functionally.

Although generally lacking in meaningful, two-way dialogue components, E-Government technologically facilitated activities further institutionalize the important requirements that the public sector fulfills duties in accordance with expectations inherent within American democracy. Doing so further reinforces, in practice, important expectations associated with deliberative democracy while creating an opportunity for later expansion into more involved participatory endeavors associated with this dynamic. Broadly speaking, E-Government efforts to disseminate information and provide services to the public plays an important role in the context of the U.S. deliberative democracy. Specifically, the U.S. deliberative democracy is expected to provide continuous, plentiful opportunities for citizens to engage with government at multiple points of contact in an effort to further commit to ensuring accountability and transparency in government. In relation, the U.S. deliberative democracy is expected to provide citizen engagement opportunities in a cyclical fashion on a longitudinal basis, which is able to be accomplished in part by establishing dynamics associated with E-Government functions. Haque and Pathrannarakul (2013, p. 25) note that ICTs are used to facilitate E-Government activities "to transform the traditional government by making it accessible, transparent, effective, and accountable." Sánchez-Torres and Miles (2017, p. 14) add that "rationales for eGovernment include increasing public services' efficiency, speed, transparency, accountability, etc., and enhancing relations between government and stakeholders (citizens, businesses, third sector organizations)." E-Government is an essential practice that can promote higher levels of government efficiency by utilizing ICTs during the provision of services delivered when interacting with a wide range of system actors such as "citizens, employees, business and agencies" (Carter and Bélanger, 2005, p. 1). Agrawal, Sethi, and Mittal (2015, p. 35) similarly explain that E-Government "uses ICT to promote efficient, cost-effective and convenient government services, allowing greater public access to information." Sprecher (2000, paragraph 10) notes that the "goals of e-government can include improving government service, reducing costs to both the government and the constituent and making agencies transparent to the constituent." Halachmi and Greiling (2013, p. 562) comment that a "greater use of information and communications technology and e-government can increase governmental transparency. This, in turn, may invite citizen participation, foster e-governance, and facilitate e-democracy." Consistent and comprehensive efforts to utilize technology to facilitate E-Government can enhance transparency systemically, which could create circumstances capable of affecting levels of "trust in government" while working to "reduce the cost of its operations" (Halachmi and Greiling, 2013, p. 579). The development of ICTs that leverage the power of the Internet has created a unique opportunity in the modern era for government to utilize innovations in the fulfillment of a wide range of responsibilities. Here, E-Government activities associated with information dissemination and service delivery create digital opportunities for citizens to engage with the public sector. In doing so, technology used to accomplish such E-Government-related tasks further institutionalizes key expectations associated with deliberative democracy as it relates to government being transparent, accountable, and cyclical in nature. Technology can dynamically augment present communication structures by providing further opportunities for system actors to engage in E-Government-related activities that includes an ever-expanding array of digital means. The usage of technology in furnishing E-Government-related tasks is also believed to provide some measure of improvement to the efficiency and effectiveness in the performance of public-sector duties. In this, ICTs being applied to fulfill E-Government activities may have the capacity to improve services and reduce costs, which reflects effectiveness and efficiency, respectively.

After the modern Internet increasingly began to be viewed societally as a more stable communicative commodity throughout the 1990s, the development of ICTs has continuously provided an increasingly diverse scope of means by which system actors may interact. In this sense, the development and proliferation of ICTs that leverage the power of the Internet to facilitate interactions between system actors is evolutionary in nature. The evolutionary nature of ICTs would eventually come to manifest in public-sector endeavors, first including those associated with E-Government. Here, the acceptance and usage of ICTs on behalf of participants, operating within a given network on a societal scale, would come to allow for such means to be applied on behalf of the public sector to fulfill interactive duties, such as those associated with E-Government. On the societal level, the development, acceptance, and wide-scale proliferation of technological means is a process that occurs longitudinally in which, eventually, the application of such innovations were later adopted on behalf of government for use. Relatedly, the process in which technological means are applied on behalf of the public sector has been accomplished in stages as it relates to the scope of activities being facilitated. The available technologies are used variably in terms of the activities being fulfilled in the context of E-Government, with each stage differing in the interactive capacity of communication and scope of tasks performed. During the fulfillment of various public-sector functions, E-Government may employ a wide range of strategies that includes the following:

(1) Simple information dissemination (one-way communication).
(2) Two-way communication (request and response).

40 E-Government and E-Governance

(3) Service and financial transactions.
(4) Integration (horizontal and vertical integration).
(5) Political participation.

Source: Moon (2002, p. 426)

Although E-Government stages provides conceptual lines of demarcation regarding communicative dynamics and scope of duties to be fulfilled, the phases themselves can be implemented in a less rigid manner on behalf of the public sector. In this sense, the employment of E-Government strategies by the public sector is not necessarily required to "follow a true linear progression" (Moon, 2002, p. 427). In relation, it is entirely possible that the employment of such E-Government strategies may be pursued in a simultaneous fashion (Moon, 2002, p. 427). Moon (2002, p. 427) illustrates this dynamic in action by noting that it is possible for government to employ "stage 5 of e-government (political participation) without full practice of stage 4 (integration)." Ultimately, government's application of E-Government evolutionary strategies is dynamic and fluid in nature, as efforts are not constrained by having to progress in a linear fashion and the usage of available strategies may be employed simultaneously or not.

A wide range of system factors—including availability of fiscal resources, levels of technical know-how held by potential participants, and substantive political pressure calling for action—could influence the decision to vest in various stages on behalf of the public-sector entities, indicating that context plays an important role in determining E-Government activities being employed. In relation, West (2004, p. 17) specifically indicates that agency behavior is generally reflective of the following four distinct phases of E-Government:

(1) The billboard stage.
(2) The partial-service-delivery stage.
(3) The portal stage, with fully executable and integrated service delivery.
(4) Interactive democracy with public outreach and accountability enhancing features.

Source: West (2004, p. 17)

West (2004, p. 217) expands on the notion that, when developing websites, every agency is not required to progress through each of the phases, nor are they required to progress through each step in a linear fashion. West (2004, p. 217) explains that, when broadly analyzing thousands of agency websites, "there is a wide variety of ways that e-government has evolved in different cities, states, and countries," with the understanding that the aforementioned four phases of E-Government are still reliably capable of providing a generalized guide as to how this process may unfold within various U.S. government entities. It is important to observe that both Moon and West provide similarly oriented explanatory models regarding the evolutionary stages of E-Government. In that, E-Government initial activities include the public sector leveraging technology for the purpose of advertising information online regarding governance in which the later stages include digital options for service delivery. Similarly, both Moon and West indicate that such evolutionary processes regarding the provision of information and delivery of services ultimately lead to a final stage that is more reflective of participatory endeavors traditionally associated with E-Governance in the context of deliberative democracy.

In general, E-Government extends the ability of interested parties to engage government through the use of ICTs, thereby enhancing the communicative opportunities of citizens to engage in a wide assortment of online activities. In doing so, the power of the Internet can be leveraged to broaden the opportunities by which government can disseminate information and deliver services. E-Government's usage of ICTs can enhance government's ability to perform its duties from a service-delivery standpoint. Here, E-Government facilitated through the Internet may provide an opportunity for government to more effectively and efficiently provide online services to the public at the federal level (i.e. pay online taxes, participate in online government auctions, etc.) and lower levels (i.e. renew online car registration, pay online parking tickets, apply for a building permit online, etc.). By utilizing ICTs to leverage the power of the Internet, E-Government initiatives can assist citizens in overcoming geographical and temporal limits that are oft attributed to traditional means associated with in-person requirements typical to the fulfillment of both activities. E-Government fulfills a key democratic function in that a dynamic government is expected to utilize emergent technology to fulfill duties such as those associated with sharing information and delivering services to the public. In the modern era, E-Government serves to provide innovative interactive means that increases the capacity of government to engage the public in specific activities, which fall outside the scope of direct meaningful deliberations between system actors, through digital events that are attributed to E-Governance. However, E-Government outcomes may provide an opportunity for system actors to parlay accumulated information into more well-informed public opinions when engaging with other system actors in deliberative events associated with E-Governance. The role of applying information generated during E-Government events brings to light the important relationship this process can later play during E-Governance-oriented activities, which are deserved of further exploration.

42 E-Government and E-Governance

The functions associated with E-Government and E-Governance each fulfill distinct expectations associated with public-sector responsibilities in American democracy. Although E-Government and E-Governance are sometimes explained in a fashion that attempts to present the practices as being indistinguishable, it is important to observe that these interrelated concepts vary greatly regarding functions fulfilled when applied in the U.S. deliberative democracy (Agrawal, Sethi and Mittal, 2015, p. 35). Qian (2011, p. 119) similarly notes that "E-Government and E-Governance are intrinsically related, however, practice shows that successful e-government and e-governance are not synonymous, but complementary." Here, it is important to view the activities associated with E-Government and E-Governance as each being capable of fulfilling important democratic expectations attached to U.S. public-sector responsibilities in related but distinctly separate ways. While both are capable of facilitating various activities expected in a democracy, E-Government is largely transactional (i.e. information dissemination, service delivery) while E-Governance is generally considered to be richly interactional (i.e. facilitating communication), indicating the differing nature at the core of each's basic conceptualization in practice (Calista and Melitski, 2007, p. 99). Although fulfilling important roles expected of the public sector in the U.S. democratic system, activities associated with E-Government and E-Governance reflect distinctly different functions associated with this dynamic. In relation, the act of leveraging ICTs in order to perform specific activities associated with either E-Government or E-Governance, which are reflective of functional differences, may correspondingly cater to variances in recipients operating within the political system. In this, the public sector's pursuit of E-Government and E-Governance is reflective of efforts to apply a wide array of modern technologies to achieve specific goals in the interest of strengthening "partnerships among all stakeholders" (Qian, 2011, p. 119). The two conceptualizations "largely serve disparate client bases" in that E-Government is mainly geared toward facilitating transactions "with customers as end-users of agency services" while E-Governance is generally focused on using technology to create opportunities for the public to interact with government to advocate for the societal values associated with various "networked democratic affiliations" (Calista and Melitski, 2007, p. 99). Marche and McNiven (2003, p. 75) expand on the complexity, in a communicative and functional sense, associated with E-Governance activities as being "a technology-mediated relationship between citizens and their governments from the prospective of potential electronic deliberation over civic communication, over policy evolution, and in democratic expressions of citizen will." E-Government and E-Governance both play an important role in fulfilling important public-sector responsibilities expected in the

American democratic system, but the activities associated with each may vary in functions performed, clientele to be engaged, and complexity in communication dynamics. In this respect, the functional differences associated with the activities for E-Government and E-Governance facilitated through ICTs may also reflect variances in the nature of the goals held by the recipients, which attempt to engage in the technological means that are used to facilitate respective interactions.

In the U.S. political system, the expected roles associated with E-Government and E-Governance may be viewed as complementary to one another, with the understanding that the activities attributed to each fall within distinctly different functional categories. On one level, E-Government duties are generally related to digitally facilitated tasks focused on information dissemination and service delivery. Here, citizens are provided greater opportunity to become engaged through a wide range of E-Government-related activities, conducted on behalf of the public sector by leveraging ICTs that are available for use within the modern era. On another level, E-Governance serves vastly different functions within the U.S. deliberative democracy, in that efforts associated with such are geared toward applying ICTs to create greater opportunities for system actors to engage in discursive events, in which outcomes later can ultimately affect some measure of identifiable and substantive change to the political system. With these distinctive differences in mind, it is important to consider how the different activities associated with E-Government and E-Governance can serve complimentary functions within the context of deliberative democracy. E-Government applies ICTs to fulfill a wide range of functions associated with information dissemination and service delivery, in the hopes that doing so will promote more efficient and effective performance on behalf of the public sector. By leveraging the power of the Internet, the public sector may integrate ICTs to allow for citizen to obtain greater levels of access to an increasingly wider range of government information. Once information is obtained by interested parties, it is preferably optimal that digitally obtained knowledge is parlayed into more informed decision making, when system actors participate through the many points of contact within the communicative structure that may provide an opportunity to impact changes to the political system associated with E-Governance. For example, a citizen-consumer going online to review voting information on proposed bills for a member of Congress in a specific jurisdiction, and to analyze details associated with bills introduced by said legislator (i.e. E-Government), can allow for the industrious educational effort by the individual to be used to make more informed decisions when participating in any number of deliberative events over policy preferences, or when voting in the upcoming elections (i.e. E-Governance). In this sense, participation in any number of E-Government opportunities involving information dissemination may ultimately be capable of providing a transitional path that leads system actors toward more responsibly taking part in later deliberative events associated with E-Governance. Ultimately, the government making information available regarding its activities (i.e. annual budget expenditures, voting on proposed bills, legislative measures passed, etc.) to ensure transparent and accountable governance is only part of the participatory equation expected in a deliberative democracy. In that, interested parties are also required to access and analyze the information in order to make more informed decisions when later engaging in deliberative opportunities, such as voting, participating in public hearings regarding proposed agency rule changes, or dialoguing with elected officials in the hopes of affecting legislative efforts. The provision of information by the public sector and the usage of information by interested parties within the political system are interrelated events that have the capacity to contribute to more informed decision making, which in turn may result in official outcomes that better reflect system needs. The potential relationship between processes focused on information gathering, associated with E-Government, and the application of such by participants in various E-Governance-related activities, highlights the interconnected nature that can be associated with each concept in practice within the American democracy.

The effort on behalf of the public sector to provide digital E-governance opportunities for citizens to engage with government through deliberative events is part of the evolutionary nature associated with the U.S. political system. In that, the U.S. deliberative democracy is expected to remain flexible and dynamic in assessing and responding to system needs, including those associated with establishing participatory opportunities. Relatedly, the decision to further integrate ICTs into the communication structures both impacts and reflects the expectations associated with deliberative democracy, regarding government efforts to integrate interactions that are transparent, accountable, and cyclical in nature. In this sense, technological means available in the modern era provide system actors with an ever-expanding set of digital tools by which to share and identify preferences held by the wider public regarding the direction of government. Qian (2011, p. 119) expands on this dynamic by noting that "without government effectively using ICTs, it is unlikely that the citizen-state-private sector interaction would have become as integrated as it is today or as widely." In the contemporary era, E-Governance activities that involves the application of modern technologies adds further substantive means by which participatory events can be facilitated. Therefore, communicative structures in the modern era, which include ICTs-facilitated discursive events, provide greater opportunity for the public sector to gauge the thoughts of system actors on items of import within the political environment. Specifically, the means available by which citizens participating in discursive events with government can be expanded by applying technology that is now available in contemporary society. These efforts are representative of the government's responsibility to maintain a political system that is actively supportive of the expectations for participation in a deliberative democracy. In this regard, E-Governance applies Internet-based technology to create opportunities for citizens to directly engage with government in which "networked interactions" promote transparent exchanges as expected in a democratic system (Calista and Melitski, 2007, p. 102). Xu and Asencio (2012, p. 117) similarly explain that the technology associated with E-Governance is used to facilitate interactive activities expected in a democracy, which are focused on "citizen participation and empowerment, collective intelligence and local knowledge, decentralization of decision/policymaking, and transparency and openness of government." In relation, E-Governance efforts are focused on applying a wide range of ICT-associated Web 2.0 technologies that can support various interactions, such as those between citizens and the public sector, which conceptually are better able to promote transparent and accountable democracy (Xu and Asencio, 2012, p. 117). Among the important aspects of deliberative democracy that are capable of being expressed through interactions associated with E-Governance is the ability for discursive events to further institutionalize transparency and accountability into political processes. Here, citizens may exchange ideas and lobby for value-based preferences for the direction of government via digital discursive events that are open to all interested parties. Regarding further institutionalizing accountability into decision making, E-Governance includes the public sector applying a variety of modern technologies that can encourage "citizen engagement," in which the interactions can result in outcomes that directly influence decisions on policymaking regarding legislation and bureaucratic activities (Xu and Asencio, 2012, p. 117). Here, the idea of meaningful deliberations is expected in the U.S. democratic system, indicating that participation in discursive events lacks legitimacy unless engaging in this process which will potentially allow for the opportunity to affect changes to the political system to occur. While recognizing the fact that the digital divide may limit "representativeness" to some degree, government usage of innovations to fulfill a wide range of activities may still be successful in enhancing levels of transparency and citizen participation (Justice, Melitski, and Smith, 2006, pp. 17–18). This includes that the usage of modern-era ICTs to facilitate E-Governance has led to growing permeability of information among network actors (Dawes, 2008, p. 86). Dawes (2008, p. 86) expands on this notion by noting that "citizens and businesses interact with government

46 E-Government and E-Governance

much more through e-mail, Web sites, and interactive voice systems, and much less in person or on paper. Government is even beginning to engage in virtual electronic worlds, crossing the boundary between physical and digital communities." E-Governance applies innovative means available in the modern era to enhance the ability of system actors to engage in meaningful deliberations. In doing so, the opportunities for citizens to participate in the modern era are expanded considerably when compared to the pre-Internet deliberative environment which includes far less options available by which to facilitate discursive events. In general, the responsibility of the public sector to consider adding communicative means that prove viable in facilitating discursive events serves as a foundational element associated with government responsiveness in the U.S. democratic system. The continuous effort on behalf of the public sector to add emergent digital means to existing traditional means to create a more expansive communicative structure is reflective of the evolutionary nature of the U.S. deliberative democracy.

As opposed to the more limited interactions from a directionally communicative and task-oriented standpoint associated with E-Government (i.e. citizens obtaining information posted on a government website, citizens receiving service delivery online, etc.), the network structures associated with E-Governance are able, and in many cases expected, to be supportive of system actors consistently engaging in a multi-directional fashion. In relation, communication structures associated with E-Governance promote the usage of various technologies to facilitate participatory activities between system actors that are both asynchronous and synchronous with the later methodology, providing a more immediately immersive deliberative experience. Although lacking in the ability to directly engage in real-time with other system actors, the provision of asynchronous communicative events can also contribute greatly to enhancing the network structure by which E-Governance activities can be facilitated. This includes providing an opportunity for system actors to engage in E-Governance-related activities that would not have otherwise existed without the establishment of asynchronous communicative means. The usage of technology to facilitate E-Governance further integrates participatory means into existing "communication networks" so that interested parties from within or outside government may engage "regardless of time or location" (Dawes, 2008, p. 86). By utilizing ICTs to facilitate more convenient "asynchronous communication" between system actors, it is possible to mitigate issues that may have otherwise limited participation due to logistical barriers that were schedule or travel oriented in nature (Justice, Melitski, and Smith, 2006, p. 17). In doing so, asynchronous means facilitating E-Governance activities are capable of extended the scope of participants by creating a more convenient opportunity which is accommodating to those in society that may have otherwise been prevented from engaging. The asynchronous participatory events integrated into the broader communicative framework serves to create digital bridges capable of increasing the opportunities for interested parties to engage in discursive events. In addition, government may apply technological means to enhance levels of participation by providing digital deliberative opportunities for citizen to engage with government via "message boards and chat rooms," which contribute to limiting issues stemming from "problems of scale" and "physical barriers to interaction" (Justice, Melitski, and Smith, 2006, p. 17). As message boards would generally be conducted asynchronously and chat rooms would be geared more toward synchronous communication, the broader communicative framework would be better served by integration of both participatory means, so that choices in participation are provided to those citizens that may wish to engage in discursive events. The idea of diversity in means is one of great importance regarding government efforts to enhance the communicative structure used to connect network actors during discursive events. Ultimately, E-Governance endeavors are designed with the intent to broaden the scope of means available for citizens to engage in meaningful deliberations with government. By integrating ICTs that facilitate asynchronous and synchronous interactions, E-Governance endeavors can expand the options available to those interested in participating and create a more expansive communications structure that reflects diversified deliberative modalities. The decision to integrate such means into the broader communicative structure may provide the opportunity for the U.S. deliberative system to generate increased levels of citizen participation by establishing a more expansive set of discursive events, which will ultimately include a combination of traditional and digital means. In relation, the ability to select between participating in traditional in-person means and digital-distanced means provides choices to citizens as to how to engage with government. These variances in venues—in person and digital—and time-related dynamics—asynchronous and synchronous—ultimately create a broader communication structure that can provide an opportunity for citizens to overcome barriers to participation that are temporal and geographical in nature. The diversity in communicative means also provides further evidence as to the importance of government remaining dynamic in developing and maintaining participatory events as expected in the U.S. deliberative democracy.

In general, there are any number of politically oriented factors that may affect public-sector decision making, including those determining whether to apply various ICTs for the purpose of digitally facilitating governmental activities within the American democratic system. In relation, analysis of

48 E-Government and E-Governance

the political environment may reveal situational and contextual cues highlighting extant preferences that can affect decision making regarding the implementation of electronically designed official activities. In reference to paving the way for the initial application of innovative means to fulfill a wide assortment of organizational goals in the public sector, situationally the burgeoning opportunity to apply newly emerging technologies requires the support of "digital champions" to begin to establish engaging "virtual outputs" (Calista and Melitski, 2007, p. 92). Essentially, E-Governance activities require support from those within government that are willing to implement processes that can integrate digital means into the communicative structure and from those outside government interested in the usage of such. Broadly speaking, in a political system, the decision for a given nation to effort to develop E-Governance endeavors is in part due to "the collective national and local capital supplying IT services and of informal social and human capital creating a demand for e-governance" (Rose, 2005, p. 5). In addition to the perception that the public is supportive of E-Governance endeavors, there are also logistical issues that may influence the degree to which digital discursive events are pursued. In this, situationally the government must possess the technical knowledge and fiscal resources required to develop, implement, and maintain discursive events associated with E-Governance. The political system can also provide contextual cues that, once assessed, can directly affect decisions to utilize ICTs to fulfill E-Governance-related responsibilities. Rose (2005, pp. 5–6) notes that "since governance is about the interaction of the state and society, e-governance is necessarily influenced by its national context," which from a longitudinal standpoint is influenced by system expectations that have developed "for generations before the Internet was invented." In the U.S. deliberative democracy, it is important to recognize that there are most assuredly a wide range of political dynamics that may affect public-sector decision making associated with pursuit of discursive events. The situational cues present within the political environment may provide information capable of influencing the scope and nature of E-Governance to be employed. From a political standpoint, the strengthening of interactive means within the communicative structure may be derived from decision makers' assessment of fiscal opportunity at a given point in time. In addition, government must have the technical know-how regarding developing, implementing, and maintaining communicative means capable of facilitating E-Governance. Relatedly, in order to enact E-Governance there must be sufficient levels of support for the undertaking, which includes system actors actively advocating for the usage of ICTs to fulfill public-sector activities. Broadly speaking, there may be some variability in levels of acceptance for E-Governance as it relates to the expectations of system actors which is partly dependent upon the jurisdictional boundaries in question. The political system also contains various contextual cues that, upon review, will highlight system expectations that can assist in guiding decision makers in the public sector regarding the usage of innovative means to facilitate various participatory opportunities. In relation, the system of government in place can play a role in the usage of ICTs in E-Governance as societal expectations often affect political outcomes especially within a democracy. Here, the system of government in place may have a direct impact on the actions of public-sector decision makers as it relates to actively maintaining a communicative structure that best reflects the expectations for participation. Relatedly, it is of importance to continue to reinforce the fact that U.S. deliberative democracy includes expectations that the public-sector efforts to apply available means—be they traditional or digital—in order to enhance the participatory opportunities available to citizens to engage in government. In this sense, E-Governance efforts are often viewed by system actors as serving as the logical progression of the participatory means expected in the modern U.S. deliberative democracy, creating an increasingly more accommodating stance societally for the perpetuation of this technologically facilitated dynamic. In all, the availability of sufficient levels of fiscal resources, the presence of technical skill in those responsible for implementation, and the widely held belief by system actors that implementing ICTs to facilitate E-Governance activities may provide the political opportunity to pursue this endeavor.

E-Government and E-Governance: Potential Concerns in Practice

E-Government and E-Governance integration of modern technologies to fulfill a wide range of governmental activities can play an instrumental role in longitudinally reinforcing the principles of transparency, accountability, and cyclicity throughout the political system, which are of great importance in American democracy. Although technological means can be used to achieve a number of important expectations inherent with the U.S. deliberative democracy, there are also cautionary concerns that are deserved of some measure of attention. E-Government activities (i.e. information dissemination, service delivery) and E-Governance activities (i.e. discursive events between system actors that allow for meaningful deliberations) may yield unintended externalities capable of impeding performance, which may limit the successful completion of corresponding goals to some degree. In the context of democracy, there are several potential issues associated with the usage of technology to facilitate E-Government-based information dissemination, such as when those working in an agency or other governmental entity practice "E-clogging," which constitutes "dumping data and documents," in massive quantities (Calista and Melitski, 2007, p. 114). This process can create "information overload" to the point where the citizen-consumer's ability to meticulously read through and properly interpret the immense amount of material published online is significantly challenged, which may correspondingly result in a diminished investment in citizen participation through available electronically facilitated means (Calista and Melitski, 2007, p. 114). The digital publication of information expands the means at the disposal of system actors by which to conduct research on a vast array of topics regarding public-sector actions. Whether intentional or unintentional, the online publication process can create an unwieldly surplus of complex information that, for a citizen, is both difficult to interpret and in such excess that it makes analysis in full an implausible task from a logistical standpoint. There may also be concerns when technology is applied to facilitate E-Governance-focused citizen participation events in which a select group of contributors intentionally inundate the provided interactive means with a "disinformation" campaign that results in "consuming agencies and jurisdictions" (Calista and Melitski, 2007, p. 114). Here, communicative structures that are strengthened by the application of ICTs available in the modern era may result in some measure of disinformation being promoted among system actors. Unfortunately, modern-era tools such as social media have increasingly been irresponsibly utilized by informal and formal actors alike to promote opinions lacking in the necessary levels of substantive, accurate information that would warrant support of the arguments being advanced regarding political preferences. In this way, using innovative means by which to express opinions as factual evidence may serve to diminish the expected threshold of participatory legitimacy that, if permitted to continue, can correspondingly degrade the faith of system actors in the deliberative processes. Relatedly, the establishment of technology-based means intended to promote meaningful deliberations between citizens and government may instead result in "disquisition" as powerful groups capture key aspects of the political environment associated with "agencies and jurisdictions" in much the same fashion as these factional interests do so through traditionally facilitated participatory events (Calista and Melitski, 2007, p. 114). Here, issues that have affected traditional participatory dynamics—in which interest groups that are well-organized, highly funded, and reflect proficient leadership may leverage greater access during government decision making—may simply extend to the digital forum to some degree. In this sense, the communicative structure is utilized more so in an expository fashion, in which digital discursive means are captured by select groups, which in such cases would serve to reduce the intended dialectic capacity of the participatory event.

facilitate delivery interactions with citizens which would no longer be conducted by the public sector in this scenario. In relation, the role of government itself may shift to be more focused on oversight of the industry now being served through privatization and the private-sector entity directly involved in this delivery process. Both E-Government and E-Governance may be affected by privacy and security concerns, which can directly affect the functionality of and the faith in digital means on behalf of system actors. In addition, the initial application and continued usage of ICTs to fulfill governance duties online will require an expenditure of resources associated with human capital and public finances. Lastly, there is a distinct possibility that decision makers in government may fail to properly institute digitally facilitated discursive events that truly provide opportunity for citizens to become engaged in meaningful deliberations that are genuinely capable of affecting changes to the political system. Should such digital efforts be perceived by system actors as being incapable of creating opportunities for meaningful deliberations, then this failure may negatively affect the levels of trust on behalf of citizens in government processes and outcomes.

The Digital Divide

In addition to the above-mentioned circumstances, the usage of technology to facilitate activities associated with E-Government and E-Governance may also be subjected to concerns for inequities associated with the digital divide. As such, it is important to define the digital divide and to expand on the concerns caused by the digital divide in relation to the public sector endeavoring to utilize technology during the fulfillment of its expected responsibilities. Rogers (2001, p. 96) defines the digital divide as "the gap that exists between individuals advantaged by the internet and those individuals relatively disadvantaged by the internet." Van Dijik (2006, pp. 221–222) similarly notes that "the digital divide commonly refers to the gap between those who do and those who do not have access to new forms of information technology." Although the digital divide most assuredly includes variances in access to Internet-based forms of communication, there are more expansive dynamics that contribute to inequities associated with technology. The digital divide includes "usability and accessibility" concerns as it relates to citizens having the technical know-how to utilize Internet-based technology and the opportunity to access these technologies so that they may employ such means to interact with government (Manoharan, Bennet, and Carrizalas, 2012, p. 89). According to the Division of Broadband and Digital Equity of North Carolina (2022, paragraph 3) the digital divide refers to "the gap between those who have access to technology, the internet

54 E-Government and E-Governance

and digital literacy training and those who do not. It affects all generations – both rural and urban communities – and a wide variety of industries and sectors." Overall, access to and understanding of the wide range of ICTs employed in the modern era contributes to determining whether an individual will be negatively affected by the digital divide. The focus here is on whether citizens have consistent access to the broad scope of ICTs and, if having so, are proficient in its usage to the point where it is possible to benefit from engaging the public sector digitally. Also of importance is recognizing that digital-divide concerns associated with access to and understanding of technology may transcend geography, in that this issue may affect those residing in both urban and rural locales. The digital divide can refer to broadly sourced inequities, whose nature may be physical (i.e. access to computer, cell phone, tablet, Internet, etc.), skill based (i.e. understanding of how and when to use a particular innovative tool), and preferential (i.e. variances in individual motivation to achieve and apply technically oriented knowledge), which together helps to explain societal disparities regarding the usage of technology (van Dijik, 2006, p. 224). Howland (1998, p. 287) explains that, broadly speaking, in the modern era the digital divide "has separated much of the world into two societies—one comfortable with computers and with adequate access to telecommunications technologies and one that neither possesses, nor has access to, these tools." Howland (1998, p. 287) adds that "technology has created a chasm, polarizing the 'technological haves' from the 'technological have-nots'." In this sense, citizens must be proficient in and have access to the Internet connected ICTs and also the devices required to facilitate digital participation (i.e. computer, smart phone, etc.). The government's application of ICTs to facilitate a wide range of activities requires citizens to use the Internet and this requirement highlights a more subtle aspect associated with access that is related to inequities in quality of the Internet service available. Rachfal (2020, p. 2) descriptively expands on the notion of the digital divide by noting that it is applied to "characterize a gap between those Americans who have access to telecommunications and information technologies and those who do not. One subset of the digital divide debate concerns access to high-speed internet, also known as broadband." Furthermore, this advancement in ICTs is more fully understood as follows:

> Broadband is provided by a variety of technologies (e.g., cable, telephone wire, fiber, satellite, and mobile and fixed wireless) that give users the ability to send and receive data at volumes and speeds that support a wide range of applications, including voice communications, entertainment, telemedicine, distance education, telework, ecommerce, civic engagement, public safety, and energy conservation.
>
> *Source: Rachfal (2020, p. 2)*

Here, the quality of the Internet creates a level of nuance that contributes to further understanding practical aspects associated with the digital divide, as access to and proficiency in broadband may further drive a wedge between members of society. The digital divide's potential to affect the levels of technology-based inequity may play a broader and deeper role in context of the U.S. deliberative democracy. Hammond (1997, p. 182) advises some measure of caution in the application of ICTs on behalf of government, in that it is important when identifying "the potential of network technology to benefit society" that those involved in its application should remain "wary that it not become a tool of disenfranchisement." This concern is deserved of further exploration, as meeting the expectations associated with deliberative democracy is a key contextual component associated with decision making on behalf of the U.S. government and perceptions regarding this dynamic in practice can affect society's trust in the public sector to some degree. As E-Government and E-Governance are facilitated through the usage of ICTs, it is prudent to consider the technologies and skillsets that are required by potential participants, which may contribute to the inequities associated with the digital divide. In doing so, it is of import to recognize the potential concerns that may be raised in the context of democracy as it relates to possibility that the digital divide could unintentionally create a disadvantage for those in society that lack access to and understanding of the innovative means required to allow for full participation in E-Government and E-Governance related activities.

The government's application of technology can be facilitated to create digital bridges between system actors including citizens and the public sector, which is intended to allow for greater access to a wide range of participatory opportunities associated with deliberative democracy. In theory, the usage of ICTs to fulfill a wide range of politically oriented activities, such as interacting directly in discursive events with system actors and forming political groups, may increase levels of citizen participation, because the application of innovation creates a measure of convenience by allowing for such to occur via the Internet (Schlozman, Verba, and Brady, 2010). As younger generations in the modern era are well-versed in and comfortable with the usage of ICTs to fulfill a wide range of activities in their personal and professional lives, E-Governance efforts may have the potential to increase levels of citizen participation for those younger adults, in part because integrating technological means is highly appealing to this age demographic (Schlozman, Verba, and Brady, 2010). Whereas the usage of ICTs to facilitate citizen participative activities via the Internet has potential to enhance the involvement of "those who have just joined the electorate," it is argued that there may be significant room for improvement regarding the potential to electronically engage citizens "who are lower on the socioeconomic ladder" and those citizens that skew older demographically

(Schlozman, Verba, and Brady, 2010, p. 503). In the modern era, the effort to integrate technology into the communicative structure, in order to facilitate interactions, may be capable of affecting system actors from different demographic groups in distinctive ways. Although it is important to avoid assuming that all those within a generational category–Baby Boomers, Gen Xers, or Millennials–behave without deviation from an expected norm, there are likely variances associated with comfort in, access to, and use of technologies in the modern era that should be considered. For example, system actors such as those representing generations that skew younger may benefit more from the opportunities to use ICTs to join in activities facilitated on behalf of government. On the other hand, in some cases the effort on behalf of government to create a digital bridge intended to increase citizen participation may inadvertently contribute to the digital divide from a demographic standpoint in relation to older generations.

Overall, the digital divide can greatly affect the integrity of the U.S. deliberative democracy in that those subject to electronic inequities may be disadvantaged by government efforts to invest too widely in innovations at the expense of foregoing traditional means of participation. Instead of creating a digital bridge capable of connecting system actors, the chasm resulting from the digital divide may serve to prevent interactions that are expected to occur in a responsive democratic government. In relation, the digital divide as a conceptualization exceeds being constrained to affecting one demographic group, governmental jurisdiction, or public-sector function. Jorgensen and Cable (2002) explains that the digital divide's effect on E-Government is applicable at the local levels of government as well, in that "politicians, management, and citizens suggest that a lack of access to e-government technology can further economic inequities within the city and limits choices and opportunities for the poor, the elderly, and historically underrepresented groups, creating a 'digital divide' in the public sector." Among any number of those in society potentially affected, the digital divide inequities are not constrained to a single jurisdictional boundary in the U.S., indicating that the scope of such issues are far from limited to a single level of government. As such, the digital divide is capable of affecting citizens' opportunity to engage with the public sector in E-Government and E-Governance activities at each of the levels of government in the U.S. federal system (i.e. national, state, and local). In relation, the following excerpt expands on the notion that the digital divide may affect the ability of some members of society to take full advantage of E-Government and E-Governance activities that are facilitated via ICTs available in the modern era:

If the government implements a whole-of-government approach to incorporate electronic means to facilitate interactions with the public, then the entirety of the populous may not actually be able to participate through these means due to the digital divide. The nature of the digital divide yields complex concerns caused in part by individuals in society that experience inequity of access to technology, a lack of opportunity to develop the requisite skills needed to utilize technology or simply have a disinterest in participating through non-traditional, high-tech means. In relation, the application of technology toward governance activities may potentially yield significant societal implications affecting those representing the digital divide disproportionately.

Source: Trotta (2018, p. 23)

In the modern era, the decision by government to use technology to continuously engage the citizenry in a wide range of activities necessitates that a responsible public sector remains aware of the inequities that may affect members of society as a result of the digital divide occurring during the employment of innovative means by which to facilitate participatory events. The previous notations regarding the possibility that society may broadly reflect technological haves and have-nots creates a fairly accurate but somewhat partial picture as to the scope of the digital divide. Gibson (2001, p. 581) notes that "even if the digital divide is overcome" as it relates to the technological "haves and have-nots," from an access and skillset standpoint, that there may still yet be "an entrenched class of 'want-nots,' " which would raise concerns regarding the effectiveness of employing E-Government and E-Governance alike. In that, there may be members of society that find the prospect of engaging with government through modern innovative means a daunting or disinteresting prospect (Gibson, 2001, p. 581). Gibson (2001, p. 581) recommends that in cases such as this "more attention needs to be paid by policymakers to questions about frequency of use in addition to issues of access in combating electronic exclusion." In some cases, lack of access to and knowledge of the ICTs used to facilitate E-Government and E-Governance may unintentionally digitize societal inequities to some degree. However, it is possible that individual choice may also contribute to the digital divide, in that there may be citizens that are averse to participating electronically. Regardless of the genesis, be it individual choice or societal inequity, it is of great importance that government recognize the presence of the digital divide and respond accordingly when necessary to avoid negatively affecting the integrity of U.S. deliberative democracy when facilitating participatory activities electronically.

The digital divide may affect any number of individuals representing various demographics in society, ranging from age, ethnicity, gender, socioeconomic status, and residency (i.e. urban setting, rural setting, etc.).

In the context of U.S. governmental interactive dynamics, the digital divide refers to those in society that may lack understanding of and access to the innovations that are necessary to participate in a wide range of activities facilitated by the public sector through the application of modern-era technology. Here, utilizing technology to facilitate activities associated with E-Government and E-Governance requires interested parties to be adept in technically oriented tools being used in these processes. Relatedly, the interested parties must also have access to the technological devices that connect to the Internet (i.e. computer, mobile phone, tablet, etc.) in order to be able to take full advantage of the digital opportunities provided by the public sector to engage in E-Government and E-Governance activities. Without the knowledge of and access to the innovative tools needed to participate, there are members of society that will be unable to engage government via this technology, which in turn renders the digital path inert for those individuals. The digital divide can create a measure of inequity by electronically separating society into two broad categories: (1) those who are electronically savvy and have access to technology; (2) those that lack the technical know-how and access to technology. Relatedly, there are also members of society that simply remain completely disinterested in the usage of technology to engage with government in any capacity. The digital divide can have a deleterious effect on the potency of participatory democracy as it relates to the important role that equity to access is expected to play in facilitation of both E-Government and E-Governance activities. For example, the digital divide may create inequities regarding the ability of citizens to engage with government electronically regarding any number of E-Government-based activities. In addition, the exclusion of those disadvantaged by the digital divide will call into question government actions that are intended to utilize discursive events to help identity the will of the public. By only identifying the policy preferences held by those participating in digital discursive events, those whose participation is absent because of the digital divide may remain underserved to some degree from a policymaking standpoint. Should the disparity be left unattended by the public sector, the digital divide may continue to unintentionally diminish levels of trust in government as it relates to a lack of opportunity for citizens to participate electronically in meaningful discourse, as is expected the U.S. deliberative democracy.

If the goal of utilizing technology is to enhance the participatory capacity of the U.S. democracy, then it is prudent to remain aware of the potential of the digital divide to inhibit full achievement of this objective. There are several actions that may be taken on behalf of government to help mitigate the negative effects of the digital divide to better reinforce the expectations associated with participation in a deliberative democracy.

This includes that government may develop, fund, and implement programs that are focused on providing educational opportunities to citizens that wish to develop the skillset necessary for participating in E-Government and E-Governance activities. In relation, government can provide access to devices that connect to the Internet through community venues, such as computers placed in libraries and public kiosks. Among the many important endeavors that decision makers can pursue in the hopes of affecting changes to the U.S. political system capable of leveling aspects of the technological playing field, those serving in government can enact legislation that is designed to address societal circumstances serious enough to be considered a problem that needs officially mandated intervention. Historically, this includes legislative efforts on behalf of Congress that are designed to combat access issues faced by the public associated with advancement in communications technologies. For example, the Communications Act of 1934, which served as the creation mandate for the Federal Communications Commission (FCC), provided the following general purposes associated with efforts to level the proverbial playing field regarding access to the communication means available then:

> For the purpose of regulating interstate and foreign commerce in communication by wire and radio so as to make available, so far as possible, to all the people of the United States, without discrimination on the basis of race, color, religion, national origin, or sex, a rapid, efficient, Nationwide, and worldwide wire and radio communication service with adequate facilities at reasonable charges, for the purpose of the national defense, for the purpose of promoting safety of life and property through the use of wire and radio communication, and for the purpose of securing a more effective execution of this policy by centralizing authority heretofore granted by law to several agencies and by granting additional authority with respect to interstate and foreign commerce in wire and radio communication, there is hereby created a commission to be known as the "Federal Communications Commission, " which shall be constituted as hereinafter provided, and which shall execute and enforce the provisions of this Act.
>
> *Source: Federal Communications Commission (1934)*

Here, the U.S. government enacted legislation that sought to institutionalize efforts to better ensure that equality of access was provided to all citizens regarding the communication technologies available at the time (i.e. phone service, radio service, etc.). In relation, the idea of "universal service" was highlighted within the Communications Act of 1934, which essentially reflects a policy effort to create equity in access regarding the

60 E-Government and E-Governance

available communication means, which has continued to find relevance in the modern era. More precisely stated:

> Universal service is the principle that all Americans should have access to communications services. Universal service is also the name of a fund and the category of FCC programs and policies to implement this principle. Universal service is a cornerstone of the law that established the FCC, the Communications Act of 1934. Since that time, universal service policies have helped make telephone service ubiquitous, even in remote rural areas. Today, the FCC recognizes high-speed Internet as the 21st Century's essential communications technology, and is working to make broadband as ubiquitous as voice, while continuing to support voice service.
>
> *Source: FCC (2022a)*

Similarly, updates to the field of communications technology over time have yielded corresponding policy responses such as the Telecommunications Act of 1996. This act updated many aspects associated with the Communications Act of 1934, including institutionalizing efforts associated with ensuring that universal service kept pace with emergent telecommunication technologies. This legislative effort was an important next step on behalf of government in further efforts to reduce the access gap to technology that is associated with the digital divide, in that:

> The Telecommunications Act of 1996 expanded the traditional goal of universal service to include increased access to both telecommunications and advanced services – such as high-speed Internet – for all consumers at just, reasonable and affordable rates. The Act established principles for universal service that specifically focused on increasing access to evolving services for consumers living in rural and insular areas, and for consumers with low-incomes. Additional principles called for increased access to high-speed Internet in the nation's schools, libraries and rural health care facilities.
>
> *Source: FCC (2022a)*

Relatedly, over time additional legislative efforts on behalf of Congress sought to further institutionalize the idea of universal service by continuing to effort to provide increased access to the Internet and connected technologies. For example, the Infrastructure Investment and Jobs Act of 2021 included statutory guidance that provided $14.2 billion to modify and extend the Emergency Broadband Benefit Program (EBB Program) to a longer-term broadband affordability program called the Affordable Connectivity Program (ACP) (Federal Communications Commission, 2022b, paragraph 2). In doing so, the ACP program is a legislative effort that "provides eligible households with a discount on broadband service and connected devices," which serves to help combat digital divide inequities as it relates to issues of access to the Internet and connected technologies (Federal Communications Commission, 2022b, paragraph 1). Although the ideal regarding what constitutes reasonable charges, and how to ensure this dynamic in practice, has seemingly shifted significantly since the creation of the FCC, the pursuit of the long-standing principle of universal service is clearly reinforced in modern legislative efforts including recent initiatives such as the mandated efforts associated with the ACP.

Although there are a wide range of options available to government that can help to reduce issues associated with the digital divide, the responsibility in this dynamic is not limited to the domain of the public sector. As such, citizens are responsible for making efforts to utilize offered educational programs and to participate in the digital activities that are made available by government. Government can implement E-Government and E-Governance activities, provide a vast assortment of training programs, and increase public access to technology, but without the effort on behalf of citizens to become engaged digitally the societal gap created by the digital divide may remain unchanged to some degree. In addition, there may also be citizens that comprise a category referred to as want-nots, who remain completely disinterested in digitally engaging with system actors for any reason. As the digital divide will likely persist to some degree despite efforts on behalf of government to close the technology gap, and there will continue to be individuals disinterested in using innovative means to facilitate activities associated with E-Government and E-Governance, the public sector will be better served by utilizing a multi-functional delivery design. In this context, activities associated with government (i.e. dissemination of information, service delivery) and governance (i.e. participatory means by which to facilitate deliberative democracy) should be facilitated via a communicative structure that is capable of simultaneously supporting traditional and digital interactions. By providing choices in means for system actors to participate, the communicative structure is maintained more broadly, providing greater opportunity for those interested to become engaged. In this sense, the application of technological means to facilitate E-Government and E-Governance activities should avoid wholly supplanting traditional means in which citizens may engage with government.

The Role of ICTs in Modern-Era American Democracy: E-Government (Web 1.0 technology) and E-Governance (Web 2.0 technology)

The implementation of E-Government (i.e. information dissemination, service delivery) and E-Governance (i.e. facilitating deliberative events) requires the application of various ICTs available in the modern era that are correspondingly capable of fulfilling tasks associated with each endeavor. Here, ICTs representing initial stage Web 1.0 technologies and the later development of Web 2.0 technologies signify the advancement in innovations that are applicable to the delivery of responsibilities associated with E-Government and E-Governance, respectively. In order to be able to understand the technological dynamics associated with fulfilling the respective duties associated with E-Government and E-Governance, it is important to elaborate on various aspects associated with ICTs. This includes the initial stage of ICTs, oft referred to as Web 1.0 technology, and how this advancement in communication means would come to be integrated into the public sector. The National Institute of Standards and Technology (2015) explains that "Information and Communications Technologies (ICTs) encompasses all technologies for the capture, storage, retrieval, processing, display, representation, organization, management, security, transfer, and interchange of data and information." In this sense, ICTs first manifesting as Web 1.0 technologies represented a previously unheard advancement in the means by which to communicate basic information between system actors. Although considered limited in functionality by today's standards, in the 1990s the Web 1.0 technology represented a significant advancement in field of communication. ICTs based on Web 1.0 technology would apply various digital tools for the purpose of facilitating basic information requests and this step would serve to augment the communicative structure, creating an interactive capacity that had not previously existed in U.S. society. After the initial introduction of Web-1.0-based ICTs, the usage of these designs generally took some time to be accepted and used societally. As society slowly became more accepting of such ICTs, its usage rate and scope correspondingly increased, yielding higher levels of proliferation for these innovative means. Once more broadly accepted by society, it became increasingly more acceptable and expected for the public sector to incorporate ICTs into the existing communicative structure. Trotta (2018 p. 20) expands on this notion by noting that "the continued developments in information technology since the early 1990s led to increasingly high levels of permeation of these means throughout society and correspondingly increased citizens' expectations for government to apply innovations toward task completion for a wide range of activities". In this initial stage of development, Web 1.0 technologies were limited to information sharing, which would be applicable to related public-sector activities associated with E-Government. Since the invention of the modern Internet in the 1990s, the initial wave of ICTs that followed was steadily applied by the U.S. government by focusing on the application of Web 1.0 technologies to fulfill E-Government functions (Xu and Asencio, 2012, p. 115). Initially, the U.S. government "at all levels" slowly began to take advantage of the opportunity to apply a wide range of Web 1.0 technologies to facilitate E-Government initiates, which were focused largely on sharing information with the citizen base and facilitating processes regarding delivering services to the public (Xu and Asencio, 2012, p. 115). Simply put, Web 1.0 technology represented an early developmental stage of communication innovations in the ever-expanded history of the modern Internet, which would allow interested parties to digitally share information through tools such as emails and webpages. Similarly, Web 1.0 would progress to the point where it would be possible to facilitate service-delivery options between citizens and government. Basic as these designs may seem today, the creation, acceptance, and proliferation of emergent innovations on a societal level would eventually lead to its acceptance for use to facilitate E-Government related activities. In relation, Web 1.0 technologies would establish an environment of acceptance and expectations that would later serve as the foundation for the usage of Web 2.0 technologies that would be introduced to society next.

By today's societal standards, Web 1.0 technology was able to facilitate relatively limited information exchanges between interested parties via the newly created Internet. To be sure, Web 1.0 technology represented an important step forward in the evolution of democratic communication, in that this innovation expanded the scope of interactive means by which interested parties could engage with government to exchange information associated with E-Government-related activities. As is often the case with emergent innovations that have survived the rigorous process associated with broadscale acceptance, Web 1.0 would have the opportunity to continue along its evolutionary path leading to the development of Web 2.0 technology. In relation, Web 2.0 technology would further enhance the communicative capacity of government, allowing for the public sector to utilize these innovative designs to facilitate more complex interactions associated with deliberative democracy. Unlike Web 1.0 technologies, which provide means that are generally used for more basic information-dissemination purposes, Web 2.0 technologies are defined in part by the ability of innovations to expand the communications capacity to include enhanced designs allowing for an exchange of ideas between interested parties (Ayanso and Moyers, 2012, p. 2). By allowing for enhanced levels of interaction, Web 2.0 technologies applied by the public sector would

64 E-Government and E-Governance

make it possible to augment the communicative structure, creating greater opportunities for more meaningful exchanges between citizens and government. The development of Web 2.0 technology would provide the public sector with an opportunity to transition to a new stage of communication in which participation with citizens via digital interactions may yield outcomes that can influence "policy making and administrative processes" (Xu and Asencio, 2012, p. 115). The application of Web 2.0 technologies by the public sector would usher in the E-Governance era in which the communicative structure would increasingly include the integration of modern innovations capable of digitally hosting meaningful deliberations. E-governance related activities that digitally provide meaningful deliberations, in which outcomes of participation are expected to be able to impact the direction of government in some ways, are often referenced as E-Democracy or E-Participation. Xu and Asencio (2012, p. 116) notes that "Web 2.0 applications are especially conducive to e-democracy, since as they can create multimodal, non-hierarchical, collaborative and deliberative networks." Best described as falling under the conceptual umbrella of E-Governance, which includes a vast array of digital participatory means, the model of "E-Participation" refers to applying "ICTs (primarily but not exclusively web-based technologies)" in order to promote "engagement and participation in the policy making process" (Tait, 2012, p. 226). The means that are provided on behalf of government to facilitate citizen participation, such as social-media-based interactions, can better serve democratic ideals by ensuring that outcomes during E-Participation are "integrated into the decision-making process in a formal and transparent way" to give indication that this process is a meaningful opportunity to affect the public sector (Tait, 2012, p. 227). Citizen participation that is perceived as being meaningful is capable of "having a positive impact on the legitimacy of policies and decision making" and this is attained in part by government taking the opportunity to mine information derived from discursive events to craft policy responses that are "more suitable to the needs of the people" (Tait, 2012, p. 228). In this sense, citizens choosing to engage in digital discursive events serve as only part of the deliberative equation, as participation is also expected to have the potential to create an opportunity to impact the policy path of government in some fashion. This is not to imply that each individual citizen, or collective group, that chooses to participate in digital discursive events will always result in affecting changes to the public sector, but instead that system actors perceive that there is a legitimate opportunity for this to occur for those successful during the policy argumentation process. Although generally capable of strengthening the public's perception regarding the legitimacy of processes and outcomes, there is a concern regarding electronically oriented discursive events possibly resulting in public-sector actions that fail to adequately represent those disadvantaged by the digital divide. In relation, it remains important to recognize the possibility that the presence of a "negative class-specific feedback loop" could threaten the legitimacy of government to some degree should democratic processes fail to effort in engaging the "marginalized and disadvantaged strata of society" who may reflect disproportionally higher levels of non-participation in activities that affect government outcomes (Habermas, 2015, p. 50). Overall, the early era of the modern Internet would initially lead to the creation and usage of a Web 1.0 technologies that were applied with the intent to fulfill a number of E-Government related activities. As technology progressed, new digital opportunities were provided to government that would allow for ICTs to be applied to activities associated with E-Governance. The usage of Web 2.0 technologies to facilitate interactive events between system actors would provide an opportunity for E-Governance-related activities to be integrated into the communicative structures, further institutionalizing participatory events expected in a deliberative democracy. In this sense, E-Governance endeavors can play a key role in expanding the scope and frequency of the available participatory means through the application of ICTs available in the modern era. In doing so, the additions of digitally facilitated participatory means can strengthen the overall communicative structure by enhancing the opportunities by which system actors may engage in meaningful deliberations, as expected in the U.S. democracy.

Further Discussion of Technological Means Used to Facilitate E-Government and E-Governance in the American Democracy

The dynamics associated with applying Web 1.0 technologies to facilitate E-Government activities and Web 2.0 technologies to facilitate E-Governance activities are further expanded on for illustrative purposes. Doing so will provide a greater measure of illustration, highlighting the technologies in practice and the role each effort respectively plays in the context of the U.S. deliberative democracy. Initially, Web 1.0 technologies allowed the public sector to leverage the power of the newly emergent modern Internet to fulfill activities associated with E-Government. Here, E-Government-related actions were first capable of facilitating basic activities associated with information dissemination and then were able to be used for transactional purposes associated with service delivery. In the modern era, interested parties operating in the U.S. system now have at their collective disposal unprecedented levels of information regarding government activities and its representatives. For example, Web 1.0 technologies create access regarding a wide range of information related to government activities (i.e. voting records by elected officials for proposed bills, contact information for members of government, mission statement of an agency, proposed changes to agency rules, signed legislation, budget proposals and approved budgets for the upcoming fiscal year, etc.). Later, emerging Web-1.0-based ICTs would employ the modern Internet in the hopes of achieving greater levels of effectiveness and efficiency to the processes associated with delivering services to the public. In relation, the usage of such ICTs can enhance the level of convenience associated with the process of service delivery by allowing for the public to use the Internet to interact with government without having to travel to a designated location during regular business hours. As such, a citizen may go online from a locale of their choosing, and at a time that is convenient to them, to engage with government as a means by which to facilitate a wide range of services at various levels of government. This includes leveraging the Internet for the purposes of digitally facilitating service-delivery options by engaging with the federal government (i.e. file federal taxes with the IRS, receive assistance obtaining affordable housing with U.S. Department of Housing and Urban Development, apply for student loans via the U.S. Department of Education, etc.) and state/local government (i.e. file state taxes, renew a driver's license with state DMV, obtain a fishing license, obtain a building permit, pay parking and traffic tickets, facilitate processes involving federally funded Supplemental Nutrition Assistance Program [SNAP] and Temporary Assistance for Needy Families [TANF], etc.). In contemporary governance, there is an increasingly extensive menu of options at each of the levels of government, which provides an opportunity for citizens to utilize ICTs to receive a wide array of public services. Here, Web-1.0-based ICTs provide citizens greater levels of opportunity to become engaged in E-Government activities associated with information dissemination and service delivery at each of the levels of government in the U.S. federal system. In doing so, the digital means allow for government to better meet expectations associated with American democracy regarding the importance that government is transparent, accountable, and provides access to the system that is cyclically longitudinal in nature.

In general, E-Government may be used with increasing frequency in part because it is viewed as a fiscally sound means by which to lower costs without diminishing the quality of the services delivered to the public at large. While recognizing the fiscal outlays associated with developing and maintaining digital means, the usage of ICTs to facilitate E-Government may digitally streamline activities, which can contribute to lowering overall costs. As the delivery of high-quality services in a cost-effective manner remains an important public sector goal, the usage of digital means to allow for interactions that are transactional can contribute to achieving this end.

However, the pursuit of efficiency at the expense of other societal values, such as equity, should be factored into decision making as well. This is due in part because the system itself should to some degree dictate the values to be applied during government decision making and that consistently applying a singular social value at the expense of all others will create disproportionate responses that fails to account for the importance of the three Es of performance measurement (i.e. efficiency, effectiveness, and equity). In relation, E-Government's usage of the Internet to exclusively deliver services to the public may negatively affect citizens in relation to the digital divide, especially in circumstances in which the online transactional methods are used to completely replace traditional in-person methods. The duplication of means to deliver services may cause a redundancy on this account that may be deemed inefficient by some. However, establishing a redundancy in means that combine traditional and digital access would be more sensitive to the equity aspect of service delivery associated with the digital divide. In relation, the redundancy in means may provide greater opportunity for government to effectively provide services to the public. In this sense, it would be prudent to require government to avoid completely investing in digital transactions without leaving any opportunity for citizens to obtain such through traditional means. If digital service delivery is used to replace all traditional means in a widespread, whole-of-government approach at any level of U.S. government, then this can negatively impact those citizens that are disadvantaged due to the digital divide. The pursuit of efficient, fiscally responsible government is of great importance, but in the context of democracy it is imprudent for the public sector to allow any singular social value to guide all decision making, including those associated with the application of E-Government endeavors.

During the early stages of the modern Internet, Web 1.0 technologies began to be applied by the public sector to facilitate E-Government-related activities associated with information dissemination and then the delivery of services. The continued proliferation of Web 1.0 technology usage in E-Government established a foundation in which citizens were increasingly amenable and expectant of emerging innovations being applied by the public sector in fulfillment of a wide range of responsibilities. As time progressed, Web 2.0 technologies were developed and eventually would also become societally accepted for use by the public sector in efforts to create deliberative opportunities associated with E-Governance. Over time, the continued development of Web 2.0 technologies would allow for corresponding ICTs leveraging the Internet to be utilized to create a wide range of richer, deeper engagement opportunities that could facilitate highly interactive events between system actors in the context of U.S. deliberative democracy. This includes utilizing Web 2.0 technologies to

68 E-Government and E-Governance

create opportunities for citizen participation to be facilitated digitally, which includes suggestion boxes, deliberative mini-publics, deliberative polls, citizen review panels, and digitally facilitated public meetings. The application of technology in the modern era is also used to facilitate meaningful interactions between system actors involving social media and crowdsourcing, in which participation in such has the potential to digitally contribute to illuminating the will of the public and that may ultimately play a role in determining the direction of government. Essentially, the emergence of later-stage ICTs, capable of supporting greater levels of participation among system actors, provide modern-era government with a continuously diverse means in which to digitally facilitate meaningful deliberations expected in the American democracy.

In the modern era, Web 2.0 technologies made it possible for government to apply digital means to facilitate deliberative events capable of expanding citizen participation opportunities. Here, the usage of technology can create greater opportunities for system actors to deliberate by adding digital venues to the existing communicative structures inherent within the U.S. political system. The increased interactive opportunities provided through digital means can further institutionalize expectations for deliberative democracy associated with transparency and accountability. Similarly, in a deliberative democracy, the government is expected to provide cyclical opportunities for interested parties to engage in meaningful deliberations in which outcomes of participating is expected to yield changes to the political system. The provision of a wide range of deliberative events via Internet-enabled communication means creates an increasing opportunity for citizens to engage with government, but for these interactions to be considered meaningful there must be some measure of ability for those engaged in this dynamic to directly impact the direction of government. In this sense, E-Governance efforts to apply digital means to facilitate citizen participation opportunities, capable of affecting the policy path of government in some way, serves as a critical component in the efforts to further institutionalizing expectations associated with meaningful deliberations in the U.S. democracy. Should the outcomes of these participatory events fail to generate some measure of identifiable change to the political system on a consistent basis, then the digital means employed will most assuredly ring hollow to citizens in the context of government's responsibility to provide discursive events that facilitate meaningful deliberations associated with E-Governance. By extension, E-Governance endeavors creating digital discursive events, which fall short of the democratic expectations associated with instituting meaningful deliberations, may to some degree lead citizens to call into question the legitimacy of government processes and outcomes. Therefore, E-Governance endeavors must ensure that digital discursive events provide meaningful dialogue that empowers those engaged in participatory proceedings with some measure of genuine opportunity to consistently impact the direction of the public sector.

The application of ICTs to promote both E-Government and E-Governance requires support from decision makers in the public sector that will dictate the pursuit of one, both, or neither option and to what degree that will be done. In this, the role of leadership at any level of government cannot be discounted as being a major contributing factor regarding the public sector's efforts to apply technology in the context of both E-Government and E-Governance. This digitally focused direction decided on behalf of leadership could broadly manifest through a wide range of formalized measures, such as laws passed by legislatures, executive orders that guide agency activity, and rulemaking procedures at the bureaucratic level that will dictate how legislative mandates are ultimately implemented. In relation, informal leadership preferences regarding the application of digital designs within a public-sector entity can have some measure of impact during the implementation of actions mandated by exterior sources, such as those put forth by the legislative branch. In this sense, leadership can opt to impede or facilitate the implementation of digital designs within the bureaucracy, which can affect the speed, frequency, and vigor in which the whole of the entity adopts technically oriented means to fulfill a wide range of duties. Similarly, the same dynamic can be extended to explain the behavioral buy-in of the career civil servants that operates with an agency. It is common that those working in a federal agency are often career civil servants whose support of or resistance to mandated actions regarding standard operating procedures guiding the fulfillment of digital duties will to some degree affect the tenacity of those applying such. This principle in practice is reflective of how the acceptance or rejection of digital design, by those working within a given bureaucratic entity, may affect the integration processes regardless of guidelines stemming from mandated actions. Whatever the source(s) of official action crafted to guide public-sector responses, the route taken by decision makers to pursue E-Government and E-Governance designs can very much be a political choice to some degree. In relation, public-sector decision makers may pursue E-Government and E-Governance in part as a calculated politically oriented response to perceived preferences held by citizen stakeholders within society. In this, the assessment of preferences held by citizens within the political environment can play a role in affecting the policy choices chosen by government decision makers in a deliberative democracy. This dynamic is applicable to public-sector decision makers choosing to pursue the means to institutionalize the application of ICTs categorized as Web 1.0 and Web 2.0, which would be applicable to the integration of E-Government and E-Governance, respectively.

70 E-Government and E-Governance

It is plausible that even today there may be levels of government—national, state, or local—in which E-Government and E-Governance activities have yet to be applied in equal measure. In this respect, it is important to recognize the possibility that the cause of a digitally oriented discrepancy between E-Government and E-Governance in place is derived, in part, from the natural progression associated with the proliferation of technologies throughout the whole of society. With the initial wave of ICTs taking place in the 1990s, the application of innovative means in government were first focused on applying Internet-based Web 1.0 technology to fulfill E-Government-based interactions with citizens. At the onset of the digital age in government, the application of early-stage ICTs associated with Web 1.0 technologies was focused on creating electronic processes to complete tasks, related to information dissemination, and then providing public services. If E-Governance efforts trail the application of E-Government initiatives, then this lag between methodologies may in part be due to the natural progression of technology proliferation on a societal scale, in which E-Government's initial usage of ICTs provided these types of activities with a temporal head start over those associated with E-Governance. In that, the ICTs usage of Web 1.0 technologies first gradually began to proliferate in society through a wide range of private-sector applications. Once these digital means were firmly established more broadly in society, the acceptance of Web 1.0 technologies began to increasingly find greater traction in government usage over time. The government responded in kind to the development and proliferation of Web 1.0 technology that was more gradually occurring in society, based on an assessment of the usage of these means being able to successfully fulfill a wide range of E-Government-based actions. In this scenario, government was largely a "second mover," as private-sector actors within broader society served as a proving ground for a wide assortment of "first movers" that would apply Web 1.0 technologies. This concept in practice is also applicable in helping to explain why E-Government initiatives may have originally outpaced E-Governance initiatives. The E-Government efforts that applied early-stage ICTs had a temporal head start in the digital sense when compared to E-Governance initiatives, which are based on the later development of Web 2.0 technologies. Naturally, E-Government based on Web 1.0 technologies would initially enjoy a greater online presence than the E-Governance efforts that are based on Web 2.0 technologies, which came about much later. In relation, the disparity that may have initially existed seems natural, in the technical sense, as some measure of time may be required to pass so that E-Governance can eventually close the gap with E-Government, allowing the presence of each to be observed on more equal digital footing. The determination of this temporal threshold to achieve a balance will require increased efforts to integrate E-Governance and the decision to do so is subject to a wide assortment of circumstances, stemming from an assessment of the political environment. This includes determining whether there is sufficient demand from the public for increased levels of E-Governance-related interactions, which will allow citizens to have greater opportunity to engage in meaningful deliberations with government. There are obviously also mitigating factors regarding the requisite levels of the public sector's fiscal capacity and technical know-how by those serving in government, which is needed to develop, implement, and maintain E-Governance endeavors. Overall, the decision to utilize Web 2.0 technologies capable of facilitating a wide range of deliberative events associated with E-Governance will require continued efforts over time, should there be a high enough demand from the public to do so and if the government has the capacity to pursue this option. Given that the previously mentioned stages of E-Government are neither classified as being linear or mutually exclusive in nature, progression to the later stages associated with E-Governance can be pursued more readily in the modern era, providing further allowance to close any possible gap in activities that may be representative of a digital carryover since the development of initial ICTs in the 1990s.

As successful technological trends increase in popularity within any given sector, usage of these innovative means may slowly begin to permeate throughout other areas of broader society. If this proliferation continues over an extended period, then the technological means can become more entrenched throughout the communicative structures on a societal scale. This reciprocity dynamic could initially manifest in the public sector or the private sector, in which the innovative design eventually grows in usage so that each sphere becomes saturated by the presence of the innovative design in a communicative sense. For example, the Internet was initially a public-sector design that, once the World Wide Web was created, allowed this pairing to eventually find greater promise for common use during the mid-1990s in the private sector. This technological development would come to manifest through the application of Web 1.0 technologies used in fulfilling a wide range of basic societal functions associated with direct communication (i.e. emails), information dissemination (i.e. websites), and then service-oriented applications (i.e. digital means by which to purchase goods and service). As the range of available Web 1.0 technologies increased, and usage of these innovations continued to proliferate society, government gradually took advantage of the opportunity to piggyback on the private-sector success by making concerted efforts to integrate these digital means into applicable public-sector activities. At that early stage of development, government began to steadily apply Web 1.0 technologies to largely fulfill an array of actions that facilitated one-way communication,

72 E-Government and E-Governance

largely focused on information dissemination (i.e. publicize emails of government employees, post information about proposed bills in the legislature, etc.) and later service-oriented functions (i.e. pay parking ticket online, renew a car registration online, etc.). Overall, the acceptance process was progressive and longitudinal in nature, so that application of such technologies would eventually first become viewed as being appropriate and then as a status quo aspect of public-sector interactive designs.

The increasing proliferation of Internet-based Web 1.0 technologies, throughout the communicative structure of broader society, was an integral step in establishing a path for the integration of technological designs into government functionalities and would eventually lead to similar considerations associated with emerging innovations associated with Web 2.0 technologies. Since the creation of the modern Internet in the 1990s, the continued advancements in and proliferation of an ever-expanding array of ICTs has affected the cultural fabric of contemporary U.S. society. These ideals are applicable to the usage of Web 2.0 technologies that have proliferated throughout modern society and affected how system actors interact within the political arena. Broadly speaking, the expansion of a multitude of Internet-based Web 2.0 technologies usage on a societal scale has greatly contributed to enhancing connectivity in a dialectic sense by providing greater opportunities by which system actors can communicate. The proliferation of Web 2.0 technologies that utilize the Internet creates digital bridges between system actors participating within a given network, which can enhance the communicative structures that facilitate a wide range of societal interactions. As accepting citizens increasingly began to adopt the role of Web 2.0 technologies to fulfill a wider range of societal functions in their private lives, it becomes prudent for government to consider which innovations may also be applicable for use in the public sector. In response to growing acceptance of technological trends, it is politically astute of those serving in various capacities, at each of the levels of government in the U.S. federal system, to make efforts to routinely integrate emerging technologies into the existing communicative structures that are used to facilitate interactions between a wide array of system actors. In addition to utilizing Web 2.0 technologies to facilitate interactions between members of government, these Internet-based innovations can provide greater opportunities for citizens to engage in meaningful deliberations with a wide array of officials serving in various positions in the public sector. Similarly, ICTs can be used to create digital bridges between those within the private sector, be they individuals or organized into interest groups. Ultimately, Web 2.0 technologies directly affect the scope and nature of means that are available to facilitate interactions between all members of the civic community from the private sector and public sector.

Closing Remarks

With the invention of the modern Internet in the 1990s, a series of evolutionary technologies have correspondingly continuously been developed, which would provide for a significantly meaningful opportunity for government to apply a variety of innovations to bolster the communicative structure present in the U.S. democratic system. In the modern era, the development and acceptance of ICTs would create an opportunity for the U.S. government to expand the scope of participatory dynamics by which system actors could engage in various activities involving the public sector. To start, Web 1.0 technologies would provide a means for the public sector to increase the opportunities for citizens to utilize the Internet to facilitate E-Government activities associated with information dissemination and the delivery of services to citizens. Later, the development of Web 2.0 technologies would be applied on behalf of government in order to provide a broader, richer participatory experience that would be capable of supporting meaningful deliberations. Here, E-Governance would allow for interested parties to engage in digitally oriented discourse at multiple points of contact within an expanding communicative structure. In all, ICTs available in the modern era has provided the U.S. government with a unique opportunity to integrate digital participatory means into the existing communicative structure to increase the points of contact available to network actors to become engaged. E-Government and E-Governance are interrelated concepts that each in their own way are capable of institutionalizing means focused on ensuring that the U.S. deliberative democracy is transparent, accountable, and cyclical in nature. E-Government and E-Governance each works to simultaneously reflect and reinforce the important expectations associated with participation in the U.S. deliberative democracy.

E-Government is capable of playing a crucial role in providing an opportunity for system actors to electronically obtain information associated with many aspects of government (i.e. voting records of elected officials, proposed agency rulemaking changes, budgeting expenditures in a fiscal year, etc.) that can be used to make more informed decisions when participating in democratic decision making at a later date (i.e. participating in voting for elected officials, participating in public hearings prior to instituting agency rule changes, etc.). Here, E-Government activities such as those associated with information dissemination can allow for more informed participation should citizens later decide to become engaged in E-Governance-based deliberative events. In addition, E-Government provides an opportunity to utilize innovation to expand the means available by which to provide a wide range of services to the public at various levels

74 E-Government and E-Governance

of government within the federal system (i.e. file online taxes, pay parking tickets, purchase fishing licenses, etc.). In doing so, E-Government's usage of technology ensures that citizens are provided enhanced opportunities for longitudinal access to government information and government services, which is an important component associated with further institutionalizing expectations associated with responsible governance in the U.S. deliberative democracy as it relates to transparency, accountability, and cyclicity. By extension, the opportunity to utilize innovation to obtain and analyze disseminated information can be parlayed by interested parties into more informed participation in deliberative events such as voting for elected officials.

Similarly, E-Governance endeavors provide a unique interactive opportunity to modern-era government in that digital means can continuously be added to the existing communicative structure, which dynamically creates a broader participatory schema on a longitudinal basis. Here, technology can initially create and then expand upon digital bridges, further connecting interested parties operating within a given network for the purposes of engaging in meaningful deliberations. The collaborative nature of a digital discursive event provides a participatory opportunity for a wide range of system actors to interact with each other for any number of reasons such as to identify societal problems, to express preferences for the agenda of government, and to contribute to the crafting of solutions. The ability of digital discursive events to facilitate collaborative interactions between system actors, which contributes to the development of collective intelligence, is an essential contribution of ICTs to modern deliberative democracy. However, collective intelligence's capacity to enhance the knowledge base of system actors from the public sphere and private sphere is not an end-game goal unto itself. Once the accumulation and analysis of collective intelligence has occurred, there should be efforts on behalf of government to parlay the shared knowledge regarding societal preferences into official actions which are more likely to accurately reflect system needs expressed by participants engaged in digital deliberative events. In this sense, the collective intelligence must first be generated and then the shared knowledge accumulated through ICTs-based deliberative events should be used to help guide government decision making regarding policy. In that, government is responsible to some degree to responsively adapt decision making to reflect public opinion, which in this case was identified through digital dialectic processes designed to generate collective intelligence regarding preferences for the public sector's policy path. The important link between the accumulation of collective intelligence, and its usage to influence policymaking, serves as evidence of deliberative democracy in action, while also increasing the possibility that trust in government will be maintained. It is equally important to note that citizens' participation in digital discursive events designed to generate collective intelligence regarding preferences for the direction of government is not wholly expected to be a perfect match to the entirety of society. In the context of E-Governance, the digital divide may naturally exclude citizens from the digitally facilitated discursive events used to generate collective intelligence. This collective intelligence can most assuredly be informative in gaining a better understanding of the public will held by those participating in digital deliberations, but this process may not always be wholly applicable to broader society, keeping in mind those who were unable or unwilling to participate in discourse facilitated through the use of ICTs.

Whether applying Web 1.0 technologies to facilitate E-Government activities or utilizing Web 2.0 technologies to create digital discursive events, there are several items of importance regarding its implementation that government must be prepared to address. There is a wide array of potential issues that may affect the effectiveness and efficiency associated with applying modern innovations to fulfill public-sector activities associated with E-Government and E-Governance. To be sure, there are general maintenance considerations associated with technical issues that may arise, which can affect the functionality of innovative means employed to facilitate E-Government and E-Governance functions. Concerns also include that there may be issues associated with privacy and security, which are oft attributed to participating in online interactions involving sensitive personal data. In this, government must make efforts to protect the privacy of those participating and to establish measures that create a safe environment, by which interested parties may interact without being subject to security-based threats. Additionally, government must plan accordingly as it relates to allocating the resources (i.e. financial, human, and time) that are necessary to monitor the security measures during implementation and to ensure that technical issues regarding functionality are limited. Both E-Government and E-Governance usage must coincide with acknowledging and addressing inequities that may exist, associated with the digital divide, which may limit participation among those in society that neither have access to nor are highly proficient in the technologies utilized to facilitate digital activities. In relation, those in society that represent the technological want-nots, who have no interest in participating digitally in E-Government or E-Governance, would also be left behind in a democratic sense should all activities be facilitated through ICTs in the modern era. As such, it is important that digital interactive means avoid wholly replacing traditional interactive means across all levels of government in the U.S. federal system. Doing so would serve to weaken the participatory structure by limiting choices in means available for citizens to engage in E-Government- and

76 E-Government and E-Governance

E-Governance-related activities. Given the advancements in technological means by which to engage with other members of government, and with others operating from within the private sector, the sole usage of traditional communication means is imprudent in the context of fulfilling the expectations associated with a deliberative democracy. To better ensure the American democracy is transparent, accountable, and provides cyclical opportunities for interested parties to longitudinally engage a wide range of participatory endeavors, government should generally be focused on maintaining a communicative structure that is simultaneously able to provide opportunities to interact via traditional and digital means. It is of great importance that modern-era governance actively works to integrate ICTs into the communicative structure while also ensuring that traditional means to facilitate citizens engaging with the public sector are maintained. This way, a more complete communicative structure is maintained that provides choices as to how citizens can engage with the public sector during E-Government and E-Governance activities.

The public sector's pursuit of integrating E-Government and E-Governance also reflects complex concerns associated with activities that are inherently unique to each. For example, E-Government may be subject to instances of information overload that results from when the entirety of entities operating across all levels of the U.S. federal system publish a wide range of data online. The level of complexity associated with the digitally published information may compound issues associated with the logistics of obtaining, analyzing, and understanding the plethora of material made available. In this sense, digitally publishing information is of great importance to a transparent and accountable government, with the understanding its availability still requires effort on behalf of the populous to decipher such in a responsible and timely fashion. In the context of deliberative democracy, information is only as good as those willing and able to parlay such into informed decision making, and on its own would be no more useful than any other tool left unused or improperly handled. As it relates to a unique concern associated with the delivery of services, E-Government may be subject to the same treacherous terrain associated with traditionally facilitated privatization from a public administration standpoint. In that, the delivery of services being outsourced to private-sector entities may shift the responsibility of the public sector to functions that are more focused on oversight than direct implementation. This regulatory responsibility associated with privatization of service delivery is focused on activities such as monitoring that private-sector firms perform as contracted and ensuring fairness in the digital bidding processes for those competing to win a contract. Despite possible concerns associated with E-Government, the application of such designs is still of great importance in the American democracy. The existence of task-specific concerns associated with implementing E-Government only indicates that it is important to recognize this possibility in practice and to consider making adjustments, if necessary, to mitigate negative impacts to the integrity of the American democracy associated with participation.

Similarly, there are a wide range of unique concerns associated with ICTs being applied by the public sector when opting to facilitate activities associated with E-Governance. E-Governance's integration of ICTs into the communicative structure can increase the participatory opportunities available to network actors by combining traditional means and digital means in order to facilitate meaningful deliberations among interested parties as expected in the American democracy. However, it would be a miscalculation in the political sense to believe that the process of expanding the communicative structure by utilizing digital means to support discursive events would somehow be exempt from many of the same pitfalls associated with participating through traditional means. For example, well-organized, well-led, and well-funded interest groups may to some degree be better able to leverage collective resources to outperform others engaged in digital discursive events. In this, powerful interest groups may play a more significant role in affecting outcomes derived from digital deliberations than less organizationally accomplished interest groups or the individual citizen participating of their own accord. Here, adding digital means to the communicative structure may simply extend the existing inequities oft attributed to traditional participatory dynamics involving interested parties, who chose to engage in discursive events in the hopes of affecting changes to the political system. This is not to imply that discursive events that are traditional or digital are somehow incapable of providing valuable insight as to the preferred direction of government held by a wide range of societal members, but that processes associated with such should consider the role that access based inequities may play in shaping outcomes of discursive events. Although system inequities regarding participation may exist, the importance of utilizing ICTs to facilitate digital discursive events associated with E-Governance should not be discounted. Ultimately, there is great merit in the possibility that increased opportunities and more convenient means to participate may in fact result in generating collective intelligence that will allow for a more accurate assessment of public preferences. In fact, modern-era government is beholden to system actors to make efforts to apply technology as a function of public-sector responsibility to integrate innovative means, if doing so will help further institutionalize expectations of participation in the U.S. deliberative democracy.

When it comes to E-Governance activities, there may be some measure of variance regarding the frequency of public-sector usage of Web 2.0

78 E-Government and E-Governance

technologies to facilitate such at each of the levels of government in the U.S. federal system. The variances in usage may stem from any number of causes such as fiscal constraints limiting the ability to develop and maintain digital means, agency leadership and career civil servants who may be averse to integrating technological means to facilitate communication with citizens, and the levels of expectations for the presence of digital interactions on behalf of the constituency base being served by a government entity. Despite possible impediments to ICTs being used to facilitate E-Governance-related activities, over time the U.S. democratic system has increasingly reflected the decision to apply societally accepted technological means to increase opportunities for system actors to engage in meaningful deliberations via digital participatory events integrated into the broader communicative structure. Doing so has proved to play an integral role in enhancing the frequency of opportunities available by which citizen can participate in meaningful deliberations through an ever-increasingly expanding array of discursive events. In the modern era, the arrival and societal acceptance of a wide scope of communication-based innovations, such as those associated with Web 2.0 technology, have caused a shift in the means utilized on behalf of government to engage with the public. As the U.S. democracy is expected to be flexible and dynamic, this ideal is applicable to the means utilized to facilitate communication events such as those occurring between government entities and the citizen base in which they serve. The evolutionary nature of the U.S. political system—in which the government is expected to actively assess system expectations held by the public and develop responsive means capable of addressing shifts in citizen demands for actions—also applies to the communicative means utilized to facilitate meaningful deliberations. As such, it would be irresponsible in the democratic sense for modern-era governance to ignore the development, increasing acceptance, and widespread proliferation of a seemingly ever-expanding array of technology-based communication means throughout society. This includes the innovations derived from any number of examples of ICTs that could be used to facilitate meaningful deliberations between a wide range of system actors. For example, Web 2.0 technologies could be used to facilitate discursive events between members of government and to create greater opportunity for citizens to participate with the public sector in meaningful deliberations. Web 2.0 technologies provide a different participatory experience when compared to first-generation technological means associated with Web 1.0, which were largely representative of limited communication dynamics that sought to disseminate information or provide services to the public, as opposed to providing an opportunity for citizens to engage in meaningful deliberations with government. Web 2.0 technologies provide an opportunity for greater levels of interactions, in which richer two-way communications allow for meaningful dialogue to exist between government and the public at large. Ultimately, the public sector in the modern era has a responsibility to consider the applicability of such emergent technologies to be able to contribute to establishing means capable of meeting expectations associated with participation in a deliberative democracy.

In general, the application of ICTs creates digital bridges between system actors, in which participation through newly structured communicative networks may yield collective intelligence that may greatly contribute to increasing the efficiency and effectiveness of government actions. In the U.S., an ever-expanding array of Web 2.0 technologies may be employed to enhance the communicative structural means that are used to facilitate a wide range of citizen-government interactions, including those that result in the public making known policy preferences. Here, Web 2.0 technologies, such as social media, can provide means by which to digitally streamline preferences held by the public to government, who is ultimately charged with addressing identified system needs through policy efforts. As a cautionary possibility, it is important to consider that choosing to pursue a public-sector agenda that fails to identify and address widely held perceptions by citizens could relatedly result in causing some measure of public-sector inefficiency and ineffectiveness in the long run. This is due in part to the possibility that the government may have enacted official means focused on affecting change to a given policy area, yielding a government agenda reflective of a disjoint between actual system needs and the official policy efforts in play. Here, it is entirely possible that the government's chosen agenda fails to pursue policymaking in a manner that is geared toward satisfying the actual preferences of the public. Obviously, it is generally politically prudent to avoid government actions that fail to consider the will of the public during decision making and that would represent a democratic deficiency in the deliberative sense. This is due in part because the end-result would be policy choices guiding government activities society is neither interested in nor accepting of, and will eventually later require official adjustments so that the agenda of government is better aligned with the preferences held by the public. The need to have to readjust the government's agenda that failed to initially make efforts to consider citizen preferences reflects a policymaking process that is lacking in both efficiency and effectiveness. To reduce the likelihood of this disjoint from occurring, the government should actively make consistent efforts to determine the public's will and the usage of Web 2.0 technologies can a useful tool in this process. The usage of Web 2.0 technologies can serve as one of many means capable of strengthening the communicative structures used to facilitate dialogue between citizens and government in

80 E-Government and E-Governance

the U.S. democratic system. Here, the application of ICTs provides further credence to the idea that modern governance has at its disposal the ability to integrate digital bridges capable of bolstering the broad communicative structure that is used to facilitate discursive events. In this, discursive events facilitated through a wide array of digital bridges provides the government with increased opportunities to actively identify issues of societal importance held by system actors within the political arena. In turn, the public-sector policy efforts designed to address identified problems yields a government that is potentially more responsive to issues that may exist and is therefore better suited to perform official duties that more accurately reflect system needs.

It is possible that any number of ICTs could be used during communication processes by which those in the private sector may share policy preferences with those serving in government (i.e. members of an agency, members of Congress, etc.). The provision of a specific type of discursive event that is publicized on behalf of and proctored by a given government entity could provide citizens with the opportunity to express their preferences directly to those responsible for initially developing and ultimately implementing policy efforts. A singular event like digital discussion boards could be flexibly open in that citizens could participate in electronically facilitated interactions at the time(s) of their choosing, without placing a limit on the temporal availability of the opportunity, and they may asynchronously make remarks on broad preferences for all manner of topics that fall within the purview of the government entity facilitating the deliberations. The singular event could also be closed-ended topically so that comments are provided on a singular issue and could be established with a limited window for participation from a timing sense (one week, one month, etc.). In addition, members serving within a government entity can routinely monitor Web 2.0 communication tools such as social media, which are always available for citizens to express preferences regarding the public-sector performance of duties. Here, citizens may post information via social media that would be extremely beneficial to officials in providing an initial introduction to and further clarification of societal preferences, which could be used to create a conceptual roadmap helping to shape the governmental agenda pursued by those serving within the public sector. Overall, the communication dynamics would provide the opportunity for those in government to utilize digitally interactive means to routinely identify any number of issues that are of significant enough concern to the citizen base that would classify such as a problem to be addressed by the public sector. In doing so, those serving in government can monitor the comments being made by citizens through social media and then use this information to help further refine the agenda of government.

In relation, social media can allow for citizens to express preferences and correspondingly for government to develop additional digital discursive means that provide further opportunity for elaboration. This includes that government can identify commonly held preferences of the public, initially shared via social media, and then provide a follow-up opportunity in a different digital venue (i.e. public meeting, crowdsourcing, etc.) for citizens to further engage in providing some additional feedback that can help to shape the agenda of government. Ideally, the multi-tiered interactions would be facilitated in an arrangement that allows for two-way communication to occur between multiple parties operating from the public sector and private sector. That way, the communications facilitated between the government and citizens would more closely follow the expectations associated with participating in a deliberative democracy. Much like the previously mentioned information overload component that is oft associated with digital sharing efforts, there may be some measure of difficulty in government discerning societal agreeance on topics expressed through the vast chorus of preferences being electronically articulated though participatory means such as social media. Recognizing such is not to imply that the effort to do so should be avoided, but that there may be some difficulty in discerning which topic(s) are agreed upon by a wide enough audience to justify considering taking policy action.

As mentioned, ICTs can be applied to create a wide assortment of interactive digital means by which citizens can directly interact with government to express policy preferences. In the contemporary American democracy, it is also of importance for government to consider instituting digital means that are capable of allowing for citizens to contribute to developing solutions to public policy problems. Once issues in society are identified as a problem that needs a policy response by government, the public sector is capable of instituting crowdsourcing endeavors that expands the scope of participation to include system actors assisting in the process of generating solutions. For example, the U.S. federal government has established a website entitled Challenge.gov (Challenge.gov, 2022), which hosts a wide array of crowdsourcing events designed to create creative solutions to dilemmas for a plethora of public policy areas (i.e. healthcare, veteran affairs, environment, education, etc.). Crowdsourcing allows for an individual or group to develop and share solutions to pre-established problems that are set to be addressed by government. To incentivize participation, the winning solutions generated via a crowdsourcing event can receive a significant monetary reward. Here, the power of ICTs is leveraged to generate collective intelligence, in which citizens may directly participate in crafting solutions that government can adopt during policymaking processes. The usage of deliberative mini-publics also provide a unique opportunity for a small group of citizens purposefully chosen to be representative of selected societal demographics, with personalized ties to a topic, to engage with government in meaningful deliberations to ascertain thoughts and preferences held by those that may be more directly affected by issues related to the subject matter in question. Similarly, deliberative polling provides an opportunity for an exchange of information between those being polled and those conducting the poll. In relation, deliberative polling allows for those conducting the interactive survey to provide an educational component so that participants can provide more informed responses to questions that are posed. On the lower levels of government, digital participatory budgeting has begun to show some promise in providing citizens with the opportunity to discuss preferences for public-sector spending options in a limited but interactive capacity. In turn, citizens can directly engage with government to express preferences regarding how the public sector should allocate limited and extinguishable fiscal resources during an impending fiscal year. For example, in 2011 the New York City Council (New York City Council, 2022) introduced participatory budgeting to provide an opportunity for citizens to give feedback on how a specific amount of public dollars should be used to fund activities. Although the feedback provided relates to a specific amount of the public budget, which is relatively small when compared to the overall fiscal outlays in a given year, participatory budgeting can serve to provide an opportunity for civically minded citizens to engage in meaningful deliberations capable of directly affecting public expenditures.

Ultimately, there is an expected level of malleability attributed to public-sector efforts to maintain the communicative framework used to facilitate a wide range of participatory events in the modern U.S. deliberative democracy. This includes the flexible usage of technology to facilitate an array of activities associated with E-Government and E-Governance, which have become integral to the modern American democracy. The digital participatory events available in the U.S. political system contribute greatly to the ability of the public sector to meet expectations associated with deliberative democracy. However, the pursuit of such innovative means at the expense of traditional opportunities to participate would be detrimental to goal achievement in the democratic sense. In the context of U.S. deliberative democracy, it is of import that the communicative structure continues to include a blend of established traditional means and emerging digital means to allow citizens to engage with government via an increasingly more diverse assortment of contact points. Today, the goal of maintaining a broadly diverse communicative structure is unable to be achieved by only pursuing digital participatory designs, which would potentially cater solely to tech-savvy participants who have access to corresponding innovative means, while alienating those potentially disadvantaged by the many dimensions of the digital divide. Essentially, doing so would be detrimental to the goal of enhancing the range of participatory opportunities available for a wider range of citizens to become involved in interactive events important to a healthy, vibrant deliberative democracy. That said, the role of E-Government and E-Governance undeniably represents an evolutionary step forward in the continuous development of deliberative democracy and each's continued usage will play a crucial role in helping to shape the future of participation in American democracy.

References

Agrawal, S., Sethi, P., & Mittal, M. (2015). E-Governance: an analysis of citizens' perception. *IUP Journal Of Information Technology, 11*(3), 34–46.

Ayanso, A. and Moyers, D. (2012). The Role of Social Media in the Public Sector: Opportunities and Challenges. In K. Kloby and M. D'Agostino (Eds.), *Citizen 2.0: Public and Governmental Interaction through Web 2.0 Technologies*. John Jay College of Criminal Justice.

Bannister, F. & Connolly, R. (2012). Forward to the past: Lessons for the future of e-government from the story so far. *Information Polity: The International Journal Of Government & Democracy In The Information Age, 17*(3/4), 211–226.

Calista, D. & Melitski, J. (2007). E-government and E-governance: Converging Constructs of Public Sector Information and Communications Technologies. *Public Administration Quarterly, 31*(1).

Carter, L. & Bélanger, F. (2005). The utilization of e-government services: citizen trust, innovation and acceptance factors. *Information Systems Journal, 15*(1), 5–25. doi:10.1111/j.1365–2575.2005.00183.x

Challenge.gov (2022). Active Challenges. https://www.challenge.gov/

Dawes, S. S. (2008). The Evolution and Continuing Challenges of E-Governance. *Public Administration Review, 68*, 86–102.

Division of Broadband and Digital Equity of North Carolina. (2022). What is the Digital Divide?. N.C. Department of Information Technology. https://www.ncbroadband.gov/digital-divide/what-digital-divide

Federal Communication Commission. (1934). Communications Act of 1934. https://www.fcc.gov/general/universal-service

Federal Communication Commission. (2022a). Universal Service. https://www.fcc.gov/general/universal-service

Federal Communications Commission. (2022b). Affordable Connectivity Program. https://www.fcc.gov/affordable-connectivity-program

Finger, M. (2010). What Role for Government in E-Government? *Journal of E-Governance, 33*(4), 197–202. https://doi-org.libproxy.troy.edu/10.3233/gov-2010-0230

Gibson, R. (2001). Elections online: Assessing Internet voting in light of the Arizona Democratic primary. *Political Science Quarterly*, (4). 561–583.

Habermas, J. (2015). *The Lure of Technocracy*. Translated by Ciaran Cronin. Polity Press.

84 E-Government and E-Governance

Halachmi, A. & Greiling, D. (2013). Transparency, E-Government, and Accountability. *Public Performance & Management Review*, 36(4), 572–584. https://doi-org.libproxy.troy.edu/10.2753/PMR1530-9576360404

Hammond, A. S. (1997). The telecommunications act of 1996: Codifying the digital divide. *Federal Communications Law Journal*, 50(1), 179–214. http://search.proquest.com/docview/213153100?accountid=32521

Haque, S. & Pathrannarakul, P. (2013). E-Government towards good governance: A global appraisal. *Journal Of E-Governance*, 36(1), 25–34.

Howland, J. S. (1998). The 'Digital Divide': are we becoming a world of technological 'haves' and 'have-nots?'. *The Electronic Library*, (5), 287–289.

Jorgensen, D. J. & Cable, S. (2002). Facing the Challenges of E-Government: A Case Study of the City of Corpus Christi, Texas. *SAM Advanced Management Journal*, 67(3), 15.

Justice, J.B., Melitski, J., & Smith, D.L. (2006). E-Government as an Instrument of Fiscal Accountability and Responsiveness: Do the best practitioners employ the best practices?. *The American Review of Public Administration*, September. doi: 10.1177/0275074005283797

Manoharan, A.P., Bennet, L.V., & Carrizalas, T. J. (2012). M-Government: An Opportunity for Addressing the Digital Divide. In K. Kloby and M. J. D'Agostino (Eds.), *Citizen 2.0: Public and Governmental Interaction through Web 2.0 Technologies*. John Jay College of Criminal Justice.

Marche, S. & McNiven, J. D. (2003). E-Government and E-Governance: The future isn't what it used to be. *Revue Canadienne Des Sciences De L'administration/Canadian Journal Of Administrative Sciences*, 20(1), 74–86.

Moon, M. J. (2002). The Evolution of E-Government among Municipalities: Rhetoric or Reality? *Public Administration Review*, (4). 424–433.

National Institute of Standards and Technology (U.S. Department of Commerce). (2015). Supplemental Information for the Interagency Report on Strategic U.S. Government Engagement in International Standardization to Achieve U.S. Objectives for Cybersecurity. *NISTIR 8074*(2). https://nvlpubs.nist.gov/nistpubs/ir/2015/NIST.IR.8074v2.pdf

New York City Council. (2022). Participatory Budgeting. https://council.nyc.gov/pb/

Norris, D. F. & Reddick, C. G. (2013). Local E-Government in the United States: Transformation or Incremental Change? *Public Administration Review*, 73(1), 165–175.

Qian, H. (2011). Citizen-Centric E-Strategies Toward More Successful E-Governance. *Journal of E-Governance*, 34(3), 119–129. https://doi-org.libproxy.troy.edu/10.3233/GOV-2011-0263

Rachfal, C. L. (2020). The digital divide: what is it, where is it, and federal assistance programs. Congressional Research Service. https://crsreports.congress.gov/product/pdf/R/R46613/4

Rogers, E. M. (2001). The Digital Divide. *Convergence: The Journal Of Research Into New Media Technologies*, 7(4), 96–111. doi:10.1177/135485650100700406

Rose, R. (2005). A Global Diffusion Model of e-Governance. *Journal of Public Policy*, 25(1), 5–27. https://doi-org.libproxy.troy.edu/10.1017/S0143814X05000279

Sánchez-Torres, J. & Miles, I. (2017). The role of future-oriented technology analysis in e-Government: a systematic review. *European Journal of Futures Research*, 5(1), 1–18. https://doi-org.libproxy.troy.edu/10.1007/s40309-017-0131-7

Schlozman, K. L., Verba, S., & Brady, H. E. (2010). Weapon of the strong? Participatory inequality and the internet. *Perspectives on Politics*, 8(2), 487–509. http://dx.doi.org/10.1017/S1537592710001210

Sprecher, M. (2000). Racing to e-government: Using the Internet for citizen service delivery. *Government Finance Review*, 16(5), 21. https://www.thefreelibrary.com/Racing+to+e-Government%3a+Using+the+Internet+for+Citizen+Service...-a067323090

Tait, E. (2012). Web 2.0 for E-Participation: Transformational Tweeting or Devaluation of Democracy? In K. Kloby and M. J. D'Agostino (Eds.), *Citizen 2.0: Public and Governmental Interaction through Web 2.0 Technologies*. John Jay College of Criminal Justice.

Trotta, A. (2018). *Advances in E-Governance. Theory and Application of Technological Initiatives*. Routledge/Taylor & Francis Group.

van Dijk, J. A. G. M. (2006). Digital divide research, achievements and shortcomings. *Poetics*, 34(4–5), 221–235. http://dx.doi.org/10.1016/j.poetic.2006.05.004

West, D. M. (2004). E-Government and the transformation of service delivery and citizen attitudes. *Public Administration Review*, 64(1), 15–27. doi:10.1111/j.1540–6210.2004.00343.x

Xu, H. & Asencio, H. (2012). E-Government in Local Government in the Era of Web 2.0: Experiences of Alabama Municipalities. In K. Kloby and M. J. D'Agostino (Eds.), *Citizen 2.0: Public and Governmental Interaction through Web 2.0 Technologies*. John Jay College of Criminal Justice.

3

TECHNOLOGICAL DETERMINISM

A Technocratic Rationale and American Democracy

In the modern era, those serving in the U.S. government are often placed in a position in which decision makers are responsible for addressing newly emerging problems distinct to a given point in time, such as those associated with determining the policy environment that will affect the role of technology in society. In the context of American democracy and policymaking associated with technology, it is of great import to understand various available political rationales that are argued to be most capable of guiding decision makers in government. Ultimately, a political rationale is used to help guide decision makers in undertakings involving crafting official responses to identified societal problems in any given area of U.S. public policy, such as those associated with technology. There is undoubtedly a wide scope of political rationales that are arguably applicable for use in guiding the processes by which government decision makers craft official responses to address potential problems associated with the field of technology. With the understanding that enumerating an exhaustive list of all possible politically oriented rationales fall outside the scope of this discussion, the following two chapters will introduce three key technology-based approaches that may be used to guide government decision making: technological determinism, permissionless innovation, and the precautionary principle. This chapter will introduce technological determinism and the next chapter will include a discussion that pairs permissionless innovation and the precautionary principle. As a note, it will be important to consider this introductory information to determine which (if any) of the rationales are better suited to government decision making in the U.S. democratic system as it relates to the cryptocurrency industry, which will be discussed

DOI: 10.4324/9781003441830-3

at length in later chapters. With that said, the first step in this chapter is to provide a reminder of the previously discussed concept referred to as technocracy, which serves as the conceptual baseline for technological determinism. After doing so, the concept of technological determinism will be expanded on at length.

Technocracy: The Foundational Concept of Technological Determinism

To briefly recap the earlier discussion regarding technocracy, this approach to government decision making favors policy choices based on expert knowledge, argued to yield efficient and effective actions, over those derived through system actors participating in deliberative means to help determine official responses as expected in a democratic system. In relation, those advocating for a technocratically oriented approach prefer to allow this technique to be used in government, even though doing so clearly circumvents the deliberative processes that are expected to help guide decision making in a democratic system. Technocrats are generally unconvinced by arguments advocating for government outcomes to be derived from discursive events which are more inclusive to a wider array of interested parties from the public sector and private sector making efforts to contribute, in the political sense, to decision-making processes. To the technocrat, deliberations among such system actors is viewed as an unnecessary and unproductive expense of time that should be avoided in favor of accepting rationally determined, technically oriented solutions posited by experts as the status quo in government decision making.

Those supportive of technocracy would prefer that decision makers operate from a frame of reference in which rational experts are empowered to expedite centralized decisions based on specialized knowledge. To the technocrat, doing so would justifiably serve to supplant traditional deliberative processes associated with system actors having the opportunity to participate in meaningful discourse, which would otherwise play a role in influencing policy outcomes in the American democracy. The technocratic approach to governance is one that advocates for experts to serve a primary role in public policymaking and, by extension, for the importance of placing specialized knowledge at the forefront of government decision making. Here, the unwavering belief in decision making based on the expertise of those holding some form of scientific or technically oriented knowledge serves as a justification for technocrats to be permitted to enact what is argued to be rational, efficient policymaking. Technocracy as a concept represents a foundational base that has spawned a wide array of similarly oriented rationales that promote the belief that less democratically oriented processes should play a paramount role in affecting governmental policymaking. Since being conceived in the early twentieth century, technocracy has consistently maintained various levels of influence in the U.S. democratic system, appearing in numerous "guises" over time, most recently manifesting as technological determinism and permissionless innovation (Sadowski and Selinger, 2014, p. 11). One such manifestation of technocracy is the concept referred to as technological determinism, in which advocates of this rationale promote the importance of recognizing and allowing the pervasive power of technology to play a primary role in affecting societal change. To further expand on this idea's potential role in the U.S. democratic system, it is important to expand on descriptive information to provide a broader foundation of understanding regarding what constitutes technological determinism. This will include efforts to provide a working definition of technological determinism to serve as a conceptual starting point to understanding this rationale. Once establishing how technological determinism can be defined, it then becomes necessary to expand on information associated with the role this concept is believed to play in society, and how those that advocate for this rationale expect government to incorporate its ideals into policymaking considerations. As it relates to decision making in U.S. government to formulate policy addressing the field of technology, the concept of technological determinism is a rationale that is supportive of technocratic tendencies that generally prefer to bypass traditional expectations associated with deliberative democracy processes. In that, the technological determinism rationale signifies an approach to government decision making that favors technocratic tendencies to guide official actions over outcomes derived from system actors participating in deliberative processes, as expected in the U.S. democratic system. It is also of import to provide some critiques of technological determinism in practice, to discuss the narrative approach as it relates to the value-based arguments for those supporting this rationale, to highlight potential variations of technological determinism that may have some merit for limited use in U.S. policymaking, and to provide some concluding remarks regarding the potential role of technological determinism in modern-era American democracy.

Defining Technological Determinism

To be able to later consider the potential role in policymaking that those supportive of technological determinism advocate for, it is first important to provide some definitional parameters that can establish an introductory understanding of what constitutes this rationale on a fundamental level. Specifically, defining technological determinism requires understanding the underlying belief held by those supporting this rationale in the capacity of technology to serve as the guiding force behind meaningful changes that occur in society. Hauer (2017, p. 1) describes technological determinism as "the belief that technology is the principal initiator of the society's transformation." M. L. Smith (1994, p. 38) defines technological determinism as "the belief that social progress is driven by technological innovation, which in turn follows an 'inevitable' course". Hughes (1994, p. 102) similarly defines technological determinism "as the belief that technical forces determine social and cultural changes." When providing a historical discussion regarding the progression of technological determinism, M. R. Smith (1994, p. 2) observes that "this belief affirms that changes in technology exert a greater influence on societies and their processes than any other factor." Hauer (2017, p. 1) adds that "the proponents of technological determinism argue that the society is influenced and shaped by technological development. It has to adjust and adapt to new technologies and innovations." Fountain (2001, p. 17) explains that technological determinism is an approach claiming that "the power and ubiquity of the Internet and the pace of technological change have overwhelmed human capacities to plan, design, or consider alternatives." Fountain (2001, p. 17) adds that, for technological determinism, "technology itself leads inexorably to new institutions that were planned and anticipated by no individual." In practice, technological determinism is a frame of reference that promotes the important role that technology plays in affecting the direction of society over all other potential sources of influence (i.e. economic factors, political ideology, crisis circumstances, etc.). Here, technological determinism is a technology-oriented rationale that posits that innovation serves as the primary driving force of system changes on a longitudinal basis in a given society. In this, the development and proliferation of technology has a transformative effect on society in a fashion that is principally powerful and irresistibly uncontestable. In relation, the technological determinist approach assumes that technology outpaces the capacity of system actors to process needs inherent within the political environment, and that such circumstances dictate that innovations should serve as the driving force in governmental decision making.

Next, it is helpful to highlight why advocates of technological determinism have come to believe so strongly in the power of technology to serve as the primary source of meaningful changes that may occur in society over time. The subscription to the primary role that technology plays in broadly affecting significant societal change is, in part, based on the increasing levels of innovation reaching a point of near omnipresence that continuously encroaches into most aspects of everyday life in the modern era. The increasing frequency and scope in which technology proliferates throughout

90 A Technocratic Rationale and American Democracy

society serves as part of the justification for viewing innovations as having an irresistible nature, which technological determinism is based upon. M. L. Smith (1994, p. 38) suggests that to better understand the cultural components associated with why innovations have become so ingrained in U.S. society it may be helpful "to venture into the murky bog of technological determinism, where machines seem to have lives of their own." It is oft the case that technology is viewed in "artifactual terms" and that the "thingness or tangibility of mechanical devices" plays a role in society being universally convinced of its power on such a grandiose level (Smith and Marx, 1994, pp. x–xi). The broad visible presence and consistently influential role in society is a driving force in technology conceived as being an "independent entity" that is essentially an "autonomous agent of change" (Smith and Marx, 1994, p. xi). Once an innovative design is integrated on a broad societal scale, the technology is oft perceived to be consequentially "far-reaching, cumulative, mutually reinforcing and irreversible," generating a momentum that is viewed as having "a life if its own" (Smith and Marx, 1994, p. xi). Here, the near omnipresent state of technology in the modern era can yield societal subscription to the inevitability of its continued growth and permeance. In addition, the highly ubiquitous and increasingly proliferative nature of technology in the modern era can lead many to broadly view innovation as being unquestionably influential and important in widely contributing to the betterment of society.

Relatedly, advocates of technological determinism place full faith in the capacity of technology to positively affect society, in a broad and uncompromising fashion, to the point that thoughts of government regulation of this field are viewed as unnecessary and irresponsible. Instead, technological determinism supporters prefer that government would allow a policy environment largely supportive of the free pursuit of innovations that are thought capable of improving society, and that this in and of itself would be reflective of responsible public-sector decision making. Here, advocates of technological determinism promote the importance of maintaining an innovation friendly environment based in part on the premise that technology is perceived to be transformative in nature, and progress resulting from such efforts is a worthy goal unto itself (D'Agostino, Schwester, Carrizales, and Meliski, 2011, p. 7). The cultural stature of technological determinism in the United States may lead some to believe that "faith in technology-as-progress can serve as a substitute for a more genuine participatory democracy" (M. L. Smith, 1994, p. 38). In this sense, those supportive of this rationale vest so completely in the power of technology to positively affect society that they are willing to promote technocratic decision making that is highly supportive of innovative freedom over government decisions derived from discourse among system actors as expected in

American democracy. From a leadership standpoint, those serving in government may promote technological determinism in part because aligning themselves with the idea that the advancement of technology and corresponding progress that results from the implementation of innovations are inevitable is a self-serving means to be viewed by other system actors as a popular pioneer leading the way into the future (M. L. Smith, 1994, p. 40). In the modern era, technology develops at an accelerated rate and its growth continues to permeate throughout many aspects of society. In relation, the ubiquitous presence of technology, and its continued societal proliferation on an increasingly broadscale, leads advocates of technological determinism to invest in the idea that innovation is an inevitable force capable of influencing positive changes in society. The perceived inevitability of technology's proliferation and the unwavering belief in the importance of innovation playing a primary role in transforming society for the better contributes to how those supporting technological determinism approach policymaking for the field of technology. To some degree, the support of technological determinism may serve to reflect the societal landscape in which technology's growth becomes increasingly more entrenched in the aspects of daily life in the public sector and private sector. In relation, those that serve in government and that comprise the citizen base may both become hard-pressed to argue against the importance of technology for fear of being politically and culturally left behind by the growing ranks of technophiles in society. This relational dynamic can create an environment in which system actors become overly protective and supportive of technology, creating a political opportunity for the advancement of technological determinism as the rationale by which to guide governmental decision making.

The belief that technology is the primary source of societal change and that its proliferation is inevitable correspondingly influences how those supporting technological determinism believe policymaking for the field of innovation should be facilitated in the modern era. Technological determinism is predicated on the idea that societally, when it comes to the regulation of innovation, it is government's responsibility to be focused on providing an environment that is conducive for each subsequent stage of "technological evolution" to thrive (Dotson, 2015, p. 102). In that, this cognitive construct promotes a hands-off approach in society to the point where it becomes nomological, or widely accepted as fact, with little-to-no deliberative consideration, to create an environment in which participants favor policy inaction over regulation (Dotson, 2015, p. 102). The belief in the importance of protecting technology development is partly rooted in the fear, by citizens, that failure to adapt to new technologies is indicative of regressive thought and that overregulation may lead one to miss out on the many benefits believed to be critical to living a full life in the modern era (Dotson, 2015, p. 102). Ultimately, technological determinism creates a collective belief widely held by system actors, such as citizens and those responsible for developing public policy, that government's role in regulating the environment should be limited to allow for the continued evolution of innovations to occur naturally, unimpeded by policy-based controls (Dotson, 2015, p. 102). In this context, the preferred focus of government activities would be to ensure the establishment of an environment favorable to "further cementing the perceived naturalness of technological determinism." (Dotson, 2015, p. 103). The deeply held belief by technological determinists—that modern innovations inevitably and undeniably play a pivotal role in providing a wide array of benefits to society—serves as sufficient reason for the advocates of this rationale to favor a protectionist approach to policymaking for the technology industry. In relation, members of government and citizens alike may adopt technological determinism of their own volition, because of their belief in its merits or because they believe that standing in opposition of this rationale in practice may unwisely create tension with the vast, and growing, legion of technophiles that support its usage. Standing in opposition of technological determinism, if this rationale has become entrenched, may yield political and social consequences that members of government and citizens may wish to avoid, which may lead to those individuals lending support for convenience's sake. Here, technological determinism may hold sway politically and societally, in part because there is a measure of acceptance by enough system actors for this rationale to guide decision making, so that policy favors prescribing great freedom to the ability of the technology industry to develop and proliferate in what is perceived as naturally.

Normatively speaking, technological determinism places technology at the forefront of societal change, and those advocating for this approach subscribe to the somewhat fatalistic idea that innovation is both primary and all-powerful in the context of transforming society. In relation, once developed, a technology that proliferates throughout society is believed to become embedded in use, which affects the expectations and actions of system actors operating within the broader network. Here, technology is both a catalyst of change and a guiding force in determining the overall direction of society moving forward. In relation, the consistently expanding presence of technology in the modern era in all facets of life, public and private, may contribute to the perception that technology itself is a change agent that plays a tremendously powerful role in transforming society. In this, the ability of technology to affect broadscale change is viewed as being extensively powerful, and the influence of innovations to alter society positively is considered so expansive that challenges to these certitudes are viewed as unnecessary and even counterproductive. Instead, technological determinists vest in the inevitability of technology as being a necessary aspect of society and advocate that government should be cognizant of such during decision-making endeavors, to avoid limiting the ability of innovation to fulfill its full potential in affecting societal change. Because of such, members of society and government alike are viewed to some degree as being subjected to the overwhelming directional pull of technology, which serves as a guiding force behind major societal progression. To those supporting technological determinism, enacting policy that limits technology is an effort that lacks functional credence, because it unnecessarily and irresponsibly holds back the natural progression of innovation in society. If technology is the primary source of positive change in society, then its members are better served by efforts to create an environment capable of facilitating its unfettered growth, so as to allow for innovations to avoid being unnecessarily restricted by government policy. In this regard, those advocating for technological determinism may espouse the importance of the societal influence of innovation over that of democratic decision making in the context of crafting policy designs suited for the technology industry.

For advocates of technological determinism, the capacity for innovations to serve as a directing force in shaping societal routines, and to positively affect broadscale change, is unquestionably important, rendering the preferred scope of policy practices friendly to technology to be both extensive and largely uncontested. Ultimately, technological determinism reflects the belief that technology should be permitted to develop, proliferate, and endure of its own volition, without being subjected to contrarian input by system actors, such as citizens or members of government, seeking to enact means designed to impede the natural progression of innovation. Taking a cue from technocrats, who advocate for policy choices being based on expertise that bypasses discursive events traditionally associated with deliberative democracy, technological determinists largely place establishing a policy environment that favors protecting technology as the status quo over the importance of maintaining expectations associated with official outcomes being derived from democratic processes. In this sense, to the technological determinist, it is permissible and preferable for traditional expectations associated with democracy, regarding participatory opportunities and government responsiveness, to assume a secondary role to the importance of maintaining a policy environment with minimal regulatory intervention that will allow technology to flourish naturally and to positively influence society with little-to-no policy impediments. For advocates of technological determinism, innovation is expected to be permitted to maintain its natural course regarding development and proliferation,

94 A Technocratic Rationale and American Democracy

without having its influence diffused by the unnecessary trapping of democratically derived policy constraints.

To the technological determinist, minimizing, or better yet omitting, democratically derived policy constraints, which are traditionally designed to serve as a check on the ability of technology to influence society, is preferable as the official standard operating procedure within the political system. In relation, this dynamic calls for government to serve in more of a supportive capacity, where meaningful deliberations between a variety of system actors, intended to help shape policymaking, takes a supplemental role to a protectionist approach to technology that is preferred to guide public-sector decision making in this field. In this, advocates of technological determinism posit that it is the responsibility of government to create a policy environment that is friendly to the technology industry, which will allow for the many positive benefits derived from innovation to continue to serve to guide major societal change. The technological determinist is content to allow for the public sector to establish a policy environment generally geared toward automatically protecting the technology industry, which will supplement democratically derived decision making as the primary means by which government decision making is based upon. Furthermore, individuals serving in government that may be supportive of assuming a lessor role in determining the scope of issues to be addressed during decision making do so because those opposing the tide of technological determinism may be viewed as taking an antiquated, politically dangerous stance by the increasing numbers of technophiles in society operating from within the private sector and public sector. In this case, to some degree, members of government willingly cede the responsibility to engage in meaningful deliberations with system actors in an effort to identify problems in society, and the decision-making authority to develop policy capable of addressing such, to the will of technological determinists. Those serving in government, and citizens alike, may be unwilling to attempt to stem the tide of technological determinism for fear of being labeled a technophobe by a technology-obsessed society which has slowly evolved into a legitimately influential assemblage since the rise of the modern Internet in the 1990s. However, acquiescing to technological determinism as an unchallenged rationale by which to base government policymaking decisions associated with technology would in many ways qualify as a direct threat to democracy, which deserves further discussion.

Ultimately, technological determinism as a rationale reinforces the technocratic preference that public-sector decision making circumvents traditional expectations for policy to be decided within a deliberative system in which actors participate in discursive events resulting in an agreement being reached regarding the direction of government. In this respect, technological determinism is related to technocracy in that there is a shared preference for traditional democratic processes to largely be bypassed when government decision makers determine policy outcomes in a given field such as technology. For the technological determinist, policy outcomes derived from interested parties engaged in a multitude of participatory events, as expected in a deliberative democracy, become secondary to the importance of government decision making predicated on supporting technology that should be above reproach in the discursive sense. In relation, the technological determinists claims that, due to technology's broad positive impact on societal change, it is the responsibility of decision makers in government to acknowledge this dynamic and to respond accordingly by creating a policy environment that is conducive to promoting the proliferation of developing innovations. Technological determinism views technology as the primary driving force behind significant positive societal changes, and because such advocates for this approach believe that it is the responsibility of government to advance policymaking based on protectionist designs capable of enhancing the potential of innovations to influence society for the better. The preference of a technological determinist to circumvent the primary role that deliberative democracy is expected to play in official decision making regarding policy in any field runs counter to the foundational principles regarding participatory and responsive governance that are of great importance to the U.S. political system.

Technological Determinism: Narrative Constructs Reflect Values and System Preferences

The technological determinism rationale is one that is deeply vested in advancing the belief that technology development plays an important role in affecting and improving society. In relation, the narratives crafted by technological determinists apply value-laden arguments that attempt to advance the importance of policy protections for the field of technology. The narrative constructs reflecting a technology-friendly approach to government regulations are deserved of further exploration. In the modern era, technology is oft promoted as being a "crucial agent of change," which is directly responsible for facilitating a broad scope of transformative measures in society resulting from the application of a newly developed innovation (Smith and Marx, 1994, p. ix). In a narrative sense, technology is often portrayed as being the major "driving force in history" (Smith and Marx, 1994, p. x). Here, "mini-fables" advance the idea that once a given innovation is developed it has an unprecedented and unstoppable capacity to greatly impact societal changes (Smith and Marx, 1994, p. x). Conceptually, this narrative perspective is largely focused on the "material artifact" of a technology

96 A Technocratic Rationale and American Democracy

(i.e. the identifiable invention themselves) and the corresponding effects that the innovation's introduction may have on a societal level (Smith and Marx, 1994, p. x). In relation, less importance is placed on describing the circumstances that contributed to the act of creation itself and the active role that individuals may play in the success of a given technology (Smith and Marx, 1994, p. x). The technological determinism narrative, promoting the inevitability of large-scale technology proliferation, may be more convincing in the contemporary system, to some degree, because there are increasing numbers of identifiable markers reflecting the benefits derived from innovation in use throughout society (i.e. digital networks increasing global communication, home-computer use allowing for expanded work venues, cellphone ownership easily facilitating a wide range of everyday tasks, etc.), which provide evidence supporting the case for maintaining an environment capable of supporting this status quo (Sadowski and Selinger, 2014, p. 10). Here, supporters of technological determinism craft narratives that highlight the undeniably essential and immense role that technology plays in advancing society, while arguing that regulatory efforts would be counterproductive in this sense. Because of the influential role that technology plays in positively affecting change on a broad societal scale, the policy environment should reflect an effort to protect this dynamic.

In contrast to those representing more democratic sensibilities, technology as a field is viewed by technological determinists as deserving of government protection even at the expense of policymaking outcomes that are expected to be influenced in part by participatory processes inherent within a deliberative political system. For the technological determinist, the role of government is to ensure that technology is continued to be permitted to flourish without being overly burdened by government regulation, which would only serve to diminish the many crucial benefits provided to society through creatively designed innovations. The value system underlying technological determinism is constructed, disseminated, and reinforced over time by its advocates that actively engage in framing the idea that innovations can, and should, drive societal change without being constrained by governmental regulations in most instances (Dotson, 2015, p. 103). The entrenchment of technological determinism, which may allow for this cognitive typology to reach the status of a protected topic beyond reproach within the policy arena, should be concerning to those who support the importance of debate that is expected within a democratic system (Dotson, 2015, p. 103). Although recognizing that there is a wide array of factors that are "social, material and political" in nature capable of affecting "nondemocratic technological decision-making," Dotson (2015, p. 99) also focused on uncovering how "cognitive or psychocultural" obstacles act to limit the ability of government to freely promote regulations of technology as deemed necessary by conducting discursive events. The cognitive impediments restricting traditional democratic responses within an area of public policy, such as those associated with technology regulation, are reflective of "technological determinism," which is essentially a strong belief that "technology autonomously drives history," and its recent incarnation "permissionless innovation" that is similarly focused on the belief that, in order for society to fully benefit from technology, those responsible for innovating should be empowered to do so in an environment that lacks expansive regulations (Dotson, 2015, p. 99). Conceptually, these cognitive constructs are normative in scope, yielding a framework for acceptability in the field of technology for a wide spectrum of system actors (i.e. government decision makers, citizens, etc.) and ultimately dictating preferences for facilitating activities such as institutionalizing topics available to be deliberated, establishing values to be widely held in society, and serving to guide large-scale societal responses (Dotson, 2015, p. 99). The biases inherent within such perspectives result in an obstructive "governing mentality" reflective of a societal path steeped in favoritism for the protection of innovation, and those that innovate, over the traditional pursuit of a more dynamically responsive system that requires malleability in choice expected of a democratic system (Dotson, 2015, p. 99). Technology is "embedded" into the fabric of society so completely that its presence in the political sense is often unnoticed until it is necessary for government "to regulate it when evidence of its risks or misuse become obvious" (Hess, 2015, p. 122). For the technological determinist, the embeddedness contributes to the perception that technology is ubiquitous and also serves to establish that government efforts should be minimal from a regulatory standpoint, only coming to the forefront in the political arena when societal harm has been proven to exist. Ultimately, the cognitive dynamic can become something of a self-fulfilling prophecy by which aspects of technological determinism are incorporated into the belief system of network participants, who in turn work to ensure the preservation of these innovation-centered values. Over time, the internalized principles associated with technological determinism may become nomological in nature, in which advocates of this approach posit the possibly of reaching a nearly unimpeachable status within the deliberative realm functionally becoming entrenched in the ability to directly affect the system on a perpetual basis. In this sense, technological determinism both reflects and influences a reality geared toward protecting innovation as a primary facet of governmental responsibility. In relation, technological determinists advocate that because technology is so completely embedded into the fabric of everyday life that government should work to ensure that the policy environment is capable of perpetuating this entrenched position in perpetuity.

A technologically deterministic approach holds that innovations are the primary driving force of transforming society and that the resulting

98 A Technocratic Rationale and American Democracy

technologically driven change is an inevitable by-product of this dynamic. Additionally, the development of technology serves as a catalyst for change throughout society, and the individual is subject to the powerful impact that such innovations have on everyday life. In this scenario, the individual (on the micro level) and society (on the macro level) are viewed as being passive actors to the technologies that drives a new standard of action in all corresponding circumstances, be they exacting or mundane. For the technological determinist, the impact of technology is irresistibly transformative in nature, serving to guide the course of society as the individuals in the larger network are expected to simply acquiesce to the direction dictated by the pull of innovation. Here, the narrative promoting the power of technology to influence society largely excludes considerations regarding the role that humans may have played in the process of developing a given innovation. This narrative approach additionally holds that the individual generally lacks the ability to choose whether to utilize a given technology and that individuals play an inconsequential role in affecting a given innovation's ability to proliferate throughout society. The narrative that favors technically oriented dynamics diminishes the potential role of the individual in affecting change in society and in having the capacity to act independently of the influence of innovations. Operating under the belief that technology is the key driving force of societal change, those promoting technological determinism craft a narrative that is supportive of this supposed dynamic by positing that government behaves accordingly. Narratively, advocates for technological determinism promote a political environment that is highly conducive to the development and proliferation of technology. In that, the responsibility of government is framed as being willing to enable technology by creating a policy environment that is permissive to the natural development of innovative designs. Additionally, technological determinists favor an environment that promotes the ability of technology to be uncontested allowing for innovations to positively affect the lives of those that together comprise society. For the technological determinist, the preferential treatment of the technology industry calls for government to maintain a supportive policy environment that provides an opportunity for the further entrenchment of vast and recurring innovative changes that positively permeate throughout society.

Technological Determinism: Questions Regarding Application During Decision Making in American Democracy

In the democratic sense, technological determinism is subject to a wide array of critiques that calls into question the political soundness of the primary usage of this rationale for government decision making in the context of expectations of the U.S. deliberative system. Critiques associated with technological determinism includes the perception that technology's role in society is based on "a unicausal explanation of historical change" without considering "the complex interaction of casual factors" that are more likely in play on a societal level (Hess, 2015, p. 121). Similarly, technological determinism views "technology as an exogenous variable," which may be inadequate in descriptive capacity due to overlooking "how society also affects technological trajectories." (Hess, 2015, p. 121). Technological determinism—viewing the functional process of technology development as being largely absent of significant input from a variety of system actors, and subscribing to the notion that technology is the driving force of societal transformations—is descriptively inadequate as it relates to the real-world development and proliferation of technology because this limited view fails to account for "the possibility of human agency" (Dafoe, 2015, p. 1052). Schnurer (2022, p. 108) expands on this idea by noting that "technologies themselves are not inherently authoritarian—or otherwise ideological—and current digital technologies certainly are not. These technologies are what we make of them." While it is plausible that a "dominant technology" in the modern era may be capable of affecting the "thoughts, actions and lives" of society, individuals still retain some measure of choice as to the usage of technology in their daily lives (Schnurer, 2022, p. 108). Overall, technocratic suppositions—regarding the indisputably dominant nature of technology to influence society and the minimal capacity of individuals to play an active role in determining preferences for usage of technology—would fall short in adequately describing societal dynamics in relation to the proliferation of innovations.

In many ways, technological determinism is largely descriptively limited and normatively questionable in that this approach provides a statically inadequate assessment of the relationship between society and technology. Technological determinism is based on a narrow relational assumption in positing that technology is and should be the major contributing factor capable of affecting significant societal change on a longitudinal level. Overlooking, or worse yet ignoring, the fact that many other situational factors may influence societal change in the U.S. political system further calls into question the logic of subscribing fully to technological determinism. Clearly, there are a wide range of factors over the course of history capable of influencing significant transformations in society that, to name a few, include situations involving armed conflicts (i.e. wars, terrorist attacks, etc.), acts of nature (i.e. hurricanes, pandemics, etc.), and ideological shifts that affect expectations for what constitutes necessary government actions. Whereas technology may be involved in the development of any number of viable responses to address concerns that arise in society, the

100 A Technocratic Rationale and American Democracy

impetus for change may be an event(s) that are unrelated to innovation. In addition, technological determinism assumes that technology affects society in a distinctly monodirectional capacity, without considering the ability of society to influence the development and proliferation of technology. The idea that technology is the most significant factor in affecting societal change, and that broadly speaking society is unable to influence the progression dynamics of innovations, is questionable. The technological deterministic approach generally lacks the ability to properly describe system dynamics in part because of the conceptual insolvency to appreciate the reciprocal influence that may exist between society and technology. Unlike the view of technological determinism that posits the actions of society are entirely subject to the directional impulses of innovations, it is important to acknowledge that individuals retain a level of deterministic power over technology in a multitude of societal circumstances. On the micro level (i.e. individual) and macro level (society on the whole), human choices may play a role in dictating whether emergent innovations will be accepted and to what degree digital designs will be permitted to proliferate through use. In this, over time choices made at the micro level on behalf of the individual can have a cumulative macro effect, which determines the role that technology will ultimately play in various aspects of society–such as those of a political, social, or economic nature. The technological deterministic approach largely fails to account for this reality, further lending credence to questioning the establishment of this rationale as the primary guiding force to determine policymaking in the field of technology.

The Continuum Approach of Technological Determinism and the Idea of Technological Momentum

Technological determinism has a wide array of conceptual and practical shortcomings that should disallow for the approach to responsibly be considered to serve as the primary guide for wide-scale governmental decision making on issues related to technology. The plethora of legitimate concerns associated with fully subscribing to technological determinism serving as the principal rationale to guide government decision making includes the questionable assumption that real-world societal changes unfold based primarily on the influence of a singular focus—technology. In this regard, technological determinism is deficient in the ability to properly assess the wide range of influential sources present within a given political environment that are also capable of affecting societal events on a longitudinal scale. In relation, the focus on the alleged primacy of technology extends to the unlikely assumption that innovations influence change in society in a one-directional fashion. The idea that occurrences, individuals, or groups present within the political landscape are completely ineffectual in determining any directional outcomes associated with technology fails to capture the true essence of the role that events, and system actors, actively may play within the U.S. political system. Furthermore, failure to acknowledge the wide range of situational elements present within the political system that affect technology, and by extension society of the whole, renders technological determinism to be descriptively and functionally inadequate for use in the manner preferred by advocates of this approach. This is especially true when considering maintaining a policy environment capable of meeting expectations associated with participatory dynamics and responsive government attributed to the U.S. deliberative democracy. Technological determinism unnecessarily limits the flexibility and dynamism expected of a wide range of system actors participating in a deliberative democracy, including those in the public sector and private sector. From a governmental standpoint, a broad investment in technological determinism would ultimately prove deleterious to the ability of the public sector to perform responsively as expected in the U.S. deliberative democracy. When guided by technological determinism, the policy options to be considered on behalf of government during decision making would include a choice matrix that is limited to ensuring that the political environment is maintained to allow for technology to thrive. This policy path would create a political environment that is nurturing to the development and proliferation of technology without being concerned for efforts to take actions that can adequately ensure that citizens are afforded protections and choice customary to those expected in a deliberative democracy.

Members of government and society alike would benefit from avoiding widely subscribing to technological determinism in an overly ambitious fashion, because this rationale is largely inadequate in fulfilling a wide range of deliberative democracy expectations such as those associated with institutionalizing participatory opportunities between system actors. Additionally, the application of technological determinism to guide public-sector decision making will largely create a technology-friendly political environment in which government lacks the capacity to remain flexible and dynamic in crafting policy responses as needed, which is a major component of the U.S. democratic system. Although technological determinism may be inadequate in identifying and responding to the wide variety of system needs present in the U.S. deliberative democracy, there may be some measure of limited applicability by slightly altering the original parameters inherent within the rationale and applying the ideal in a more restrained localized manner. Dafoe (2015, p. 1052) similarly suggests that technological determinism can be better served by emphasizing a moderate approach that considers "the autonomy of technological change" in

102 A Technocratic Rationale and American Democracy

conjuncture with "the technological shaping of society". The concept of technological determinism can be viewed with some measure of causal nuance in which the concept can be assessed along a horizontal continuum, which on opposite ends calls for "hard" or "soft" interpretations of the role technology plays in affecting changes in society (Smith and Marx, 1994, p. xii). Here, the understanding of technological determinism can be based on a broader "continuum" that includes "harder determinants putting more emphasis of the autonomy and power of technology" and "softer determinists allowing for more social control and context" (Dafoe, 2015, p. 1052). On one end of the continuum, the harder view of technological determinism affords technology a great deal of influential power in that, once developed, the innovations themselves are attributed a significant measure of "agency (the power to effect change)" (Smith and Marx, 1994, p. xii). In this, the growth of technology is viewed in a somewhat fatalistic fashion, in which innovations are both an "inescapable necessity" and the most important determinant in transforming society. On the other end of the continuum, the softer view of technological determinism acknowledges that technology's development and eventual roles in society are the result of "multivalent explanation" in which it is implausible to completely factor out the influence of humans on this longitudinal change process (Smith and Marx, 1994, p. xiii). The soft view of technological determinism perceives technology as being less of an "independent agent" of change by granting that the individual still retains a measure of choice that can affect the overall direction of society and the scope in which innovations are ultimately adopted (Smith and Marx, 1994, p. xiii). The soft view of technological determinism is more accommodating to system dynamics in American democracy and is reflective of aspects associated with social construction. Hughes (1994, p. 102) explains that the idea of social construction is based on the presumption "that social and cultural forces determine technical change." The technological determinism continuum seeks to establish a more flexible interpretation of this rationale, which expands the discussion to allow for some level of interactivity between the advancement of technology and society to be recognized. For example, the soft interpretation adopts a social constructionist element by at least accounting for the possibility that society may influence how technology develops and proliferates. In relation, the soft interpretation of technological determinism also introduces the possibility that technology is one of many environmental factors that may directly influence how society progresses over time. As such, the continuum's soft interpretation of technological determinism may find some limited applicability as a contributing factor in assisting in determining policymaking decisions regarding technology. In that, technological determinism advocates representing the soft interpretation may still adamantly argue for a policy environment that is highly protective of the technology industry while also conceding the role that society may play in affecting its development, growth, and proliferation. In doing so, this view may provide some measure of allowance for a broader interpretation of policymaking that may be more accommodating to the human factor involved in the lifecycle of technology.

The continuum approach to technological determinism is more inclusive in efforts to assess extant relational dynamics by accounting for the possibility that technology and society may have the capacity to affect the other to some degree. Within the continuum, the softer view of technological determinism allows for an account of the potential impact of the human element, helping to counter the idea that technology reigns as the supreme source in guiding societal change. This includes acknowledging that technology is created by humans and that, once an innovation is developed, the acceptance of, or resistance to, its usage by individuals operating within society will contribute to determining the scope of proliferation longitudinally. In this, the human element plays a role in which innovations are developed and to what degree the technology will be able to play in a role in society. In relation, allowing for the possibility that societal preferences held by system actors may influence the development and proliferation of technology promotes a humanistic deterministic element associated with the availability of innovations in the modern era. The individual retains some measure of choice regarding the buy-in for using technology (i.e. whether to utilize an innovation, to what degree an innovation will be accepted, etc.) that has both functional and historical implications for society. Whereas technology may play a role in shaping the field of choices available in topical areas such as those associated with governance, the constraints are not absolute in influence as the individual will have a role in affecting the proliferative power of innovation on a societal scale. In developing and proliferating technology, the relational dynamics between innovation and users ultimately contribute to transforming society which in turn affects the trajectory of history. Unlike the harder perspective, the softer approach to technological determinism posits that individuals in society are not hapless pawns to innovation only seemingly along for the technologically charged ride without input or choice on any level. In this sense, the soft aspects of the continuum approach at least in part introduces aspects features of social constructivism into the technological determinism rationale, which provides some measure of expansiveness to the conceptualization because it more realistically accounts for interactive system dynamics present regarding the relationship between society and technology. The process of recognizing the vast array of relational dynamics that may broadly affect aspects of societal change, including those

104 A Technocratic Rationale and American Democracy

associated with technology, may contribute to creating a political environment that is more capable of accurately identifying and addressing system needs during policymaking.

As noted previously, accepting an unaltered technological deterministic approach to governance is wholly inadequate in the modern U.S. democracy, in part because this conceptualization fails to properly account for the wide scope of system dynamics that can affect societal change over time. Technological determinism is essentially far too limited in scope to be used to guide government decision making, in part because it is based on the idea that significant societal change is primarily determined by technology's all-powerful influence, rendering this rationale as being limited in the ability to truly explain real-world system dynamics within the U.S. deliberative democracy. As such, the only opportunity for technological determinism to maintain any measure of descriptive and functional utility in the U.S. democratic system is to consider undertaking modifications to the rationale that allow for a more progressive understanding of the relationship between technology and society. The continuum approach accounts for the possibility for a soft interpretation and hard interpretations on either extreme end along this conceptual spectrum, which creates a more nuanced understanding of technological determinism. In doing so, the continuum approach to technological determinism considers relational dynamics associated with society and technology that may allow this rationale to be more appropriately applied in government decision making regarding innovation-focused policy endeavors. Without acknowledging the influence of expansive bi-directional factors established by the aforementioned continuum, an approach to apply technological determinism would largely remain ill-suited for use in the U.S. democratic system as a descriptive or normative conceptual tool. Altering the original approach to technological determinism will help the rationale to be better suited for playing at least a limited role in governmental decision making and in contributing to facilitating a better understanding of the relationship between technology and society in a modern democratic system. The modified approach to technological determinism, which is based on a continuum including hard and soft interpretations, represents a subtle shift in scope, but the effort to do so allows for greater applicability in real-world circumstances because it integrates a broader understanding of the relationship between society and technology. In addition, the continuum approach also allows for a better accounting of the role that the human element plays in affecting societal change. Although application of the softer interpretation of the technological determinism continuum may better recognize relational dynamics that are present in the U.S. deliberative democracy, the preference to promote a political environment that favors being overly protective to the technology industry would still place limits on the viability of this approach. Still, the idea of adapting technological determinism to ensure that is more politically palatable for use in the U.S. democratic system deserves further consideration and expansion.

Another such interpretative approach to assessing the relational dynamics attributed to society and technology is reflected in the more malleable and flexible conception referred to as technological momentum. While recognizing potential flaws in adopting a limited view of relational dynamics often associated with technological determinism, there may be an opportunity to effort to broadly "develop a vigorous politics of technology" that more aptly reflects how society and technology interacts and influences the other (Hess, 2015, p. 121). A more "holistic," environmental, system-oriented approach that diverts from the limited "unicasual" explanatory perspective may allow for a more accurate account of how other dynamic factors in the real-world affect the two-way relationship between technology and society (Hess, 2015, p. 122). Hughes (1994, p. 102) expands on this idea by noting that "technological momentum infers that social development shapes and is shaped by technology." In relation, the idea of technological momentum includes a mutually dynamic element, which in part acknowledges that social development and technology may enjoy different levels of influence on the other at a given point in time dependent upon the situation at hand (Hughes, 1994, p. 102). Because the concept of technological momentum represents a dynamically reciprocal relationship, allowing for society and technology to mutually influence the other, depending on context at a given point in time, this idea can serve as a conceptual bridge between the interpretive limitations of pure technological determinism and social construction of technology that better accounts for the existence of a wide range of system factors capable of affecting changes to society (Hughes, 1994, p. 112). In this sense, technological momentum recognizes that societal and technological circumstances present in the moment may dynamically impact the ability of one to influence the other. The role of circumstance inherent within the technological momentum perspective provides insight, as it relates to the situational and temporal components present at a given time that impact the levels of influence society may have on technology and vice versa. The rationale of technological determinism is largely lacking the capacity for real-world application in U.S. governance, but a modified approach such as technological momentum that takes a different perspective on understanding the relational aspects associated with society and technology may find some measure of relevance in policymaking endeavors regarding technology. Similar to the technological determinism continuum's soft interpretation, technological momentum moves toward providing a more accurate depiction of the many

106 A Technocratic Rationale and American Democracy

interrelated societal factors that are in play within the policy environment, which implies that this alternative approach may have some contributing merit in public-sector decision making in the U.S. deliberative democracy. Although still focused on the singular policy topic of technology, potential applicability of technological momentum is based on actors subscribing to this design being more cognizant of extant relational dynamics in American democracy, which would allow for more fluid and dynamic interpretation of the many interrelated factors capable of affecting change within the political environment. In doing so, technological momentum represents a more accurate depiction of change processes within the U.S. political system by noting the reciprocity between technology and a wide array of social factors capable of influencing each other. Furthermore, the observance of the role that time plays in shaping the political setting is one of many important contributing factors affecting the progression of policymaking in the American democracy. In all, technological momentum is better suited to influence government decision making in American democracy than is pure technological determinism, because the former more accurately assesses the dynamic relationship between the nature of change involving society and technology, which, in turn, increases the capacity of governmental actions to be more responsive to the contextual elements at play at a given time.

Closing Remarks

There are legitimate concerns associated with technological determinism's efforts to promote that technology is the primary determining factor capable of impacting all significant changes within society in a monodirectional fashion, as this idea is arguably insufficient in understanding the nature of dynamic interactions that transpire in a deliberative democracy. In some cases, technological determinism being focused on the assumption that technology is the driving force of all significant societal change is descriptively inadequate as the real-world environment is subject to a wider array of factors that may yield transformative events. Although the capacity of innovation has undeniably been pivotal in advancing society from a historical standpoint, there is a concern associated with the premise of technological determinism because it may overlook other determining factors for major social change. Technological determinism is highly speculative regarding the possibility that technology affects society without accounting for other sources of input and in the belief that society is unable to affect technology. Relatedly, technological determinism fails to account for the human element, in that people who together comprise society are active participants whose choices to some degree can impact the world in which they live. Technological determinism's subscription to the idea that technology's influence on society is a one-way dynamic fails to account for the reality—that societal members play a role in determining the initial acceptance and proliferation of technology. Arguable assumptions regarding technological determination also includes the idea that all technologically driven changes to society are positive in nature and that government should not intervene in the natural development and proliferation of innovations, because doing so would unnecessarily deprive system actors of the opportunity to reap the many benefits that would have otherwise been enjoyed without government regulatory intervention. In all, the technological determinist would prefer to create a political environment that would be highly protective of the technology industry even at the expense of the needs of broader society, despite if doing so would result in diminishing the deliberative dynamics expected in the American democracy.

The social constructivist approach applied to the field of technology interprets innovations as being influenced by socially and culturally relevant factors. The idea of social construction accounts for the human and contextual intertwined influence on technology's progression with the understanding that this process should avoid mistakenly omitting the ability of technology to actively affect societal change in any significant way. Technological determinism is a technocratically oriented, fatalistic approach that rigidly dictates that technology is the driving force behind societal change and that individual members operating within the networked society are unable to influence technology regarding its development and proliferation. A rationale such as technological determinism that automatically subscribes to the idea that technology is the main force behind all change in society is ill-suited to broadly explaining real-world dynamics in the U.S. deliberative democracy, which generally means that its application during policymaking endeavors is less than ideal. In relation, technological determinism is far too restrictive in scope, failing to acknowledge that in addition to technology there are multiple sources of influence that may affect how society develops. Similarly, technological determinism is insufficient when it comes to recognizing that humans can affect technology, especially regarding the extent to which innovations are accepted and are able to proliferate throughout society. The technological determinism approach is unable to adequately recognize the plethora of societal factors that may affect system outcomes and may often tend to overestimate the importance of technology's role in determining the direction of society. Ultimately, the one-dimensional and limited nature of technological determinism renders this rationale as wholly insufficient in being able to properly describe the relationship between technology and society in a modern democratic system. As many of the foundational components inherent within the rationale of technological determinism that refer to system dynamics are inadequate descriptively, normative arguments for the public sector to subscribe to this approach as the status quo means by which to guide policymaking regarding technology in the U.S. deliberative democracy raises serious questions regarding its substantive applicability. The decision to apply technological determinism to public-sector decision making may result in policy that is incapable of properly addressing extant system needs and can serve to diminish the perceptions that government outcomes are legitimate as it relates to the expectations that participatory opportunities should be readily available to system actors in a deliberative democracy. By bypassing policy outcomes derived from discursive events in favor of creating a decision-making environment that automatically favors the growth of technology, the advocates of technological determinism adopt a path that runs counter to the established expectations for government action in the U.S. deliberative democracy system. The decision-making processes promoted by advocates of technological determinism largely run counter to expectations for participatory opportunities and government responsiveness that are important to U.S. deliberative democracy, which significantly diminishes the capacity for this technocratic approach to play a primary role in policymaking endeavors.

If technological determinism is inadequate in properly expressing the situational and contextual dynamics between innovation and society that are present within the U.S. political system, then this rationale would also be lacking in potency to serve as the principle guiding government decision making on policy related to technology and society. As it relates to the role that government is responsible for playing in the policy environment, an approach that is based on technological determinism is problematic in part because it fails to properly account for the presence of important system expectations associated with the U.S. deliberative democracy. In a deliberative democracy, government is expected to monitor the political arena and engage with a wide range of system actors from the private sector and public sector to determine whether problems of great consequences are believed to be present. Should the deliberative processes yield an agreement among system actors that a significant problem is present that requires an official response, then the government is responsible for developing policy that can address such. If the government created a standard operating framework to guide policy development that automatically and unequivocally favors technology, then the deliberative power of system actors to affect changes to the political system is significantly diminished, rendering participation in discursive events as a largely inconsequential endeavor in the democratic sense.

In addition to falsely assuming that society is unable to influence the path of technological growth in any way, and that technology is the driving force behind all societal change, the technological determinist approach to policymaking lacks the opportunity for system actors to engage in meaningful deliberations capable of influencing government decision making. The technological determinist promotes a policy environment that operates under the assumption that a protectionist approach to the technology industry is preferable to preserving the important role that system actors participating in discursive events plays in contributing to government decision making in a democracy. For advocates of technological determinism, promoting an environment supportive of the development and proliferation of technology takes precedence over institutionalizing requisite interactive avenues for system actors to engage in meaningful deliberations through a plethora of discursive events along multiple points of access within communicative structures. In this sense, technological determinism is a rationale that promotes significantly limiting the participatory means provided for network actors that are expected to be prevalent within the existing communicative structures for the U.S. deliberative democracy. In essence, policymaking based on technological determinism would supplant the democratically oriented expectations for system actors to participate in discursive events with systemic support for granting primacy to a technology friendly approach to government decision making. To attempt to bypass the opportunities for system actors operating from within and outside the public sector to engage with each other in meaningful deliberations, by replacing this hallmark of democracy with an approach that favors protecting technology sans discourse, is an idea ill-suited for use as the primary factor guiding government decision making in the U.S. democracy. It is paramount to the integrity of democracy that both the participatory processes and subsequent policy outcomes, which result from a plethora of discursive events along many points of contact within the broader communicative structure, are viewed by system actors as being legitimate. If the participatory processes are perceived as being incapable of providing a genuine opportunity for system actors to conduct meaningful deliberations, whose outcomes can affect changes to government, then both the procedures and outcomes may both potentially be viewed as illegitimate in the context of deliberative democracy. Therefore, attempts to advance technological determinism as the standard rationale used to guide decision makers on technology policy would serve as a detriment to the integrity of U.S. deliberative democracy.

Technological determinism narratives call for a political environment that holds being highly protective of technology above governmental responsiveness, even though doing so would fail to promote principles of deliberative democracy such as transparency and accountability. In allowing for policymaking to be predicated based on favoring unfettered support of the

110 A Technocratic Rationale and American Democracy

development and proliferation of technology, the ideals behind transparent and accountable government processes may be bypassed by applying technological determinism to guide public-sector decision-making processes. In aligning government decision making with technological determinism, official actions based on this approach would be neither transparent nor accountable to a wide array of system actors in the context of expected participatory opportunities in a deliberative democracy. Additionally, technological determinism is an approach that endorses government wholly institutionalizing a technology-friendly policy environment at the expense of maintaining expectations associated with system actors having the opportunities to participate in the U.S. deliberative democracy. In relation, the narratives used to promote technological determinism largely advance values that run counter to those associated with the firmly established expectations for deliberative democracy, such as those that call for system actors to be able to participate in cyclical discursive events over time, in which persuasive arguments are used to support policy preferences in the hopes of affecting changes within the political system. By applying technological determinism as the status quo rationale to guide governmental decision making, the opportunity for interested parties to engage in meaningful deliberations that can affect political outcomes is diminished or, worse yet, bypassed completely. Those advancing narratives used to promote technological determinism posit that it is beneficial to society that democratic processes are subjugated to the power of technocratic dominance when government decision makers go about enacting policy choices. Technological determinism narratives advancing the call for system actors to extend unwavering allegiance to government efforts to establish an environment in which being supportive of technology is the primary determinant of public-sector decision making is representative of an unconventional plea, as doing so would require supplanting the tenants of deliberative democracy that are so important in the U.S. political system. This lends further credence as to the importance of negating the suggested primary influence of technological determinism by instead advancing narratives that promote the importance of ensuring that the U.S. political system adheres to deliberative democracy expectations. This includes advancing narratives that supports further integrating participatory means into the existing communicative structures, so that expectations associated with responsive governance in a deliberative democracy have greater opportunity to be institutionalized within the U.S. political system.

The preference to create a policy environment that supplants democracy with technology-friendly decision making, as posited by advocates of technological determinism, lacks broad applicability in the U.S. democracy. However, the technological determinism continuum and technological momentum represent variant ideals that represents conceptual steps

A Technocratic Rationale and American Democracy **111**

forward that may modify the far too rigid ideas inherent within traditional technological determinism--by promoting efforts to broaden the scope of the analysis to include the possibility that dynamic relationships exist between society and technology. Although still allowing for the possibility that traditionally oriented, fatalistic agency is attributed to technology's exclusive role in affecting society (i.e. hard determinism), the technological deterministic continuum approach would also permit considerations for human elements to be aptly attributed some measure of agency in affecting the role of technology in society (i.e. soft determinism). Similarly, the idea of technological momentum is an even more fluidly responsive interpretation of the interconnectivity of technological system dynamics because it allows for the possibility that there is a reciprocal relationship between society and technology. Technological momentum is an approach that is cognizant of the fact that at a given point in time situational factors within the U.S. political system can affect the degree to which society influences technology and vice versa. Technological momentum is more malleable and reciprocal in the assessment of the mutually directional relationship between society and technology, while also promoting the understanding that the greater role of one in affecting the other is at least partly due to a variety of situational factors present. As such, technological momentum more accurately depicts the shared power of society and technology to influence the other as being fluid, multidirectional, and situational. Policy argumentation rooted in technological momentum may be suited to serve as one of many rationales advocated for by the multitude of interested parties participating in discursive events. This possibility would provide some measure of opportunity for this technologically focused rationale to contribute to decision making in the U.S. political system, and if chosen may still yield technology-friendly policy but that is more considerate of, and responsive to, extant system dynamics. In this sense, advocates of technological momentum would represent one of many value-based arguments that join in the deliberations involving system actors to determine the policy path of government as expected in American democracy. As a political rationale, pure technological determinism lacks the necessary descriptive power to functionally serve as the primary theory used to explain the nature of technology's influence on society, and is therefore largely rendered ineffectual as a guide in policymaking in U.S. deliberative democracy. Only modified ideals, such as technological momentum, may find a limited role in U.S. decision making providing supplemental guidance capable of contributing to—as opposed to exclusively dictating—the policy direction of government. It will be helpful to keep this in mind when reading the next chapters regarding alternative political rationales, which may be considered to guide government decision making on issues of technology and the present state of the regulatory environment in the United States.

References

D'Agostino, M, Schwester, R., Carrizales, T., & Meliski, J. (2011). A study of e-government and e-governance: An empirical examination of municipal websites. *Public Administration Quarterly, 35*(1), 3–25.

Dafoe, A. (2015). On Technological Determinism. *Science, Technology & Human Values, 40*(6), 1047–1076. https://doi.org/10.1177/0162243915579283

Dotson, T. (2015). Technological Determinism and Permissionless Innovation as Technocratic Governing Mentalities: Psychocultural Barriers to the Democratization of Technology. *Engaging Science, Technology, and Society, 1,* 98–120.

Fountain, J. (2001). *Building the Virtual State: Information Technology and Institutional Change.* Brookings Institute Press.

Hauer, T. (2017). Education, Technological Determinism And New Media. *International Journal of English Literature and Social Sciences (IJELS), 2*(2). https://ijels.com/detail/technological-determinism-and-new-media/

Hess, D. J. (2015). Power, Ideology, and Technological Determinism. *Engaging Science, Technology, and Society, 1,* 121–125. https://doi.org/10.17351/ests2015.010

Hughes, T. P. (1994). Technological Momentum. In M. R. Smith and L. Marx (Eds.), *Does Technology Drive History? The Dilemma of Technological Determinism.* The MIT Press.

Sadowski, J. & Selinger, E. (2014). Creating a Taxonomic Tool for Technocracy and Applying it to Silicon Valley. *Technology in Society, 38,* 161–168.

Schnurer, E. B. (2022). Democracy Disrupted: Governance in an Increasingly Virtual and Massively Distributed World. *Hedgehog Review, 24*(2), 106–130.

Smith, M. L. (1994). Recourse of Empire: Landscapes of Progress in Technological America. In M. R. Smith and L. Marx (Eds.), *Does Technology Drive History? The Dilemma of Technological Determinism.* The MIT Press.

Smith, M. R. (1994). Technological Determinism in American Culture. In M. R. Smith and L. Marx (Eds.), *Does Technology Drive History? The Dilemma of Technological Determinism.* The MIT Press.

Smith, M. R. and Marx, L. (1994). Introduction. In M. R. Smith and L. Marx (Eds.), *Does Technology Drive History? The Dilemma of Technological Determinism.* The MIT Press.

4
PERMISSIONLESS INNOVATION AND THE PRECAUTIONARY PRINCIPLE

The previous chapter focused on introducing what constitutes technological determinism and discussing the potential role that a technocratically motivated political rationale could play in affecting the policymaking environment in the context of the U.S. deliberative democracy. Technological determinism is one of many rationales whose existence is attributed to being predicated in part on the founding ideals associated with technocracy. However, the technological deterministic approach is largely ill-suited to take a primary role to guide government decision makers in the American democracy in efforts to determine the scope and nature of policy endeavors in any given field including that of technology. In general, technological determinism largely lacks direct applicability for decision making in the U.S. political system in part because the inherent preference to maintain a technology-friendly policy environment runs counter to traditional expectations associated with establishing participatory opportunity and responsive government in a deliberative democracy. In addition, technological determinism is an approach that remains overly optimistic of the need for the technology industry to be able to develop innovations freely in society and is conceptually limited regarding the belief that technology monodirectionally serves as the driving force of all changes within society. Instead of being widely adopted at all levels of government as the status quo rationale that will be used to guide decision making when government officials craft policy to address the technology industry, technological determinism may find a limited role in contributing to discursive events as one of a plethora of political rationales being argued on behalf of various interested parties attempting to influence policymaking. In this sense, this approach likely may find only a measure

DOI: 10.4324/9781003441830-4

114 Permissionless Innovation and the Precautionary Principle

of supplemental relevance in shaping the U.S. policy environment in the modern era as its very design—calling for automatic preferential treatment of the technology industry in the policy sense—runs counter to expectations of participatory dynamics in deliberative democracy.

This chapter will begin by introducing the conceptual premise inherent within permissionless innovation and the precautionary principle that serves to guide preferences for policymaking intended to address the field of technology. The idea that innovators should seek government permission to act when developing technology is a highly subjective concept, in which assessment of this ideal plays a key role in determining support for permissionless innovation or the precautionary principle. This chapter will also provide a discussion as to how advocates for permissionless innovation firmly believe that this rationale should take a primary role in guiding government decision making regarding policy and will highlight critiques associated with permissionless innovation, which calls into question its applicability for use in the U.S. deliberative democracy. In addition, the chapter will introduce the precautionary principle that largely serves as a conceptual counterbalance to the ideals held by those advocating for technology-friendly rationales such as permissionless innovation. The scope and nature of the discussion will also extend to efforts to determine to what extent permissionless innovation, or the precautionary principle, is suited to facilitate technology-based policymaking while also honoring participatory expectations within the context of U.S. deliberative democracy. In doing so, it will be essential to integrate into the discussion the presence of value-laden arguments that are inherent in the opposing narratives used to promote the benefits of subscribing to either permissionless innovation or the precautionary principle.

Permissionless Innovation and the Precautionary Principle: Opposing Perceptions of the Preferred Role of Government in Regulating the Technology Industry

In many ways, the ideas associated with technocracy serves as the conceptual precursor to the development of similarly oriented rationales that also favor a policy environment focused on allowing expertise and expediency to take a primary role in government decision making. In relation, technological determinism, and its more recent iteration permissionless innovation, are both adequately described as conceptually progressive subvariants of the broader theoretical perspective of technocracy. Having previously expanded on technological determinism, it will now be helpful to introduce information that expands on what constitutes permissionless innovation, and to determine if this concept serves as viable rationale in guiding policymaking endeavors in the U.S. democratic system. In doing so, it will also be of great importance to coincidingly discuss aspects associated with the precautionary principle, which is a rationale that largely stands in opposition of the preferred parameters for policymaking set forth by permissionless innovation. Ultimately, permissionless innovation and the precautionary principle represent vastly different perceptions regarding the preferred role of government in U.S. policymaking that will result in official means capable of affecting the field of technology. As it relates to public policy considerations applicable to the field of technology, a key conceptual discussion that will affect preferences for the scope of government intervention is centered on how to address "the permission question" (Thierer, 2016a, p. 1). This question is focused on determining whether it should be required of "the creators of new technologies" to obtain the "blessing of public officials before they develop and deploy their innovations" (Thierer, 2016a, p. 1). If the answer to the permission question is believed to be yes, then one would be an advocate for the rationale referred to as the "precautionary principle" (Thierer, 2016a, p. 1). This perspective is focused on the importance of government actively and preemptively having the ability to develop policy means to regulate technology with an underlying assumption attached to this dynamic calling for government intervention over industry freedom (Thierer, 2016a, p. 1). In that, the burden of responsibility is shifted to the technology industry to prove that a given innovation "will not cause any harms to individuals, groups, specific entities, cultural norms, or various existing laws, norms, or traditions" (Thierer, 2016a, p. 1). The precautionary principle requires that government remains dynamically active by promoting flexibility in policymaking to ensure that the public sector can identify and address system needs as they arise. In this sense, the technology industry is not provided permission to have an unlimited free rein to act and is instead subjected to a dynamic regulatory environment expected in the U.S. deliberative democracy. Should the answer to the permission question be no, then one would subscribe to a policymaking approach that promotes a rationale termed "permissionless innovation" (Thierer, 2016a, p. 1). This perspective supports self-regulation of the technology industry over government enacting stringently preemptive regulatory measures (Thierer, 2016a, p. 1). Unless there is convincing evidence that a specific innovation will cause societal damage, industry practitioners should be free to experiment with emerging innovations in order determine if significant issues exist and, if so, how best to address said problems (Thierer, 2016a, p. 1). Here, preferences regarding whether the technology industry's freedom to innovate should be subject to government regulatory constraints, and to what degree this intervention should be pursued, serves as the foundation by which support of permissionless innovation, or the precautionary principles, are based.

On one hand, permissionless innovation is an approach favoring the freedom of the technology industry to develop and implement innovations in

116 Permissionless Innovation and the Precautionary Principle

a policy environment that is largely lacking in preemptively designed regulatory constraints. Here, permissionless innovation places protecting technology as the default setting for governmental decision making regarding the broad field of innovations. The advocates of permissionless innovation believe that all technology should be permitted to develop and proliferate largely without being subjected to government interference, which is deemed burdensome and unnecessary. For those supporting permissionless innovation, a political environment in which government preemptively and excessively crafts policy that is restrictive of the ability of technology to develop and grow is both unnecessary and undesirable. Apart from cases in which undeniable evidence exists that proves significant harm was caused to society by a given innovation, those supporting permissionless innovation operate under the assumption that a policymaking environment should largely be accommodating to the field of technology. Without convincing proof being readily available ensuring that no harm will come from the application of innovation, there is little need to allow government to maintain the ability to remain actively vigilant in the policy landscape. For the advocate of permissionless innovation, it is preferrable that government supports the unfettered growth of technology instead of opting to develop restrictive policy that will potentially deprive society of the many benefits that would have otherwise been enjoyed by the public if government had taken a hands-off approach to innovation in the policymaking sense. In this, government is expected to tacitly provide permission for the technology industry to grow and adapt with very little regulatory interference. On the other hand, the precautionary principle is an approach to governance that errs of the side of caution by placing the responsibility to protect society from potential harm caused by technology in the hands of government decision makers. In this sense, those advocating for the precautionary principle believe that allowing the technology industry to expand without governmental checks in place is irresponsible in a democratic sense. Instead, the regulatory environment is better served by requiring the technology industry is subject to mandated guidelines that are actively and dynamically updated based on perceived system needs. In the modern era, permission can be viewed in terms of degrees of influence that may affect the policymaking process and outcomes that contributes to regulating the technology industry. An overly restrictive approach to permission would proactively create a policy environment that affords little-to-no flexibility for the technology industry to develop of its own volition. This choice could result in creating highly restrictive policy to address a developing technology, which includes banning a specific innovation outright or which significantly limits its development, which essentially halts both growth and proliferation. However, a judicious approach to the influence of permission on policy could create an environment that allows for a measure of creative freedom of the technology industry while still retaining the government's ability to develop policy proactively and reactively as deemed necessary. Here, the application of the precautionary principle would create a policy environment that is better suited to responsive and dynamic governance as expected in the U.S. deliberative democracy. Ultimately, how the idea of permission is viewed will be a contributing factor for choosing to support permissionless innovation or the precautionary principle to serve as the political rationale by which the regulatory environment will be based upon in American democracy. In relation, this preference regarding permission is capable of playing a direct role in government decision making, which is intended to affect the technology industry.

Permissionless Innovation: The Case for Limited Government Intervention

Those supportive of permissionless innovation advocate for government to avoid actively pursuing a policy environment that is overly restrictive of technology in a general sense. To some, permissionless innovation is deemed preferable as the standard by which public sector policymaking is conducted, because of the belief in the importance of protecting the wide array of benefits to society that innovations are capable of delivering, especially if permitted to do so with little, or preferably, no government intervention. Permissionless innovation is predicated on arguments focusing on simultaneously advancing the possibility of an endless of array of unparalleled benefits that will, most assuredly, be reaped by society only through the unencumbered advancement of technology and the assumption that, broadly speaking, any outcomes resulting from the proliferation of technology will be overwhelmingly positive, certainly outweighing any and all possible ill effects that may have resulted from integration of such on a comprehensive scale (Dotson, 2015, p. 106). In this sense, those supportive of permissionless innovation look unfavorably on a highly restrictive regulatory environment that unnecessarily limits the boundless possibility of technology to positively affect society. In this sense, it is argued that it is more favorable for government to adopt a permissionless innovation approach to regulating the field of technology, which would require decision makers avoiding the temptation to officially pursue an overly restrictive, pre-emptive path based on the precautionary principle (Thierer, 2016a). Thierer (2016a) observes that reasons to support a minimalistic regulatory environment guiding policy endeavors associated with technology that is founded in permissionless innovation can be summarized as followed:

> An automatically apprehensive approach to developing public policy intended for regulating technology that is based on the precautionary principle may unnecessarily serve to stymie the natural growth of that

118 Permissionless Innovation and the Precautionary Principle

industry. An environment with strict regulatory guidelines designed to actively constrain innovative growth reduces, and in some cases even eliminates, the opportunity to access knowledge that would have otherwise been gained via organic social learning.

Active learning, and the subsequent accumulation of resulting knowledge, occurs over time in a field such as technology. This dynamic process involves continuous trial and error by innovators and practitioners to determine what works and what doesn't work. Experimentation on a longitudinal basis can allow participants to gain first-hand knowledge regarding what causes failures and successes which are both equally important to the advancement of technology as a field.

Accepted social practices, industry benchmarks and ethical standards prevalent within a given field should avoid being automatically translated into public policy initiatives in a somewhat misguided effort to further institutionalize even more broadly said values within society.

The most suitable solutions to complicated issues in society are most often derived via a trickle-up approach empowering participants in a field such as technology who are cognizant of the established legal, social, and ethical parameters by providing the latitude needed to determine means to best adjust to circumstances.

Source: Thierer (2016a, pp. 2–3)

Permissionless innovation is a rationale with a premise that is generally very supportive of the belief in the capacity of technology to better society in incalculable ways and that places a great deal of faith in those that create technology to solve issues inherent to the industry without the burden of government intervention. Those supportive of permissionless innovation are oft vehemently opposed to government intervention in the industry based on the premise that doing so would unnecessarily limit the natural development of technology, restrict the role that active learning plays in discovery within the technology industry, unnecessarily integrate industry values into broader society by enacting legislative mandates that attempt to constrict the technology industry, and hold back the ability of active participants within the industry to rectify issues of their own accord. Those advocating for permissionless innovation generally prefer a policy environment in which government largely takes a hand-off approach, which allows for the industry and society to both take an active part in reaping the benefits of technology while contributing to designing solutions as needed should any issues arise that are caused by innovations usage.

Those advocating for permissionless innovation argue there is evidence that this approach to policymaking has enjoyed some measure of success in practice in the U.S. political system. Permissionless innovation supporters believe firmly that there is sufficient evidence of cases in which an industry's creative freedom has greatly benefited a wide range of societal members and that these instances serve as precedent, lending further credence to the merit of this approach. Since the early 1990s, the U.S. government has often pursued a public policy path that has been supportive of an environment conducive to permissionless innovation, including when it came to the regulation of Internet-based commercialism endeavors (Koopman, 2018, p. 1). The regulatory environment in the U.S. has generally been encouraging of the ability of innovators to develop and implement a wide array of new technology-based for-profit designs without having to first obtain permission from the government to do so (Koopman, 2018, p. 1). In the modern era, the continued marketization of profit-based endeavors, facilitated by way of the Internet, have often been left to proceed unfettered, sans preemptive strict regulatory guidelines by the U.S. government, to allow for an environment that is generally permissive in scope in order to encourage such innovative means (Koopman, 2018, p. 2). In addition, regulatory efforts in the digital domain are typically initiated on a more reactionary scale in response to a perceived need for government to address an emerging problem that is believed to cause significant societal strife in some way (Koopman, 2018, p. 2). Here, permissionless innovation in practice is focused on maintaining a public policy environment that favors being highly nurturing to the continued development of technological endeavors by default, while still allowing for some measure of reactive regulatory means to be developed by government should a significant need arise. For those advocating for permissionless innovation, the adoption of a policy approach favoring a reactionary government response arguably would find some measure of justification in the context of the U.S. democracy. A reactionary, as opposed to preemptive, approach to regulating the technology industry serves to contribute to maintaining a level of system malleability, in that government is able to respond on a case-by-case basis to societal concerns that may occur over time, and there is some historical precedent for the acceptance of this practice as a function within the U.S. deliberative democracy. In this context, the reactionary component associated with permissionless innovation may serve to compliment aspects of modern democratic governance, which often requires responsiveness over prevention involving official actions, because of the need to account for the natural constraints of governance that may inhibit being able to consistently take broad preemptive measures in all areas of public policy. However, allowance for some measure of reactionary regulatory responses is a far cry from subscribing to a political environment that is highly permissive of innovation or that completely forgoes government regulation of the technology industry. In that, it is irresponsible of modern U.S. government

120 Permissionless Innovation and the Precautionary Principle

to pursue a policy path that attempts to justify supplanting the ability of the public sector to preemptively act if deemed necessary by offering only a limited quality of reactionary responsiveness in its place. In addition, regulatory allowance providing some measure of developmental freedom in one area of technology, such as Internet-based commercialism, wouldn't necessarily mean that this tactic would be responsibly or successfully employed broadly for all aspects of innovations.

In addition, permissionless innovation advocates would suggest subscribing to an action template that places government responsiveness as being secondary to industry efforts to regulate itself based on experiential preferences generated through use to guide change derived from those directly immersed in the technology industry. In this context, favoring permissionless innovation means supporting innovators and practitioners by allowing them the opportunity to identify potential issues that may occur when technology is in use and to have the freedom to develop means within the industry to rectify any weaknesses prior to government regulation. In this sense, advocates of permissionless innovation favor a policy environment that is supportive of interested parties maintaining significant levels of self-determination, providing an opportunity to research, develop, market, and disseminate innovative designs. This aspect of permissionless innovation is geared toward establishing a protectionist approach to the technology industry as the status quo rationale to guide policymaking in the field. Doing so considers technology development and proliferation as providing diminished risk to cause societal harm to the point that the preferred policy environment recommends government intervention only as a reactionary response to proven problems derived from innovation. Here, permissionless innovation supports favoring participants operating in connection to the technology industry to serve as the primary influential factors to identify and address issues that may stem from technology's development and expanded usage. This idea allows industry leaders and societal practitioners to contribute to self-regulation, which is tantamount to undemocratically giving those vested in innovation a level of dominion over the whole of society as it relates to technology. In practical terms, adopting permissionless innovation as the rationale to guide policymaking would largely be undemocratic in the sense that participatory and responsive governance is supplemented in the process of deferring to those involved in the technology field whose pursuit of protecting the industry may place society at risk. Although the reactionary response component inherent to the permissionless innovation is a useful tenant in policymaking that is applicable for use within a complex, heterogenous society such as the U.S., advocates of this approach prefer the application of such is only limited to allowing government regulation in cases in which there is proof that technology in practice has caused harm to society. Overall, the reactionary role for regulations applied in a limited fashion only in extreme cases where there is proof of technology-based harm caused to society and recommendation for establishing a technology-friendly policy environment that willingly overlooks traditional decision making required in a democracy are representative of concerns associated with widescale usage of permissionless innovation in the American system.

Inherent within the permissionless innovation rationale is also the belief that government efforts to limit the initial development and continued growth of technology may potentially create artificial impediments in shaping the industry to the point that innovations are no longer permitted to remain on course naturally. To those supporting permissionless innovation, the choice to pursue competing rationales such as the precautionary principle will likely create a regulatory environment that constrains the organic development and proliferation of the technology industry that has far-reaching implications in many aspects of society. For example, technology has greatly affected the manner in which members of society may engage in various industries within the broader economy. Therefore, to those advocating for permissionless innovation, a political environment that actively and preemptively seeks to regulate the technology industry could yield a domino effect that impedes how other industries develop, which may unnecessarily cause harm to the economy. In the modern era, technological advancements such as the Internet has provided means capable of reducing, or even eliminating, many of the traditional barriers to entry, especially those associated with geography and costs of production, which had previously long stood to prevent higher levels of participation in an industry that renders "artificial barriers—particularly licensing and regulatory restrictions" as the primary preventative means to become involved (Koopman, 2018, p. 2). An effort to move away from a public policy approach based on permissionless innovation can create an artificially restrictive regulatory environment that may mitigate many of the benefits that would otherwise be derived by applying technology to overcome natural barriers to entry in an industry serving to hamper the participation of interested parties (Koopman, 2018, p. 2). Furthermore, it can be argued that governmental efforts to adopt a public policy plan that preemptively creates strict regulations of the technology industry may cause innovators to relocate to other more accommodating jurisdictions in the hopes of finding an environment that is more supportive of such pioneering efforts (Koopman, 2018, p. 2). Thierer (2016b) refers to this phenomenon as "innovation arbitrage," which is described as "the idea that innovators can, and will with increasingly regularity, move to those jurisdictions that provide a legal and regulatory environment more hospitable to entrepreneurial

122 Permissionless Innovation and the Precautionary Principle

activity" (Thierer, 2016b). In that, those responsible for developing innovations may look globally to locate jurisdictions that provides "more friendly regulatory treatment" on behalf of government (Thierer, 2016b). Similarly, on the domestic level, those at the forefront of technology development may also actively "play state and local governments off each other" in the hopes of finding more favorable regulatory conditions that will allow for a greater ability to compete in the market (Thierer, 2016b). Here, official decision making rooted in permissionless innovation is viewed as being able to play an invaluable primary role in protecting the technology industry from experiencing potentially irreparable harm to its natural growth, which would have occurred if subjected to artificially restrictive government policy. In that, advocates of permissionless innovation posit that this rationale is well suited to ensure that artificially created policy designs do not unnecessarily limit the range of interested parties that may wish to participate in contributing to the expansion of the technology industry and in participating in other fields that benefits from the application of innovations. Here, the government can largely avoid instituting official means that will limit participating in the progression of the technology industry and in doing so generally circumvent potentially depriving society of the many benefits that are surely to be derived from emerging innovations. Relatedly, the usage of permissionless innovation would assist in the prevention of the technology industry simply moving its operations in order to pursue a locality, state, or even a nation that is more willing to provide a policy environment that is favorable to those vested in the innovation industry. If this industry movement should occur, then the previous locale that served as its home base of operations will be less immediately able to enjoy the benefits that may be derived from the industrious endeavor because of the logistical implications associated with production occurring elsewhere. This may negatively affect the ability of the government, the economy, the industry in question, and the members of society to benefit from technology that would have otherwise been nurtured within the jurisdictional boundaries of the original locality.

Granted, in some cases this dynamic aspect may only create a temporary disadvantage to the original locale should the technology development achieve a high permeability rate in which increased mobility may later permit digital access to or a physical return of the innovation in question. It is possible that arbitrage in this case would serve to highlight the migratory capacity of innovation as the recently re-located technology industry is otherwise able to flourish elsewhere in a more friendly policy environment. Although the geographical element may create a delay in porting technology back to the original jurisdiction, the resulting dynamic is not necessarily completely prohibitive of innovation migration from the new base of operations back to the original locale. To avoid the flight of an entire industry to an alternate location that has a policy environment favorable to technology, the supporters of permissionless innovation recommend the use of this rationale in the context of technology-related policymaking. Thus, permissionless innovation as a practice reflects a preference to avoid policy that would artificially create geographical and logistical barriers that would only ultimately serve to delay the natural progression of technology in another locale, as regulatory efforts were functionally circumvented by industry movement. If these strict regulations in a given locale could be easily circumvented by industry movement, then the supporters of permissionless innovation could argue that it would be more prudent to develop a policy environment that is conducive to the technology industry. Otherwise, the technology industry will be motivated to move elsewhere, develop innovations from afar, and then attempt to port these designs in some way back to the original locale anyway. In this case, regulating the technology industry may not be as successful in limiting its growth as originally intended by lawmakers. Whereas regulation may slow the development process considerably, unless the regulations are broadly draconian in scope, completely preventing the presence of the technology in the locality at any time, then the arbitrage route may only serve to delay the progression and proliferation of technology.

Further Narrative Analysis of Permissionless Innovation: Inherent Values Argued For, System Preferences Held and Determining Applicability in U.S. Deliberative Democracy Policymaking

In the narrative sense, those supportive of the permissionless approach attempt to advance this rationale by incorporating a normative component (i.e. what should be) that portrays its usage in the policy environment as necessary for the sake of bettering society. For the advocates of permissionless innovation, the narrative designs used to promote this rationale often focus on arguing that a policy environment friendly to technology is both traditional in practice and should be allowed to persist unaltered. The normative element of permissionless innovation is in part advanced through a rhetorical approach that frames the development and proliferation associated with the technology industry as one that should largely be detached from "political oversight and control" (Dotson, 2015, p. 104). Similarly, advocates of permissionless innovation view this typology to be nomological, meaning that the importance of this approach should be widely accepted at face value, free of debates that would only likely result in government actions that could possibly hinder the unfettered growth of innovations throughout society (Dotson, 2015, p. 104). Dotson (2015, p. 104) argues against permissionless innovation being normative and

124 Permissionless Innovation and the Precautionary Principle

nomological, indicating that the underlying narrative of this approach that claims the status quo in the U.S. political system is one that favors an environment promoting absolute freedom to innovate without regulation is something of a fallacy. In that, advocates of permissionless innovation that attempt to frame the public policy landscape as one in which the status quo has long supported a totally regulation-free environment that is suddenly under threat by those prejudiced against technology clamoring for unnecessarily comprehensive restraints lacks credence (Dotson, 2015, p. 104). The technocratically oriented preferences inherent within permissionless innovation narratives calling for a landscape with little-to-no official intervention can be critiqued on the basis that it is important to recognize that promoting innovation in society can actually be facilitated by government actions designed to reduce obstacles to participation, that the claim innovators have been unnecessarily hampered by a harshly restrictive environment fails to account for the growing neoliberal impact on government regulatory efforts, and that the utopian assumption all technological changes automatically have a positive effect on the whole of society fails to recognize there may be many who are negatively influenced by a wide scale technology adoption (Dotson, 2015, p. 104). In sum, the narrative designs that argue permissionless innovation is normative and nomological in many ways lack persuasive power partly because there are many factors that call into question claims associated the circumstances surrounding the technology-focused regulatory environment in theory and practice. In that, the assumption that government should, and largely has, taken an entirely hands off approach to the field of technology to allow it to develop and spread unconditionally is questionable on a number of accounts. While the policy environment in the U.S. may allow some measure of freedom in innovation, the government is far from entirely permissive in providing allowances for such in the policy sense. In addition, the idea that the policy environment should be maintained in a manner that is favorable to all things technology related raises some valid concerns regarding the legitimacy of government processes and outcomes in the context of deliberative democracy. The narrative promoting permissionless innovation as the status quo rationale that should guide government decision making would yield a policy environment that falls dangerously short of many of the key expectations associated with deliberative democracy. Permissionless innovation calls for deliberative democracy expectations associated with transparency and accountability to be bypassed in favor of accepting that the policy environment should allow for the growth of the technology industry to be unchallenged, unregulated, and undeterred. Essentially, the narratives supporting permissionless innovation promote a policy environment that also circumvents the expectation associated with deliberative democracy that calls for system actors to routinely have the opportunity to engage in meaningful deliberations in the hopes of affecting changes to the political system. If the policy environment largely removes the possibility of regulating technology from the debates, then the opportunity for meaningful deliberations among interested parties is significantly diminished or, worse, eliminated. Furthermore, the perception that meaningful deliberations are unavailable in the context of developing technology policy may in some cases understandably lead system actors to question the legitimacy of the democratic processes and outcomes. In this sense, allowing permissionless innovation to achieve and maintain unchallenged status as the rationale that guides technology-oriented policymaking would serve as a direct threat to the integrity of the U.S. deliberative democratic system. Additionally, permissionless innovation advocates may fail to account for the fact that there is a positive and necessary role that government can play in crafting policy capable of enhancing the development of technology and further integrating its broad usage in society. This includes that public policy efforts may work to reduce barriers to participation that may have occurred naturally as it relates to becoming involved in the production of technology, which may serve to benefit consumers and industry competitors alike. Although regulatory efforts are potentially viewed by advocates of permissionless innovation as intrusive and detrimental to the natural flow of competition in the economy, the U.S. government policy initiatives such as those associated with enacting anti-trust laws are developed in part to prevent the existence and persistence of a monopoly in any given industry, such as technology, creating some measure of balance that is intended to protect both consumers and potential competitors. In addition, policy efforts may reduce participation obstacles to the extent that citizens may have greater access to, and knowledge of, the modern technologies that are more frequently used to facilitate a wide range of government activities that involves the public (i.e. disseminate information, deliver services, engage in discursive events, etc.). Therefore, narratives crafted by permissionless innovation advocates—arguing that the only role that government should play in crafting technology-focused policy is in the rare instances in which there is a need to rectify undisputable harm caused to society by a given innovation—misses the mark regarding the reality of the capacity and responsibility of the public sector in this regard. Therefore, the role of the U.S. government exceeds this rather one-dimensional and overly minimalistic approach argued on behalf of those advocating for permissionless innovation, which fails to paint a full picture of the positive impact that the public sector may responsibly play in this dynamic.

Those advocating for permissionless innovation to serve as the rationale that guides decision making for technology policy arguably includes some overly ambitious assumptions regarding the scope and nature of the role that innovations play in society. Permissionless innovation narratives are extremely complimentary in advocating that technology is consistently capable of providing a slew of necessary benefits, which society should never be denied access to, and in claiming that any negative effects that may result from when innovations are applied is minimal at best. In this, narratives utilized to promote permissionless innovation inherently reflect a tendency to understate the potential risks posed to society by technology and to overvalue the extent that applying technology will provide benefits in all aspects of life that will be widely enjoyed equally by all members of society. Permissionless innovation can be viewed as being somewhat unrealistic regarding the assessment of technology's potential to impact the system, due to the belief that changes resulting from technology are always overwhelmingly beneficial to society and the positive assessment of risk serving as the foundation for arguing that regulation generally should be avoided, except in rare instances in which undeniable harm is caused by the application of innovation is clearly identified (Dotson, 2015, p. 105). This overly optimistic view of the capacity of technology to influence society fails to account for the possibility that during the application process there could very well be negative repercussions and that those in society who are negatively affected would be less inclined to view an environment supporting technology without restraint as being worth the risk (Dotson, 2015, p. 105). This technocratic rationale inherent within permissionless innovation rhetoric overlooks the existence of real-world consequences that could result from a system in which technology is largely left unchecked by government, and this is why it can be so important that public policy is crafted to protect "the interests of those potentially harmed" (Dotson, 2015, p. 105). The narratives used to promote permissionless innovation generally hold an excessively, and arguably unrealistically, positive view of the role that technology plays in society without properly acknowledging the scope of issues that also may result from innovations is use. Relatedly, permissionless innovation advocates craft narratives that underestimate the dangers associated with technology in practice, which is an approach that inherently believes that innovations pose a minimal risk to society and that government can retroactively address a rare problem that develops if need be. Through the act of assuming a minimalistic assessment of risk inherent within this approach, technology's capacity to negatively impact society is devalued to the point where it is believed that the policy environment should allow innovation to freely flourish without being unnecessarily hampered by excessive regulations. In this, permissionless innovation is subject to some measure of scrutiny because the overly positive assessment of technology may create a policy environment that fails to expeditiously recognize developing problems and that may be incapable of adequately responding to issues that occur. Contrary to preferences held by advocates of permissionless innovation, the decision to institutionalize a policy environment that is capable of actively and responsibly monitoring the need to officially address problems caused by technology is both more realistic and responsible in a political sense in the context of U.S. deliberative democracy.

In essence, permissionless innovation is a rationale that favors supporting innovation's industry over those that may in some way be negatively affected by the very technology that is alleged to be largely incapable of causing harm to the members of society. This idea runs counter to system expectations of the U.S. democratic system, in which a key responsibility of government is to remain flexible enough to be able to actively work to protect its citizens from being subjected to harm if the need should arise. By permissionless innovation narratives promoting the importance of a policy environment that is automatically set to protect an industry, there are questions that will naturally be raised as to the merits of using this approach when regulating technology, because doing so places the nation's citizenry in a secondary position of importance to that of protecting innovation. Furthermore, subscribing to permissionless innovation requires advocating for a policy environment that is supportive of those that are in a position to profit from the undertaking of technology development at the expense of protecting "democratic decision-making rights of stakeholders," who may be negatively affected should innovations be permitted to be disseminated throughout society largely unchecked by government (Dotson, 2015, p. 105). Permissionless innovation advocates would argue that safeguarding the rights, freedoms, and choices of those seeking to develop, and disseminate, innovation on a wide scale would take precedence over "conscious democratic steering," which they view as a policy approach that is far too restrictive because it unnecessarily limits the ability of society to take advantage of the many benefits that may be universally enjoyed within an environment that is largely devoid of technology focused regulations (Dotson, 2015, p. 106). The act of favoring prospective societal advantages, which are expected to be derived from innovation usage in a largely regulation-free environment, over the preference to allow decision makers to remain flexible in the ability to develop means capable of preventing harm caused by technology serves as a legitimate threat to expectations associated with the responsibility of government in a democracy (Dotson, 2015, p. 106). In this sense, permissionless innovation grants precedence to safeguarding the "liberties of innovators" over "risk mitigation typically assured through democratic process" (Dotson, 2015, p. 107). In that, there is a technocratic view of risk and reward that

128 Permissionless Innovation and the Precautionary Principle

favors a policy path giving priority to allowing innovation to freely develop preferably with minimal regulation over that of supporting deliberative democracy processes that may have otherwise resulted in regulatory efforts to safeguard the public if necessary. The advocates of permissionless innovation promote a policy environment that runs counter to the traditional system expectations that are of great importance to the maintenance of preserving the U.S. deliberative democracy. The recommendation on behalf of permissionless innovation advocates to place the protection of technology above an active, participatory government misses the mark regarding the importance of a policy environment that is flexible, dynamic, and vigilant in determining system needs that will require official actions to solve said problems. Instead, permissionless innovation advocates prefer a protectionist approach, placing the ability of the technology industry to flourish free of restrictions over the participatory dynamics inherent within a deliberative democracy, in which a wide range of system actors are expected to debate over the preferred direction of government through multiple points of contact integrated in modern communicative structures. Permissionless innovation advocates view a public-policy approach that calls for exercising caution as being far too risk adverse, which ultimately serves as the enemy of progress, and because of this they remain in opposition of routinely facilitating meaningful deliberations among interested parties to determine if the need for regulation of technology exists. Permissionless innovation advocates favor granting near-limitless freedom to innovators to create technology in a largely unrestricted manner, over the traditional processes expected within a democratic system in which participants would not otherwise largely exempt precaution as a policy path during the deliberative process. Advocates of permissionless innovation actively work to frame those subscribing to the precautionary principle who call for responsibly regulating the technology industry as the enemy of progress, representing an overly guarded policy approach that will simultaneously serve to diminish the natural progression of innovation development and deprive the populous of an undoubtedly endless array of benefits that are assumed to occur throughout society with minimal-to-no negative consequences. The protection of creative freedom, which is believed to be necessary to yield innovations capable of providing any number of potential benefits as new technologies proliferate society, is essentially framed by supporters of permissionless innovation as an either-or proposition. For the supporters of permissionless innovation, government decision makers must choose between a public policy path that allows for technology to progress largely free of regulatory control so that society may reap resulting rewards or a public policy path that facilitates timely deliberations among participants to determine if there is agreement regarding the need to regulate the technology industry as expected in traditional democratic processes. In reality, the decision-making environment within the U.S. political system is suitably designed to allow for some measure of responsible co-habitation of regulatory preferences, optimally creating a balance between both policy paths dependent on an assessment of situational and contextual factors. However, this cooperative design is largely unfavorable to advocates of permissionless innovation, who prefer public-policy responses only in cases in which extreme harm to the citizenry has been proven. The permissionless innovation rationale frames efforts to actively regulate the technology industry as being reflective of an overly cautious approach, whose application in the policy environment unnecessarily threatens the development of innovations. In relation, advocates of permissionless innovation view the decision to actively regulate or grant developmental freedom to the technology industry as policy approaches that are in direct opposition to the other, without considering the opportunity for a more responsibly balanced approach to government decision making that may account for both.

Those supporting permissionless innovation view the precautionary approach as creating an unnecessarily strict regulatory environment that threatens the natural growth of innovations that potentially limits the ability of society to reap the benefits that are sure to be enjoyed by applying technology on a wide scale. The opposition's disinclination to the usage of the precautionary approach is also predicated on the idea that the promise of frequently remarkable rewards derived from technology that will be enjoyed by all far outweighs any minimally impactful, negative outcomes that may occasionally affect individuals in society. The overly optimistic, one-dimensional assessment of risk significantly diminishes the existence, and impact, of the potential for those in society to incur significant harm caused by technology in real-world circumstances. As such, those advocating on behalf of permissionless innovation place the technology industry's ability to freely innovate with minimal intervention over the responsibility of government to be able to flexibly develop public policy as expected within a deliberative democracy. Doing so relegates the rights of those in society who could potentially be harmed by negative externalities directly stemming from the proliferation of innovation and the ability of government to be able to respond as needed to potential problems by creating public policy to secondary system concerns placed below the needs of innovators to freely develop technology without restraints. This idea is irresponsible in respect to the important role that government is expected to play within a deliberative democracy, in that the public sector must remain flexible and dynamic during the process of assessing the political landscape to identify, and respond to, newly emerging problems within the system. By removing the idea of actively regulating the field of technology as needed from the purview of government, permissionless innovation reflects a failure of sorts as it relates to the ability of the public sector to maintain participatory processes and achieve deliberatively derived outcomes as expected in the American democracy. By promoting a narrative claiming that the unfettered proliferation of technology will result in minimal risks and maximum benefits to society, advocates of permissionless innovation attempt to advance the idea that it is viable to limit regulatory control by government in the hopes of allowing the innovation industry to reach its full potential. In doing so, permissionless innovation advocates favor a technologically friendly environment, in which innovators are free to develop and apply innovations as they see fit without being subjected to the rigors of deliberation in the political arena that are an essential part of American democracy. The narrow, and arguably unrealistic view, of risk, the utopian assumptions regarding outcomes incurred by society being overwhelmingly positive, and the pursuit of an environment largely free of regulatory control, except in the rare cases that verifiable harm to society has been established in reality, all serve as questionable underlying ideals inherent within the permissionless innovation approach. Promoting such industry-friendly, one-dimensional, and undemocratic ideals serve to further reduce the credibility for permissionless innovation to be the status quo rationale guiding U.S. government decision making associated with regulating technology.

The rationale of permissionless innovation serving to guide technology-based policymaking may yield a political system that lacks the ability to protect deliberative democracy expectations associated with transparent and accountable governance. The usage of permissionless innovation may also fall short of a policy environment that adheres to additional expectations associated with deliberative democracy. This includes the expectations that interested parties have an opportunity to participate in discursive events in a cyclical fashion over time and that involvement in said opportunities are open to system actors that seek to craft narratives in the hopes of affecting changes to the system that represent specific values regarding society. Regarding crafting public policy intended for the purpose of regulating the technology industry, this task is accomplished in part by interested parties shaping persuasive arguments designed to draw support that some type of action, or inaction, is required. Advocating that the processes associated with the development and dissemination of technology should be conducted by innovators without having to seek permission to do so, within a largely regulation-free environment, is incongruent with the expectations that meaningful deliberations will be facilitated that can provide the opportunity for interested parties to impact the U.S.

political system. The pursuit of a protective path supporting the technology industry in all cases except when there is certainty regarding verifiable harm to the public is lacking substance in the context of deliberative democracy, which dictates that government is expected to actively work to remain flexible in being able to respond to the rapidly changing circumstances within society. By largely exempting the technology industry from the public-policy debate, permissionless innovation fails to uphold critical elements related to expectations of deliberative democracy in the United States. Doing so hampers the ability of government to assess if problems will or have developed within the system, which by extension results in a diminished range of topics available for deliberation among interested parties. If the topic of regulating technology is largely removed from the debate platform, then the opportunity for interested parties to cyclically engage in participatory events, with the goal of affecting changes to the political system that will address this industry as expected in a deliberative democracy, is diminished significantly. In relation, the scope of topics to be debated in this deliberative process is expected to be open to any ideals held by system participants who are interested in crafting value-laden arguments with the hopes of advancing a specific viewpoint. Therefore, the attempt by supporters of permissionless innovation to create a de facto immunity within the political arena for the preference to support a technology friendly policy path—except in supposed rare instances in which harm to society is proven to have occurred—runs counter to the key expectation of deliberative democracy associated topical openness.

The Precautionary Principle: Narrative Analysis and a Potential Role in Policymaking for the Technology Industry in the U.S. Deliberative Democracy

The technocratic idealism embedded in permissionless innovation narratives are applied, in part, to argue against the notion that discursive events should consistently be used to help develop means capable of regulating the technology industry. The narratives used in advancing permissionless innovation may generate some measure of persuasive power by tapping into the readily available evidence that society experiences immeasurable advantages that make technology an invaluable resource, which should not be limited in scope by policy endeavors on behalf of government. Interestingly, the permissionless innovation narratives may work to paint technology as both common in its routine occurrences that have permeated essentially all aspects of society and extraordinary in its ability to positively impact all those that become vested in its usage. Routinely experiencing benefits that better one's life that are derived from technology

132 Permissionless Innovation and the Precautionary Principle

is a positively reinforcing process that cognitively contributes to the further entrenchment of the idea that innovations are 'primarily freedom enhancing" (Dotson, 2015, p. 114). In relation, the experiential dynamic can make the task of convincingly framing the need for government intervention more difficult on the basis that regulation may be perceived by many as placing unwanted limits on an individual's freedom to enjoy the benefits of technology without being restricted by a slew of official rules (Dotson, 2015, p. 114). Linguistic attempts to persuade the target audience as to the benefits of the precautionary approach that are perceived to be largely, or completely, critical of technocratic rationales may be met with firm resistance, because such an effort may largely be viewed as a threat to the status quo widely believed to provide a level of comfort and order (Dotson, 2015, p. 112). Those seeking to counter "technocratic governing mentalities," such as technological determinism and permissionless innovation, may find some success by constructing "stable-feeling counternarratives" (Dotson, 2015, p. 115). On a longitudinal basis, individuals being constantly exposed to positive personal experiences associated with technology can contribute, on a societal scale, to establishing a cognitive tendency to view regulatory efforts potentially limiting innovation-based conveniences, known and unknown, as being unappealing, intrusive, and unnecessary. In the modern era, there are countless examples of this personalized benefits dynamic in action throughout a wide range of tasks in broader society, which includes an individual saving time by completing a driver's license renewal by utilizing convenient online services provided by the state's DMV website, instead of standing in lines at the local office, engaging in banking options facilitated at home via computer and using a delivery app to place a dinner order by smart phone. In this regard, it may be increasingly more difficult to stem the tide of technology-based dependency that continues to rapidly permeate the everyday lives of many, resulting in the growing belief that the conveniences derived from such innovations are unquestionably necessary. With a seemingly diminishing cogent heuristic path forward on this account to provide evidence to the contrary, it may be prudent to consider the potential contributions of a narrative method to help promote the important role that the precautionary principle can play in shaping technology-based public policy in the U.S. deliberative system. In short, undermining the unquestioned acceptability of permissionless innovation and technological determinism as the primary rationale(s) used to create a technology-friendly regulatory environment will require the construction of narratives, supportive of the precautionary approach, that are capable of persuading recipients as to the many societal benefits that will come of regulatory efforts in the field of technology. During this process, being cognizant of the tonal focus and supporting evidence used in value-laden arguments is one of many techniques associated with the construction of narratives that can affect the capacity to persuade recipients to subscribe to ideals inherent within the precautionary approach. If the precautionary principle is going to be capable of challenging permissionless innovation, then it may be helpful that such a narrative counter effort avoids being constructed in a fashion that is solely critical of the technology-friendly views holding that the policy environment should be protective of the many wonders that innovations readily provide to U.S. society. A narrative that is only focused on being overly critical of permissionless innovation may understandably illicit a reactionary response on behalf of the target audience that seeks only to defend the rationale that is perceived as being under siege in the linguistic sense. This narrative process to promote the precautionary principle may include providing some measure of acceptance for updated technocratic approaches to serve as of one of many political rationales added to the wide range of value-based arguments used by participants in deliberations regarding government actions to address the field of technology. Additionally, a narrative approach that is also focused on framing the benefits of the precautionary principle, as opposed to solely launching a linguistic offensive, which is functionally tantamount to harshly criticizing those supporting technocratic ideals, may allow for the counter-narrative to be better received by the target audience. In this respect, the precautionary principle's narratives may be more effective in the ability to persuade by also focusing on highlighting the multitude of benefits associated with applying this rationale. This approach may be received better than narratives that solely condemn the more extreme views associated with permissionless innovation, which are rooted in promoting the need to maintain a policy environment that will protect everyone's ability to keep enjoying the benefits of technology without interruption. Relatedly, the narratives supporting the precautionary principle can pragmatically highlight evidence to provide illustrative examples that support the importance of government maintaining the ability to actively regulate the technology industry in the context of the important expectations for participatory opportunities and responsive government in American democracy. If successful, then this narrative approach may increase the precautionary principle's chances of being considered a more legitimate option in the public policy arena for those focused on the importance of actively regulating technology.

In addition, the narrative method can be used to counter the attempts by technocratic advocates to paint the precautionary principle as one that is unnecessarily focused on creating regulations that will deprive the public of limitless and irreplaceable freedoms derived from technology. A narrative comprised of value-laden arguments designed to persuade recipients to subscribe to the merits of the precautionary principle is a potentially promising means by which to diminish any entrenched rhetorical potency of various technocratic approaches, such as permissionless innovation, that favor promoting an environment largely devoid of regulating technology. The narrative effort supporting considerations of precaution as a responsible policy path forward would need to work to linguistically challenge any techno-centric beliefs that government should protect the technology industry, at all costs, by allowing innovators to operate freely within an environment with little-to-no regulation, and that timely deliberations among decision makers regarding government intervention as needed is somehow the enemy of all meaningful societal progress. A precautionary-based narrative will be required to argue against a technocratic status quo in which government automatically protects innovators' freedoms instead of considering official action that may prevent harm to citizens caused by technology, and the widely held nomological faith in the ability of technology to provide unprecedented benefits to society with little-to-risk of harm. In that, providing evidence of harm to society caused by technology, and highlighting the important role that government plays in enacting policy designed to mitigate the effects of this damage, would be paramount during the process of disseminating a narrative supportive of the precautionary principle. Doing so would provide evidence of circumstances in which it was necessary for government to be able to have the discretion to act to protect citizens that may have been caused harm in some way. This includes highlighting government efforts to level the proverbial playing field for members of society, as it relates to enacting policy means designed to overcome externalities derived from the digital divide, such as various iterations of the Federal Communications Act of 1934 and the important role that anti-trust laws play in maintaining a competitive balance within an industry. This effort can be supported by highlighting a slew of government actions designed to protect citizens from incurring digital harm because of nefarious uses of technology, such as those established regarding electronically facilitated identity theft (https://www.usa.gov/identity-theft) and IRS imposter scams (https://www.usa.gov/irs-scams). Ultimately, narrative persuasiveness of the precautionary principle will be better achieved through argumentation that this political rationale is well-suited to achieve expectations associated with meaningful deliberations and government responsiveness that are foundational components of American democracy. In doing so, it will be helpful to highlight the active role that the government has played in enacting flexible policy actions designed to protect citizens from potential harms derived from technology that may have otherwise been overlooked if decision makers pursued technocratically oriented rationales.

It is of great import that narratives promoting the precautionary principle are framed in a manner that highlights that this approach is capable of yielding actions better suited to meet the expectations of a functional modern democracy. In this, the narratives supporting the precautionary principle would be well-served by highlighting that this rationale would reinforce the importance of maintaining a political system in which a wide range of interested parties are provided opportunities to deliberate over defining problems to be addressed by policy, which is an integral foundational element associated with the U.S. democratic system. Promoting the capacity to protect democratic processes by maintaining participatory opportunities, in which system actors may influence government decision making, is an important function of the narratives used to advocate for the use of the precautionary principle to shape the policy environment. Here, a precautionary-focused narrative should promote the fact that adhering to expectations associated with deliberative democracy are, by design, capable of yielding a policy path that promotes societal freedom regarding participation in a way that approaches such as permissionless innovation are wholly ill-equipped to fulfill. In this, the U.S. system is predicated on the belief that it is important that the opportunities to participate in discursive events at multiple points of contact help to legitimize government processes and outcomes. In relation, rationales such as permissionless innovation and technological determinism recommend a technology-friendly policy environment that would circumvent the opportunity for interested parties to participate in discursive events in the hopes of affecting changes to the system.

In all, the ideals inherent within the precautionary principle promote a vision of governance that is more closely aligned with expectations associated with deliberative democracy than competing rationales, such as permissionless innovation and technological determinism. Functionally speaking, the precautionary principle is far better suited to fulfilling the promise of participatory opportunities in which system actors may engage in meaningful deliberations to contribute to determining government outcomes. To help strengthen the precautionary narrative and increase the likelihood that it will be received positively, it will be important to linguistically integrate key democratic values into supporting arguments that are widely appealing to the intended audience in the United States. This includes that the narrative should highlight the ability of the precautionary approach to preserve the integrity of the U.S. deliberative democracy by promoting timely and responsible debate among interested system participants regarding the possible need to craft public-policy responses to issues defined as a problem. The narratives supporting the precautionary principle should argue that this approach is more capable than technocratic

136 Permissionless Innovation and the Precautionary Principle

rationales to adhere to key expectations associated with the U.S. deliberative democracy by ensuring that the policy arena is open to all who are interested in participating, by allowing for all interested parties the opportunity to routinely impact the system through deliberative involvement, and by ensuring that, once agreement among participants is achieved, public-policy changes will reflect the values inherent within the winning arguments. Deliberative democracy also requires that government decision making is the result of a process that is both transparent in actions and accountable to the public, which is more readily attributed to government's usage of the precautionary principle. In that, narratives promoting the precautionary principle are best served by highlighting how this approach is more supportive of the expectation that decision-making processes are open so that all interested parties may be able to hold government accountable for its public policy choices. If permissionless innovation and technological determinism are permitted to protect the innovation industry from regulations without this policy path legitimately being subject to rigorous and routine discourse, then the transparency and accountability aspects expected in a deliberative democracy are bypassed without the required level of dialogue among system participants. Ultimately, the narrative effort to promote the precautionary principle as the rationale to guide government decisioning making should make note of the fact that permissionless innovation and technological determinism reflect democratically oriented deficiencies associated with participatory and responsive government in the context of the U.S. deliberative democracy.

Closing Remarks

The preference to support the application of permissionless innovation or the precautionary principle for use as the foundational rationale guiding policy action to address the field of technology is dependent in part on how one views the role of government in the U.S. democratic system. The competing rationales reflect alternate perspectives regarding the role that government should play in regulating technology, in part because of the differences inherent within each approach regarding interpreting the very nature of deliberative democracy that is such a foundational aspect of U.S. governance. The preference for a limited role for government, in which the policy environment is highly supportive of the technology industry, would coincide with accepting permissionless innovation as the standard by which decision making is based upon. Conversely, the precautionary principle would be favored by those wishing to closely adhere to expectations associated with deliberative democracy, in which the policy environment allows for participation by system actors to help guide responsive government action. In addition, either rationale includes variances associated with the assessment of risk regarding the impact of technology on society if innovation is left largely, or completely, unchecked in the regulatory sense. In this regard, supporters of permissionless innovation favors a technology-friendly policy environment that is focused on protecting the industry, because innovation is largely viewed as having a positive impact on society that renders regulation unnecessary and counterproductive. In this case, the risk of technology negatively impacting society is viewed as minimal, so it is preferable to correspondingly create a policy environment that reflects this perspective. For those supporting permissionless innovation, the risk assessment is overly positive to the point where it is viewed that the appropriate role of government in a policy sense is to intervene in rare cases in which technology has been proven to cause harm to society. On the other hand, advocates of the precautionary principle prefer erring on the side of caution by empowering government to maintain the capacity to be flexible and dynamic enough to take policy action if need be. Here, those advocating for the precautionary principle differentiate on risk assessment by prioritizing a policy environment that includes participatory opportunities associated with deliberative democracy and responsive governance as primary components needed to ensure that government is capable of addressing problems within the field of technology. Those that support the precautionary principle avoid placing full faith in the ability of technology to provide nearly limitless benefits to society if permitted to progress undeterred by the constraints of regulatory intervention, and instead believe that responsible government is required to mitigate potential and existing threats in an appropriately responsive fashion as expected in a deliberative democracy.

Both permissionless innovation and the precautionary principle are advanced by its advocates crafting narratives that reflect value-laden arguments, who use these linguistic devices in an attempt to persuade a wider audience as to the benefits associated with subscribing to one ideal over the other in the context of U.S. policymaking endeavors focused on the field of technology. The advocates of permissionless innovation and the precautionary principle construct competing narratives that contend for the entrenchment of vastly differently value systems to guide the U.S. policy environment that will affect the ability of government to regulate the field of technology. Permissionless innovation is an approach that favors government maintaining a policy environment that is highly protective of the ability of the innovators to freely develop the field of technology sans regulatory constraints, unless in rare instances in which innovation-based harm to society has been proven to occur. The preference for adopting permissionless innovation is partly based on the firm belief that technology

138 Permissionless Innovation and the Precautionary Principle

plays such an all-encompassing and important role in society that official efforts to protect innovation should be of primary importance to government. Except in rare instances in which technology has been proven to cause societal harm, those advocating for permissionless innovation prefer a minimal policy role for government in which the public sector's primary responsibility is to focus on maintaining a regulatory environment that encourages the development and proliferation of technology. By assuming that the risk of technology to routinely cause great harm to society is negligible and uncommon, permissionless innovation calls for a limited and reactionary role of government as it relates to crafting policy to address this field. Furthermore, those favoring permissionless innovation utilize narratives that argue persons that seek to regulate the technology industry are irredeemably out-of-touch technophobes who are unable or incapable of appreciating the countless wonders that innovations provide to society, which will most assuredly vanish into the ether under the heavy burden of government regulation. The advocates of permissionless innovation posit that those in government only serve to stand in the way of progress by insisting on routinely and actively regulating the technology industry. In the eyes of those supporting permissionless innovation, those that insist on government making significant efforts to regulate the technology industry would be actively depriving members of society, from the private sector and public sector alike, the opportunity to benefit from innovations that would have otherwise regularly emerged in a less restrictive policy environment. Here, advocates of the permissionless innovation rationale frames technology as playing a pivotal role in society's growth and claims that those that seek to nurture its evolution are avant-garde protectors of the public good whose actions serve the best interest of society. Those subscribing to permissionless innovation firmly believe that this approach is well-suited to safeguard society from the unnecessary efforts by those supporting an interventionist government who are intent on pursuing official means that will undoubtedly reduce the overall quality of life of societal members by routinely enacting regulations of innovation. Ultimately, permissionless innovation is a rationale that supports the public sector actively pursuing means that are protective of technology over the use of the democratic processes that are expected to guide government action in a deliberative system such as the United States.

The institutionalization of any technocratically oriented approach supportive of essentially granting innovators the opportunity to develop technology as they please in a largely, if not completely, regulation-free environment is fundamentally undemocratic because it fails to consider the entire scope of society that may be affected by the widescale usage of innovations. Permissionless innovation applied in this context would prohibit a full range of interested parties from actively participating in deliberations during the public-policy process to determine if an innovation-related problem exists, or is likely to soon exist, that would ultimately require government regulation to protect those in society from potentially being harmed. Permissionless innovation as a rationale is largely unsuccessful in creating a policy environment that upholds many of the expectations for a deliberative democracy because this approach supports protecting the technology industry over the importance of maintaining a participatory and responsive system in which government is able to flexibly adjust to address rapidly emerging problems in any field. An automatic allegiance to a technocratically oriented rationale such as permissionless innovation would create a policy environment lacking in opportunity for those representing opposing views to challenge this perspective in the political arena. A policy path based on permissionless innovation would render government's role in protecting freedoms for all members in society as secondary to the more elitist goals of safeguarding the liberties of those that enjoy the benefits derived from technology and those that create, and most often profit from, innovations disseminated throughout society. As was the case in the last chapter, in which technological determinism was argued disqualified for primary usage as the rationale to guide governmental decision making regarding the field of technology, the modern incarnation of this approach, permissionless innovation, would also lack applicability in this sense in the modern U.S. political system.

In theory, given an either-or proposition regarding the applicability of a political rationale, the precautionary principle is better suited to ensure the institutionalization of deliberative democracy expectations, including those associated with participatory opportunities to engage in meaningful deliberations and the corresponding effects associated with responsive government action. In reality, it is possible to create a regulatory environment that is simultaneously static in the effort to provide some measure of protection to the technology industry while also reflecting the necessary levels of flexibility as expected of government in American democracy. This may manifest by employing the precautionary principle judiciously, which would allow for a more nuanced application of permission to create a regulatory environment that allows for some measure of freedom for technology to develop while also retaining the capacity of government to enact policy measures as deemed necessary by system actors participating in deliberative events. In the context of U.S. deliberative democracy, a judiciously flexible approach to the precautionary principle is arguably better suited to ensure the government's ability to fulfil expected democratic responsibilities by maintaining a policy environment that can regulate technology as needed. In this sense, the precautionary principle can allow government to work to preserve the interests of the public in a timely manner through enacting policy measures responsively, and as deemed necessary, after responsible debate among interested parties has been facilitated. It is of the utmost importance to the integrity of the U.S. democracy that the participatory environment is actively maintained so that meaningful deliberations may occur in which end results of discourse between interested parties will result in verifiable system changes. In relation, the precautionary principle can serve as an important rationale in guiding public policy development in the field of technology, which is better suited to creating a political environment that is able to uphold deliberative democracy expectations. Instead of having the default setting of decision makers favor the needs of innovators over the general public, which may be harmed by regulatory indifference or outright inaction, the application of the precautionary principle to guide decision makers within a deliberative democracy will allow for a policy environment that better ensures official actions to address the technology industry are taken if necessary. In this sense, decision makers may be better equipped to fulfill deliberative democracy expectations, in the participatory and responsiveness sense, if the precautionary principle is chosen over technocratic options to guide government during policymaking processes. Such possibilities should be considered when progressing through the later chapters, which are focused on U.S. government responsibilities and corresponding official reactions associated with the emergent cryptocurrency industry and its most popular manifestation: Bitcoin.

References

Dotson, T. (2015). Technological Determinism and Permissionless Innovation as Technocratic Governing Mentalities: Psychocultural Barriers to the Democratization of Technology. *Engaging Science, Technology, and Society*, 1, 98–120.

Koopman, C. (2018). Creating an Environment for Permissionless Innovation. U.S. Congress Joint Economic Committee. Hearing: Breaking through the Regulatory Barrier: What Red Tape Means for the Innovation Economy. May 22.

Thierer, A. (2016a). *Permissionless Innovation: The Continuing Case for Comprehensive Technological Freedom, Revised and Expanded Edition*. Mercatus Center at George Mason University. https://www.mercatus.org/system/files/Permissionless.Innovation.web_.pdf

Thierer, A. (2016b). Innovation Arbitrage, Technological Civil Disobedience & Spontaneous Deregulation. *Medium* (December 7). https://medium.com/techliberation/innovation-arbitrage-technological-civil-disobedience-spontaneous-deregulation-eb90da50f1e2

5

THE CONCEPT OF MONEY

To begin the conversation about money, it is important to first establish definitional parameters regarding the broad qualities attributed to describing this concept, many of which have a rich historical background. The process of defining money is of important in part because "conceptions of money influence social and public policy" (Mellor, 2019, p. 2). Therefore, defining money will help to establish a foundation by which to later analyze whether traditional qualities associated with such are applicable in describing the emergent field of non-fiat virtual currency such as those associated with cryptocurrency and correspondingly in determining the appropriate role that government is to play in efforts to regulate this newly developing field of public policy. To start, it is prudent to provide a brief introductory definition of money, which is encapsulated as followed:

> Something generally accepted as a medium of exchange, a measure of value, or a means of payment: such as a: officially coined or stamped metal currency newly minted *money* b: money of account c: paper money.
>
> *Source: Merriam-Webster Dictionary (2022)*

Here, money is capable of taking tangible form, be it coin or paper, can be accepted by system actors as a means by which to transact in market exchanges, and may serve as a unit of account that allows for items of comparable value to be exchanged for it in the market. Relatedly, the following

DOI: 10.4324/9781003441830-5

142 The Concept of Money

basic characteristics contribute to establishing a definitional foundation for understanding money:

> Money should be generally accepted as a medium of exchange.
> Money should be a unit of account so that we can compare the costs of goods and services over time and between merchants.
> Money should be a store of value that stays stable over time.
>
> *Source: Peters et al. (2016, p. 244)*

Dobeck and Elliott (2007, p. 1) similarly explains that money is used "to buy and sell things" and therefore fulfills "three important purposes within the economy: (1) it acts as a medium of exchange, (2) it is a standard unit of account, and (3) it has the ability to store value." There are additional attributes of money that include qualities such as: divisibility (able to be broken down into smaller denominations), portability (able to be transported easily, which in the modern era includes convenience in the physical and digital sense), durability (coins and paper money last for an extended period of time; should coins or paper money be damaged they are replaceable), stability (dependably consistent value in the relative sense on a longitudinal basis), and difficulty of duplication or counterfeiting (extraordinarily difficult to reproduce as a requisite of production in order to preserve value of and trust in the money in use) (Dobeck and Elliott, 2007, pp. 2–3). Money is defined in part as being an identifiable unit of currency (i.e. paper money, coins, commodities like fur or sugar, etc.) that is (or was) widely accepted by system participants as a medium of exchange enabling whatever item(s) being used in this commerce dynamic to be considered to be viable means by which to base a wide array of economically oriented transactions upon. The idea of money requires that there is a clearly established and universally accepted fiscal worth that allows for system actors to determine the corresponding value of goods and services being transacted for in conventional economic exchanges. In this sense, money serves as a transactionally based fiscal device that is used comparatively to establish the value of goods and services being transacted for in the market. Here, money is a tool providing comparative means by which system actors are able to gauge the value of items within the market creating some measure of transactional stability. Although there may be some measure of variability of worth over time, the value of the unit of currency used as money is intended to be relatively stable, which allows it to remain viable for extended use when purchasing goods and services on the market. This last aspect of money speaks to the relative degree of stability of the worth of the unit of currency over an extended period, which allows for the development of confidence by all parties to be able to trust in the usage of such to facilitate a wide range of transactions within the economy.

The Concept of Money **143**

Having established some basic characteristics that are used to define money, it will be helpful to expand the discussion to focus on understanding the processes by which money comes to be broadly accepted by system actors. The early origins associated with the establishment and usage of money avoided entirely being that of an act of the state and instead is oft recognized as being a socially contrived conceptualization. The following observations are focused on the origins of money as it relates to the possibility of being initially derived from a social process of collective acceptance:

> …money has not been generated by law. In its origin it is a social, and not a state institution. Sanction by the authority of the state is a notion alien to it. On the other hand, however, by state recognition and state regulation, this social institution of money has been perfected and adjusted to the manifold and varying needs of an evolving commerce, just as customary rights have been perfected and adjusted by statute law.
>
> *Source: Menger (1882, p. 51)*

Here, the establishment, acceptance, and usage of something to be used as money is initially derived from a process that is social in nature, in which collective approval on behalf of system actors is required. In this sense, money may initially be created as a function of necessity within a societal setting and its continued usage can be augmented by government efforts that may further legitimize its role in that community. Ultimately, the force of law may be wielded by government to either promote or suppress socially accepted items that have been granted community approval to serve as money. However, the trust and confidence generated, and held, on behalf of system actors serves as key foundational elements associated with establishing emergent money as viable for use within a given society. Without a societal buy-in from a trust standpoint, money—regardless of its origin point—would fail to achieve the requisite levels of acceptance on behalf of system actors that would allow such to steadily proliferate various aspects of an economy, including those involving conventional transactions.

In the historical sense, there have been a wide assortment of socially accepted items serving as money that have collectively been deemed to have value, which grants such articles permission for use in transactions. Galbraith and Galbraith (2017, p. 6) notes that money should be viewed simply in that whichever form it may take it is "commonly offered or received for the purchase or sale of goods, services or other things." In this sense, early money often lacked uniformity of form allowing for societal acceptance of an item to serve as the primary means by which it would qualify as currency. Historically, money has taken various forms, including

144 The Concept of Money

denomination-based tangible currency that—except for examples in which coinage was made of precious metal (i.e. gold, silver, etc.)—more often than not reflect "no intrinsic value" while still having the capacity to reflect "immense social value" (Mellor, 2019, p. 4). In whatever form it may manifest, it is the idea of money's value being prescribed and accepted by system actors that contributes greatly to determining whether a unit of currency is able to thrive or perish within a given economy. Money is attributed a mutually accepted value, which serves as a trusted replacement for the otherwise lengthy and complicated requisite bartering processes that would be used to transact in the economy that was without an accepted medium of exchange (Dobeck and Elliott, 2007, p. 1). Relatedly, Dobeck and Elliott (2007, p. 1) observe that "money has value because a society collectively agrees or trusts that it does." The trust in something used as money that is held by system actors lacks randomness in that this faith is not spontaneously achieved in a vacuum without input from those in society that are directly involved with determining its viability. Essentially, money is something of a "social phenomenon" whose widespread acceptance in society requires a "monetary community" to trust in the ability of something being used as currency to behave as expected (Mellor, 2019, pp. 6–7). The trust is derived in part by establishing a "perceived value and dependability" in which the worth of monetary denominations can be exchanged for "goods and service" (Mellor, 2019, p. 7). Trust in money is also partly generated by its transferability in that system actors universally "accept it as payment" with the understanding that it may later be conveyed to others for a variety of purposes including "settlement of a debt, a gift or in making a purchase" (Mellor, 2019, p. 7). Trust derived from transferability also requires that the value during the transfer of money, whether it be tangible or digital format, is generally unaffected during the exchange (Mellor, 2019, p. 7). Money is an ideal that is socially constructed and that, once agreed upon in principle, is then capable of manifesting as a medium of exchange to be used in the economy. Here, money must be trusted and valued by the community by which its usage will be facilitated to fulfill a wide assortment of transactional endeavors within the economy. Trust in money is at least partly rooted in the perception by system actors that the currency in question is relatively stable in value and is broadly accepted as a means by which to facilitate transactions. In relation, the transferability of money on a comprehensive scale contributes greatly to its ability to be perceived as a trusted medium of exchange. Ultimately, the acceptance of a medium of exchange from a societal point of view is derived from whether system actors perceive the value of something being used as money as being able to be utilized to facilitate market transactions in a dependable and reliable manner. Although the origin of money is often considered to be

The Concept of Money **145**

derived from an amalgamation of longitudinal social processes reinforcing its acceptance, the state undoubtedly can play a key role in enhancing the capacity of currency to become trusted as a medium of exchange. In the modern era, government's consistent presence and expansive involvement (i.e. coining, regulating, etc.) continues to play a key role in the continued evolution of the socially constructed concept of money. Government intervention manifesting through the creation of guidelines and regulations, by which an industry is expected to operate, is a common aspect associated with, and expected of, the state. This ideal is equally applicable to the concept of money even though its origins were largely considered to be the end-result of system actors socially constructing the accepted means by which a variety of economic events are facilitated.

There is a social dynamic that contributes to determining whether money will ultimately be able to reach the requisite levels of trust to allow for such to be utilized as a medium of exchange. As such, the social processes occurring outside state influence by which system actors contribute collectively to determining if money reaches a point of broad acceptance as a medium of exchange is deserved of further attention. In 1912, Mises wrote *The Theory of Money and Credit*, which provides a broad, in-depth discussion regarding how money comes to be valued societally and how this process ultimately affects the usage of a given unit of currency in question to effectively act as a medium of exchange. The process of valuing something to the point where the unit in question can reach the status of money used to facilitate exchanges in the market is a progression that has an inherent historical element, and can aptly be encapsulated by the following observations on behalf of Mises regarding what is termed as the Regression Theorem:

Demonstration of the fact that search for the determinants of the objective exchange value of money always leads us back to a point where the value of money is not determined in any way by its use as a medium of exchange, but solely by its other functions, prepares the way for developing a complete theory of the value of money on the basis of the subjective theory of value and its peculiar doctrine of marginal utility.

Source: Mises (1912, p. 62)

The theory of the value of money as such can trace back the objective exchange value of money only to that point where it ceases to be the value of money and becomes merely the value of a commodity.

If in this way we continually go farther and farther back we must eventually arrive at a point where we no longer find any component in the

146 The Concept of Money

objective exchange value of money that arises from valuations based on the function of money as a common medium of exchange; where the value of money is nothing other than the value of an object that is useful in some other way than as money. But this point is not merely an instrumental concept of theory; it is an actual phenomenon of economic history, making its appearance at the moment when indirect exchange begins.

Before it was usual to acquire goods in the market, not for personal consumption, but simply in order to exchange them again for the goods that were really wanted, each individual commodity was only accredited with that value given by the subjective valuations based on its direct utility.

Source: Mises (1912, p. 66)

Mises (1949) further discussed that the value of items that come to serve as money is determined in part by understanding the progression of the attached mutually perceived worth that develops over time, which correspondingly affects the demand placed upon its continued, and potentially increased, usage as a medium of exchange. The conceptualization of this process is rooted in understanding how a given item is capable of becoming valued as a medium of exchange, which Mises discussed as follows:

As soon as an economic good is demanded not only by those who want to use it for consumption or production, but also by people who want to keep it as a medium of exchange and to give it away at need in a later act of exchange, the demand for it increases. A new employment for this good has emerged and creates an additional demand for it. As with every other economic good, such an additional demand brings about a rise in its value in exchange, i.e., in the quantity of other goods which are offered for its acquisition.

Thus the demand for a medium of exchange is the composite of two partial demands: the demand displayed by the intention to use it in consumption and production and that displayed by the intention to use it as a medium of exchange. With regard to modern metallic money one speaks of the industrial demand and of the monetary demand. The value in exchange (purchasing power) of a medium of exchange is the resultant of the cumulative effect of both partial demands.

Source: Mises (1949, p. 405)

In this dynamic process, the exchange value of something is determined in part by tracing the unit of currency in question to a time in which its subjective worth was derived from the direct utility that was shared by system participants. For example, a commodity (i.e., sugar, salt, etc.) was viewed as being permissible as a medium of exchange, because the value of the unit was translatable to real-world usage that is relatable in terms of consumption or production itself. The utility factor associated with such a commodity plays a key role in determining whether the unit in question can reach broad acceptance as a medium of exchange to be used by system actors as money during various transactional circumstances. In relation, the acceptance of an economic good as a medium of exchange may increase the perception of its overall value in relation to other goods/services that are obtained in the trade. In this sense, acceptability of a medium of exchange is directly correlated with demand that system actors place on its usage in transacting for goods and services because it is deemed mutually valuable.

The Landscape of Modern-Era Currency: From Official U.S. Legal Tender to Non-Fiat Virtual Currency

In the contemporary era, the government plays a more significant role in determining whether money is trusted and accepted on behalf of those in society who are expected to actively engage in its usage. In the modern U.S. system, understanding money relates to defining what constitutes fiat currency, which serves as the standard in practice by which official legal tender is predicated upon. Here, the conceptualization of money expands to include government taking an active role in creating a stable legal tender that is accepted on behalf of the populous as the means by which goods/services will be valued and that is collectively acknowledged as the medium of exchange in transacting for such. Lee, Johnson, and Joyce (2021, p. 76) explain that, in the traditional sense, "money is cash-paper money and coinage" in which the quantity of such "is strictly controlled by the government." In the modern era, government issuance of official fiat currency within a given nation can be represented tangibly or digitally. Virga (2015, p. 514) notes that "fiat currencies, also known as 'real money' or 'national currencies,' are the coin and paper money that a nation assigns as its legal tender. E-money is a digital representation of fiat money used to electronically transfer money that has a legal tender status." Lansky (2018, p. 19) adds to this definition by noting that "electronic money is a digital equivalent of cash." Here, the idea of digital money or electronic money is that of virtual representations of fiat currency, which is the official legal tender created, regulated, and backed by the government. Ultimately, it is constitutionally faithful and functionally acceptable for fiat money to manifest tangibly and digitally in the modern era. In the United States, the creation, regulation, and backing of fiat currency in tangible form or digital form is the sole responsibility of the Congress. In that, the U.S. government exercises its constitutional power to fulfill duties such as coining,

148 The Concept of Money

valuing, taxing, and preventing the counterfeiting of fiat money. Together, the tangible manifestations of fiat money (i.e. bills, coins) and the digital representations of fiat money comprise what constitutes a legal tender landscape, which is thusly able be utilized for a wide range of purposes in the public and private sector.

In the modern U.S. system, tangible or digital fiat money is utilized to facilitate numerous economic activities such as transacting for goods/services, banking, and investing, in which either manifestation is able to serve as an acceptable fiscal means of engagement. However, technological advancements in the modern era have raised some concerns regarding the emergence of alternate forms of currency that are seemingly attempting to masquerade as fiat currency. Today, the usage of digital technologies has been impactful in affecting the scope and nature of currencies that may potentially create constitutional and functional concerns to be addressed by government. This includes that, due to modern-era innovations, there now exists the continuously expanding concept of digital currencies. The U.S. Department of the Treasury (2021) notes that "digital currency includes sovereign cryptocurrency, virtual currency (non-fiat), and a digital representation of fiat currency." As the U.S. presently has yet to officially adopt a sanctioned sovereign cryptocurrency, considerations regarding digital currency are dedicated to broadening the understanding of this technology in the context of digital fiat currency and virtual currency that is designated as being non-fiat. As mentioned previously, electronic money or digital money would fall under the definitional purview of digital currency that represents fiat money. For example, banking wire transfers are digital currency, in which the existence of these manifestations is intangible in transit but is clearly representative of fiat currency that can be treated accordingly once a transaction between parties has been completed. Conversely, the variation of digital currency referred to as non-fiat virtual currency, facilitated electronically, would not generally be representative of official legal tender and would include types of cryptocurrencies such as Bitcoin.

Of the three-fold conceptualizations of digital currency, virtual currency that fails to represent fiat money, created in accordance with the powers granted to Congress via the U.S. Constitution, is a burgeoning industry that has caused a great deal of skepticism and confusion from among a wide scope of system actors. Broadly speaking, the manifestation of non-fiat virtual currency adds a new fiscal dynamic that is unique to the modern era, requiring an attentive analysis regarding what constitutes this emergent technological endeavor. To this end, providing further definitional parameters as stated by U.S. federal bureaucratic entities regarding virtual currency will help to begin to establish a broader understanding of this innovative design in practice, which has more recently come into greater prevalence in contemporary society. The U.S. Department of the Treasury (2021) states that "virtual currency is a digital representation of value that functions as (i) a medium of exchange; (ii) a unit of account; and/or (iii) a store of value; and is neither issued nor guaranteed by any jurisdiction." The U.S. Internal Revenue Service (2021) similarly defines virtual currency as "a digital representation of value that functions as a medium of exchange, a unit of account, and/or a store of value. In some environments, it operates like "real" currency (i.e., the coin and paper money of the United States or of any other country that is designated as legal tender, circulates, and is customarily used and accepted as a medium of exchange in the country of issuance), but it does not have legal tender status in the U.S." The U.S. Financial Crimes Enforcement Network (2013, p.1), or FinCEN, which is a bureau within the above-mentioned U.S. Treasury Department, explains that "in contrast to real currency, 'virtual' currency is a medium of exchange that operates like a currency in some environments, but does not have all the attributes of real currency." FinCEN (2013, p. 1) continues by observing that "in particular, virtual currency does not have legal tender status in any jurisdiction." The U.S. Commodity Futures Trading Commission (2021, p. 1) defines virtual currency as "a digital representation of value that functions as a medium of exchange, a unit of account, and/or a store of value." The Commodity Futures Trading Commission (2021, p. 1) adds that "in some cases, you can spend it like money, but it does not have legal tender status in the United States." Here, virtual currency is non-fiat in nature and, even though there may be instances in which its usage in the market may be similar to fiat money, it is not granted legal tender status by the U.S. government. Despite not achieving fiat money status, non-fiat virtual currency is still used in some cases in the modern economic system as the fiscal basis by which system actors facilitate a wide array of market activities. Instances of such potentially represent a novel threat to the constitutional powers granted to Congress that traditionally empower this governmental body to have exclusive domain in determining the processes associated with coining, taxing, valuing, and regulating money.

On the topic of potentially challenging constitutionally generated fiat money as an accepted medium of exchange to be used in the economy, non-fiat virtual currency raises another concern as it relates to the concept of convertibility. The Commodity Futures Trading Commission (2021, p. 1) explains that "some virtual currencies have an equivalent value in other currencies, such as U.S. dollars or Euros, or can be traded for other virtual currencies. These are referred to as convertible virtual currencies." FinCEN (2013, p. 1) notes that convertible virtual currency "either has an equivalent value in real currency, or acts as a substitute for real currency." The Internal Revenue Service (2021) similarly states that "virtual currency

150 The Concept of Money

that has an equivalent value in real currency, or that acts as a substitute for real currency, is referred to as 'convertible' virtual currency." The Internal Revenue Service (2021) expands on this concept by noting that "Bitcoin is one example of a convertible virtual currency. Bitcoin can be digitally traded between users and can be purchased for, or exchanged into, U.S. dollars, Euros, and other real or virtual currencies." Peters et al. (2016, p. 244) explain that the fiscal relevancy of "virtual currency is rapidly growing. It can be redeemed in fiat money but is not necessarily backed by such currency as a representative currency would typically be." Virga (2015, p. 514) adds that "virtual currencies are a digital representation of value that can be exchanged through the Internet for goods and services. However, virtual currencies have no physical counterpart with legal status and are largely unregulated." Here, virtual currency may mimic the behavior of money regarding value and convertibility but generally does so without government officially being involved in the corresponding support processes. Understandably, convertible virtual currency being used in the market causes legitimate constitutional concerns (i.e. only Congress is empowered to coin money) and potential regulatory dilemmas (i.e. what if any existing laws are applicable to this industry; how should new policy efforts be designed to address this, etc.) as only government-sanctioned fiat currency, tangible or digital, is expected to play a significant role in transactions among system actors. The fact that non-fiat virtual currency may be convertible to fiat currency in some instances creates several legitimate questions regarding understanding its role in society and in determining how government will eventually go about developing policy designed to regulate its usage.

Interestingly, there seems to be some similarities between the previously mentioned definitional parameters of money and non-fiat virtual currency, which is likely to cause further confusion regarding establishing the participatory guidelines and regulatory efforts that will ultimately be required to be developed by the U.S. government. For example, money should be broadly accepted as a trusted means by which to facilitate a market transaction, be used as a unit of measurement by which to gauge the value of items being transacted for and be able to maintain a relatively stable value longitudinally to engender confidence in its application during exchanges. Relatedly, non-fiat virtual currency surprisingly seems to have a gradually improving case to begin to qualify to meet at least two of the three criteria used to define money in the most basic sense. Today, those interested in pursuing such options are slowly being provided an increased opportunity to utilize non-fiat virtual currency to facilitate transactions to purchase goods, to qualify as payment for services rendered, and to even use for a wide array of investment purposes. However, longitudinally the value of non-fiat virtual currencies in use has been somewhat volatile thus far, so that the necessary levels of stability traditionally associated with U.S. fiat currency is lacking. The fluctuation in the value of virtual currencies will be discussed at greater length and in more detail in later chapters. For now, it will be sufficient to simply raise awareness that this dynamic in practice would serve as reason to argue against non-fiat virtual currency from becoming used too widely by system actors, because at present there are insufficient means in place to ensure the value will be relatively stable over time.

Importantly, the type of digital currency whose status would be classified as non-fiat virtual currency constitutionally places this innovative design in direct contradiction to the powers associated with money granted to Congress. Despite being congruent with some of the previously mentioned definitional parameters of money, at present non-fiat virtual currency is unequivocally categorized as a form of digital currency that is not representative of official legal tender issued by Congress, which is the only entity within the federal government that is exclusively empowered to coin fiat money via the U.S. Constitution. Among the key areas of concern is the fact that, although there may be examples in practice regarding its convertibility to U.S. legal tender, non-fiat virtual currency is conceptually problematic in the context of constitutional powers to coin money that are granted exclusively to Congress. In relation, there are some circumstances in which non-fiat virtual currency has been used in place of fiat money to facilitate various types of activities within the economy, such as the purchase of goods and services. In this context, non-fiat virtual currency would serve as a clear violation of the exclusive right to coin and place value on money in circulation that is afforded to Congress by way of the U.S. Constitution. The convertibility and replaceability factors of non-fiat virtual currency potentially supplanting, to some degree, the usage of official U.S. legal tender runs counter to the powers granted to Congress, creating a constitutional crisis because fiat currency is intended to serve as the form of money used by all members of society. In relation, non-fiat virtual currency also creates issues associated with determining the appropriate role of government in regulating the industry, which will be discussed at greater length in the subsequent chapters.

Pros and Cons: Non-Fiat Virtual Currency

There are arguably a wide assortment of pros and cons associated with the usage of virtual currencies (non-fiat) that deserve some exploration. Although the concepts will be expanded on in greater detail in the coming chapters, for the purposes of this discussion simply consider cryptocurrency

152 The Concept of Money

(and its most popular incarnation Bitcoin) to be a form of non-fiat virtual currency. Virga (2015, p. 515) notes that there are a wide range of positives associated with the usage of virtual currency, including potentially creating a "common medium of exchange" to be used broadly within the international community, that can reduce (or in some cases eliminate) fees typically associated with the process of exchanging fiat currency. Virga (2015, p. 515) further explains that another possible positive associated with virtual currencies is the ability to reduce "transaction costs" that are typically charged when using a credit/debit card to purchase items. Virga (2015, p. 515) adds that virtual currency may provide a means by which the "unbanked" and "underbanked" are able to have a greater capacity by which to participate financially that was not previously available. When compared to official legal tender, there are potentially a number of additional benefits associated with using types of non-fiat virtual currency, such as cryptocurrency, including facilitating micropayments (i.e. providing the ability to represent value in decimal points considerably less than that of fiat currency), allowing for greater ease of use in international purchases as it relates to enhanced transaction time when compared to fiat currency, providing a means for a more stable payment option in nations that may suffer from highly variable inflation rates of fiat money from that jurisdiction, and preserving transaction information through the use of blockchain technology (Lansky, 2018, pp. 26–27). Despite many potential benefits associated with the usage of non-fiat virtual currency, there are understandably concerns that should also be acknowledged. Although there may be a number of significant concerns associated with non-fiat virtual currencies, the opportunity for use in circumstances of a criminal nature are of great import to consider. Virga (2015, p. 512) notes that, "while virtual currencies have many benefits, they also create many opportunities for crimes such as money laundering. Virtual currencies are not controlled by any state entity, they allow users to transfer goods anonymously, and they cross borders effortlessly via the Internet." Virga (2015, p. 512) adds that "all these characteristics make it difficult for individual states to regulate virtual currencies in isolation." Virga (2015, p. 515) explains that criminals may find appealing the combination of "anonymity," "global reach," and an "absence of a central oversight body" associated with virtual currency, because those factors may afford those interested in doing so with the opportunity to circumvent detection and regulatory efforts present with a nation's boundaries. Among the many benefits of non-fiat virtual currency is the opportunity provided, to those residing in nations with an unstable financial system, to now have at their digital disposal a less volatile fiscal means by which to transact with relative confidence in the domestic and international marketplace. In comparison to traditional financial institutions (i.e. credit-card companies, banks, wire-transfer business, etc.), the usage of virtual currency provides a less fiscally burdensome means because there are lower transaction fees during purchases and there are allowances for microtransactions. Ultimately, those that may be underserved by traditional financial institutions would be provided an opportunity to become more engaged in the economic system that would otherwise be unavailable to them. In this sense, non-fiat virtual currencies may provide some measure of equity by providing participatory options in the fiscal sense to those previously underserved by traditional financial institutions to become further engaged in the economy. This may create an opportunity to those generally underserved in the traditional sense to become more empowered economically by leveraging non-fiat virtual currency to allow for some measure of engagement in the market. When compared to fiat currency, non-fiat virtual currency benefits—such as lower transactions fees, expansive participatory dynamics that transcend temporal and geographical limits, minimalization of negative impacts associated with traditional exchange rates, and the usage of micropayments—may provide an increased opportunity for a wider array of individuals to more legitimately participate in the broader economy. However, it is still important to note that despite all these potential benefits, at present non-fiat virtual currency, such as cryptocurrency, may still be dependent to some degree on traditional financial institutions such as banks and credit-card companies. In that, in order to create a crypto account and engage in purchasing/exchanging cryptocurrency, the individual consumer is generally required to attach a bank account or credit card that initially serves to fund this process. Once a crypto account is created and fiat funds are utilized to purchase a cryptocurrency, then the user is able to enjoy the aforementioned benefits associated with transacting in this type of non-fiat virtual currency. In addition, there are other potential items of note that can be attributed to non-fiat virtual currency that should be recognized. Among the most important of concerns is the potential difficulties associated with government creating regulatory guidance of decentralized non-fiat virtual currency, in which an absence of official oversight may make this industry more appealing to those seeking to utilize this type of innovation to engage in criminal activities. In relation, the relative anonymity, and the capacity for a global scope of usage associated with non-fiat virtual currency transactions, may increase its appeal to those seeking to utilize such for criminal purposes. Although this brief introduction helps to move the discussion forward, in the next chapter the pros and cons associated with non-fiat virtual currency will be expanded on in greater detail. In relation, doing so will provide an opportunity to later expand the discussion to include potential role(s) that government is expected to play in maintaining a policy environment in which decision makers will go about regulating non-fiat virtual currency.

The U.S. Constitution and Congress: The Power to Shape the Dynamic Field of Money

The previous sections delved into broadly defining money, expanded on types of money that may be fiat or non-fiat, and introduced some pros/cons associated with non-fiat virtual currency. Now, a brief primer will be provided of relevant constitutional powers mandated to Congress that helps to dictate the role that the legislative branch and correspondingly empowered federal bureaucratic entities may play in potentially regulating examples of non-fiat virtual currency in the future. Doing so will help to provide a conceptual foundation by which to later discuss the policy path available to the U.S. government that is intended to address manifestations of non-fiat virtual currency such as the growing field of cryptocurrency. The selection of two constitutional components is intentionally inexhaustive in scope to avoid providing an excess of statutory analysis, which falls outside the general focus of this discussion. Therefore, two key constitutional components were selected to provide a foundational analysis as it relates to validating government actions to address modern-era technologically innovative events, in which doing so represents an effort to protect and promote traditional conceptualization associated with American democracy. Specifically, this includes the following constitutional elements that grant Congress powers related to policymaking associated with addressing non-fiat virtual currency such as cryptocurrency: (1) the Necessary and Proper Clause and, (2) the powers granted to Congress associated with money, especially exclusive rights to coining such.

To those that wish to further familiarize themselves with the U.S. Constitution, a copy of the entire document can be viewed online (https://constitution.congress.gov/constitution/). In addition to including the original Bill of Rights, which was a landmark first step in the extensive process of creating essential civil liberties for U.S. citizens, the U.S. Constitution includes articles that created and correspondingly enumerated powers to the three branches of government as followed: Article I (legislative branch), Article II (the executive branch), and Article III (the judicial branch). Broadly speaking, there are a number of sections inherent within Article I of the U.S. Constitution that enumerates a wide range of powers that are granted to Congress. This includes the U.S. Constitution granting this branch of the federal government the power to craft legislation (Article I, section 1), establishing a bi-cameral legislature that includes the House of Representatives and Senate (Article I, section 2 and Article I, section 3, respectively) and indicating that all budgetary bills will originate in the House with advice granted from the Senate (Article I, section 7). This also includes the powers granted to Congress that are directly related to the

The Concept of Money **155**

ability to remain flexible in drafting legislation as indicated in Article I, section 8 that states the following:

> To make all Laws which shall be necessary and proper for carrying into Execution the foregoing Powers, and all other Powers vested by this Constitution in the Government of the United States, or in any Department or Officer thereof.
>
> *Source: U.S. Constitution (1788, Article 1, section 8, clause 18)*

The Necessary and Proper Clause (aka the Elastic Clause) is an essential element of the U.S. Constitution that provides Congress with the power to enact legislation capable of addressing issues of import that become prevalent at any given point in time. The Framers of the U.S. Constitution understood that it was impossible to foresee all possible future issues that would materialize in what has now become centuries after the original drafted document became the law of the land, but they still provided those serving in contemporary government with the means by which to use mandated authority to develop policy measures to address newly emerging societal problems as needed. When originally writing the document, for example, the Framers of the U.S. Constitution could not have foreseen the many technology-based modern issues that would come to develop over time, such as those stemming from air pollution caused in part by modern advancements associated with widescale industrial manufacturing and exhaust from automobiles. The Necessary and Proper Clause of the U.S. Constitution is the statutory means by which Congress is empowered to actively identify issues of societal import and to create legislation intended to address identified problems in a given field of public policy, including those associated with newly emergent non-fiat virtual currency such as cryptocurrency.

Among the many powers enumerated via Article I, section 8 of the U.S. Constitution is that of the ability of Congress to craft responsive legislation to identified problems as a function of flexible and dynamic government action. There is a certain measure of elasticity that is afforded to, and expected of, Congress, in which the legislative branch is granted the opportunity to assess issues of importance that may become prevalent in the U.S. system and to also be empowered to flexibly construct public policy in an effort to address such. In this sense, the Necessary and Proper Clause provides constitutional justification for Congress to respond when there are sufficient levels of agreement among system actors that societal issues are perceived to be a problem deemed to be in need of a government response. If there is agreement among system actors supporting drafting an official policy response to an identified problem, then decision makers in Congress

156 The Concept of Money

are empowered to do so via the Necessary and Proper Clause. To further illustrate this dynamic in action, the final chapter will be dedicated to an expansive analysis associated with the present policy environment in which a responsible U.S. government is tasked with efforts to devise official means by which to address concerns associated with non-fiat virtual currency, such as those attributed to the rapidly growing field of cryptocurrency. The concept of elasticity associated with the Necessary and Proper Clause is most assuredly relatable to policy dynamics that will ultimately determine the U.S. government's responses to the development and proliferation of cryptocurrency. The decision as to whether the government will craft new legislation to broadly address the cryptocurrency industry represents a major challenge that Congress faces regarding policymaking endeavors that are reflective of issues unique to the modern era and that involve newly emerging advancements in technology. In addition, there are a multitude of federal agencies that will be expected to develop internal measures to address cryptocurrency in accordance with each entity's mandated duties, which includes the Internal Revenue Service (IRS) and the Securities and Exchange Commission (SEC), that ultimately creates a fragmented policy approach to address this topic.

As the U.S. has a federal system in place in which decision-making powers are shared to some degree with each of the levels of government (i.e. national, state, and local), it is also possible that, in accordance with the tenth amendment, Congress may defer to the discretion of the states allowing for that level of government to exercise preference in determining what constitutes the official stance on cryptocurrency. Briefly stated, the tenth amendment indicates that powers not expressly granted to the federal government are reserved for the states. Therefore, the tenth amendment simultaneously indicates that federal government powers are limited to some degree, and that state governments have vast discretionary powers to address localized policy concerns. Ultimately, Congress may choose to act by establishing broad legislative parameters that can assist in determining how cryptocurrency will be addressed at all levels of government in the United States. At present, the U.S. is largely lacking a Congressionally designed unifying policy plan that broadly and directly details how all levels of government will be required to address issues stemming from the proliferation of cryptocurrency. A more detailed discussion of significant policy efforts that have been developed thus far will be introduced in the final chapter, to paint a broad picture of the present policy environment through which decision makers will endeavor to address the growing cryptocurrency industry. At this point in the discussion, it is more important to recognize that Congress is constitutionally empowered through the Necessary and Proper Clause to develop policy endeavors in order to address emerging problems in society such as those potentially posed by cryptocurrency.

In relation, the Necessary and Proper Clause provides Congress with the constitutional authority to develop official means by which to address how the emerging cryptocurrency industry conflicts with another power expressly granted to the legislative branch, regarding its ability to serve as the sole source of designing determining factors associated with money such as coining, valuing, taxation, and preventing counterfeiting. As such, it is important to next address what constitutes Congressional powers in this regard especially in the context of coining money. Doing so will allow for later considerations of the potential threats to this Congressional authority potentially posed by the decentralized cryptocurrency industry, which may be subject to legislative actions in accordance with the Necessary and Proper Clause. The emergence of cryptocurrency, a form of non-fiat virtual currency, is indicative of one of many technologically oriented challenges facing government that is unique to the modern era. Specifically, the emergence of cryptocurrency legitimately raises concerns regarding how this innovative, decentralized, non-fiat virtual currency may conflict with the powers associated with money that is enumerated to Congress via the U.S. Constitution. The following excerpts from Article I, section 8 highlights relevant powers enumerated to Congress related to a wide range of components focused on aspects of money, including:

> The Congress shall have Power To lay and collect Taxes, Duties, Imposts and Excises, to pay the Debts and provide for the common Defense and general Welfare of the United States; but all Duties, Imposts and Excises shall be uniform throughout the United States.
>
> To borrow Money on the credit of the United States Section.
>
> To coin Money, regulate the Value thereof, and of foreign Coin, and fix the Standards of Weights and Measures.
>
> To provide for the Punishment of counterfeiting the Securities and current Coin of the United States.
>
> *Source: U.S. Constitution (1788, Article 1, section 8)*

As previously noted, the Necessary and Proper Clause empowers the federal government to take actions that are designed to create on opportunity for officially mandated influence in a given field of public policy. In this sense, Congress is constitutionally empowered to take action that is geared toward mandating activities associated with many dynamic aspects associated with money. To this end, Congress in the modern era is faced with a

158 The Concept of Money

unique dilemma regarding how to respond to the presence of cryptocurrency as this non-fiat virtual currency may present a slew of constitutional threats that may require official actions. This is not to imply that each individual member of Congress themselves becomes directly involved in coining money, taxing money, valuing money, or punishing counterfeiters of money. Instead, Congress drafts public policy, yielding mandates that can create the very agencies that are directly responsible for completing acts as directed by the legislative branch and that serve to guide administratively oriented actions in a given field. Here, a legislative mandate on behalf of Congress creates a government agency and the corresponding statutory directives guiding the created entities actions that follow in subsequent years is reflective of progressively dynamic action cycle. In the context of Congressional powers associated with addressing evolutionary societal events affecting fiat currency, such as those associated with cryptocurrency, the U.S. Department of the Treasury serves as one of many federal agencies that was created to address a multitude of items concerning the field of official legal tender. Lee, Johnson, and Joyce (2021, p. 76) note that "in the United States, only the U.S. Treasury Department may print currency or mint coins." In the context of fashioning a policy foundation that would later establish governmental capacity on the topic of fiat, tangible currency, Congress first created the U.S. Department of the Treasury at the initial stages of developing the federal government, as indicated by the following:

> The First Congress of the United States was called to convene in New York on March 4, 1789, marking the beginning of government under the Constitution. On September 2, 1789, Congress created a permanent institution for the management of government finances:
> Be it enacted by the Senate and House of Representatives of the United States of America in Congress assembled, That there shall be a Department of Treasury, in which shall be the following officers, namely: a Secretary of the Treasury, to be deemed head of the department; a Comptroller, an Auditor, a Treasurer, a Register, and an Assistant to the Secretary of the Treasury, which assistant shall be appointed by the said Secretary.
> *Source: U.S. Department of the Treasury*
> *(2022a, Section 2, paragraph 1)*

At that stage, the Department of the Treasury under the leadership of this agency's first Secretary of the Treasury, Alexander Hamilton, was focused on enacting policy means that would help to establish a path forward for the field of governmental financing. Since the creation of the U.S. Department of the Treasury, Congress has enacted additional legislative mandates that would shape the role the federal government would play in addressing many different policy aspects capable of influencing the dynamic field of money. In short, the U.S. Department of the Treasury would become further empowered to affect the financial landscape in various ways, which can be best summarized as followed:

> The Department of the Treasury is organized into two major components: the Departmental Offices and the operating bureaus. The Departmental Offices are primarily responsible for the formulation of policy and management of the Department as a whole, while the operating bureaus carry out the specific operations assigned to the Department. The basic functions of the Department of the Treasury include:
> Economic, international economic, and fiscal policy
> Government accounting, cash, and debt management
> Promulgation and enforcement of tax and tariff laws
> Assessment and collection of internal revenue
> Production of coin and currency
> Supervision of national banks and thrifts
> *Source: U.S. Department of the Treasury*
> *(2022b, section 1, paragraph 1)*

After creating the U.S. Department of the Treasury, Congress would then draft legislation that would further institutionalize mandates guiding actions in the field of public-sector finance and that would create additional government entities that would play a key role in overseeing a wide range of aspects associated with money, many of which will be discussed in the final chapter of this book. This includes that, after creating the Department of the Treasury, Congress would later go on to establish many bureaus within this agency's operational umbrella, such as the U.S. Mint, which would become directly responsible for the production processes associated with coining money. For example, in 1792 the U.S. Mint was created via the legislative effort entitled the Coinage Act, and this entity would serve as the first national mint under the new Constitution (U.S. Mint, 2022, paragraph 1). In relation, the Coinage Act literally provided guidelines for the exact types of coins that would be furnished, and the composite corresponding metallic make-up associated with each as indicated by the following information:

> The Act specified the following coinage denominations:
> In copper: half cent and cent
> In silver: half dime, dime, quarter, half dollar, and dollar
> In gold: quarter eagle ($2.50), half eagle ($5), and eagle ($10)
> *Source: U.S. Mint (2022)*

160 The Concept of Money

It would not be until 1861 when Congress authorized the U.S. Treasury Department to create "greenbacks" that the federal government would become involved in the production of paper money (U.S. Currency Education Program, 2022, paragraph 12). In doing so, the federal government would soon create another entity called the Bureau of Engraving and Printing (BEP), which would become involved in the production of paper money. The origins of this entity would be rooted in the newly mandated requirement that the official legal tender in the form of paper currency was to be issued, in that "The Bureau of Engraving and Printing had its foundations in 1862 with workers signing, separating, and trimming sheets of Demand Notes in the Treasury building" (Bureau of Engraving and Printing, 2022a, paragraph 1). The Bureau of Engraving and Printing is one of several bureaus that fall under the organizational umbrella of the U.S. Department of Treasury. Ultimately, the functional focus of the parent organization (i.e. the Department of the Treasury) regarding the production of fiat money is carried out by the parent agency's subsidiary bureaus (BEP and U.S. Mint) as followed:

What is the difference between the BEP and the Mint?

The Bureau of Engraving and Printing is the Nation's sole producer of U.S. paper currency. The BEP advises other federal agencies on document security matters and also produces engraved documents such as military commissions and award certificates, and special security documents for a variety of government agencies.

The United States Mint is the Nation's sole manufacturer of circulating coins. The Mint also produces numismatic coins and coin-related products, including proof, uncirculated, and commemorative coins; medals; and silver and gold bullion coins.

Source: The Bureau of Engraving and Printing (2022b, paragraph 1)

In sum, Congress utilized the powers granted via the Necessary and Proper Clause to enact legislation that created the U.S. Department of Treasury, whose mandated responsibility included tasks such as establishing fiscal policy for the public sector and coining money in accordance with the standards set forth by the federal government. In relation, the U.S. Mint was established as a subsidiary entity within the U.S. Department of Treasury via the Coinage Act, empowering the bureau to fulfill duties related to the production of fiat coinage. When the U.S. federal government opted to add paper money into circulation, the BEP was tasked with directing the effort to create this form of fiat currency. The U.S. Department of the Treasury and the subsequent bureaus (U.S. Mint and BEP) are among the many examples in which Congress has exercised its constitutional powers to address the fluid policy dynamics associated with addressing the field of fiat currency. In relation, Congress has crafted a wide assortment of legislative efforts to create guidelines and corresponding federal agencies that will be responsible for taxing money (Internal Revenue Service: https://www.irs.gov/about-irs), valuing money (Federal Reserve: https://www.federalreserve.gov/aboutthefed.htm), punishing counterfeiters of money (Secret Service: https://www.secretservice.gov/investigation/counterfeit), and preventing anti-money laundering and counter-terrorism financing (Financial Crimes Enforcement Network: https://www.fincen.gov/what-we-do). Correspondingly, working within the confines of each's Congressional mandate, a bureaucratic entity is responsible for developing internal measures that allow for a public-sector organization to fluidly address a specific area of policy through official actions as needed.

The emergence of types of non-fiat virtual currency, such as those associated with the cryptocurrency industry, potentially may serve as a direct threat to the constitutionally mandated roles that Congress is intended to play, such as those associated with being exclusively empowered to coin money. In relation, the Necessary and Proper Clause of the U.S. Constitution empowers Congress to create policy responses to address emerging problems, which serves as the authority by which the legislative branch can enact means to address the cryptocurrency industry at the federal level. In this regard, the federal government is empowered to enact legislation that will then require a wide range of bureaucratic entities to respond in kind by becoming actively involved in regulating the cryptocurrency industry as mandated. Relatedly, bureaucratic entities generate internal efforts that will affect how an agency goes about addressing an area of public policy, such as the challenges posed by the cryptocurrency industry. In addition, the U.S. is a federal system of government in which there is also a certain measure of discretion afforded to the state and local levels of government. Without unifying examples of federal legislation that indisputably provides universally mandated actions regarding how the government at all levels should address non-fiat virtual currencies, such as cryptocurrency, the present policy landscape in the U.S. is somewhat inconsistent, fragmented, and in a constant state of flux. Determining what the role of government should be in addressing the emergence of cryptocurrency will in part be based on the preferences held by system actors as to what degree it is deemed permissible for the public sector to intervene in shaping the trajectory of the industry through policymaking. Here, such discussions would largely be centered on how technology-based policy will be capable of affecting the cryptocurrency industry if either permissionless innovation or the precautionary principle serve as the primary rationale guiding decision making. In relation, it would be imprudent to overlook the role that

162 The Concept of Money

deliberative democracy plays systemically in serving as the narrative venue by which interested parties may argue over which technologically focused rationale is better suited to decision making to address the cryptocurrency industry in the U.S. political system. The U.S. deliberative democracy includes a wide range of expectations associated with maintaining opportunities for interested parties to engage in meaningful deliberations over policy matters such as those associated with the field of cryptocurrency regulations. This policy landscape and several corresponding official actions at various levels of government in the United States will be discussed at greater length in the final chapter.

Closing Remarks

The concept of money has a rich history regarding the dynamics of its creation, acceptance, and usage on a broad societal scale. In relation, the analysis of the historical context allows for the identification of money characteristics that remain relevant in the modern era. In this sense money has specific characteristics that includes its ability to serve as a medium of exchange, to act as a reliable unit of measurement by which goods/services are comparatively valued during transactions in the market and to instill trust in system actors that can come to rely on the relative stability of the established worth in a fiscal sense. Relatedly, money is also expected to reflect qualities associated with being divisible, portable, durable, stable, and difficult to counterfeit. The initial idea of money was essentially a socially contrived construct, derived of necessity, in which system actors collectively developed trust in the value of something being considered for usage as a medium of exchange. In addition, the original manifestations of money were not necessarily constructs of the state, as system actors would often take the lead in establishing an accepted medium of exchange. In relation, the collective value attached to a unit of something would reflect its utility to some degree, which in turn would contribute to the basis by which it became widely accepted as a medium of exchange. These broad ideas that establish contextual parameters for understanding money are historical in nature, in which the early conceptualization has had long-lasting effects well into the modern era. Money cannot function as a medium of exchange unless there is some measure of value associated with it and system actors must be able to trust in the fact that the many qualities of money that are present will continue to persist, allowing the accepted medium of exchange to remain viable in perpetuity. Over time, the state has taken an increasingly larger role in actively shaping operational dynamics associated with money to the point where, in the modern era, the government assumes a primary role in coining money, taxing money, valuing money, and punishing counterfeiters of money. This act of government legitimacy helps to further promote the acceptance and usage of money on behalf of system actors who are actively engaged in various types of interactions within the economy.

In the modern era, the nature of official legal tender has changed somewhat to reflect the shifting technologies of the time. For example, traditional fiat money now manifests in tangible form (i.e. bills, coins, etc.) and also in electronic format oft referred to as digital money. Regardless of whether it is found in tangible or digital form, fiat money serves as official legal tender, to be used societally, to fulfill a wide range of economically based activities. The advent of the modern Internet and various other advanced technologies has led to the creation and growth of various forms of digital currency. For example, digital currency could manifest as official, state-sanctioned cryptocurrency, which is not presently adopted by the U.S. government. Digital currency could also represent electronically transacted versions of fiat currency or non-fiat virtual currency, such those associated with cryptocurrency. As the U.S. government has yet to develop its own official cryptocurrency, and electronic fiat currency is considered to fall within the constitutional purview of Congress, the area that would require greater attention in the modern era from a descriptive and regulatory perspective would be non-fiat virtual currency, such as cryptocurrency. In relation, the most prominent form of cryptocurrency in use in the modern era is Bitcoin, which has dominated the international and domestic market thus far. There is an assortment of considerations regarding the development and proliferation of cryptocurrency that will ultimately yield a wide range of unique concerns derived from this particular manifestation of modern-era technology. This includes refining an understanding of why this form of non-fiat virtual currency came to be, discussing how cryptocurrency is transacted and identifying potential pros/cons associated with cryptocurrency as it slowly begins to become used more societally.

The continued growth and proliferation of the newly emergent cryptocurrency industry has raised some concerns regarding this non-fiat virtual currency's ability to challenge the constitutional authority solely held by Congress to fulfill responsibilities, such as coining money, and to contest the role that fiat currency plays as the accepted monetary mechanism used within the U.S. system. Among the many concerns that non-fiat virtual currency, such a cryptocurrency, presents regarding its classification is the idea that the existence of such is neither created by nor officially supported by the U.S. government. Although non-fiat virtual currency is not classified as official U.S. legal tender, there are instances in which examples such as cryptocurrency are convertible to fiat currency, which further complicates understanding of this innovative design in practice. The possibility that

164 The Concept of Money

cryptocurrency may continue to permeate the system, as actors become more comfortable with and confident in its usage, will ultimately create an opportunity for government to design policy means by which to establish guidelines to regulate such to some degree. The U.S. legislative landscape at present is considerably disjointed, generally lacking in a unifying statutory presence of Congressional actions directly designed to broadly address the field of cryptocurrency and to clearly provide a policy template by which federal agencies are expected to comply when dealing with this type of non-fiat virtual currency. In the next chapters, further descriptive information will be provided regarding the most popular form of cryptocurrency, Bitcoin, and a discussion will ensue regarding a wide range of policy measures presently in place at each of the levels of government in the U.S. federal system, which are designed to address different aspects of the cryptocurrency industry.

References

Bureau of Engraving and Printing (2022a). History. https://www.bep.gov/currency/history

Bureau of Engraving and Printing (2022b). FAQs. https://www.bep.gov/currency/faqs

Dobeck, M. F. & Elliott, E. (2007). *Money.* Greenwood Publishing Group.

Financial Crimes Enforcement Network (FinCEN) (2013). Application of FinCEN's Regulations to Persons Administering, Exchanging, or Using Virtual Currencies. https://www.fincen.gov/sites/default/files/shared/FIN-2013-G001.pdf

Galbraith, J. K. & Galbraith, J. K. (2017). *Money : whence it came, where it went.* Princeton University Press.

Internal Revenue Service (2021). Virtual Currencies. April 30. https://www.irs.gov/businesses/small-businesses-self-employed/virtual-currencies

Lansky, J. (2018). Possible state approaches to cryptocurrencies. *Journal of Systems Integration,* 9(1), 19–31. https://www.proquest.com/scholarly-journals/possible-state-approaches-cryptocurrencies/docview/2000967598/se-2?accountid=38769

Lee, R. D. Jr., Johnson, R. W. & Joyce, P. G. (2021). *Public Budgeting Systems.* Jones & Bartlett.

Mellor, M. (2019). *Money : myths, truths and alternatives.* Policy Press.

Merriam-Webster Dictionary. (2022). Money. https://www.merriam-webster.com/dictionary/money

Menger, C. (1882). *On The Origins of Money.* Ludwig von Mises Institute. https://mises.org/library/origins-money-0.

Mises, L. V. (1912). *The Theory of Money and Credit.* Ludwig von Mises Institute.

Mises, L. V. (1949). *A Treatise on Economics: Human Action (The Scholar's Edition).* The Ludwig von Miss Institute. https://cdn.mises.org/Human%20Action_3.pdf

Peters, G. W., Chapelle, A., and Panayi, E. (2016) Opening discussion on banking sector risk exposures and vulnerabilities from Virtual currencies: An Operational Risk perspective. *Journal of Banking Regulation,* 17(4), 239–272.

The Commodity Futures Trading Commission (2021). An Introduction to Virtual Currency. https://www.cftc.gov/sites/default/files/idc/groups/public/%40customer protection/documents/file/oceo_aivc0218.pdf

U.S. Constitution (1788). Constitution Annotated: Analysis and Interpretation of the U.S. Constitution. https://constitution.congress.gov/constitution/

U.S. Currency Education Program (CEP). (2022). The History of U.S. Currency: "Greenbacks." https://www.uscurrency.gov/history

U.S. Department of the Treasury (2021). Frequently Asked Questions: Questions on Virtual Currency. October 15. https://home.treasury.gov/policy-issues/financial-sanctions/faqs/topic/1626/print

U.S. Department of the Treasury. (2022a). History of the Treasury. https://home.treasury.gov/about/history/history-overview/history-of-the-treasury

U.S. Department of the Treasury. (2022b). Organization and Functions. https://home.treasury.gov/about/history/history-overview/organization-and-functions

U.S. Mint. (2022). History of the U.S. Mint. https://www.usmint.gov/learn/history/overview

Virga, J. M. (2015). International Criminals and Their Virtual Currencies: The Need for an International Effort in Regulating Virtual Currencies and Combating Cyber Crime. *Brazilian Journal of International Law*, *12*(2), 512–527.

6
CRYPTOCURRENCY, BITCOIN, AND THE CONCEPT OF MONEY

Although outside the scope of the constitutional parameters of official legal tender, non-fiat virtual currency has managed to increasingly gain momentum in expanding its fiscal viability domestically and abroad. In the modern era, virtual currency is increasingly being represented by emergent cryptocurrency such as Bitcoin, which is not qualified as U.S. fiat currency. Therefore, the concept of cryptocurrencies such as Bitcoin and the potential role(s) in society as a factor in the economy will receive further consideration in this chapter. To assist in moving the understanding of this form of non-fiat virtual currency forward, a broad discussion regarding what constitutes cryptocurrency will be provided to help shed further light on this relatively new industry, which has increased in relevance in recent years. This includes introducing blockchain technology, which is a highly technical means by which Bitcoin transactions are securely verified. Additionally, some of the pros and cons associated with Bitcoin will be introduced. Any potential role of Bitcoin for widescale usage will require the presence of sufficient levels of trust in this form of cryptocurrency held by system actors and plentiful opportunities for which to use this cryptocurrency for various activities within the economy. In relation, determining whether Bitcoin meets the previously discussed characteristics of money will help to shed some light on the capacity of this form of cryptocurrency to operate as a medium of exchange, despite being classified as non-fiat virtual currency.

DOI: 10.4324/9781003441830-6

Cryptocurrency: Key Systemic Features

Among the most intriguing fiscal aspects unique to cryptocurrency is the fact that this form of non-fiat virtual currency is decentralized in nature. Unlike fiat currency, which is created by a centralized governmental authority, cryptocurrency such as Bitcoin are generated as the result of a digitally facilitated, decentralized process. The U.S. Internal Revenue Service (2014, paragraph 6) explains that "cryptocurrency is a type of virtual currency that utilizes cryptography to validate and secure transactions that are digitally recorded on a distributed ledger, such as a blockchain." Cryptocurrency has no "issuing authority" and exists exclusively in the form of "electronic records" in which its creation is the "product of a computer program" (Mellor, 2019, p. 4). Lerer (2019, p. 40) notes that "cryptocurrency is digital currency that used encryption techniques, rather than a central bank, to generate, exchange, and transfer units of currency." Daj (2017, p. 222) states that, due to the precipitous proliferation of cryptocurrencies in the modern era, there may be potential in the future for a broad government strategy, allowing for traditionally sanctioned forms of currency to exist in a monetary ecosystem with "Central-Bank-Issued Digital Currencies (enjoying legal tender status)," in which this approach may serve as an official means by which to simultaneously endorse and lay a foundation for the regulation of such types of virtual currency. Although the likelihood that countries develop a nationally sanctioned fiat form of cryptocurrency is potentially relevant in the future, the United States has presently avoided pursuing such considerations on this account. Unless in a case where a nation may opt to develop a fiat cryptocurrency, this industry has remained highly vested in maintaining its decentralized nature in which government involvement is largely circumvented. This is an intentional construct and, more often than not, the preferred path forward in perpetuity for the staunch advocates of this industry whose support is, in large part, due to the perceived benefits derived from the capacity of cryptocurrency to circumvent government intervention in its creation, distribution, regulation, and usage. Peters et al. (2016, p. 250) note that "cryptocurrencies were introduced for use in the real economy, in order to remove the need for financial intermediaries and central banking authorities, and reduce transaction costs." Lansky (2018, p. 19) expands on this notion by stating that "cryptocurrencies usually achieve a unique combination of three features: ensuring limited anonymity, independence from central authority and double-spending attack protection. No other group of currencies, including fiat currencies, has this combination of features." At present, the most popular form of cryptocurrency is Bitcoin, which falls

168 Cryptocurrency, Bitcoin, and the Concept of Money

well within the definitional parameters regarding being digitally created by relatively anonymous actors engaged in a decentralized process that generally falls outside the scope of government involvement. Bitcoin is a globalized, intangible, "decentralized currency" in which no "institutional owner" or "specific country" is directly, and solely, responsible for regulating this form of cryptocurrency (Parveen and Alajmi, 2019, p. 3). Ngai (2014, p. 36) adds that "Bitcoin is also not dependent on governments, which can occasionally fail. These unstable governmental events could trigger hyperinflation or a complete collapse of their fiat currency." The usage of technology to facilitate decentralized transactions involving cryptocurrency in a relatively secure fashion runs counter to fiat currency dynamics, which relies on traditionally oriented, centralized actors (i.e. government, banks, etc.) working in concert to establish, maintain, and perpetuate existing financial network arrangements. The nature of cryptocurrency is vastly different than traditional fiat currency in that this form of non-fiat virtual currency presently circumvents the constitutional dynamics associated with official parties in government being involved in all aspects associated with official legal tender, including creating, valuing, taxing, and preventing counterfeiting. Instead of government's centralized authority applied to create legal tender, the majority of cryptocurrency is generated on behalf of decentralized, non-governmental entities utilizing technological means associated with blockchain. Cryptocurrency attempts to bypass involving participants traditionally associated with the development, facilitation, and regulation of fiat currency, by allowing for decentralized parties to incorporate technological means that play a primary role in lifecycle dynamics associated with this form of non-fiat virtual currency. The cryptographic means used to generate, transact, and regulate non-fiat virtual currency intended for use in various economic events poses a unique threat to the status of fiat money that has maintained relatively unchallenged fiscal primacy in the U.S. economic system.

Bitcoin's Primary Standing Within the Cryptocurrency Industry

With the understanding that cryptocurrency is a particular type of non-fiat, decentralized, and digitally facilitated virtual currency, it is important to further expand on a specific example to broaden this discussion. Among the many types of cryptocurrencies that continue to develop in the modern era, presently Bitcoin is inarguably the most recognizable and prominent in usage domestically and internationally. Due to the perpetual popularity in name recognition and increasing levels of usage in economically oriented circumstances, for many across the globe Bitcoin has largely become synonymous with the idea of decentralized cryptocurrency. To illustrate this point, information regarding Bitcoin's enhanced market share in the cryptocurrency industry is deserved of further exploration. Bitcoin's industry presence has reflected a variable but largely dominant percentage of the cryptocurrency market for an extended period, including the recent yearly highs that includes ranges such 84.84 percent (March 2017), 71.89 percent (January 2021), and 47.49 percent (June 2022) (CoinmarketCap, 2022a). Although defined as a type of non-fiat virtual currency, Bitcoin has reached an operational status and a level of acceptance in society that has led this form of cryptocurrency to be assessed in terms of its value in relation to the U.S. dollar. Similarly, Bitcoin in comparable U.S. dollars is also significantly more valuable than the other types of cryptocurrencies registered on the top ten in market capitalization, which on October 24, 2022 was as followed: Bitcoin (BTC) $19,353.14, Ethereum (ETH) $1,346.61, Tether (USDT) $1, USD Coin (USDC) $1, BNB (BNB) $273.56, XRP (XRP) $0.457, Binance USD (BUSD) $1, Cardano (ADA) $0.36, Solana (SOL) $28.83, Dogecoin (DOGE) $0.05 (CoinMarketCap, 2022b). Relatedly, at that time Bitcoin registered as the number one ranked cryptocurrency in value and market cap from a list that included over 9,000 different cryptocurrency brands (CoinMarketCap, 2022b). Although Bitcoin generally holds steady in being ranked the most valuable cryptocurrency in both U.S. dollars and market cap, it is important to note that the dollar value in Bitcoin is generally subject to fluctuations, the overall rankings of the cryptocurrencies is subject to change and the total number of cryptocurrency entities available at any given time may vary. Among the many thousands of cryptocurrency brands, Bitcoin is by far the most popular, and most valuable, available to system actors interested in becoming involved in this market. Relatedly, Bitcoin is often the focus of many academic works (including this one) in which this speculative spotlight continues to provide analysis that further gives credence to the popularity of this form of cryptocurrency. With its primary status firmly established, Bitcoin is deserved of additional attention in an effort to provide greater insight regarding this form of cryptocurrency.

Origins of Bitcoin

As Bitcoin has dominated the industry in relation to market presence and fiscal worth, it is important to expand the discussion regarding its origins to develop a better understanding of the nature of this form of cryptocurrency, which has contributed to its ability to flourish. By providing a discussion regarding the relatively short history of Bitcoin, it will shed light on the impressive rise to dominance in the emergent cryptocurrency market, which is still in the fledging stage of development. In this sense,

170 Cryptocurrency, Bitcoin, and the Concept of Money

the rise of Bitcoin and the whole of the cryptocurrency industry have recently developed along parallel paths, in which the growth of the first has provided the second the opportunity to persist in its societal presence. The conceptual impetus for the creation of this example of cryptocurrency was established in a document called the Bitcoin white paper. This document was written by Satoshi Nakamoto in 2008, whose identity thus far is frequently speculated about but still unknown and could even be a moniker for a consortium rather than an individual. A number of key excerpts from Nakamoto's Bitcoin white paper are provided below to help establish an understanding of the innovative ideas that created the framework for what would eventually become the cryptocurrency known as Bitcoin. The introduction to Nakamoto's key ideas, which would eventually allow for Bitcoin to be developed and flourish, will then be followed by further explanatory discussions regarding the nature of this form of cryptocurrency.

Nakamoto's (2008, p. 1) white paper provided a lengthy, industry-shaping discussion regarding the recommendation to establish a "peer-to-peer electronic cash system," which would eventually pave the way for the birth of Bitcoin. The expansive discussion on behalf of Nakamoto includes the following key excerpts, which introduces foundational elements that would ultimately contribute to the development of this new payment system:

A purely peer-to-peer version of electronic cash would allow online payments to be sent directly from one party to another without going through a financial institution.

Digital signatures provide part of the solution, but the main benefits are lost if a trusted third party is still required to prevent double-spending. We propose a solution to the double-spending problem using a peer-to-peer network. The network timestamps transactions by hashing them into an ongoing chain of hash-based proof-of-work, forming a record that cannot be changed without redoing the proof-of-work. The longest chain not only serves as proof of the sequence of events witnessed, but proof that it came from the largest pool of CPU power. As long as a majority of CPU power is controlled by nodes that are not cooperating to attack the network, they'll generate the longest chain and outpace attackers.

[...]

By convention, the first transaction in a block is a special transaction that starts a new coin owned by the creator of the block. This adds an incentive for nodes to support the network, and provides a way to initially distribute coins into circulation, since there is no central authority to issue them. The steady addition of a constant of amount of new coins is analogous to gold miners expending resources to add gold to circulation. In our case, it is CPU time and electricity that is expended.

[...]

Cryptocurrency, Bitcoin, and the Concept of Money **171**

A peer-to-peer network using proof-of-work to record a public history of transactions that quickly becomes computationally impractical for an attacker to change if honest nodes control a majority of CPU power.

Nodes can leave and rejoin the network at will, accepting the proof-of-work chain as proof of what happened while they were gone. They vote with their CPU power, expressing their acceptance of valid blocks by working on extending them and rejecting invalid blocks by refusing to work on them. Any needed rules and incentives can be enforced with this consensus mechanism.

Source: Nakamoto (2008, pp. 1, 4, and 8)

Here, Nakamoto discussed foundational components that would contribute to Bitcoin's development, which includes a peer-to-peer network, timestamping innovations, mining processes, double-spending prevention, and blockchain. When discussing the white paper written by Nakamoto in 2008, it has been observed that the general tone of the work indicates that Bitcoin as a "currency is for computer technicians, not economists nor political pundits" (Tucker, 2014, p. 13). To some degree, the suggested technical distancing may help to explain why the concept of Bitcoin has broadly elicited a lack of congruence in understanding as to how this form of cryptocurrency is assessed, defined, and applied throughout society. However, the idea that Bitcoin was not originally meant for experts in fields other than that of computer technicians does not make understanding this form of cryptocurrency unimportant to students, academics, and practitioners in public administration, public policy, and political science. With this idea in mind, this chapter will generally be focused on discussing cryptocurrency such as Bitcoin from a minimally technical perspective that is intended to be relatively accessible in nature. In that, the discussion of Bitcoin will generally avoid focusing on providing highly technical information such as illustrating in detail how computers are used to solve the complex mathematical equations associated with blockchain during verification processes. Instead, this chapter will focus on topics such as introducing the basic underlying technical components contributing to the developmental lifecycle of Bitcoin, discussing pros/cons associated with Bitcoin usage on behalf of system actors, and expanding on the potential for this technologically generated non-fiat virtual currency to play a contributing role within the broader U.S. economic system.

The Security of Blockchain: Technical Building Blocks and the Participation of Bitcoin Miners

Although various forms of cryptocurrency may share some of the traditional characteristics used to define money, industry manifestations such as

172 Cryptocurrency, Bitcoin, and the Concept of Money

Bitcoin would still technically be classified as being non-fiat in nature, and the means used to create such presently falls outside the practice of government as no officially sanctioned U.S. sovereign cryptocurrency exists. Until the U.S. government decides to create an official fiat cryptocurrency, Bitcoin must be classified and discussed in terms of being non-legal tender. In relation, types of non-fiat cryptocurrencies such as Bitcoin are created, transacted, and verified by non-governmental actors participating in the decentralized peer-to-peer network that utilizes blockchain technology to maintain systemic perpetuation. Bitcoin is understood in part by acknowledging that this form of cryptocurrency is inseparably intertwined with the blockchain technology that is used to verify and perpetuate its existence. As the blockchain process is in part based on the application of timestamping, it will be first helpful to summarize the origin of this conceptualization in practice that is applicable to the cryptocurrency in question. The early work of Haber and Stornetta in 1991 focused on developing timestamp verification technology that was irreversible and unable to be tampered with, in which this innovation would set the stage for the modern-day usage of blockchain technology used in Bitcoin transactions first suggested by Nakamoto (Fadilpašić, 2018). To address the growing need to verify the creation of, and identify possible modifications to, many types of digital documents (audio, video, text, etc.) that were increasingly proliferating in modern society, the "time-stamping" process was developed, which reflected two criteria (Haber and Stornetta, 1991, p. 453). Haber and Stornetta (1991, p. 453) explain that "first, they must time-stamp the actual bits of the document, making no assumptions about the physical medium on which the document is recorded. Second, the date and time of the timestamp must not be forgeable." The idea behind timestamping technology would come to serve as one of the foundational components of blockchain technology when Bitcoin was ultimately created in 2009.

Although timestamping was first conceived by Haber and Stornetta in 1991, it was not until 2009 that it would become a foundational aspect of the blockchain technology used in the cryptocurrency verification process for transactions associated with the newly created Bitcoin. As such, a minimally technical introduction to the conceptual and procedural dynamics associated with blockchain as applied to Bitcoin is provided next. Nakamoto (2008, p. 1) promoted the creation of Bitcoin in part based on the possibility that this form of cryptocurrency would serve as "an electronic payment system based on cryptographic proof instead of trust." Instead of viewing Bitcoin as a "stand-alone currency," it is more realistically considered "a unit of accounting attached to an innovative payment network" (Tucker, 2014, p. 17). In part, the payment system is inseparable from Bitcoin itself and is reflective of traditional currency qualities such as being "portable, divisible, fungible, durable, and scarce." (Tucker, 2014, p. 17). The blockchain technology is an innovative design that is specifically geared toward creating cryptocurrency, such as Bitcoin, whose existence is not generated by centralized government involvement. Boxerman and Schwerin (2017, p. 2) reminds us that Bitcoin is decentralized in that "no one person, company, or government controls Bitcoin." Lerer (2019, p. 40) adds that "unlike cash transactions, no bank or government authority verifies the transfer of funds. Instead, these virtual transactions are recorded in a digitized public ledger called a 'blockchain'." Parino, Beiró, and Gauvin (2018, p. 1) expand on this notion by stating that "Bitcoin is a digital currency created in 2009 as an alternative to the banking system. Not only does it offer a payment mechanism without any centralized control (i.e. by institutions, governments, or banks), but it has also introduced the revolutionary concept of the blockchain." The integrated protective workings of this technological endeavor are based on Nakamoto's suggested usage of a "private key" and "blockchain ledger" in facilitating interactions associated with this payment system (Coinbase.com, 2022a, section 3, paragraph 2). The private key constitutes an encoding method in which a sequence of "randomized numbers and letters" is generated, which is used to gain digital access to a corresponding acquisition while the process is tracked longitudinally via "virtual ledger" referred to as a blockchain (Coinbase.com, 2022a, section 3, paragraph 2). In this interactive dynamic, the private key adds an additional layer of security to Bitcoin transactions, involving blockchain that is designed to help prevent instances of criminality such as fraud and theft. Ultimately, the blockchain process is a broad technological safeguard designed to create a level of protection for users during the verification processes. During the early development stages of Bitcoin, standard desktop computers had sufficient power to allow for all interested parties to attempt to engage in the mining processes (Coinbase.com, 2022a, section 4, paragraph 3). Coinbase.com (2022a, section 4, paragraph 3) indicates that today "specialized computers" referred to "mining rigs" are leveraged on behalf of "businesses or large numbers of individuals" working collectively to "perform the equations required to verify and record a new transaction." The leveraging of computational power required to participate in blockchain may have once been more easily facilitated by a wider audience through conventional computers, but this process now requires technological tools that are reflective of enhanced processing capabilities in which access to such devices is far more limited. With that said, the important participatory role of miners and the power that networked computers plays in blockchain processes to verify Bitcoin transactions is further expanded upon.

174 Cryptocurrency, Bitcoin, and the Concept of Money

In general, the blockchain technology is utilized for the purposes of verifying newly created Bitcoin and to confirm the validity of transactions involving Bitcoin. Here, participants work simultaneously to leverage computer "processing power" to be the first to solve "complex mathematical problems" associated with a blockchain designed to verify the presence of Bitcoin on the public ledger (Parveen and Alajmi, 2019, p. 3). In this sense, miners' collective participation—to leverage the computational power of CPUs to solve equations associated with blockchain technology during Bitcoin verification processes—serves to provide a measure of system stability. Bitcoin's usage of "miners" participating in a community-based verification process, derived from reaching an agreement for solutions to mathematical computations that records transactions to a "public ledger," is an innovative means that is intended to protect users against double-spending (Tu and Meredith, 2015, p. 281). Bitcoin implements digitally savvy means, associated with blockchain and digital signatures, by which to help prevent double-spending, which increases the levels of security associated with transacting with this type of cryptocurrency (Naheem, 2018, p. 569). Naheem (2018, p. 569) notes that blockchain is a "irreversible mathematical algorithm" yielding a "unique standardized identifier to each transaction" called a "hash." Naheem (2018, p. 569) observes that the next step involves adding the subsequent identifiers "to a block that then places that transaction into a chain of other blocks," which creates a "chronological stamp" that logs the transaction's "value and sequence." Naheem (2018, p. 569) explains that the verification processes then require "the sender and receiver" to provide their respective "digital signature" that signifies agreeance on the transactions (Naheem, 2018, p. 569). Here, the application of the private key and the timestamp technology play a key contributing role in securing the complex, technologically oriented process. In this sense, the use of blockchain technology serves as a means by which transactions are responsibly and accurately verified to protect against nefarious acts, such as forgery of cryptocurrency like Bitcoin (Harwick, 2016, p. 571). As cryptocurrency such as Bitcoin are generated in a decentralized fashion without government intervention, the blockchain technology plays a pivotal role in helping to create a secure environment by which to verify transactions through an internally maintained process.

The increasing attractiveness of Bitcoin as a legitimate method of payment relates to a wide range of distinctive system factors that appeal to potential users who wish to transact with this form of cryptocurrency. This includes that Bitcoin payments are enacted via a "private cryptographic key," the "decentralized" nature of transactions, and online facilitation occurs via a relatively secure structure "without having a single authority backing it as a payment system" (Parveen and Alajmi, 2019, p. 2). Those

Cryptocurrency, Bitcoin, and the Concept of Money **175**

participating in the decentralized blockchain process used in Bitcoin verification are expected to behave in a trustworthy manner and motivational rewards may be used to help ensure that this takes place. At present, there are two key rewards available that serve to provide Bitcoin miners with motivation to participate honestly during the blockchain verification process: Bitcoin and transaction fees. Ciaian, Rajcaniova, and Kancs (2016, p. 88) echo this notion by noting that miners "in return for this service they receive transaction fees and newly minted Bitcoins." The honesty of those participating in the mining of Bitcoin is maintained in part by providing incentives such as rewards that includes newly created Bitcoins, which is expected to serve as motivation to participate in the blockchain verification process in good faith (Chiu and Koeppl, 2017). Harwick (2016, p. 571) explains that Bitcoin placed in circulation is derived from the incentivized mining process, referred to as blockchain, in which "the network rewards verifiers with a certain number of coins after they have successfully verified a block of transactions." Böhme et al. (2015, p. 218) expand on the concept of rewards provided by noting that "at first, miners solving the puzzle received a reward of 50 Bitcoins. This reward is periodically cut in half, and it stands at 25 as of March 2015." Böhme et al. (2015, p. 218) add that once "21 million Bitcoins have been minted, the reward falls to zero and no further Bitcoins will be created." When Bitcoins will no longer be viable as a reward, miners will have to rely solely on being rewarded by receiving a transaction fee awarded to the miner successful in solving the mathematical equation "that verifies the transaction" (Böhme et al., 2015, p. 218). Harwick (2016, p. 571) adds that the numbers of Bitcoin in circulation are restricted and this certainty is maintained in part because "the adjustable difficulty ensures that computing advances will not affect the rate of expansion." When the intended limit of Bitcoin in circulation is reached, coins being granted as a reward for honest participation by those verifying this form of cryptocurrency through blockchain will be entirely supplanted by transactions fees. Until then, Bitcoin and transactions fees can serve as appealing rewards that can incentivize honest behavior on behalf of those participating during blockchain verification processes.

The Double-Spending Dilemma, Confirmation Lags and Possible Threats to the Security of Bitcoin

Unlike fiat money, the fact that Bitcoin presently only manifests digitally is a factor of circumstance in determining the scope of its usage in market transactions and in shaping the range of challenges to prevent counterfeiting this form of cryptocurrency. In relation, the nature of the double-spending dilemma associated with digital fiat currency is different when

176 Cryptocurrency, Bitcoin, and the Concept of Money

compared to cryptocurrency, due to its decentralized nature, and thusly requires different considerations as to how to solve this problem. In a conventional in-person marketplace interaction, there is traditionally an exchange of tangible good(s) for a mutually agreeable form of payment such as "shells, gold coins or bank notes" that results in a timely conclusion to the transaction (Chiu and Koeppl, 2017, p. 3). The advent of e-commerce, in which direct proximity between sellers and buyers is not required, shifts purchasing dynamics to include forms of digital currency via a "string of bits" and introduces the potential dilemma regarding transactions referred to as double-spending, in which the purchaser endeavors in "re-using the same bit" (Chiu and Koeppl, 2017, p. 3). With traditional forms of digital currency used in e-commerce, it is possible to circumvent the double-spending dilemma by utilizing a trusted third party (i.e. Google Pay, PayPal, etc.) who maintains a "centralized ledger and transfers balances by crediting and debiting buyers and sellers' accounts" (Chiu and Koeppl, 2017, p. 5). However, this transaction process is not universally applicable in all circumstances, including those involved cryptocurrencies such as Bitcoin, which is a decentralized digital payment method without typical third-party verification (Chiu and Koeppl, 2017, p. 5). When utilizing Bitcoin, the issues stemming from the double-spending dilemma are assuaged in part by "the usage of the blockchain and by introducing confirmation lags" (Chiu and Koeppl, 2017, p. 6). The blockchain technologies associated with the authentication process of Bitcoin are broken down into a combination of component parts: block (identifiable record of the current transaction facilitated by the parties involved in the singular use of cryptocurrency) and chain (history of all previous transactions creating a lengthy, archived register used in public verification of the ownership of Bitcoins) (Chiu and Koeppl, 2017, p. 6). In addition, the usage of a "confirmation lag" allowing a delay for the duration of several blocks before the transactional dynamic is completed will postpone the buyer's receipt of items purchased with Bitcoin while making it "harder to alter transactions in a sequence of new blocks" (Chiu and Koeppl, 2017, p. 6). In general, there is a uniqueness to cryptocurrency in that it is borne of and perpetuated through technologies of the time, which introduces a degree of difficulty in counterfeiting or theft that requires a novel approach to prevent double-spending. Instead of a third-party verification process to address the double-spending dilemma, Bitcoin utilizes uniquely tailored technological means to verify transactions facilitated via this form of cryptocurrency. The usage of blockchain technology and instituted confirmation lags during the verifying process serve as complimentary means by which the decentralized Bitcoin may limit the double-spending dilemma and increase the levels of trust that system actors may have in utilizing this form of cryptocurrency to facilitate a number of transactional endeavors in the economy.

As with any innovative tool, the blockchain technology used to verify Bitcoin transactions is highly effective but far from foolproof, as there are instances in which this form of cryptocurrency may be subject to an attack, highlighting the presence of potential vulnerabilities. Although blockchain is largely successful in preventing cryptocurrency exposure to risk, this digital security technique falls short of being deemed completely infallible, including possible susceptibility to "transaction malleability" (Naheem, 2018, p. 570). In order for this to be successful, a miner participating in the blockchain verification process will attempt to be first in submitting a "rouge version" in the hopes of creating a "duplicate copy of the transaction," which will actually cause the original to be rejected based on the fact that it inaccurately appears to be "duplicate double spending." For Bitcoin to be forged, it would require the blockchain of the digital assailant to exceed that of the "legitimate one," which would require maintaining "more computing power than the total of the honest nodes" in what is referred to as a "51 percent attack," making this illicit action quite difficult (Harwick, 2016, p. 571). Relatedly, Bitcoin can also be stolen by conducting a more traditionally oriented action, in which the exchange service responsible for transactions simply pilfers the funds, keeping them in the embezzlement of this form of cryptocurrency (Naheem, 2018, p. 570). Although digitally counterfeiting cryptocurrency such as Bitcoin is difficult, due to the number of safeguards in place associated with blockchain, there are rare instances in which this may be possible. In this sense, the honesty and integrity of the community of miners is expected to, and in most cases largely capable of, applying CPU power to solve the complex mathematical equations associated with blockchain that is required to verify that Bitcoin transactions are valid. Although Bitcoin's use of blockchain is largely successful in maintaining the integrity of transactions involving this type of cryptocurrency, there are still means by which industrious, tech-savvy criminals may be able to circumvent these structural protections. This includes the most famous case of this type of theft to date, in 2014, when hundreds of millions of dollars' worth of cryptocurrency was stolen from the cryptocurrency exchange (i.e. an entity that facilitates purchasing, vending, and storage) called Mt. Gox. At that time, this Japanese exchange firm, which represented approximately 70 percent of the world's cryptocurrency industry, was the victim of a hack that financially decimated the entity, which was forced to declare bankruptcy. In addition to being the victim of a targeted digitally conducted theft by external actors, those operating within a firm that serves as a cryptocurrency exchange may themselves resort to traditional fraud and embezzlement, in which

Bitcoin is intentionally falsely misrepresented for personal financial gain or outright stolen by internal actors, respectively. Such was the situation for the recent 2022 case involving FTX, an international cryptocurrency exchange, in which the company's CEO and founder was indited on December 13, 2022 by the U.S. Justice Department on various counts, including several alleged acts of cryptocurrency-based fraud and embezzlement. In cases of theft (i.e. externally stolen from), embezzlement (i.e. internally stolen by), and fraud (i.e. internal criminal deception for the purpose of financial gain) involving an exchange, this can cause real-world fiscal consequences to those directly involved, while also serving to diminish societal trust in the cryptocurrency industry.

In general, it would be imprudent to oversell Bitcoin as having an absolute ability to circumvent theft, embezzlement, and fraud that may befall cryptocurrency exchanges, because this may occur in much the same fashion as fiat currency can similarly be stolen by external sources, stolen from internal sources, and misappropriated for individual financial gain in any number of traditional financial institutions. The existence of a wide range of criminal acts such as theft, embezzlement, and fraud are far from unique to the virtual currency industry, but at this stage of development the presence, or worse yet persistence, of such may raise concerns as to the fiscal viability of cryptocurrency, such as Bitcoin. Because fiat currency which manifests as tangible money and electronic money are also susceptible to a wide range of criminal acts, the possibility that this may occur to those transacting in Bitcoin would not necessarily be grounds to automatically eliminate this form of cryptocurrency from consideration for use, on some level, if the industry was managed properly internally and in conjuncture with government regulation if necessary. In the most conventional sense, tangible fiat currency used to facilitate in-person transactions requires a physical exchange of legal tender for goods or services, which renders the double-spending problem in this context as inconsequential in this transactional dynamic. However, it is this same tangibility of fiat currency that makes it susceptible to traditional, physical counterfeiting efforts. Unlike tangible fiat currency, Bitcoin is unable to be counterfeited in the traditional sense because, at present, this form of cryptocurrency generally lacks a widely used physical counterpart in this stage of its development. Although the future may yield a tangible version of Bitcoin, at present this form of cryptocurrency is not subject to the same counterfeiting threats posed to legal tender in the physical sense.

As noted, the double-spending dilemma is something of a concern regarding the intentional digital duplication of Bitcoin by nefarious actors seeking to game the system by launching an attack to disrupt the community, which is otherwise cooperating to honestly verify a blockchain under review. The blockchain verification process serves to create an intentionally contrived protective layer that allows for technology to provide a communal check on the integrity of each Bitcoin, which is intended to prevent double-spending. At present, the field of cryptocurrency largely must rely on the inherent industry protections, such as the use of blockchain, that are designed to limit instances of criminality associated with theft, embezzlement, and fraud that, if permitted to run rampant, would otherwise cause enough distrust from among system actors to relegate Bitcoin to niche status permanently. The internally generated safeguards and incentives associated with blockchain technology are intended to provide a multi-layered schema of protections to those engaged in various Bitcoin market-based transactions, so that participants may have some measure of trust in the process. The blockchain provides a means by which to review transactions at a given point in time and to assess the resulting de facto ledger of historical transactions, which serves as a mechanism for verification of Bitcoin ownership. In relation, instituting a confirmation lag provides a means by which to create additional time to further ensure the viability of the subsequent Bitcoin transaction, which serves as another layer of defense against criminality. The application of such means used in conjuncture can increase the likelihood of preventing double-spending attempts by dishonest participants during Bitcoin transactional dynamics. Success in such cases can ultimately increase the levels of trust held on behalf of system actors that may work to further cement the practical usage of this form of cryptocurrency on a wider scale. In addition, the efforts to incentivize honesty in the miners engaged in verification efforts via blockchain provides yet another layer of protection, which contributes to establishing perceptions that this form of cryptocurrency can be considered a relatively dependable and safe means by which to engage in various market-based events in the U.S. economy. In this, the verification process involves a multitude of miners working together to authenticate the existence of Bitcoin that is intended for use in a transactional affair, such as purchasing goods/services in the market. In relation, any attempts to double-spend Bitcoin is intended to ultimately be deemed invalid by the protections associated with the blockchain verification process. As such, it is important to recognize that blockchain technology serves as a technological design working to enhance efforts to provide greater levels of security to those choosing to use Bitcoin. The usage of blockchain serves as an important and largely effective means by which system actors may be able to develop trust in the idea of engaging in circumstances involving transacting in Bitcoin. In relation, trust in the use of Bitcoin may be established and maintained to the point where this form of cryptocurrency may eventually achieve a broader measure of legitimacy by system actors, allowing it to achieve

180 Cryptocurrency, Bitcoin, and the Concept of Money

a greater societal role in various economic scenarios, including those associated with being considered for use as a medium of exchange. Lastly, it is important to observe that, because of Bitcoin's decentralized nature, the above conversation, regarding enacting efforts capable of maintaining system trust, omits analysis of the potential role(s) that government, a centralized authority that exists outside blockchain verification proceedings, plays in ensuring the security of this form of cryptocurrency.

Bitcoin: Pros/Cons of Usage, Potential Role(s) in the Stock Market, Effects of Scalability and Digital Wallets

As the most popular form of cryptocurrency at present, it is important to further elaborate on potential benefits and detriments that are oft associated with Bitcoin. As a note, many of the benefits associated with Bitcoin highlighted here mirror the positives attributed to non-fiat virtual currency, which were enumerated in the previous chapter. The attributable benefits of both share commonalties because Bitcoin is by extension a form of non-fiat, virtual currency and enumerating conceptual harmony on this account here serves to further reinforce the important role that such may play in promoting trust, potentially capable of further cementing this industry within the U.S. economy in various circumstances (i.e. transacting, investing, etc.). In addition to the previously discussed safeguards against double-spending, Bitcoin's unparalleled global success is due in part to the many perceived benefits held by those choosing to engage in its application, which includes some measure of shelter against government control, a degree of transaction anonymity, reduction in costs of usage, and inherent protections against fluctuations of inflation rates (Tu and Meredith, 2015, p. 278). Among the many participants that have interest in Bitcoin, there are some that view the promise of transacting in anonymity and a lack of government involvement as highly appealing. Bitcoin is generally considered to be relatively anonymous as "every transaction is posted on the ledger, the transferors and transferees of the bitcoins in each transaction are identified by code and not by actual name" (Boxerman and Schwerin, 2017, p. 2). Boxerman and Schwerin (2017, p. 2) additionally explain that a potential benefit of Bitcoin is that some system actors may prefer that it is decentralized, in which "no one person, company, or government controls bitcoin." On this account, part of the appeal of Bitcoin to some is that potential users avoid being dependent on traditional actors (i.e. government and banks) during the process of facilitating various types of transactions on a global basis (Tucker, 2014, p. 13). In this sense, Bitcoin is not dependent on conventional means used to establish "trust and identity" typical to monetary transactions facilitated via the traditional financial structure

(Tucker, 2014, p. 13). In brief, Bitcoin's appeal to some is derived from the non-traditional nature of the decentralized, peer-to-peer network, in which blockchain processes circumvent government involvement, and transacting in this form of cryptocurrency may allow for some measure of anonymity to those involved. As there are still means by which U.S. government has efforted to conduct digital investigations to determine network actors involved in blockchain processes that were involved in acts of criminality, the identity aspects may be more aptly termed as reflecting pseudo-anonymity.

Bitcoin may provide system actors with increased opportunities to become engaged within the market and this prospect may be especially beneficial to those negatively affected by the sometimes prohibitive nature of traditional financial institutions. This includes the possibility that those using Bitcoin as a payment system can avoid being restricted by time or geographical constraints associated with conventional means used to conduct transactions. On some level, Bitcoin may have the potential to globally compete with the traditional banking industry in part because transactions via this form of cryptocurrency can be rapidly facilitated without restrictions that are temporal (i.e. limitations imposed by having to adhere to regular business hours) or geographical (i.e. physical location provisions not required for use) as long as parties have access to the Internet (Parveen and Alajmi, 2019, p. 3). More broadly speaking, this form of cryptocurrency has the potential to create "financial access for countries with underdeveloped financial sectors" that can serve to provide alternatives to international banking systems (Parveen and Alajmi, 2019, p. 3). Bitcoin as a payment system has the potential to appeal to interested parties from both "poor countries without vast banking infrastructures" and "developed countries" (Tucker, 2014, p. 13). This broadly focused appeal from a nation standpoint is due in part to many perceived positive qualities attributed to Bitcoin garnering some measure of interest to users, including the fact that a third party is not required to facilitate the transfer, exchanges are "nearly costless," there is certainty in the quantities available of this form of cryptocurrency, and that it is reflective of key qualifications expected of money (i.e. durability, fungibility, etc.) (Tucker, 2014, p. 13). In general, a nation that has an unstable financial and economic system may be buoyed in these domains by the influx of Bitcoin that is more stable than existing fiat currency. On a more individual level, the flexibility provided by Bitcoin can allow for users to engage in fiscal activities such as those associated with facilitating purchases outside of the limits of traditional hours of operation, and this type of cryptocurrency has also proven to have an increasingly global reach, helping to overcome geographical limitations that may otherwise limit economic participation. Bitcoin may

182 Cryptocurrency, Bitcoin, and the Concept of Money

enhance economic equity by providing individuals alternative access to fiscal tools necessary to participate in a variety of transactional activities. Here, an individual may choose to transact with cryptocurrency such as Bitcoin instead of relying on traditional financial institutions, in which interactions include various logistical hurdles and impose greater costs to facilitate this process. As noted in the previous chapter, at present cryptocurrency such as Bitcoin may still be subject to involvement of traditional financial institutions to some degree (i.e. banks, credit cards, etc.) because the establishment of a crypto account and subsequent crypto purchases requires an initial funding of some manner of fiat currency. In this case, individuals may still be somewhat reliant on traditional financial institutions when setting up crypto accounts, but once this occurs the potential benefits associated with utilizing cryptocurrency may be enjoyed during transactions. This includes that, unlike a savings account or checking account, cryptocurrency does not require that an individual establish a minimum balance in order to become engaged in a wide assortment of market transactions within the economy. Additionally, high costs associated with fiat monetary exchange rates are comparatively negligible for cryptocurrency and, due to the decentralized nature, a third party is not required to facilitate the cryptocurrency transactional dynamics. Lastly, Bitcoin is appealing to many users because cryptocurrency is not subject to traditional supply-oriented inflation rates that are attributed to fiat currency, which may affect its overall value and levels of trust in its usage to some degree.

In various economically oriented events, Bitcoin's systemic qualities may provide advantages that allow for this form of cryptocurrency to serve as a rival to established financial institutional options, such as those associated with banks and credit cards. Relatedly, Bitcoin may provide an array of benefits regarding transactions facilitated with this form of cryptocurrency that are attractive to both venders and consumers alike. When compared to the traditional banking industry, Bitcoin transactions reflect markedly lower fees that can prove fiscally beneficial to small business and individuals the world over (Parveen and Alajmi, 2019, p. 3). Bitcoin can also be a more attractive option than facilitating purchases via credit-card purchases for small businesses because of the lower transaction costs, elimination of the possibility that a customer may reverse payments after purchases, and significantly quicker turnaround times for payouts (Tu and Meredith, 2015, p. 289). Bitcoin also provides a unique advantage over traditional payments systems regarding the ability of this form of cryptocurrency to allow for transactions in denominations that were previously unavailable. In this regard, the fact that Bitcoin provides allowances for micropayments is oft considered to be a very appealing aspect of this form of cryptocurrency (Turpin, 2014; Luther, 2016; Peters et al., 2016;

Lansky, 2018; Parino, Beiró and Gauvin, 2018). Bitcoin may be an especially intriguing option in transactions as Bitcoin is able to be broken down into eight decimal places through micropayments (Turpin, 2014; Luther, 2016). Ultimately, micropayments allow for transactions that can "be transmitted in amounts previously not possible before Bitcoin" (Turpin, 2014, p. 366). When compared to more traditional forms of payments such as credit cards, Bitcoin offers a number of benefits that are attractive to both venders and consumers. Venders would appreciate the possibility that Bitcoin would provide some measure of fiscal freedom, because this form of cryptocurrency reflects lower transactions costs than traditional payment means such as credit cards. In relation, the irreversibility of Bitcoin transactions would be viewed as beneficial to vendors because, unlike with credit cards, the consumer is unable to reverse the purchase of goods and services. The irreversibility dynamic associated with Bitcoin provides vendors with a greater degree of confidence in the dependability of each sale. Relatedly, consumers may appreciate the advantages derived from Bitcoin, such as the savings that may be provided based on micropayments and the increased ability of those underserved by traditional financial institutions to become involved economically.

As one of the key benefits attributed to Bitcoin usage is a potential retention of savings stemming from transactions fees that are lower than those associated with traditional financial institutions, it will be helpful to further expand on dynamics associated with this process. The cryptocurrency transaction fees are applicable to a wide range of activities, which includes the relatively basic task of "sending a cryptocurrency or digital asset" to a recipient and more complex endeavors such as utilizing a decentralized application (or DApp) to facilitate loans (Bitcoin.com, 2022, paragraph 1). In addition, charges for transactions involving Bitcoin or Ethereum are paid in that specific form of cryptocurrency because "transaction fees are paid in a blockchain's native cryptoasset" (Bitcoin.com, 2022, paragraph 1). The nature of the task being performed can affect the transaction fee in that facilitating "complicated actions cost more" than less complex activities (Bitcoin.com, 2022, paragraph 1). It is also important to observe that "different blockchains have lower or higher transaction fees for similar actions" (Bitcoin.com, 2022, paragraph 1). DeJesus (2022, paragraph 3) notes that ordinarily when "Bitcoin is involved in a transaction—making a payment using Bitcoin, buying Bitcoin, etc.—transaction fees will be charged." DeJesus (2022, paragraph 3) explains that "the data volume of the transaction and the speed at which the user wants their transaction completed" are two key considerations capable of influencing the value of the fees for transacting with Bitcoin. In August of 2022, the medium for transactions fees associated with Bitcoin was "0.000044 BTC, or $0.957" (DeJesus, 2022, paragraph 4). Between August 2021 and August 2022, the transaction fees for Bitcoin varied "from less than $1 to nearly $5," while in April of 2021 the medium price exceeded $60 (DeJesus, 2022, paragraph 4). Leonard and Bottorff (2022, paragraph 1) note that "the average credit card processing fee ranges between 1.5% and 3.5%" of the value of each transaction. Leonard and Bottorff (2022, paragraph 2) add that "credit card processing fees are the fees that a business must pay every time it accepts a credit card payment." The transaction fees associated with Bitcoin are fulfilled in corresponding cryptocurrency attributed to that brand, there are variances in payment fees based on the complexity of tasks being performed, and transaction fees may vary for the same task based on the cryptocurrency in use. These dynamics associated with Bitcoin transaction fees contribute to better understanding the nature of operational dynamics attributed to cryptocurrency usage. Comparatively, the transaction fees charged by credit-card companies are generally higher than those associated with Bitcoin. As such, this may eventually cause vendors to more frequently consider allowing patrons to use cryptocurrency such as Bitcoin when purchasing goods and services. Something to consider is that there is possibly a concern regarding the relative volatility of transactions fees ($1 vs. $60) that if permitted to persist may be unappealing to both vendors and consumers, especially if the costs longitudinally fluctuate too highly. Ultimately, the promise of reliably low transaction fees associated with cryptocurrency, such as Bitcoin, would most assuredly serve as a boon to the acceptance process on behalf of all parties involved in economic activities.

The Cryptocurrency Industry: Volatility of Value and a Potential Role in the Stock Market

The potential volatility of the assessed fiscal worth of Bitcoin may be viewed positively by some, in the same way that investors willingly engage in the uncertainty of the value of equity shares traded on the stock market for publicly owned corporations. Although there may be some questions regarding the volatility of the value of Bitcoin at present that may be unattractive to some potential users, investors may view this dynamic as attractive in the same manner that provides fiscal motivation to invest in the stock market (Tu and Meredith, 2015, p. 292). In this sense, Bitcoin being less stable in value longitudinally than U.S. fiat currency may serve as an appealing attribute to those that are keen on being involved in high-risk/high-reward investments. Interestingly, although Bitcoin is not representative of official legal tender, this form of cryptocurrency has its value comparatively framed in the context of the U.S. dollar. Since its inception in 2009, a single Bitcoin has been valued in U.S. dollars at as little as $0 and as much as \$68,789.63 in 2021 (Coinbase.com, 2022d). Despite being volatile in price longitudinally, Bitcoin is increasingly becoming viewed by some as a viable investment opportunity and is starting to draw some measure of attention as a speculative venture in this regard. Although still yet to reach the status of fiat currency backed by the U.S. government, providing the value of Bitcoin in U.S. dollars is a fiscal measuring stick that can conceptually create some measure of legitimacy for this form of cryptocurrency, which may help to advance its acceptance of wider scale use on a societal level. Further representation of this legitimizing process in progress is that Bitcoin is beginning to have a presence in well-established financial institutions such as U.S. stock exchanges. At present, U.S. stock exchanges such as the New York Stock Exchange (NYSE) introduced a unique tool called the NYSE Bitcoin Index (NYXBT: https://www.nyse.com/quote/index/NYXBT), which potentially provides further legitimacy regarding the value of Bitcoin in U.S. dollars. When the NYSE Bitcoin Index was developed in 2015, the transaction information from Coinbase was used to report on how the "NYXBT will represent the daily US dollar value of one bitcoin at 4pm (BST) and will be published on the NYSE Global Index Feed (GIF)" (Perez, 2015, paragraph 1). The fact that the NYSE made efforts to provide data on the value of Bitcoin in U.S. dollars, and that there has been a recent emergence of crypto-related stocks broadly available, may indicate that stock exchanges are beginning to set the stage to more directly play an increased role in the cryptocurrency industry in the future. This is a speculative opportunity that, before coming to full fruition on a widescale basis, may require adjustments on behalf of stock exchanges and corresponding government oversight entities alike to be better able to accommodate this newly emerging investment opportunity. In relation, for this to occur there will need to correspondingly be U.S. policy endeavors to create greater levels of transparency and accountability in the cryptocurrency industry to allow for more appropriate levels of consumer protections, which are traditionally expected for stock exchange transactions. For example, the U.S. Congress enacted legislation that created federal agencies and corresponding statutory guidelines, by which consumer protections are facilitated including the Securities and Exchange Commission (SEC: https://www.sec.gov/) and the Federal Trade Commission (FTC https://www.ftc.gov/). Information regarding the creation of the SEC and the FTC will be provided in the next chapter, that is dedicated to assessing examples of how the federal government has begun to develop policy intended to address the field of cryptocurrency. Among the many aspects to be highlighted at that time is the role that the Securities and Exchange Commission plays in regulating the stock market and educating potential investors.

186 Cryptocurrency, Bitcoin, and the Concept of Money

At present, cryptocurrency such as Bitcoin being linked in value to U.S. dollars and advertising this value via established financial institutions can be likened to serving as something of a guerilla marketing tactic. In general, guerilla marketing is a technique used by smaller, less established entities in an industry that leverages innovative and low-cost marketing techniques to compete with larger, more conventional entities operating in the same market. Here, providing a value in U.S. dollars for Bitcoin, and having such advertised via the NYSE, draws consideration as a guerilla marketing tactic allowing for a niche industry, such as cryptocurrency, to leverage the promotional power of a stalwart of the financial establishment to be perceived more legitimately by system actors. Interestingly, at this stage of its development, the cryptocurrency industry marketing efforts could be considered to reflect a blend of guerilla marketing tactics, such as leveraging the NYSE's efforts to advertise on behalf of the industry and grassroots word-of-mouth dialogue among users, and traditional marketing tactics associated with large-scale advertising campaigns, such as naming rights for Crypto.com Arena where the Los Angeles Lakers of the NBA play home games (https://www.cryptoarena.com/). Despite the crypto-winter of 2022, in which cryptocurrency was widely devalued as an industry, crypto-stock may potentially become an increasingly more viable consideration for those involved in the stock market. Additionally, the encroachment of crypto-stock into stock market exchanges, evidenced by recent listing on venues such as NASDAQ (https://www.nasdaq.com/market-activity/cryptocurrency), has provided an opportunity for this industry to begin to establish a foothold in the market. In relation, it is possible to invest in entities that deal in cryptocurrency, such as Coinbase Global, Inc. (COIN), which is available on the U.S. stock market through the National Association of Securities Dealers Automated Quotations (NASDAQ: https://www.nasdaq.com/market-activity/stocks/coin) and the New York Stock Exchange (NYSE: https://www.nyse.com/quote/XNGS:COIN). Coinbase Global, Inc. is a publicly traded entity originally headquartered in San Francisco, U.S.A. (before recently opting for a remote-first environment), which is one of the largest global cryptocurrency exchange platforms (https://www.coinbase.com/). According to Coinbase (2022b), this entity indicates that "approximately 103 million verified users, 14,500 institutions, and 245,000 ecosystem partners in over 100 countries trust Coinbase to easily and securely invest, spend, save, earn, and use crypto." The wide assortment of clients that utilize Coinbase domestically and internationally reflects well the mission of this cryptocurrency exchange platform, which is as follows:

Everyone deserves access to financial services that can help empower them to create a better life for themselves and their families. If the world economy ran on a common set of standards that could not be manipulated by any company or country, the world would be a more fair and free place, and human progress would accelerate.

Source: Coinbase (2022c)

The future of stock market investing for cryptocurrency is uncertain, as this is a newly emerging industry, but should this prospective opportunity become a more widely accepted practice it will provide a rich field of research regarding financial markets and public-policy responses. This will be one of many challenges to consider for businesses that will be involved in facilitating Bitcoin investments, consumers that are interested in pursuing this opportunity, and government entities that will be responsible for regulating the expansion of Bitcoin as an investment opportunity in this context.

Bitcoin: Scalability and Digital Wallets

Bitcoin's global presence and proliferation in the longitudinal sense is in part directly related to the economic concept referred to as scalability, which affects inclusiveness and participation dynamics. According to the Merriam-Webster dictionary (2022), scalable is defined as "capable of being easily expanded or upgraded on demand." Daj (2017, p. 221) notes that decentralized cryptocurrency use of technologically innovative computational means (i.e. distributed ledgers, blockchain, etc.) may result in system scalability issues, due in part to the requirements for "high computing power" and "energy consumption," yielding a somewhat insular design capable of limiting participation to some degree. The computational and energy demands associated with blockchain technology used in Bitcoin transactions is one that may raise some legitimate concerns regarding the scalability of this popular form of cryptocurrency. The necessary computational power of CPUs and the sources of readily available, affordable energy needed to perform such acts would serve as factors in determining whether Bitcoin is able to sustain a level of scalability over extended periods of time. If CPU and energy demands needed to facilitate innovative elements associated with computationally oriented tasks are routinely too high, then this may impact the degree of scalability of cryptocurrencies, which would render Bitcoin as less viable for widescale blockchain participation. In relation, the high energy consumption and expansive CPU power for a computer(s) that is required to participate in keeping records and verifying transactions involving Bitcoin via blockchain is somewhat exclusionary in nature. Therefore, these prohibitive participatory requirements associated with blockchain processes may serve as a natural barrier to entry that may prohibit those without access to such to be disadvantaged or excluded

188 Cryptocurrency, Bitcoin, and the Concept of Money

entirely from directly engaging in verification procedures. Whereas this reality may create scalability concerns regarding participatory dynamics in blockchain processes, system actors involved in usage of Bitcoin for a variety of transactional purposes in the market would remain unencumbered in this context.

In addition to the scalability dilemma potentially affecting widescale participation in blockchain verification processes for Bitcoin, the usage of digital wallets by consumers may add a different type of concern as it relates to securely transacting in this form of cryptocurrency. The previously discussed anonymity and double-spending protections associated with Bitcoin provide security-based benefits that may be appealing to a wide range of parties interested in being economically involved through this form of cryptocurrency. Although considered to be relatively private and secure, blockchain used in authenticating cryptocurrency may be subject to criminality in instances where nefarious participants are successful in carrying out a double-spending scheme (i.e. 51 percent attack). In addition, in an attempt to facilitate a high-tech, digital theft it is possible for sophisticated, technically proficient criminals to target the virtual wallet (i.e. digital wallet) in which an owner of Bitcoin may store this form of cryptocurrency. In this case, the digital wallet likely serves as an easier target than having to leverage sufficient CPU processing power and to access necessary levels of energy that would be required to successfully complete a double-spending attack. The owner of the crypto digital wallet, sometimes referred to as a non-custodial wallet, is ostensibly a more attractive target than attempting to perpetrate a blockchain attack resulting in double-spending, which is a much more complex, technically proficient endeavor. For example, nefarious actors may utilize an emailed phishing scheme to obtain account details and a password that would provide the opportunity to steal the contents of the owner's digital wallet. Ultimately, the process is far more easily facilitated by attackers opting to target the owner of a digital wallet than attempting to strike at more secure means used to matriculate cryptocurrency such as Bitcoin, which would be more complicated from a technical standpoint.

Bitcoin: Is it Money?

There was a discussion in an earlier chapter regarding the three basic characteristics that contribute to defining money, and this information will be further expanded in this section as it relates to cryptocurrency such as Bitcoin. This includes that one of the key characteristics often associated with defining money is whether an item is accepted as a medium of exchange by system actors operating within the economy. In essence, the process of determining if a unit of something is to be accepted as a medium of exchange requires that there be shared societal acceptance of being valued as a basis of transactional enterprises in the market. In the past, this relational dynamic was the foundation by which items such as commodities came to be accepted as a medium of exchange, in part because there was a direct utility associated with each that led to an increased perception of value in transacting and would ultimately lead to wider demand for usage by system actors. If this perceived value of a commodity can affect its ability to be used as a medium of exchange, then items capable of serving as money in this dynamic reach this status procedurally over time based on the collective perception of system actors. Outside of the minimal value of the metal now used to produce fiat coins, the stand-alone value of money in the modern era is divergently determined as tangible currency may have a worth that is partly measured in terms of its ability to be exchanged for other goods and services. Furthermore, fiat paper money is lacking in traditional functional utility, as tangible bills provide no purpose unto themselves outside of the role in transactional usage. To potentially garner consideration to meet this basic characteristic of money, Bitcoin in this context must reach a level of societal acceptance in that it is valued in a manner that would allow for it to be considered as a viable medium of exchange on behalf of system actors, despite lacking in worth outside of use in transactional events.

The capacity of cryptocurrency, such as Bitcoin, to act as a legitimate medium of exchange is still subject to great scrutiny and this possibility is expanded on here. Despite not being created and backed by government like fiat currency, cryptocurrency potentially has a role within the modern financial system in that it, to various degrees, may seem capable to begin to behave like money in relation to three basic requisite criteria (i.e. accepted medium of exchange, unit of account comparable to market goods, and able to store value reliably). Firstly, the increasing acceptance of Bitcoin as a viable medium of exchange by which transactions are facilitated have provided some measure of potential for this form of cryptocurrency to be classified as money based on this singular characteristic. In this sense, the levels of acceptance of Bitcoin in having a measure of functionality to serve as money, since being incepted in 2009, make it possible for this type of cryptocurrency to slowly permeate the broader economic system. The second criterion of money is based on understanding if Bitcoin is able to be used to establish a comparative worth of goods and services to be transacted for. In this regard, Bitcoin has begun to establish a fiscal foothold in the broader market that may allow for greater consideration as money. Similarly, Bitcoin being attached to a value in U.S. fiat currency may provide some measure of assistance in this process over time. In that, the value of Bitcoin in U.S. dollars is able to be used to measure the worth of items to be transacted for in the market in the similar manner that fiat currency would be used in this respect. However, Bitcoin only partially qualifies as money in these regards, because there are still insufficient levels of opportunity to broadly transact for comparably valued goods and services by utilizing this form of cryptocurrency. Thirdly, Bitcoin has an established, albeit volatile, value in U.S. dollars. The third criterion is where there is some additional concern in Bitcoin's ability to be considered money, as there is a level of volatility regarding the value of this form of cryptocurrency since its inception in 2009. Thus far, the attribute of worth stability may remain just outside the reach of Bitcoin's ability to function as money based on the criterion associated with relative avoidance of value volatility. Although Bitcoin is making inroads in many aspects of the economic market that will illicit strong consideration for use as a medium of exchange, this form of cryptocurrency has yet to meet fully and consistently all three of the discussed criteria here that are used to determine whether something is classified as money.

The case of classifying Bitcoin as money in the future may be strengthened by expanding the discussion to include additional criteria that can contribute to this process. For Bitcoin to be considered a viable means by which to facilitate various market-oriented events it must be capable of achieving, and maintaining, a measure of functionality proving capable of having a collectively agreed upon use as money in the modern economic system. In brief, Bitcoin has shown some additional promise in some regards by reflecting money qualities associated with portability (i.e. able to be used in transactions by a person with a device connected to the Internet), divisibility (i.e. value able to be broken down into eight decimal points during transactions), fungible (i.e. increasing, albeit still limited, acceptable use for exchange of goods and service), durable (i.e. non-tangible Bitcoin cannot be destroyed in the traditional sense), and scarcity (i.e. limited total number of Bitcoin allowable). The idea of Bitcoin's scarcity potentially affecting its value, and the role that supply-oriented limits play in influencing the capacity of this form of cryptocurrency to qualify as money based on this criterion, deserves some additional analysis. The number of Bitcoin in circulation has risen steadily since being created, on January 2, 2009, to 19,231,313.244 on January 10, 2023 (Blockchain.com, 2022). Bitcoin is considered to be scarce in part because it has been decided in advance that this form of cryptocurrency will never exceed an intentionally created hard cap of 21 million coins to be mined, which is projected to take over 100 years to reach (Lee et al., 2015; Richter, Kraus and Bouncken, 2015; Ciaian, Rajcaniova, and Kancs, 2016; Peters, Chapelle, and Panayi, 2016; Boxerman and Schwerin, 2017; Dumitrescu, 2017; Berentsen and Schar, 2018).

Relatedly, limiting Bitcoin to 21 million coins is intended to play a role that can protect against supply-oriented inflation, which is intended to serve as a natural barrier to help safeguard the value of this form of cryptocurrency (Tu and Meredith, 2015;Wenker, 2014; Peters, Chapelle, and Panayi, 2016; Dumitrescu, 2017). Richter, Kraus, and Bouncken (2015, p. 580) note that "due to the fixed number of bitcoin, a devaluation of the currency cannot occur in terms of the classical multi-production of money." Angel and McCabe (2015, p. 606) explain that "as the number of bitcoins that have been issued increases, the relative difficulty of mining bitcoins will also increase." Angel and McCabe (2015, p. 606) add that "there is a theoretical limit of 21 million bitcoins that will ever be issued. This limit prevents a government or monetary authority from inflating the currency." A key appeal of Bitcoin is that it has a "low inflation risk" in part because the number of Bitcoin is "finite" as there will only ever be possible to mine "21 million Bitcoin," which is the pre-established cap on this form of cryptocurrency (Ngai, 2014, p. 36). Ngai (2014, p. 36) further notes that because of such "the value will not be eroded due to inflation and the purchasing power will remain static." Those placing faith in Bitcoin do so in part because they believe that "Bitcoin's limited supply will result in deflation" and are "convinced that its value will forever increase." (Berentsen and Schar, 2018, p. 7). Since being introduced in 2009, the value of Bitcoin in U.S. dollars has been variable in nature and has increased considerably on a longitudinal basis since initially being worth $0. By capping the lifetime limit to 21 million Bitcoins, it is believed that this may serve as a preventive measure against supply-oriented inflation and in this context doing so can contribute to limiting the volatility in value for this type of cryptocurrency. However, it is important to reiterate that although the value of Bitcoin in U.S. dollars is believed to largely be inflation resistant in this context there is still evidence that this form of cryptocurrency has fluctuated considerably since its inception in 2009. Whereas the internally generated technical designs, creating a hard cap on the total number of Bitcoin to be produced, may serve to limit availability in the effort to combat supply-oriented inflation, the value of this form of cryptocurrency has still managed to reflect a certain measure of value volatility since being created. In this case, efforts to limit instability traditionally derived from supply-oriented inflation may be insufficient as a stand-alone means by which to reduce, or eliminate, value volatility, indicating that, like with fiat money, there is a wider scope of system stimuli that may contribute to the continued fluctuations in Bitcoin's worth in U.S. dollars that has been evidenced during its lifecycle.

At present, the relative lack of stability in the value of Bitcoin in U.S. dollars remains a significant impediment to its ability to reach all the qualities of money discussed earlier. Relatedly, it may understandably be

192 Cryptocurrency, Bitcoin, and the Concept of Money

difficult for system actors to trust Bitcoin, when establishing the value in U.S. dollars is a process that is both mercurial and mysterious in nature. In addition, public confidence in Bitcoin's viability for use in various transactional circumstances can be directly affected by perception of a combination of factors such as whether this form of virtual currency is user friendly, if appeal is diminished as an investment or in market transactions by being overly regulated by government and the relative ability to facilitate Bitcoin transactions with minimal risk (i.e. avoid loss of Bitcoin, no personal information breaches, etc.). In addition, confidence in the cryptocurrency industry may be significantly diminished by continued publicizing of high-profile cases such as Mt. Gox and FTX, which have portrayed this industry in an extremely unfavorable light. Ultimately, public confidence is an amalgamation of singular perceptions, based on a wide range of factors, that contribute to either building or diminishing faith in the usage of Bitcoin to perform various functions in the economy. In relation, public perception can affect the evolution of Bitcoin and influence the level of proliferation of the usage of this form of non-fiat virtual currency on a global level. Although progress has been made in meeting many of the criteria traditionally used to determine whether something qualifies as money, there is still some ways to go before enough trust is placed in Bitcoin to allow for widescale societal acceptance in this regard. Additionally, this form of cryptocurrency is still classified as non-fiat virtual currency, regardless of the degree of acceptance held by system actors that Bitcoin may eventually reach, further complicating its understanding and potential use in the economy.

To be sure, widescale acceptance of cryptocurrency, such as Bitcoin, to be commonly used in exchanges within the broader economy would require achieving greater levels of support in numerous avenues of society. In this, Bitcoin would be required to overcome system support that has created longitudinal inertia for the usage of existing fiat currencies in the economy. Serving as a key impediment to the proliferation of Bitcoin as a universally accepted medium of exchange is the "incumbent-monies problem," which in this context essentially indicates that participants in an economic system are deeply vested in the use of traditional fiat currency (Luther, 2016, p. 398). In relation, Bitcoin would have to overcome the many advantages held by incumbent monies associated with both "switching costs" and "network effects" (Luther, 2016, p. 398). Switching costs require comprehensive updates to a multitude of physical equipment, which traditionally handle incumbent money to facilitate transactions (i.e. vending machines, ATMs, etc.), and to conventional means in a wide array of settings that customarily reflects the use of fiat currency (i.e. menus at restaurants, records of business transactions, etc.) (Luther, 2016, p. 398).

In addition to the fiscal costs of implementing system changes of a physical nature when introducing Bitcoin on a wide societal scale, there would also be educational efforts needed on behalf of system actors regarding exactly how to "calculate in terms of a new unit of account" (Luther, 2016, p. 398). Because such broad changes on a societal level would be needed to accommodate transitioning from incumbent money to Bitcoin, this form of cryptocurrency would be required to reflect significant benefits comparatively to justify the time, effort, and fiscal cost associated with undertaking such as full-scale integration (Luther, 2016, p. 398). To better compete with incumbent money in the economy, cryptocurrency such as Bitcoin would require a vast, nuanced societal transition that would be both logistical and educational in nature. If the structural dynamics and educational efforts are established, then this may contribute to the network effect that is associated with the acceptance of cryptocurrency such as Bitcoin. Luther (2016, p. 398) explains that circumstances in which "the value of a good or service" is directly contingent upon the aggregate numbers of users epitomizes a network effect (Luther, 2016, p. 398). In the context of understanding the applicability of this conceptualization to "mediums of exchange," the network effect essentially requires wide acceptance by system participants so that use of money is essentially universal to complete transactions (Luther, 2016, p. 398). As it relates to surmounting the network effect, an emerging Bitcoin also must overcome historical societal preference and the corresponding institutionalized frameworks supporting the status of incumbent monies, which had long-ago reached widescale levels of acceptance on a longitudinal basis (Luther, 2016, p. 398). Switching costs include making changes that require funding widescale retrofitting needed when integrating a new monetary entrant into the economic system, such as Bitcoin, and the time, energy, and effort on a societal basis required to educate potential users regarding navigating the emerging framework. In the context of determining the scope of Bitcoin's acceptance, the network effect is directly linked with the sheer numbers of those using this form of cryptocurrency to complete a wide array of economically oriented transactions. For a cryptocurrency such as Bitcoin to be considered for use—in conjunction with, or as a replacement for, extant money firmly embedded within the broader modern system—there must significant enough numbers of participants willing to utilize this emerging non-fiat virtual currency across a wide spectrum of activities. In sum, the potential of newly emerging forms of currency such as Bitcoin to ascend to relevancy requires widespread application within society (i.e. network effects) and a process by which transitioning to use is deemed warranted on merit (i.e. switching costs). Bitcoin's acceptance for use in various economic events will involve overcoming a number of societal dynamics that are presently skewed to

194 Cryptocurrency, Bitcoin, and the Concept of Money

favor incumbent money. In that, fiat currency meets all the aforementioned characteristics of money including being widely accepted as the medium of exchange by members of the public and private sectors as the means by which to transact. Additionally, the economy is established in a manner that is supportive of fiat currency, which further reinforces legal tender as the primary medium of exchange. As the most popular and highly valued cryptocurrency, Bitcoin's early success may create a similar advantage over all other types of crypto that are attempting to become accepted as viable for use in the U.S. economy. This dynamic is one that is deserved of further observation in the coming years and may provide interesting comparative analysis to the growing field of cryptocurrency. Ultimately, for Bitcoin to be capable of competing with incumbent money, there will be a need for societal trust that translates to broad changes so that the economy is far more cryptocurrency friendly. One way that this could be established is through government efforts designed to create greater understanding of cryptocurrency and to create a broad regulatory framework that is capable of engendering confidence in a more expansive role for Bitcoin in the economy.

Closing Remarks

Since Nakamoto's Bitcoin white paper was issued in 2008, the creation, growth, and proliferation of Bitcoin throughout the global economy has been considerable despite its relative short lifespan thus far. This rapid rise in levels of popularity is evidenced in part by the fact that, among the vast field of cryptocurrency brands, Bitcoin is consistently the highest valued in U.S. dollars and has long enjoyed ownership of the largest market share in the industry. The role of cryptocurrency such as Bitcoin in the U.S. economy is yet to be fully determined, and its future will ultimately be dependent, in part, upon the levels of acceptance by system actors in relation to a broad scope of considerations. As was the case historically regarding items used as mediums of exchange, in which transactional acceptance was often socially contrived based on mutual convenience, the levels of trust in Bitcoin by system actors to some degree may play a role in helping to determine a potential role within the economy. In relation, it is plausible that cryptocurrency such as Bitcoin may provide a wide range of benefits to a plethora of system actors that may determine whether such non-fiat, virtual currency will be useful as a viable medium of exchange in various transactional circumstances in the U.S. economy. This includes that Bitcoin's usage may be preferred by venders and consumers alike, because when compared to traditional payments systems like credit cards this form of cryptocurrency generally reflects lower transaction costs. This is due in part because third parties are not involved in facilitating the transactions, so associated fees levied are considerably lower during the purchase of goods or services. This can benefit vendors and consumers alike if savings derived from Bitcoin transaction fees are able to be shared by all parties. The usage of Bitcoin may provide unique benefits to venders, which may yield some measure of support for this cryptocurrency to become increasingly embedded in common use societally. Vendors may prefer Bitcoin to facilitate transactions because, unlike credit-card purchases, the consumer is unable to reverse transactions when it comes to this form of cryptocurrency. This protects the vendor from purchases being canceled by disingenuous patrons seeking to falsely claim credit-card transactions are fraudulent or are dissatisfied with the goods/services, demanding a refund. If Bitcoin allows vendors to quickly process transactions at a lower rate and to promptly receive the payments, then this form of cryptocurrency would most assuredly be more appealing on those accounts than using competing traditional means, such as credit cards, which would include longer wait times, higher transactions fees, and purchase reversibility. Bitcoin may provide greater fiscal opportunity to a wider audience allowing vendors and consumers alike to take advantage of several benefits derived from utilizing cryptocurrency. Doing so may make it possible to create greater levels of inclusiveness in the economy, especially as it relates to the ability of those generally underserved by traditional institutions (i.e. banks, credit cards, etc.).

The development of trust in Bitcoin for use in various economic circumstances will also depend in part on the perception by system actors that this form of cryptocurrency is reliable and safe. In relation, it is important to recognize that blockchain technology serves as a technological design that works to enhance efforts to provide greater levels of security to those choosing to use Bitcoin. Should dishonest participants gain the advantage in blockchain verification processes, then it would be possible for a false chain of events to be approved that could potentially result in digitally savvy theft of the Bitcoin during said transaction event. To help prevent such an occurrence, the majority of those harnessing the collective power of networked CPUs are expected to act in good faith and avoid attempting to attack nodes to falsely verify an inaccurate chain. Although security concerns attributed to cryptocurrency are valid, the usage of blockchain technology to facilitate Bitcoin transactions provides a proven measure of protection to active participants, which can enhance levels of trust widely held by system actors. This includes that blockchain's peer-to-peer transfer design to confirm proof-of-work uses timestamping and collective endorsement measures by network participants during the process, by which to verify the existence of Bitcoin and corresponding transactions.

The cooperatively dynamic means to facilitate the verification process is intended to consistently serve to overcome the double-spending problem to prevent nefarious actors attempting to create a circumstance in which the same unit of currency was duplicated and spent twice. The application of confirmation lags during the process also increases the ability of those participating in blockchain to prevent the success of those seeking to conduct a 51 percent attack and to largely prevent such, which would increase the effectiveness of Bitcoin in practice. Of great import to the integrity of this design in practice, blockchain technology requires honest participants utilizing vast CPU power and harnessing high energy consumption in a collective effort to verify transactions associated with Bitcoin. Although there are a number of established means intentionally designed to help protect against unscrupulous blockchain participants seeking to fraudulently obtain Bitcoin, there are also incentives derived from rewards that help to promote honesty among those participating in such verification processes. The honesty of miners is achieved in part by providing rewards such as transaction fees or payment in Bitcoins as long as there is availability based on the duration of the artificial hard cap. In relation, those participating are incentivized in part by creating a reward-based dynamic, in which the initial transaction in a newly created node results in the creation of a coin that is then placed into the system. Essentially, Bitcoin applies blockchain technology as the means by which participants work cooperatively to verify recent transactions and to generate new coins for circulation. The mining process in which new Bitcoins are created and placed in circulation within the system through the verification process utilizes CPU computational power to solve a complex mathematical equation. The proof-of-work dynamic allows a miner that solves this mathematical equation first to earn the rewarded Bitcoin. By successfully and consistently incentivizing the mining process, system actors may come to trust the usage of blockchain to verify Bitcoin transactions, which would correspondingly enhance the confidence in this form of cryptocurrency as a medium of exchange in the economy. Together, the natural system protections attributed to blockchain technology and presence of incentives to reward honest participants serves to help maintain the integrity of this form of cryptocurrency in use.

As there have been slowly increasing levels of acceptance on behalf of some system actors for the use of cryptocurrency as a medium of exchange in various transactional opportunities, and there are some measurables associated with Bitcoin regarding being valued in U.S. dollars that would allow for comparative worth to be assigned to goods/services available in the market, there may be some measure of initial validity in considering this type of non-fiat virtual currency as being capable of meeting these two basic characteristics of money. However, there would need to be much greater opportunities in the future for system actors to use Bitcoin to transact with comparably valued items in the economy to meet these two basic characteristics of money more fully. In addition, cryptocurrency such as Bitcoin is presently subject to perceptions of volatility associated with significant fluctuations in value that have persisted since its inception in 2009, indicating that it may fall somewhat short of this third basic classification of money. Although boasting inherent protections against traditional supply-oriented inflation, which are derived from the established hard cap of total coins to be produced, the apparent volatility of Bitcoin may understandably create some issues regarding the ability of system actors to fully trust in its usage in conjuncture with, or instead of, legal tender, as relative stability regarding value is a key attribute associated with money in practice. Without some further combination of internally and externally generated means that make it consistently possible to attain a more predictably consistent measure of equilibrium in being valued in U.S. dollars, Bitcoin may be unable to become more widely accepted by system actors as a means by which to legitimately facilitate various transactions in the market. This volatility in U.S. dollar value may still make Bitcoin a promising speculatory endeavor as it would be likened to risk–reward dynamics attributed to the stock market. However, the process of system actors developing the requisite levels of trust in cryptocurrency, such as Bitcoin, for widespread usage in the various activities within the economy may prove elusive should value volatility persist. In part, this is the premise that led to the more recent development of a specific type of cryptocurrency referred to as stablecoin. Stablecoin attempts to provide stability to the value of cryptocurrency by backing them with other reserve assets such as gold, Euros, or U.S. dollars.

The trust in Bitcoin is derived in part by its ability to be perceived as a safe and effective means by which system actors may transact in the economy. This process is presently underway as evidenced by the slow growth in the usage of Bitcoin in the broader U.S. economy as a means by which to become involved in various transactional events. The development of trust in Bitcoin by system actors is a major part of the equation behind the potential success in its ability to become more broadly accepted as a medium of exchange. Should this trust be developed and maintained, the other part of the equation that will contribute to the ability of Bitcoin to act as a medium of exchange in the market is that the system itself will have to accommodate this form of cryptocurrency. This includes greater acceptance of Bitcoin by system participants in a wider array of real-world circumstances so that this cryptocurrency is able to become functionally useful in the economy. In relation, Bitcoin may presently have an advantage over other forms of cryptocurrency in the economy as it relates to trust, brand

198 Cryptocurrency, Bitcoin, and the Concept of Money

name, and institutionalized means in the system to allow for wider usage in transactions. In sum, enhanced levels of societal trust in Bitcoin may create a path leading to its broader acceptance as a medium of exchange. However, the economic infrastructure would still require conceptual and physical retrofitting to some degree to accommodate Bitcoin usage in order for this form of cryptocurrency to become functionally viable as a medium of exchange.

There are other factors that may potentially affect whether Bitcoin is viewed as being viable for use in the U.S. economic system. For example, technology used to facilitate Bitcoin transactions require an immense amount of CPU power and energy to solve the complex mathematical equations used during verification processes through blockchain. As such, the high CPU and energy requirements may create a natural barrier to participation, preventing all those that may be interested from becoming involved in blockchain verification processes associated with Bitcoin. If participation in blockchain is viewed as being the domain of only a small group of technical elites, then this insular activity may cause some measure of distrust and feelings of alienation by those left out of the process based solely on technical limitations. Similarly, such an isolated process fails to lend itself to demystifying the slew of unknowns that many in society are concerned with about Bitcoin's existence, which can impede the progression of trust in this form of cryptocurrency. In relation, blockchain may further raise some questions regarding its ability to provide an entirely secure payment system. Although there are a number of systemic means that are capable of limiting theft, the blockchain technology used to ensure security for Bitcoin-related transactions is not entirely foolproof. It is also notable that Bitcoin theft may also be facilitated by way of a successful attack to a participant's digital wallet and by nefarious internal actors embezzling Bitcoin from the exchange company, respectively. Relatedly, recent high-profile failures of cryptocurrency exchanges will lend further credence to the groundswell of growing support for government to become more heavily involved in regulations of the cryptocurrency industry. This includes the recent clamoring from system actors for significant government intervention in this industry that resulted from the precipitous fall from grace on behalf of FTX, which caused this once third-largest cryptocurrency exchange to abruptly and surprisingly file for chapter 11 bankruptcy in November of 2022. Soon after that, the U.S. Justice Department issued an indictment to the CEO and founder of FTX, who allegedly committed various acts of illegality that included fraud, money laundering, and campaign finances offenses. Here, the efforts by the U.S. Justice Department represent an example in which public-sector intervention is required, in that it is the responsibility of government to take action in order to protect citizens from various types of harm. An item, such as Bitcoin, may initially be a socially contrived concept that comes to be considered for use as a medium of exchange, and a wide array of government actions can serve to help legitimize its existence in this context. The efforts on behalf of government can vary in scope, ranging from educational endeavors to enforcement of established regulatory guidelines that provide clarity and a structural template of expected actions to be applied to the field. In this way, government actions may simultaneously contribute to legitimizing the item in question and provide measures that work to establish levels of trust on behalf of society to catapult such to be more widely accepted by system actors as a viable medium of exchange.

By intentional design, cryptocurrency is created and regulated internally, so that the lifecycle of this non-fiat virtual currency exists largely outside the scope of government involvement. The fact that the lifecycle of cryptocurrency is insular and internally managed, to the point in which government involvement in this process is deliberately circumvented, may require careful consideration on behalf of public-sector decision makers moving forward to determine whether it will be permitted to achieve a greater measure of viability within the system. Relatedly, the usage of cryptocurrency such as Bitcoin by system actors to engage in various activities within the economy may serve to challenge the constitutional authority associated with Congress's exclusive role in officially shaping the permissive landscape of money, which may require specialized attention on behalf of government to address potential concerns stemming from this practice. In that, the U.S. Constitution provides Congress with exclusive domain regarding many aspects of fiat currency (i.e. coining, taxing, valuing, and preventing counterfeiting) and allows this branch of government to create all laws necessary and proper that are capable of addressing such. Here, the creation of fiat currency is within the purview of Congress, and Congress is expected to create policy that can address problems associated with legal tender that may arise in the society. This includes that Congress may wish to more aggressively regulate the cryptocurrency industry that, if left permitted to flourish unchecked, may increasingly serve as a direct threat to fiat money. Although Bitcoin was created in 2009 and is still in its infancy stages of development when compared to U.S. fiat money, any continued proliferation of this form of cryptocurrency places the importance of governmental intervention as an increasingly greater priority. The malleability of the system is an intentional design on behalf of the Framers of the U.S. Constitution, and this is an important component regarding the evolutionary nature of the regulatory environment in any area of public policy, including that associated with cryptocurrency. With this idea in mind, the next chapter will provide a discussion of the present regulatory

200 Cryptocurrency, Bitcoin, and the Concept of Money

environment in the United States and expand on the dynamic nature of policymaking efforts focused on the cryptocurrency industry at various levels of government in the American democracy.

References

Angel, J. J. & McCabe, D. (2015). The Ethics of Payments: Paper, Plastic, or Bitcoin? *Journal of Business Ethics*, *132*(3), 603–611. http://www.jstor.org/stable/24703614

Berentsen, A. & Schar, F. (2018). A Short Introduction to the World of Cryptocurrencies. *Federal Reserve Bank of St. Louis Review*, First Quarter, 1–16. https://doi.org/10.20955/r.2018.1-16

Bitcoin.com (2022). What are transaction fees? https://www.bitcoin.com/get-started/what-are-transactions-fees/

Blockchain.com (2022). Total Circulating Bitcoin. https://www.blockchain.com/explorer/charts/total-bitcoins

Böhme, R., Christin, N., Edelman, B., & Moore, T. (2015). Bitcoin: Economics, Technology, and Governance. *Journal of Economic Perspectives*, *29*(2), 213–238.

Boxerman, S. J. & Schwerin, M. F. (2017). Its Bark is Worse Than Its Bit(E). *Criminal Justice*, *31*(4), 10–15.

Ciaian, P., Rajcaniova, M., & Kancs, d'A. (2016). The digital agenda of virtual currencies: Can BitCoin become a global currency? *Information Systems and e-Business Management*, *14*, 883–919. https://doi.org/10.1007/s10257-016-0304-0

Chiu, J. & Koeppl, T., (2017). The Economics of Cryptocurrencies – Bitcoin and Beyond. *SSRN Electronic Journal*, September.

Coinbase (2022a). What is Bitcoin? https://www.coinbase.com/learn/crypto-basics/what-is-bitcoin

Coinbase (2022b). About Coinbase. https://www.coinbase.com/about

Coinbase (2022c). Mission. https://www.coinbase.com/mission

Coinbase (2022d). Bitcoin price (BTC / USD). https://www.coinbase.com/price/bitcoin?utm_source=google_search_nb&utm_medium=cpc&utm_campaign=1658290220&utm_content=111894785026&utm_term=bitcoin&utm_creative=580598118895&utm_device=c&utm_placement=&utm_network=g&utm_location=9003815&gclid=EAIaIQobChMIibWUl-3z9QIVA8iUCR2kNAsvEAAYASABEgIGqPD_BwE

CoinMarketCap (2022a). Major Cryptoassets By Percentage of Total Market Capitalization (Bitcoin Dominance Chart). https://coinmarketcap.com/charts/

CoinMarketCap (2022b). Today's Cryptocurrency Prices by Market Cap. https://coinmarketcap.com/

Daj, A. (2017). Virtual Currencies – monetary policy dilemmas and regulatory challenges. *Bulletin of the Transilvania University of Brasov. Series V: Economic Sciences*, *10*(2), 217–222.

DeJesus, T. (2022). How Much Are Bitcoin Transaction Fees? *Nasdaq*, August 26. https://www.nasdaq.com/articles/bitcoin-transaction-fees%3A-a-full-guide-and-how-to-save

Dumitrescu, G. C. (2017). Bitcoin – A Brief Analysis of the Advantages and Disadvantages. *Global Economic Observer*, 5, 63–71.

Fadilpašić, S. (2018). *A Key Insight For the Blockchain Came in 1991*. Cryptonews. com. May 30. https://cryptonews.com/news/a-key-insight-for-the-blockchain-came-in-1991-1895.htm

Haber, S. & Stornetta, W.S. (1991). How to Time-Stamp a Digital Document. In A. J. Menezes and S. A. Vanstone (Eds.), *Advances in Cryptology – CRYPTO '90, LNCS 537.* Springer-Verlag.

Harwick, C. (2016). Cryptocurrency and the Problem of Intermediation. *The Independent Review*, 20(4), 569.

Internal Revenue Service (2014). Frequently Asked Questions on Virtual Currency Transactions: What is cryptocurrency? https://www.irs.gov/individuals/international-taxpayers/frequently-asked-questions-on-virtual-currency-transactions

Lansky, J. (2018). Possible state approaches to cryptocurrencies. *Journal of Systems Integration*, 9(1), 19–31. https://www.proquest.com/scholarly-journals/possible-state-approaches-cryptocurrencies/docview/2000967598/se-2?accountid=38769

Lee, J., Long, A., McRae, M., Steiner, J., & Handler, S. G. (2015). Bitcoin Basics: A Primer on Virtual Currencies. *Business Law International*, 16(1), 21–48.

Leonard, K. & Bottorff, C. (2022). Credit Card Processing Fees. *Forbes*. https://www.forbes.com/advisor/business/credit-card-processing-fees/Lerer, M. (2019): The Taxation of Cryptocurrency: Virtual Transactions Bring Real-Life Tax Implications. *The CPA Journal*. January, 2019.

Luther, W. J. (2016). Bitcoin and the Future of Digital Payments. *Independent Review*, 20(3), 397–404.

Mellor, M. (2019). *Money: myths, truths and alternatives.* Policy Press.

Merriam-Webster Dictionary. (2022). Definition of scalable. https://www.merriam-webster.com/dictionary/scalability

Nakamoto, S. (2008). Bitcoin: A Peer-to-Peer Electronic Cash System. https://archive.org/details/bitcoin_20171228/mode/2up

Naheem, M. A. (2018). Regulating virtual currencies – the challenges of applying fiat currency laws to digital technology services. *Journal of Financial Crime*, 25, 562–575.

Ngai, K. (2014). Regulating Cryptocurrency to Prevent Fraud and Money Laundering. Utica College.

Parino, F., Beiró, M. G., & Gauvin, L. (2018). Analysis of the Bitcoin blockchain: socio-economic factors behind the adoption. *EPJ Data Science*, 7(38). https://doi.org/10.1140/epjds/s13688-018-0170-8

Parveen, R. & Alajmi, A. (2019). An Overview of Bitcoin's Legal and Technical Challenges. *Journal of Legal, Ethical and Regulatory Issues*, 22(S1), 1–8.

Perez, Y.B. (2015). The New York Stock Exchange (NYSE) has announced the launch of a bitcoin price index (NYXBT). *Coindesk*. https://www.coindesk.com/markets/2015/05/19/new-york-stock-exchange-launches-bitcoin-price-index/

Peters, G.W., Chapelle, A., & Panayi, E. (2016) Opening discussion on banking sector risk exposures and vulnerabilities from virtual currencies: an operational risk perspective. *Journal of Banking Regulation*, 17(4), 239–272.

Richter, C., Kraus, S., & Bouncken, R. B. (2015). Virtual Currencies Like Bitcoin As A Paradigm Shift In The Field Of Transactions. *International Business & Economics Research Journal, 14*(4).

Tu, K. V. & Meredith, M. W. (2015). Rethinking Virtual Currency Regulation in the Bitcoin Age. *Washington Law Review, 90*(1), 271–348.

Tucker, J. A. (2014). What Gave Bitcoin Its Value? Those who use the work of Mises to challenge bitcoin should think again. *Freeman: Ideas on Liberty, 64*, 13–17.

Turpin, J. B. (2014). Bitcoin: The Economic Case for a Global, Virtual Currency Operating in an Unexplored Legal Framework. *Indiana Journal of Global Legal Studies, 21*(1), 335–368. https://doi.org/10.2979/indjglolegstu.21.1.335

Wenker, N. L. (2014). Online Currencies, Real-World Chaos: The Struggle to Regulate the Rise of Bitcoin. *Texas Review of Law and Politics, 19*, 145.

7

GOVERNMENT REGULATORY EFFORTS OF THE CRYPTOCURRENCY INDUSTRY IN THE U.S. FEDERAL SYSTEM

In the United States, non-fiat virtual currency, such as cryptocurrency, potentially reaching significant levels of societal acceptance, and subsequent increased proliferation throughout various dimensions of the economy, can create several constitutional challenges to the traditionally oriented aspects of government-generated legal tender. This includes that cryptocurrency such as Bitcoin, if left to develop of its own volition, may be uniquely positioned and tacitly empowered to begin to compete with fiat currency in the economy in select circumstances, which would be in direct contradiction to the constitutional powers exclusively granted to Congress to coin and regulate money. If this should be the case, then the government cannot generally be expected to permit non-fiat, virtual currencies to run rampant throughout the economic system without making efforts to provide some measure of regulatory guidance in the moment, and perhaps even develop a state-run cryptocurrency alternative in the future. The regulatory guidance on behalf of the federal government can typically manifest through actions based on legislative designs developed by Congress, and is implemented by government bureaucratic entities that are responsible for public administration in accordance with mandated duties. The development and implementation of public policy designed to address problematic circumstances inherent within a given field serves as the expected domain of governance within the American democracy. In relation, this expected dynamic provides the structural framework by which the government operates from as it relates to fulfilling the promise to remain flexible in determining official actions to be taken when an issue has been raised to the level of a problem in need of government intervention. It is

DOI: 10.4324/9781003441830-7

204 Government Regulatory Efforts of the Cryptocurrency Industry

the responsibility of the government in a democratic system to actively generate policy that can address newly identified societal problems and the emergence of cryptocurrency provides an opportunity for the U.S. government to foster official means to confront concerns that unfold, which may stem from this industry.

When the government is faced with assessing newly emergent societal subject matter, determining the means to fulfill expected regulatory duties may be problematic to some degree as, initially, there may be insufficient evidence available to properly guide decision making that would allow adequate governmental policy responses. In this sense, a disjoint between an emergent societal topic of interest and the identification of many of the still yet to be fully known potential problems, which will require policy intervention, helps at least in part to explain why government regulation often lags behind innovations. In relation, the unknown nature of an emergent innovation has yielded vastly different preferences associated with the tactics that government should employ when considering how to regulate new technologies that have themselves yet to gain a foothold in broader society, to the point where full understanding of its benefits and costs have been revealed. On the one hand, should the rationale of permissionless innovation win the day in the deliberative arena, the resulting regulatory environment will reflect a preference for a largely hands-off approach for government intervention in the policy sense. In relation, this rationale is partly based on the possibility that overly regulating cryptocurrency may undermine its natural progression in the early stages of its development, causing irreparable harm to the industry's growth. On the other hand, the regulatory environment will be markedly different in the context of policymaking should those advocating for the precautionary principle be successful in arguing for this approach. If given an either-or choice of applying said political rationales, then the selection of the precautionary principle is arguably better suited to policymaking in the U.S. deliberative democracy. Unlike permissionless innovation, which favors a regulatory environment that is overly supportive of the technology industry and is largely resistant to traditional discourse among system actors in determining the need for government action, the precautionary principle better reflects the expectations of participatory and responsive government in accordance with the U.S. deliberative democracy. Although the full extent of the need for government to regulate the still relatively novel Bitcoin industry remains unknown at present, those advocating for applying the precautionary principle choose to avoid exempting this form of cryptocurrency from the possibility of oversight through dynamically flexible government regulation enacted on an as-needed basis. Here, Bitcoin's potential growth as a viable medium of exchange in the U.S. economy should lead the government to strongly consider an approach to crafting policy efforts that leans toward favoring the judicious use of the precautionary principle, which allows for a more nuanced application of the concept of permission. As such, this policy path should avoid adopting an overly restrictive hold over the industry to ensure that there is some measure of allowance for the natural growth of the cryptocurrency industry, which protects the freedom to innovate expected by advocates of permissionless innovation. Instead of adopting a policy approach that reflects extreme regulatory tendencies, such as instituting an outright ban of cryptocurrency, the government should seek to maintain the ability to flexibly identify and address developing problems stemming from the industry as expected in the U.S. democratic system. Doing so may provide a strategically balanced approach that allows for government to actively develop policy efforts designed to protect the public from harm that may be caused by cryptocurrency, while also providing some measure of opportunity for the industry to develop under a regulatory regime that is empowered to act when necessary. This balanced approach to policy responsiveness, in which government refuses to willingly cede absolute control to cryptocurrency's unfettered growth, as would be preferred by those supportive of permissionless innovation, will still allow for the industry to maintain some measure of freedom to innovate at this stage of development. Also, actively creating policy to address identified emerging problems caused by cryptocurrency on an as-needed basis will allow for further generated information to be accumulated that may later prove invaluable to informing decision makers as to how best to develop a more comprehensive regulatory approach. The maintenance of an active and flexible regulatory environment that avoids being overly restrictive of cryptocurrency at this stage in its development is a policy path that is more reflective of the precautionary principle, and that remains diligently loyal to the expectations associated with government responsiveness in the U.S. deliberative democracy. It is this conceptualization that may be best suited presently to guide U.S. government decision making when addressing emerging concerns associated with the cryptocurrency industry that may arise within the federal system. This includes that existing statutory means provide guidance for government regulating the cryptocurrency industry while allowing responsive policy measures to be developed in real-time as needed. The incremental approach provides regulatory substance to public sector efforts to address the cryptocurrency industry in the present while allowing for flexible policy designs to be crafted proactively or reactively as events unfold over time.

The following chapter will expand on the present state of U.S. policymaking regarding cryptocurrency, such as Bitcoin, as it relates to applicable legislative and bureaucratic efforts, with the understanding that this

206 Government Regulatory Efforts of the Cryptocurrency Industry

structural guidance provided by government is still in its very earliest of stages. Furthermore, the present state of the U.S. regulatory environment is extremely fragmented at each of the levels within the federal government, as indicated by the highly disjointed, incremental responses that are in place. Relatedly, the present state of government legislative efforts within the federal system, or more accurately the general lack thereof, which are directly applicable to regulating the cryptocurrency industry, will be expanded upon. This includes noting that the present state of the legislative efforts that provides substantive cohesion on behalf of Congress is generally lacking, often leaving federal bureaucracies to attempt to apply preexisting legislation to guide internal responses to address the cryptocurrency industry within the context of the entities' mandated duties. In all, the lack of recent federal legislation that is expressly designed to broadly and clearly provide guidance regarding the cryptocurrency industry has resulted in a regulatory environment involving bureaucratic entities at each of the levels of government, which are largely left to their own volition to develop responses. Therefore, the federal agencies and entities existing within the lower levels of government have thus far gone about developing policy to address various aspects of regulating Bitcoin in a vastly different manner in many cases. Overall, the present U.S. regulatory environment focused on the field of cryptocurrency essentially reflects a policy landscape that is fragmented and incremental in nature, which is still in the very early stages of development. Similarly, this dynamic is represented well by the individualized responses from various agencies acting in the attempt to provide initial guidance for the cryptocurrency industry. In relation, the preliminary stages of agency action oft reflect various approaches that include providing educational-based guidance that is informative to system actors interested in engaging in cryptocurrency for various purposes, or that may attempt to create policy inroads by providing initial instructional requirements that are more traditionally regulatory in nature.

The development of non-fiat virtual currency has yielded a variety of cryptocurrencies, including the most popular and persistent form known as Bitcoin. In earlier chapters, it was discussed that cryptocurrency, such as Bitcoin, may adequately reflect some of the qualities of money that presently allows for such to be considered for use by limited numbers of system actors in various economic circumstances. It was previously discussed that Bitcoin may qualify as money in the context that it is divisible (transactions can be rounded to eight decimal places), portable (able to be digitally facilitated the world over with access to the Internet and a device, with the understanding that it is important to recognize impediments derived from digital divide concerns), stable (decentralized operations limiting the numbers of coins available is designed to serve deflationary function with the understanding that the value of Bitcoin in U.S. dollars has fluctuated since 2009), durable (non-fiat, virtual currency is not subject to the same physical damage as fiat, tangible money), and some degree of protection against counterfeiting (instituted by blockchain). Despite being non-fiat virtual currency, cryptocurrency such as Bitcoin seems to qualify as money in several respects, adequately reflecting a wide assortment of qualities needed to begin to viably function in various transactional endeavors within the economy. Because of this, since being created in 2009, Bitcoin has slowly become more accepted for usage by societal actors as it becomes further embedded into the U.S. economic system. This is evidenced in part by more vendors (i.e. Microsoft, Overstock, etc.) allowing for consumers to transact with Bitcoin in which goods/services are attributed comparable pricing measures that allow for traditional market exchanges. In relation, the domestic stock market daily advertisement of Bitcoin in U.S. dollars, and the introductory offering of limited crypto stocks, serves as additional means by which valuing this form of cryptocurrency is present in the U.S. economy. Although meeting many of the qualities of money, Bitcoin still falls short of consistently achieving all of the necessary characteristics to be defined as such, which helps to explain its relatively limited role in the U.S. economy at present. Because the value of Bitcoin in U.S. dollars has fluctuated since being incepted in 2009, and the acceptance of Bitcoin as a medium of exchange by system actors in the economy is still quite limited, this form of cryptocurrency would be unable to fully qualify as being widely accepted as money, therefore reducing its transactional usefulness to system actors operating with the economy. Relatedly, a key conceptual roadblock that reduces the ability of Bitcoin to qualify as money is the fact that, despite having inherent measures to guard against supply-based inflation, the valuing of this form of cryptocurrency in U.S. dollars has a history of vast fluctuations, which may contribute to system actors being distrustful in its transactional usefulness in the economy.

Although not fitting neatly into the conversation regarding defining money, Bitcoin does reflect enough of the qualities needed to be used as a medium of exchange in market transaction in a limited capacity within the U.S. economy. If Bitcoin meets many of the characteristics of money, allowing its accepted usage by some members of society, then this raises a slew of concerns regarding the existence of this non-fiat, virtual currency within the economic system. This includes the concerns derived from the possibility that cryptocurrency contradicts the U.S. Constitution, which extends exclusive powers to Congress regarding money such as those associated with its coining (i.e. create fiat currency), valuing (i.e. establishing face value of money, taking actions that affect inflation rates which influences the value of money), taxing (i.e. devising and implementation

208 Government Regulatory Efforts of the Cryptocurrency Industry

taxing schema), and protecting against counterfeiting (i.e. preventive actions to thwart counterfeiting efforts). Bitcoin's existence within the economy poses a threat to the constitutional authority exclusively granted to Congress regarding fiat currency, in the sense that cryptocurrencies may attempt to, and often succeeds in, masquerading as money in many transactional circumstances within the U.S. system. Since being created in 2009, Bitcoin has undergone a slow metamorphosis from being relegated to the outskirts of the U.S. economy to slowly gaining some traction as a viable medium of exchange, as this form of cryptocurrency has begun to proliferate an increasingly broader array of opportunities within the economy. As the creation of money as legal tender was intended by the Framers of the Constitution to be an exclusive function of Congress, the existence of non-fiat, virtual currency such as Bitcoin being used within the economy may cause some measure of concern from a statutory standpoint. In addition to the exclusive power to coin money, the Framers of the U.S. Constitution empowered Congress to enact legislation that created agencies and a broad policy infrastructure that would establish guidelines associated with a number of foundational aspects of fiat currency (i.e. coining, valuing, taxing, and preventing counterfeiting). Bitcoin being "coined" (i.e. created) by a decentralized collective, through a process that is outside constitutional involvement, runs counter to the modern expectation that all money in the U.S. economic system would be fiat in nature and be under the statutory purview of a centralized governmental authority. Although excluded from directly being involved in decentralized processes associated with Bitcoin creation, the U.S. government should consider remaining diligent, from a policy effort standpoint, to be able to address the fact that that this form of cryptocurrency has more steadily begun broadly to proliferate the U.S. economy. In this sense, the continued proliferation of Bitcoin throughout the economic system increasingly creates a growing need for the U.S. government to officially enact systemic efforts to address the possible permanence of this form of cryptocurrency.

From a political rationale standpoint, there are some questions as to how the policy environment to address cryptocurrency should be skewed, essentially pitting those traditionally supporting technocratically oriented approaches—technological determinism or permissionless innovation—against those in favor of the precautionary principle. Here, those advocating for the support of technological determinism, or the more recent technocratic manifestation, permissionless innovation would prefer a hands-off approach to government—for regulatory responses to largely be in allegedly rare instances in which it has been proven that harm to society was the direct result of technology's usage. On the other hand, those advocating for the precautionary principle support a more proactive approach to regulation that is as preventive in nature as it is far more encompassing in scope. At this early stage in the development of Bitcoin, it is unrealistic to expect to be able to fully understand the scope and nature of all benefits and problems that may be caused by the usage of cryptocurrency within the U.S. economy. In addition, a regulatory environment that is overly restrictive or permissive of this industry may inflexibly inhibit the growth of technology, causing its stagnation (or demise), or comprehensively causing harm through inaction to those in society that government is charged with protecting, respectively. As such, fully subscribing to permissionless innovation or the precautionary principle in a manner that is mutually exclusive would be inadequate in establishing a regulatory environment suited to address Bitcoin's growing role in the economy since being created in 2009. At this point, a balanced and incremental approach, which reinforces the ability of government to simultaneously pursue protective policy recourse to the public through active regulation while granting some measure of allowance to the technological growth of the industry, may be prudent. In doing so, a dynamic approach that avoids overly investing in being too restrictive or permissive better reflects the expectations associated with decision making in a deliberative democracy. It is with these ideas in mind that the information in this chapter regarding the regulatory environment in the U.S., and actions taken thus far at each of the levels of government in the federal system, should be considered.

The relative newness of cryptocurrency such as Bitcoin invokes an expected lack of full understanding regarding what issues will eventually ascend to be classified as problems that will require government responses from a policymaking standpoint. Without knowledge of such it may be imprudent to rashly enact a policymaking approach that is rationally comprehensive and overly restrictive, because this may prove to be too inhibitive of the natural growth of the cryptocurrency industry. However, the cryptocurrency industry also cannot be permitted to run amok throughout the U.S. economy without some measure of regulatory guidance working to ensure that its growth is proactively managed by government. At present, there is no concentrated unifying legislative effort on behalf of Congress that directly provides universal guidelines for Bitcoin to be implemented in a whole-of-government approach. As such, there is something of a piecemeal, incremental approach at all levels of government in the U.S. federal system regarding policymaking to address the cryptocurrency industry. In relation, there are several existing agencies that have been functionally required to develop means by which to address Bitcoin, because this form of cryptocurrency has begun to encroach in topical fields that fall within the mandated responsibility of the federal governmental entities. This includes federal entities such as the Internal Revenue Service

210 Government Regulatory Efforts of the Cryptocurrency Industry

(IRS), which is responsible for determining how Bitcoin will be defined and correspondingly addressed in the context of taxation. There are also government entities such as the Securities and Exchange Commission (SEC), the Commodity Futures Trading Commission (CFTC), and the Federal Trade Commission (FTC), which enact means that play a role in consumer protection for those transacting, investing, and trading in cryptocurrency such as Bitcoin. It also includes federal entities such as the Department of the Treasury, and its subsequent bureaus, who provide guidance that may contribute to preventing potential threats to the U.S. financial system, including those that may be caused by the presence of Bitcoin. Relatedly, entities such as the Financial Crimes Enforcement Network (FinCEN), who have been mandated by Congress to address different aspects of illegality that are facilitated with fiat money, will now to some degree include efforts to thwart criminal activity that are associated with Bitcoin. Additionally, there is a rich and diverse effort on behalf of government at the state and local level to develop means that can serve to guide the Bitcoin industry that is deserved of some attention. Together, the national, state, and local government efforts to develop means to address the proliferation of cryptocurrency, in a wide array of policy areas, serves to create a piecemeal, ever-evolving, and incremental approach to regulating the industry in the United States.

The Regulatory Environment in the United States

As noted previously, the U.S. government does not presently promote a fiat version of cryptocurrency and is not directly involved in the creation of decentralized cryptocurrency, such as Bitcoin. Ultimately, modern-era U.S. governance is now faced with a unique responsibility in that there is a growing need to officially recognize the proliferation of cryptocurrency, such as Bitcoin, by crafting policy responses capable of addressing this non-fiat type of virtual currency, which has slowly become more popular for use in certain portions of the American economy. Without unifying federal legislative mandates and supportive structural statutes to dictate how to regulate cryptocurrency in all areas of public policy, there is presently a lack of congruence at each of the levels of government in the U.S. federal system as to how address manifestations such as Bitcoin. If novel policy endeavors are present, then they are largely developed at the federal agency level or localized levels of government. In relation, there has been some measure of acceptance of the practice of addressing cryptocurrency by extending existing legislative mandates, which may have technically pre-dated this industry but that may find some measure of applicability to the oversight of the newly emergent innovation. However, it would be prudent for some measure of attention to be paid in the future as to the possibility of a federal policy effort(s) by Congress that is capable of broadly addressing potential problems that will be caused by the continued use of cryptocurrency. In general, the act of implementing legislative efforts on behalf of Congress would be accommodated by any number of U.S. federal agencies responsible for enacting corresponding internal efforts, so that each government entity will be capable of addressing a broad policy mandate designed to address cryptocurrency. Until then, a whole-of-government approach capable of uniformly providing statutory guidance is presently unavailable in the U.S., leaving official actions at each of the levels of the federal system to be facilitated incrementally, largely in a piecemeal fashion. Additionally, the U.S. federal system allows for lower levels of government to exercise policy discretion as long as doing so avoids conflicting with national mandates set forth. As such, state level and local-level government presently enjoy an opportunity to freely address cryptocurrency through the development of localized policy efforts.

At present, the policymaking efforts in the U.S. federal system that are intended to regulate the cryptocurrency industry, such as Bitcoin, has yielded an environment that is highly malleable, fragmented, and in a relative state of flux. Although it is important to recognize that, to assist in increasing the overall effectiveness of regulation, a more coordinated, international effort would ultimately be required, there are obviously still means by which the U.S. government can enact policy designed to address domestically oriented problems derived from virtual currencies, such as cryptocurrency (Virga, 2015, p. 512). Boxerman and Schwerin (2017, p. 1) note that "the number of federal and state agencies that regulate or have taken a position with respect to virtual currency is increasing." Since virtual currencies were introduced in the late 1990s, this industry has provided unique challenges to decision makers in "the financial and regulatory sector" (Naheem, 2018, p. 563). This was due in part to the fact that virtual currencies, such as cryptocurrency, largely function "outside the current structure of the formal financial services," which to some degree would allow this industry to "evade the regulation and licensing regime that was currently in place" (Naheem, 2018, p. 563). Thus far, the development of policy efforts to regulate many aspects of the cryptocurrency industry have largely been "fairly slow" throughout the United States (Naheem, 2018, p. 563). As the virtual currency industry and corresponding regulatory efforts are still collectively in the infancy stages, it is important that policy makers consider the "consequences of not regulating as well as the potential harm that increased regulation could cause within society generally, especially if digital technology innovation is stifled" (Naheem, 2018, p. 572). Policy makers must remain cognizant of the possibility that the emergence of this rapidly changing industry may cause difficulties in policy application to some degree, because the mercurial nature of the industry may cause unforeseen problems that could potentially outpace regulatory measures that are put in place (Naheem, 2018, p. 563). In general, government agencies within the U.S. federal system have begun to develop means that are intended to address the proliferation of the cryptocurrency industry in accordance with the duties mandated to each entity on behalf of legislative directives. At this stage of the development of the cryptocurrency industry, decision makers in broader government are tasked with crafting policy that will protect the public at large from potential harm caused by the emergent technologically oriented field of cryptocurrency, while also avoiding overly regulating the industry, which could potentially cause irreparable damage to its natural development. On one hand, decision makers in government should be aware that a chosen policy path forward may serve to be overly lenient in granting technological developmental freedom, which may cause greater levels of harm to society because the industry was largely left unchecked. On the other hand, policy measures that may be too aggressive could limit the development of the cryptocurrency industry and cause its practitioners to take flight, seeking jurisdictions that provide a more favorable regulatory environment. Investment in either approach in absolute would result in a regulatory environment that is either tilted to one conceptual extreme or the other, which would result in pursuing policy that favors permissionless innovation, which may allow the industry to run amok if left unchecked by government (i.e. no policy efforts to address the industry at all, only policy efforts in which harm to society is proven to be derived from the industry, etc.) or the precautionary principle if applied too stringently, which may cause irreparable harm in the industry during its developmental years (i.e. outright ban of the industry, overly restrictive measures that causes the demise of the industry in its development stage, or that causes the industry to relocate to a more favorable jurisdiction). When crafting policy to address the relatively early stages of the cryptocurrency lifecycle, decision makers in government may be best served by attempting to strike a balance to achieve some measure of regulatory guidance as deemed needed when problems arise, while avoiding inducing overly strict designs that would result in stamping out the industry before it reaches maturity. As such, it is of great importance to continue to monitor the industry to determine if regulatory efforts remain viable and, if so, to what degree. If regulatory efforts in place are deemed ineffective in goal achievement, then it will be beneficial to make the necessary adjustments to existing policy or enact new policy that will be better suited to address the newly identify problems associated with the cryptocurrency industry. This speaks to the dynamic nature of policymaking in the U.S., which requires constant flexibility in identifying and responding to newly emerging problems that may develop in a deliberative democracy.

Before providing select illustrative examples to illuminate how the government, at each level of the U.S. federal system, has thus far developed means by which to address the growth of Bitcoin and its spread into the economy, it will be helpful to further expand on the present nature of the American regulatory environment for this industry. On this matter, the U.S. regulatory environment in many ways is reflective of the same policy hodgepodge that exists on the global level, in which various nations have adopted a wide array of actions to address the cryptocurrency industry. Although when Bitcoin was created in 2009 its limited usage and relegation to fringe status in the economy meant that efforts focused on regulation were relatively non-existent, the continuous growth of Bitcoin usage on an international scale would require regulation efforts more befitting of the expansion of this form of cryptocurrency (Tu and Meredith, 2015, p. 296). On a global level, regulatory responses to various forms of virtual currency—be it cryptocurrency such as Bitcoin or other examples—have been highly diverse (Tu and Meredith, 2015, p. 296). The emergence and global proliferation of Bitcoin has presented a slew of "unique challenges" that have garnered "little consensus" as to how government entities—be they international or domestic—should regulate this form of cryptocurrency within their respective jurisdictions (Tu and Meredith, 2015, p. 314). As virtual currency is an emerging technology, and global usage is still relatively nominal, government regulatory efforts have largely reflected a "wait-and-see approach," which is not necessarily uncommon as "regulation often lags behind innovations in the market" (Tu and Meredith, 2015, p. 302). On the global level, there has been very little consensus from the international community as to how to best regulate the Bitcoin industry. Thus far, this ideal also holds true for the U.S. government's efforts to address this burgeoning field that has undoubtedly grown in popularity since its inception in 2009.

From a regulatory standpoint, the U.S. Congress has largely been slow in crafting new legislative efforts to address the Bitcoin industry directly and comprehensively. Marinova (2018, p. 1) noted that "the cryptocurrency market is still in its 'Wild West' phase as regulators try to figure out how to proceed." The U.S. Commodity Futures Trading Commission (2023, p. 1) stated:

[T]he market for digital coins and tokens is still very young, and there is no widely accepted standard for placing a value on a particular digital coin or token. This includes coins or tokens sold today with the claim that they can be used to purchase goods, services, or platform access in the future.

214 Government Regulatory Efforts of the Cryptocurrency Industry

With the understanding that Bitcoin and Blockchain are intertwined innovations, whose usage is simultaneously growing in global popularity, regulatory efforts may prove difficult as no present domestic scheme is wholly applicable to the burgeoning cryptocurrency industry (Parveen and Alajmi, 2019, p. 7). The initial U.S. efforts at different levels of government facilitated by various official entities—agencies, courts, and legislatures—that provide situational regulatory guidance to those choosing to conduct a diverse assortment of transactions via virtual currency have largely been focused on applying existing laws to this relatively new fiscal innovation (Tu and Meredith, 2015, p. 303). In general, the regulatory efforts in the United States have reflected a fragmented approach in which public-sector entities address the topic of virtual currency within the framework of pre-existing legal directives, which, at least tacitly, provides evidence that the government recognizes the importance of regulating this non-traditional payment option in the modern era (Tu and Meredith, 2015, p. 301). The establishment of official guidelines to classify and govern virtual currency usage in the United States is largely fragmented and incremental in nature, by which various federal agencies, levels of the U.S. court system, and individual state legislatures to some degrees have been left to their own volition resulting in a somewhat incongruent and piecemeal regulatory framework (Tu and Meredith, 2015, pp. 305–306). Without a universally implemented, whole-of-government legislative approach on behalf of Congress, the U.S. regulatory responses to virtual currency will continue to largely be a piecemeal, incremental endeavor, in which decision making is disjointed and incongruent dependent upon an official review of circumstances by a wide array of public-sector entities from various levels within the federal system. This observation is critical to understanding the present state of the cryptocurrency industry in general and the likelihood that U.S. government efforts to effectively monitor types of cryptocurrencies such as Bitcoin may remain highly disjointed in the immediate future. The processes for government to both conceptually define and develop actions capable of adequately addressing the burgeoning field of cryptocurrency, which is rapidly becoming more economically endemic, domestically and globally, in the modern era are in many ways presently mercurial. These dynamic system circumstances may affect policymaking designed to address the cryptocurrency industry as the field itself is extremely flexible, fluid, and volatile in many respects. Ultimately, as cryptocurrency such as Bitcoin continues to proliferate more widely, there may become more evidence of issues defined as problems that will give a clearer picture as to the need(s) for government regulatory responses to be crafted.

At present, there are a wide range of system dynamics to consider that may influence governmental efforts associated with the regulation of the cryptocurrency industry in the American democracy. This includes the constitutional concerns created by the cryptocurrency industry as it relates to challenges posed to conventional monetary practices and government involvement in the United States. Kim (2015, p. 1) notes that, traditionally, "management of currency has been a responsibility and a right of a central authority." In the modern era, the rise of virtual currencies like Bitcoin potentially challenges conventional monetary practices in part because "the creation and management of these currencies are done by non-government entities" (Kim, 2015, p. 1). Cryptocurrency usage as money by some system actors in specific circumstances creates a dilemma because this non-fiat virtual currency falls outside of the government's expected scope of formative control and creates regulatory issues that challenge conventionally led centralized efforts on this account. In relation, the decentralized nature of cryptocurrency, such as Bitcoin, provides regulatory challenges for government that will require creative and flexible actions to specify guidance that is capable of addressing problems associated with this emergent industry. The usage of a peer-to-network by Bitcoin, a decentralized cryptocurrency, renders regulatory efforts problematic to some degree because of the inability of the regulators to directly issue executable mandates to a centralized authority and to consequently enforce compliance with such (Tu and Meredith, 2015, p. 297). To address the lack of decentralization associated with Bitcoin transactions, regulatory efforts can focus on providing guidelines to the readily identifiable "exchanges and other intermediaries," whose centralized nature are more easily subjected to enforcement efforts (Parveen and Alajmi, 2019, p. 7). In this sense, the government may seek to regulate cryptocurrency exchanges that operate from a transactional standpoint, as these are likely more easily monitored than the individuals and entities that are engaged in the industry from a creation standpoint in a highly diffused, decentralized fashion. The regulation of Bitcoin is also further complicated by the fact that users have some measure of anonymity, increasing the difficulty in enforcing mandates (Tu and Meredith, 2015, p. 297) and the irreversibility of electronic transactions means that theft of Bitcoin from individuals or vendors makes retrieving losses an uncertain proposition (Tu and Meredith, 2015, p. 299). Ultimately, the continued development in use and the global proliferation path of virtual currencies, such as Bitcoin, will be subject to a wide array of key factors. This includes (but is not limited to) how Bitcoin is going to be officially defined (i.e. security, commodity, currency), the "legislative and regulatory treatment of virtual currencies," "public confidence in Bitcoin," concerns associated with "technical protocols" capable of causing usage issues and security flaws, and the viability of this form of virtual currency in the commissioning of illegal acts such as "terrorism and money laundering"

(Lee et al., 2015, p. 26). The development of statutory means raises concerns associated with the ability to broadly administer such regulations in a manner this will allow successful prevention of the use of virtual currencies for illicit purposes, based on variances in jurisdictional scope of influence, which domestic regulatory designs may lack the requisite power by those utilizing this technology to commit crimes from other countries (Lee et al., 2015, p. 47). The intent associated with developing mechanisms of enforcement is critical to the overall regulatory process, but there may be natural limits to implementation based on the international nature associated with non-fiat virtual currencies such as Bitcoin. Additionally, there is understandably some skepticism regarding federal efforts to regulate newly emergent cryptocurrency in the U.S. by applying existing legislative mandates, as they may fail to adequately address the industry problems that unfold in real-time. The effectiveness of applying existing regulations, which were initially designed to address other public-policy issues, may yield some measure of uncertainty based in part "as to how virtual currencies should be characterised and regulated" (Lee et al., 2015, p. 48). Although difficult to definitively predict the proliferation arc of Bitcoin, its continued evolution will be dependent in part on whether virtual currency is classified as "currencies, commodities or mediums of exchange," which, in turn, can affect public-policy designs having the capacity to guide regulatory efforts and ultimately impact usage diffusion (Lee et al., 2015, pp. 47–48). It has also been observed that should Congress play a more limited role in developing public policy to regulate virtual currency, a greater opportunity may be provided to state-level government and those responsible for enforcing existing federal regulations applicable to monitoring Bitcoin (Lee et al. 2015, p. 48). The discretion afforded to the lower levels of government may allow for resulting successful regulatory endeavors to serve as a policy template that can later be employed horizontally or vertically within the federal system. With the understanding that there is still some debate regarding the applicability of existing regulations to the newly emerging, and rapid expansion of, virtual currencies such as Bitcoin, this reality will yield a certain measure of trial and error that will be required with upcoming policy endeavors. In addition, the very act of defining cryptocurrency from a policy standpoint will determine the scope and nature of government involvement in the U.S. federal system.

Cryptocurrency and Energy Consumption

Before continuing to the next section, which will highlight several key U.S. policy efforts within the federal system, it is important to take a brief detour to consider the relationship between cryptocurrency production and

Government Regulatory Efforts of the Cryptocurrency Industry **217**

energy consumption. The fact that cryptocurrency's production affects energy consumption is an important consideration for those working in the industry and governments that must choose how to address this dynamic from a policymaking standpoint. To start, it is important to consider how cryptocurrency production directly affects energy consumption as it relates to integrated processes, such as blockchain, that are pivotal in verification processes involving Bitcoin. Unlike competing cryptocurrencies such as Ethereum, which now uses the proof-of-stake option, requiring lower levels of energy expenditures associated with blockchain protocols (Stoll, Klaaßen, and Gallersdörfer, 2019, p. 1657), Bitcoin's use of a decentralized consensus mechanism, proof-of-work, to facilitate verification of "ownership and transactions" requires higher level of energy consumption, as participants actively endeavor to leverage the computational power of computers to solve hash puzzles, of variable difficulty, designed in part to provide about ten minutes to allow for participants to confirm blockchain integrity (Stoll, Klaaßen, and Gallersdörfer, 2019, p. 1648). Stoll, Klaaßen, and Gallersdörfer (2019, p. 1647) further explain that "participation in the Bitcoin blockchain validation process requires specialized hardware and vast amounts of electricity, which translates into a significant carbon footprint." Stoll, Klaaßen, and Gallersdörfer (2019, p. 1655) discuss the potential for the Bitcoin mining industry to locate "near large sources of renewable energy," and the important role that expanding the growth of "renewable generation resources" will play in enhancing the production of available energy to better accommodate the increased power consumption at the physical facilities on-site. Here, it is important to recognize that cryptocurrency that utilizes blockchain technology to verify existence of and transactions with Bitcoin will require consistent access to abundant levels of energy to maintain the industry. The consumption of energy associated with the cryptocurrency mining industry can be significant and, should the energy consumed be derived exclusively from fossil fuels, the carbon footprint may be significant depending on the scope of the production in question. In relation, the energy consumption and environmental dynamics are aspects that should be considered during future regulatory endeavors for the cryptocurrency industry.

A key metric used in assessing energy consumption associated with the cryptocurrency industry is the concept referred to as hashrate. Specifically, hashrate is used in determining the size, scope, and location of the participants in the cryptocurrency mining industry on a global scale, as it relates to measurable markers associated with energy consumption. Hertig and Leech (2021) defined hashrate as "the total combined computational power that is being used to mine and process transactions on a Proof-of-Work blockchain, such as Bitcoin and Ethereum (prior to the 2.0 upgrade)."

The measurement of hashrate is a key indicator that can be used to assess where the cryptocurrency mining industry is located, and this global indicator is a useful tool used to track energy consumption to determine such. Rauchs (2021) observes that the Cambridge Centre for Alternative Finance's (CCAF) efforts to track the "geographical evolution of Bitcoin mining" are based on assessing data from "four Bitcoin mining pools – BTC.com, Poolin, ViaBTC and Foundry" that together constitutes 37 percent of the total Bitcoin network worldwide. In doing so, the CCAF is able to provide data that makes it possible to infer findings in relation to the larger scale representation of Bitcoin production internationally. Rauchs (2021) further expands on the Cambridge Bitcoin Electricity Consumption Index (CBECI), which studies Bitcoin mining in relation to its "sustainability and environmental impact," that provides the following comparative data illustrating the shift of "total Bitcoin mining power" from among select countries leading in production. According to the Cambridge Centre for Alternative Finance (2021), looking at the "average monthly hashrate share by country and region for the selected period, based on geolocational mining pool data," the nations that led in Bitcoin production shifted, from December 2019, for China (72.69 percent), the Russian Federation (6.05 percent), the United States (3.44 percent), and Kazakhstan (3.49 percent) vs. December 2021 for China (21.11 percent), the Russian Federation (4.6 percent) the United States (37.84 percent), and Kazakhstan (13.22 percent). The shift in Bitcoin production in China was indicative of the policymaking endeavors inherent with that nation that systematically began to target the cryptocurrency mining industry for expulsion from its jurisdictional borders. Despite being a world leader in cryptocurrency production and trading, starting in 2013, China methodically began to officially establish "a hostile relationship with its local crypto industry" through a number of legislative mandates leading up to 2021, which would ultimately lead to a complete ban at that time (Sergeenkov, 2021, section 2, paragraph 1). Relatedly, Chinese policy efforts would cause the cryptocurrency industry to seek to relocate at least temporarily to other nations such as nearby Kazakhstan, whose jurisdictional controls provided a more favorable policy environment, and in which there was seemingly an abundance of energy (Maidan, 2022; Sigalos, 2022; Volpicelli, 2022). Based on the hashrate data, it is observable that, in the two years leading up to the Chinese government's outright ban of cryptocurrency in 2021, the prior public-policy measures implemented had a significant impact on the mining industry not only in that nation, but in other nations as well. Since 2021, China's hashrate numbers fell while nations such as the U.S. correspondingly rose. In brief, this speaks to the notion that the cryptocurrency mining practices represents a globally interconnected dynamic associated with its existence,

Government Regulatory Efforts of the Cryptocurrency Industry **219**

in which localized policy endeavors can affect both the international economy and the industry itself. In this, major regulatory shifts in one nation may greatly affect the industry as it relates to migratory patterns of physical components needed for cryptocurrency production, energy consumption, and environmental impacts. Although there is clearly an international component to cryptocurrency, this chapter will only continue to focus on the regulation of the industry in the context of the American democracy.

The U.S. Federal System: Congressional Legislative Mandates and Agency Actions

There is a level of interconnectivity in government in which agencies may often work separately, but simultaneously in concert, to address the same area of public policy in accordance with each entity's mandated responsibilities. In relation, the U.S. system is constructed in a fashion that often creates a good measure of redundancy regarding official efforts to address a given topical area of importance. This redundancy is a purposeful attempt that institutionalizes erring on the side of caution as it relates to ensuring government is actively working to address an issue(s) of importance in society at a given point of time. Conceptually, ensuring that multiple government entities are responsible for contributing to fulfilling expectations for goal achievement in an area of public policy can increase the overall effectiveness of government doing so (with the recognition that institutionalized redundancy may create less efficiency because of the increased costs associated with such). In the modern era, instead of adopting a classic silo approach to goal achievement, a more collaborative bureaucratic system is often accepted as practice, in which an area of public policy may require some measure of interagency cooperation to help increase the chances of success. In this scenario, with many key public-sector responsibilities, such as national defense and public safety, it is often better to have redundancy in means as opposed to an insufficient ability to ensure such is provided to the general public. Here, each agency goes about fulfilling its expected mandated duties on its own while also making an effort to cooperatively share information and to become collectively engaged in shared exercises toward goal achievement in an area of public policy. For example, at the federal level there are a number of agencies that are tasked with coordinating efforts such as those fighting against criminality that may cause harm to U.S. citizens, such as the Central Intelligence Agency (CIA), Federal Bureau of Investigations (FBI), and the many bureaus that fall within the Department of Homeland Security (DHS: https://www.dhs. gov/operational-and-support-components). To be sure, in many cases the coordination and cooperation of government entities operating within the same policy arena is of great importance to broader success in achieving goals, as singular agencies acting in an insular fashion may prove ineffective, or worse counterproductive. Similarly, in the U.S. federal system, legislation passed by Congress, and corresponding agency actions developed in accordance with said mandates, may also require some measure of coordination at the state/local levels of government. To continue on with the theme of government entities that are tasked with protecting the well-being of citizens and keeping them from harm, state and local-level police forces are intended to work in conjecture with the aforementioned federal agencies. In essence, the political ecosystem in the U.S. federal system has a number of government entities at each level of government (i.e. national, state, and local) that are simultaneously individually and collectively responsible for addressing areas of public policy. Sometimes, there is congruence in the effort in which each level of government works in concert to achieve goals with very little deviation from the federal mandates. Other times, the state/local levels of government develop policy of their own volition in conjuncture to what is believed to reflect the constituent base within that jurisdiction. Unless expressly granted to the federal government, by way of the tenth amendment, state governments (and by extension local governments within that state) are empowered to develop policies that are reflective of the preferences within that locality. Therefore, there may be variances in laws from state to state on issues in which the federal government has yet to codify action on a topic through Congressional legislation (see abortion laws in the U.S.). In addition, lower levels of government may challenge the constitutionality of federal law by taking a case to the federal Supreme Court to receive a ruling as to the legal merits of such. At this early stage of development, prior to 2022 government efforts to address potential concerns stemming from cryptocurrency is largely insular, as individual agencies at each of the levels of government in the U.S. federal system have largely been left to their own volition to develop internal means by which to address this burgeoning industry. In doing so, agencies may attempt to apply preexisting legislation that was initially enacted to provide regulatory guidance for a different purpose, or may simply adopt new internal measures that will address cryptocurrency in the context of the duties assigned to the entity by Congressional mandate. As legislative mandates by Congress and agency actions continue to be developed, the policy landscape may eventually become more accommodating to continued joint cooperative endeavors at each of the levels of government in the U.S. federal system. In addition, new legislative efforts on behalf of Congress on a longitudinal basis may eventually create a broadly focused statutory environment that will allow for a whole-of-government approach to regulating the cryptocurrency industry.

In the U.S., longitudinally enacting consistent legislative designs can allow for the broad entrenchment of a whole-of-government approach intended to address an area of public policy in a manner that incorporates aspects associated with public-sector responsiveness expected in the federal system. In such cases, the Constitution empowers the U.S. Congress to pass federal legislation that is intended to be implemented at each of the levels of government (i.e. national, state and local). In relation, the pursuit of a broad approach at the federal level, designed to address cryptocurrency, could eventually be applicable should legislative efforts on behalf of the U.S. government create a policy path forward that directly provides clear guidance for the regulation and enforcement of this burgeoning industry, which has become increasingly more prevalent in the modern era. Although sound conceptually, the present structure of the legislative landscape, at the federal level, to address the cryptocurrency industry largely lacks a cogent, congruent policy path that is applicable for implementation at all levels of government in the United States. Relatedly, the lack of broad sweeping legislative mandates has left something of a void among federal agencies regarding how to address the cryptocurrency industry. As such, at the federal level there are a wide range of agencies that are responsible for regulating and monitoring the expansive role of cryptocurrency in the United States. In this sense, these federal agencies are focused on the same area of public policy (i.e. cryptocurrency) with each entity making efforts that are responsively unique to the responsibilities inherent within each's respective creation mandate. As previously mentioned, there is also a measure of redundancy in responsibility that flows down to the lower levels of government as allowed by the U.S. Constitution. The tenth amendment allows for lower levels of government to address issues deemed to be of political importance when the U.S. federal government has not been expressly empowered to do so. In relation, there are a number of vastly different regulatory approaches to the cryptocurrency industry at the lower levels of government. In all, the regulatory environment in the United States is incremental and fragmented, so that presently from a policy perspective the public sector is largely lacking in the capacity to address the cryptocurrency industry in a unified, whole-of-government approach.

With the U.S. federal system dynamics in mind, the following sections will provide a broad overview of select official actions on behalf of the U.S. government, which are intended to address various aspects of the cryptocurrency industry. This includes discussing existing legislative endeavors by Congress that, by extension, may be applicable to efforts to address potential issues that may be associated with Bitcoin's increasing usage in the economy. As previously mentioned, there are presently a relative absence of unifying federal legislative effort and supportive structural statutes that have been enacted by Congress that directly provide universal guidance regarding all aspects of Bitcoin (i.e. creating, valuing, taxing, etc.). However, there have been some attempts to apply components of existing legislation such as the Bank Secrecy Act (BSA) to address the cryptocurrency industry. Ultimately, without unifying legislative efforts newly created on behalf of Congress, the federal agencies are often largely left to their own volition to assess means by which to address the emergent cryptocurrency industry. Similarly, without consistently crafted, strong federal legislation to serve as a guide, the government entities at the state/local levels have been permitted some measure of freedom to enact policy that can address societal problems that may be caused by the cryptocurrency industry. Largely absent from the impending discussion is the analysis of the role that the court system may play in affecting the cryptocurrency industry. For example, in SEC vs. Shavers, a U.S. district court in Texas offered a landmark ruling on Bitcoin that was used in a Ponzi-scheme-type endeavor. In this ruling, the court found that investments in Bitcoin equated to securities that may provide some measure of clarity regarding future efforts to regulate this industry. The U.S. court system at all levels will most assuredly play a pivotal role in the years to come that will help to shape the policy landscape associated with the cryptocurrency industry, and is deserved of attention as this dynamic unfolds in the legal system.

At present, U.S. governmental efforts to address manifestations associated with the virtual currency industry is representative of a policy landscape that is still very much in the early stages of development, which yields a somewhat disjointed, free-for-all regulatory approach at each of the levels of the federal system. Similarly, the impending discussion of select key federal entities, to some degree, will mirror the relative nature of disarray and fragmentation that is reflected in governmental policy efforts designed to address the cryptocurrency industry. In the U.S., there are a wide range of organizational units at the federal-government level that may share some measure of responsibility in monitoring and correspondingly providing regulatory guidance for the broad field of virtual currencies in relation to each entity's mandated duties. This includes (but is not limited to) federal entities that are traditionally focused on policy dynamics involving various conceptualizations of fiscal value within the U.S. economy, such as the Internal Revenue Service (IRS: https://www.irs.gov/), Securities and Exchange Commission (SEC: https://www.sec.gov/), Commodity Future Trading Commission (CTFC: https://www.cftc.gov/), and Federal Trade Commission (https://www.ftc.gov/). In addition, the Department of the Treasury (https://home.treasury.gov/) houses a number of bureaus under its organizational umbrella that may play a role in shaping an understanding of the cryptocurrency industry, such as the U.S. Mint (https://

www.usmint.gov/), Bureau of Engraving and Printing (https://www.bep. gov/), and the Financial Crimes Enforcement Network (FinCEN: https:// www.fincen.gov/). Although falling outside the scope of the impending analysis, it is important to recognize government agencies such the Central Intelligence Agency (CIA: https://www.cia.gov/), the Department of Justice (https://www.justice.gov/), Secret Service (https://www.secretservice.gov/), Federal Bureau of Investigations (FBI: https://www.fbi.gov/), and the many bureaus that fall within the Department of Homeland Security (DHS: https://www.dhs.gov/) all play individualized roles in mitigating threats to U.S. security and economic interests, which may now include considerations of dynamics stemming from the field of cryptocurrency.

As the regulatory landscape is highly disjointed, a wide assortment of U.S. federal agencies is oft left to their own volition to develop policy means by which to address various types of virtual currency that may increasingly proliferate society. Each of the government entities may be involved with oversight in the field of virtual currency, which includes cryptocurrency, but with a slightly different focus as mandated by law. For example, the IRS is focused on defining cryptocurrency as property and then, based upon establishing said definition, taking actions such as determining if taxes have been collected for those making profits on transactions involving cryptocurrency. On the other hand, government bureaus such as FinCEN, which operates under the organizational umbrella of the Department of the Treasury, have different responsibilities associated with the regulation of those using cryptocurrency. In relation, this government entity is more focused on determining who is facilitating the exchange of cryptocurrency and if those individuals are indirectly or directly committing various criminal acts with such. In addition, there are government entities at the lower levels of government that also seek to address virtual currency usage in various circumstances. For example, the state of New York was the first to enact means that require those that deal in Bitcoin to obtain a license, and the state of Wyoming has instituted policy actions that have made that state more appealing to the cryptocurrency industry. The New York Bitcoin license (i.e. BitLicense) and Wyoming policy efforts to become an appealing destination for the cryptocurrency industry are good examples of the idea that states can serve to create policy templates that, if deemed a success, may be applied at any of the levels of government including that which is federal in scope. This idea was espoused by Supreme Court Justice Brandeis, whose comments in dissent for the case New State Ice Co v. Liebmann were as followed:

To stay experimentation in things social and economic is a grave responsibility. Denial of the right to experiment may be fraught with serious

224 Government Regulatory Efforts of the Cryptocurrency Industry

consequences to the nation. It is one of the happy incidents of the federal system that a single courageous state may, if its citizens choose, serve as a laboratory; and try novel social and economic experiments without risk to the rest of the country.

Source: Brandeis (1932)

In this sense, the state of New York may be viewed as acting as a "policy laboratory," serving at the forefront of the efforts to develop means to address issues associated with non-fiat virtual currency, which can ultimately provide a template in full, or partially, as to how other city governments, state governments, and even the federal government may initiate official means to address the same area of public policy. Similarly, the state of Wyoming may fulfill the same role by attempting to institute policy that creates a regulatory environment that is accommodating to the cryptocurrency industry, so that those involved in its mining and transacting will consider relocation to that jurisdiction.

The U.S. Federal Government and the Cryptocurrency Industry

Since being created in 2009, Bitcoin has slowly begun to proliferate the outer edges of the U.S. economy, in which there has been some measure of societal acceptance from system actors who have opted to pursue purchases of goods and services with this type of cryptocurrency. Relatedly, the major U.S. stock exchanges have started to report on the daily value of Bitcoin in U.S. dollars and have begun to allow for trading on select cryptocurrency exchanges such as Coinbase. Despite the encroachment of cryptocurrency into the U.S. economy, Congress has thus far taken very little initiative in developing broad legislative efforts designed to directly address a wide range of problems that may be attributed to this industry. In that, the contemporary Congress has yet to pass wide sweeping legislation regarding cryptocurrency, such as Bitcoin, that would allow the U.S. government to pursue a stable, whole-of-government approach to addressing this industry. At present, there may be sufficient momentum based on an assessment of situational and contextual circumstances to allow for strong considerations on behalf of the federal government to begin to develop policy that will contribute to sustaining a whole-of-government approach to the cryptocurrency industry. For example, support for such policy actions can be justified in part as being a necessary response to high-profile cases in which cryptocurrency exchanges such as FTX or Mt. Gox had their reputations tarnished, and, by extension that of the whole industry. The continued relative volatility in the value of Bitcoin in U.S.

dollars, the growth of the perceived need to protect consumers, and the still widely held societal confusion regarding the industry in general may provide a policy window by which the federal government may justify more broadly enacting policy initiatives designed to regulate aspects of cryptocurrency. Recently, there has been some minimal movement in this regard as the federal government has slowly begun to establish a policy path to more broadly recognize the need to officially address the cryptocurrency industry. In November of 2021, President Biden signed into law the Infrastructure Investment and Jobs Act (U.S. Congress, 2021), which included Sec. 80603, providing direction associated with "information reporting for brokers and digital assets." Sec. 80603 would serve as a step forward regarding federal efforts to develop statutory structure to help guide specific aspects of the cryptocurrency industry. Here, Sec. 80603 was representative of one of many topics of importance to be addressed through the broadly constructed Infrastructure Investment and Jobs Act, which may represent that there may be an opportunity in the future for Congress to create a wide range of legislation solely designed to directly and comprehensively regulate all aspects of the cryptocurrency industry. Relatedly, in March of 2022, President Joe Biden issued "Executive Order on Ensuring Responsible Development of Digital Assets" (https://www.whitehouse.gov/briefing-room/presidential-actions/2022/03/09/executive-order-on-ensuring-responsible-development-of-digital-assets/), which sought to begin to create a more unified path forward for federal agencies regarding a wide array of aspects associated with the cryptocurrency industry. Executive orders such as this can send a clear message to system actors within and outside government regarding a president's agenda in any area of public policy, including cryptocurrency. Relatedly, the entire qualifying bureaucratic structure of the executive branch is expected to acquiesce to the president's preferred agenda regarding the cryptocurrency industry, by taking agency actions that reflect the directives inherent within the executive order. In addition, the executive order serves as a situational and contextual cue indicating to Congress that it may be time to begin to broadly enact legislative guidelines that directly and comprehensively addresses the cryptocurrency industry.

Without a unifying legislative effort to create a singular set of guidelines for all levels of government to follow, many governmental agencies are left to their own volitation to develop internal actions that will allow for them to address this industry within the context of the responsibilities that are mandated by Congress for each respective government entity to perform. Although there is a wide assortment of government agencies that have issued guidelines associated with cryptocurrency, the following sections will only be focused on providing illustrative information

226 Government Regulatory Efforts of the Cryptocurrency Industry

regarding how a few select government agencies at the federal level have begun to address this industry. These select agencies are traditionally focused on addressing a wide array of fiscally oriented functions within the U.S. political system and the performance of these respective responsibilities will now be considered in the context of cryptocurrency. This includes the Internal Revenue Service (IRS: https://www.irs.gov/), Securities and Exchange Commission (SEC: https://www.sec.gov/), the Federal Trade Commission (FTC: https://www.ftc.gov/), and Financial Crimes Enforcement Network (FinCEN: https://www.fincen.gov/), which is one of the many bureaus within the Department of the Treasury (https://home.treasury.gov/). As providing a complete history of each federal agency is not the purported focus of this discussion, the following sections will only be concentrated on assessing how each's mandated mission is fulfilled through adaptive internal efforts in relation to the cryptocurrency industry. The cryptocurrency industry is still relatively new and, correspondingly, the efforts on behalf of government entities in American democracy are largely still very much in the early stages of development in most cases. In relation, the scope of agency initiatives is still somewhat limited to providing means to facilitate educational guidance and to provide clarity for how each entity expects system actors to behave when being involved in the industry.

The Internal Revenue Service and Cryptocurrency

As is the case with each bureaucratic entity within the U.S. federal government, the Internal Revenue Service (IRS) was granted a mandate by Congress that provides statutory guidance determining the policy purview for which it will be responsible. In relation, the IRS website provides the following information regarding the agency's mission and statutory authority, respectively:

The IRS Mission
Provide America's taxpayers top quality service by helping them understand and meet their tax responsibilities and enforce the law with integrity and fairness to all.

This mission statement describes our role and the public's expectation about how we should perform that role.

> -In the United States, the Congress passes tax laws and requires taxpayers to comply.
> -The taxpayer's role is to understand and meet his or her tax obligations.

-The IRS role is to help the large majority of compliant taxpayers with the tax law, while ensuring that the minority who are unwilling to comply pay their fair share.

Statutory Authority

The IRS is organized to carry out the responsibilities of the secretary of the Treasury under section 7801 of the Internal Revenue Code. The secretary has full authority to administer and enforce the internal revenue laws and has the power to create an agency to enforce these laws. The IRS was created based on this legislative grant.

Section 7803 of the Internal Revenue Code provides for the appointment of a commissioner of Internal Revenue to administer and supervise the execution and application of the internal revenue laws.

Source: IRS (2022)

Among the many functions performed, the IRS plays a key role in providing guidance as to how assessment processes are to be facilitated regarding a wide assortment of taxable items. As noted previously, non-fiat virtual currency is represented by cryptocurrency and Bitcoin is the most popular form of cryptocurrency. With this relational dynamic in mind, the IRS is responsible for deciding how cryptocurrency will be classified, which in turn will determine how this industry will ultimately be subject to taxation. In this, the classification of cryptocurrency and determining how gains/losses are defined will contribute to determining the nature of taxation for this industry. In relation, the IRS has issued official notices that sought to establish some clarity as to how cryptocurrency will be treated from a taxation standpoint. This includes the IRS notice 2014-21, which has served as a pivotal effort by the IRS in providing some measure of clarity regarding taxation and types of virtual currency. As cryptocurrency is a form of non-fat virtual currency these guidelines would be applicable to various examples in practice such as Bitcoin.

The IRS notice 2014-21 provides extensive taxation guidelines for virtual currency but only a select number of applicable aspects are excerpted from the "Frequently Asked Questions" section. The original Question (Q) and Answer (A) layout is provided here as it represents a natural conversation format that is more readily illuminating of key points in a relatively non-technical manner:

Q-1: How is virtual currency treated for federal tax purposes?
A-1: For federal tax purposes, virtual currency is treated as property. General tax principles applicable to property transactions apply to transactions using virtual currency.

Q-2: Is virtual currency treated as currency for purposes of determining whether a transaction results in foreign currency gain or loss under U.S. federal tax laws?
A-2: No. Under currently applicable law, virtual currency is not treated as currency that could generate foreign currency gain or loss for U.S. federal tax purposes.

Q-3: Must a taxpayer who receives virtual currency as payment for goods or services include in computing gross income the fair market value of the virtual currency?
A-3: Yes. A taxpayer who receives virtual currency as payment for goods or services must, in computing gross income, include the fair market value of the virtual currency, measured in U.S. dollars, as of the date that the virtual currency was received.

Q-4: What is the basis of virtual currency received as payment for goods or services in Q&A-3?
A-4: The basis of virtual currency that a taxpayer receives as payment for goods or services in Q&A-3 is the fair market value of the virtual currency in U.S. dollars as of the date of receipt.

Q-5: How is the fair market value of virtual currency determined?
A-5: For U.S. tax purposes, transactions using virtual currency must be reported in U.S. dollars. Therefore, taxpayers will be required to determine the fair market value of virtual currency in U.S. dollars as of the date of payment or receipt. If a virtual currency is listed on an exchange and the exchange rate is established by market supply and demand, the fair market value of the virtual currency is determined by converting the virtual currency into U.S. dollars (or into another real currency which in turn can be converted into U.S. dollars) at the exchange rate, in a reasonable manner that is consistently applied.

Q-6: Does a taxpayer have gain or loss upon an exchange of virtual currency for other property?
A-6: Yes. If the fair market value of property received in exchange for virtual currency exceeds the taxpayer's adjusted basis of the virtual currency, the taxpayer has taxable gain. The taxpayer has a loss if the fair market value of the property received is less than the adjusted basis of the virtual currency.

Q-7: What type of gain or loss does a taxpayer realize on the sale or exchange of virtual currency?

A-7: The character of the gain or loss generally depends on whether the virtual currency is a capital asset in the hands of the taxpayer. A taxpayer generally realizes capital gain or loss on the sale or exchange of virtual currency that is a capital asset in the hands of the taxpayer. For example, stocks, bonds, and other investment property are generally capital assets. A taxpayer generally realizes ordinary gain or loss on the sale or exchange of virtual currency that is not a capital asset in the hands of the taxpayer. Inventory and other property held mainly for sale to customers in a trade or business are examples of property that is not a capital asset.

Q-8: Does a taxpayer who "mines" virtual currency (for example, uses computer resources to validate Bitcoin transactions and maintain the public Bitcoin transaction ledger) realize gross income upon receipt of the virtual currency resulting from those activities?
A-8: Yes, when a taxpayer successfully "mines" virtual currency, the fair market value of the virtual currency as of the date of receipt is includible in gross income.

Q-9: Is an individual who "mines" virtual currency as a trade or business subject to self-employment tax on the income derived from those activities?
A-9: If a taxpayer's "mining" of virtual currency constitutes a trade or business, and the "mining" activity is not undertaken by the taxpayer as an employee, the net earnings from self-employment (generally, gross income derived from carrying on a trade or business less allowable deductions) resulting from those activities constitute self-employment income and are subject to the self-employment tax.

Q-10: Does virtual currency received by an independent contractor for performing services constitute self-employment income?
A-10: Yes. Generally, self-employment income includes all gross income derived by an individual from any trade or business carried on by the individual as other than an employee. Consequently, the fair market value of virtual currency received for services performed as an independent contractor, measured in U.S. dollars as of the date of receipt, constitutes self-employment income and is subject to the self-employment tax.

Source: IRS (2014)

The IRS Notice 2014-21 established several parameters regarding virtual currency, which under this internally generated policymaking endeavor encompasses cryptocurrencies, such as Bitcoin. This includes that IRS Notice

2014-21 indicates that, for federal taxing purposes, cryptocurrency would be classified as property (Q1) and is not treated as currency when reporting foreign currency gain or loss for transactions involving virtual currency (Q2). Additionally, it is required that the receipt of virtual currency as payment for goods or services must be included by the taxpayer when computing gross income and that fair market value of the virtual currency is measured in U.S. dollars (Q3, Q4, and Q5). This notice also designated that the taxpayer has a responsibly to indicate that gain or loss occurred based upon an exchange of virtual currency for other property (Q6). If the virtual currency is determined to be a capital asset or not, then IRS Notice 2014-21 indicates that this classification will affect the taxpayers gain or loss during the sale of virtual currency (Q7). Taxpayers that mine virtual currency such as those involved in blockchain verification processes for Bitcoin must include the corresponding rewards in virtual currency from completing this process as gross income (Q8). In relation, this notice specifies that miners that undertake this practice outside of their primary employment would be considered self-employed in this process and subject to self-employment tax (Q9). IRS Notice 2014-21 directs that an independent contractor in receipt of virtual currency as payment for services rendered constitutes self-employment income and is taxable as such (Q10). The IRS Notice 2014-21 serves as an important early step as it relates to providing taxation guidelines for cryptocurrency such as Bitcoin.

With Bitcoin coming into existence in 2009, it would be a few years before IRS Notice 2014-21 was created. This is likely due in part because cryptocurrency such as Bitcoin was still in the very early stages of development and had yet to even remotely be validated as medium of exchange in the economy that would then require the attention of the IRS in relation to taxation. The lag in official actions to address an emerging topic is quite common in cases in which new technology has yet to proliferate in significant levels throughout society, which then would require governmental considerations from a policymaking standpoint. As time passes, more information is generated about a given innovation, which can provide greater insight to policy makers as to whether problems have developed requiring official responses on behalf of government. Relatedly, this provides an opportunity for information gathering about the problem(s) in need of government intervention, which can contribute to determining the best policy choices to address said problems. Since 2014, the IRS has efforted to provide further guidance regarding the field of virtual currency, including the guidelines associated with digital assets, which expounds more specifically on cryptocurrency such as Bitcoin. This includes the 2019 IRS Revenue Ruling 2019-24 that addresses the tax implications of a hard fork. In brief, a hard fork involves a change in the blockchain protocol creating two simultaneous divergent validation branches at the disposal of miners, which can create cryptocurrency spawned of either chain. Ultimately, miners must choose which of the divergent protocol paths to follow during the blockchain verification processes. Eventually, it is expected that miners abandon the original, now outdated protocol in favor of the newest upgraded version of blockchain. Until that time, miners' retention of cryptocurrency may be held in the original blockchain protocol and the new blockchain protocol, which would affect taxation schemes dependent upon the following results:

(1) A taxpayer does not have gross income under § 61 as a result of a hard fork of a cryptocurrency the taxpayer owns if the taxpayer does not receive units of a new cryptocurrency.
(2) A taxpayer has gross income, ordinary in character, under § 61 as a result of an airdrop of a new cryptocurrency following a hard fork if the taxpayer receives units of new cryptocurrency.

Source: IRS (2019)

In relation, the IRS Revenue Ruling 2019-24 regarding hard forks addresses how this process may affect gross income, which in turn influences taxation guidelines associated with the cryptocurrency in question. Thus far, the IRS has issued a number of internal policy initiatives that helps to provide greater clarity as to circumstances that may affect how taxation of cryptocurrency, such as Bitcoin, will be facilitated. Doing so provides direction to those that may be utilizing cryptocurrency to engage in various activities within the economy, illuminating how the IRS will expect taxation filing to be conducted in this regard. It is noteworthy that, since 2014, the IRS sought to establish early guidance regarding taxation of cryptocurrency, indicating that this federal agency avoided opting to simply ignore the growing presence and growth of this industry throughout modern society. In this sense, aspects of permissionless innovation initially served as the rationale used to guide internal policymaking on behalf of the IRS regarding taxation of the cryptocurrency industry. Between 2009 and 2014, the IRS seemingly avoided rushing to pass a slew of significant internal guidelines without the benefit of having first generated helpful information regarding the usage of Bitcoin in the U.S. economy. With sufficient time passing allowing for such, the IRS then opted to lean more moderately toward the application of the precautionary principle, in which information gathered during the initial stages of Bitcoin presence in the U.S. economy was utilized by decision makers to provide cogent, responsible internal policy responses to address the growth of this form of cryptocurrency. The actions of the IRS provide further credence as to the possibility that the regulatory environment in the U.S. represents something of a sliding scale in terms of application of competing rationales used to guide governmental decision making. In this case, the IRS opted to apply permissionless innovation during the earliest stages of Bitcoin's development, followed by the incremental usage of the precautionary principle to begin to establish a more informed, responsible response to this industry. By avoiding the provision of strict statutory guidance focused on ousting or overly penalizing the cryptocurrency industry as it relates to the domain of taxation, the judicious use of the precautionary principle eluded being overly bombastic from a policy sense. Here, cryptocurrency began to be incorporated into the taxation scheme in a manner that would allow for its continued development while still ensuring its proper contributive role from a taxing standpoint. After initially employing permissionless innovation, the IRS policy efforts soon reflected an approach that judiciously adopted the precautionary principle in a moderate capacity in the attempt to begin to bring cryptocurrency into the taxation fold.

The Securities and Exchange Commission and Cryptocurrency

When it comes to the cryptocurrency industry, there may be concerns over a lack of transparency and accountability associated with investment opportunities involving variations, such as Bitcoin, that would otherwise be present with traditional fiat currency-based exchanges. Without such official oversight efforts, it may be difficult for cryptocurrency to be able to break free of the perceptual and functional constraints that may limit Bitcoin to being viewed as a viable investment opportunity, relegating it further to a niche status and limiting its ability to more fully proliferate the economic system. Wolfson (2018, paragraph 2) notes that "the Securities and Exchange Commission (SEC) and the Commodity Futures Trading Commission (CFTC) are the two federal agencies that serve as the primary regulators of cryptocurrencies in the U.S." Here, each government entity defined cryptocurrency as either a security (SEC) or commodity (CFTC), and then subsequently developed policy to guide the agency based on the authority granted on behalf of Congressional mandates (Wolfson, 2018, paragraph 4). In the interest of brevity, only information regarding the SEC and cryptocurrency will be expanded on at length below. Essentially, the Securities and Exchange Commission (SEC) seeks to address the cryptocurrency industry through the policy lens of a specific regulatory domain that is mandated by Congress. In general, the Securities and Exchange Commission (SEC) plays an important regulatory role in dynamically maintaining a variety of protections associated with the following three broad categories within the agency's mandated purview:

(1) Protecting Investors: Companies offering securities for sale to the public must tell the truth about their business, the securities they are selling, and the investment risks. Those who sell and trade securities and offer advice to investors – including, for example, brokers, dealers, investment advisers, and exchanges – must treat investors fairly and honestly.
(2) Facilitating Capital Formation: In 2020, nearly $5 trillion was raised in public and private securities offerings, promoting economic growth and job creation.
(3) Maintaining Fair, Orderly, and Efficient Markets: We monitor the activities of more than 28,000 entities in the securities industry, including investment advisers, broker-dealers, and securities exchanges.

Source: U.S. Securities and Exchange Commission (2022a)

Among the many responsibilities performed by the SEC, this federal entity provides educational endeavors designed to inform consumers as to the potential dangers of investing in a given field, which has now begun to include cryptocurrency examples such as Bitcoin. This includes the SEC's Office of Investor Education and Advocacy, which issues a series of investor alerts including the 2014 entitled "Investor Alert: Bitcoin and Other Virtual Currency-Related Investments," which provided the following educational information associated with issuing a broad warning attributed to those interested in investing in this type of cryptocurrency:

The rise of Bitcoin and other virtual and digital currencies creates new concerns for investors. A new product, technology, or innovation – such as Bitcoin – has the potential to give rise both to frauds and high-risk investment opportunities. Potential investors can be easily enticed with the promise of high returns in a new investment space and also may be less skeptical when assessing something novel, new and cutting-edge.

Source: U.S. Securities and Exchange Commission
(2022b, paragraph 1)

Furthermore, the SEC investor alert provided potential consumers with expansive information regarding Bitcoin, including the following working definition:

Bitcoin has been described as a decentralized, peer-to-peer virtual currency that is used like money – it can be exchanged for traditional currencies such as the U.S. dollar, or used to purchase goods or services, usually online. Unlike traditional currencies, Bitcoin operates without central authority or banks and is not backed by any government.

Source: U.S. Securities and Exchange Commission (2022b, paragraph 4)

The SEC's mandate requires for this agency to take a specifically tailored approach to action that is ultimately linked to the process of defining cryptocurrency as a security. In the context of the SEC mandate, this investor alert also provided the following educational information which warns potential consumers as to the high risk often associated with investing in emergent technologies and provides an illustrative example of this dynamic in action, in which the SEC filed charges via the U.S. court system to address a circumstance in which Bitcoin was used in a nefarious circumstance that reflected aspects of a Ponzi scheme, respectively:

Innovations and new technologies are often used by fraudsters to perpetrate fraudulent investment schemes. Fraudsters may entice investors by touting a Bitcoin investment "opportunity" as a way to get into this cutting-edge space, promising or guaranteeing high investment returns. Investors may find these investment pitches hard to resist.

[...]

Bitcoin Ponzi scheme. In July 2013, the SEC charged an individual for an alleged Bitcoin-related Ponzi scheme in SEC v. Shavers. The defendant advertised a Bitcoin "investment opportunity" in an online Bitcoin forum, promising investors up to 7% interest per week and that the invested funds would be used for Bitcoin activities. Instead, the defendant allegedly used bitcoins from new investors to pay existing investors and to pay his personal expenses.

Source: U.S. Securities and Exchange Commission (2022b, paragraphs 6 and 7)

This SEC investor alert also highlighted several warning signs of investment fraud that are applicable to potential investors in Bitcoin, which are summarized as followed:

"Guaranteed" high investment returns. There is no such thing as guaranteed high investment returns. Be wary of anyone who promises that you will receive a high rate of return on your investment, with little or no risk.

Unsolicited offers. An unsolicited sales pitch may be part of a fraudulent investment scheme. Exercise extreme caution if you receive an unsolicited communication – meaning you didn't ask for it and don't know the sender – about an investment opportunity.

Unlicensed sellers. Federal and state securities laws require investment professionals and their firms who offer and sell investments to be licensed or registered. Many fraudulent investment schemes involve unlicensed individuals or unregistered firms. Check license and registration status by searching the SEC's Investment Adviser Public Disclosure (IAPD) website or FINRA's BrokerCheck website.

No net worth or income requirements. The federal securities laws require securities offerings to be registered with the SEC unless an exemption from registration applies. Most registration exemptions require that investors are accredited investors. Be highly suspicious of private (i.e., unregistered) investment opportunities that do not ask about your net worth or income.

Sounds too good to be true. If the investment sounds too good to be true, it probably is. Remember that investments providing higher returns typically involve more risk.

Pressure to buy RIGHT NOW. Fraudsters may try to create a false sense of urgency to get in on the investment. Take your time researching an investment opportunity before handing over your money.

Source: U.S. Securities and Exchange Commission
(2022b, paragraph 8)

Similarly to the IRS, the SEC also sought to address cryptocurrency such as Bitcoin in relation to the mandated activities within this agency's purview of responsibilities. Relatedly, the SEC has begun to offer guidance to potential consumers regarding an emerging market for securities investment involving cryptocurrency: Initial Coin Offerings (ICOs). This includes providing information that introduces potential investors to the fact that ICOs provide an opportunity to investors to provide start-up costs for various forms of cryptocurrency. Regarding potential dangers associated with investing in ICOs, the SEC provides the following guidance, which echoes the stance taken on behalf of the agency that continuously provides cautionary advice, alerting potential consumers as to the fiscal dangers associated with investing in emerging markets such as cryptocurrency:

While these digital assets and the technology behind them may present a new and efficient means for carrying out financial transactions, they also bring increased risk of fraud and manipulation because the markets for these assets are less regulated than traditional capital markets.

Source: U.S. Securities and Exchange Commission (2022c)

As providing educational parameters are an important part of the agency's responsibility, the SEC's initial efforts provide helpful guidance

236 Government Regulatory Efforts of the Cryptocurrency Industry

to those that may be interested in various investing opportunities associated with cryptocurrency. This is done in part as a proactive effort by which the SEC sought to provide information regarding this emergent industry capable of establishing a foundation of knowledge, for consumer and market protections alike, for those interested in investing in cryptocurrency. In fulfillment of its duty to protect potential investors and monitor various types of markets involved in securities exchanges, the SEC has thus far provided a wide array of information to potential consumers that may help to stymie cryptocurrency-based fraud. In addition to providing educational information to potential investors, the SEC also performs an important enforcement function, in that this agency levies legal charges against those alleged to have committed various market illegalities involving crypto assets. This includes instances in which the SEC has sought legal actions against those believed to have committed fraud facilitated through cryptocurrency-based Ponzi schemes, promoted investments in a fictious cryptocurrency company, and when a social media influencer may have failed to disclose payments received for offering an endorsement of a cryptocurrency company (https://www.sec.gov/spotlight/cybersecurity-enforcement-actions). In all, the SEC's present policy actions are often focused on enacting a blend of initiatives that are designed to be educational or enforcement in nature, which are each capable in their own way of guiding the behavior of system actors as it relates to the cryptocurrency industry.

The Federal Trade Commission and Cryptocurrency

In the context of cryptocurrency such as Bitcoin, the Federal Trade Commission also may play a role in regulating this industry. The Federal Trade Commission Act of 1914 was the legislative foundation by which the corresponding federal agency (i.e. the Federal Trade Commission) would be established in 1915 and that would establish a wide range of responsibilities, which are summarized below:

> The Federal Trade Commission Act is the primary statute of the Commission. Under this Act, as amended, the Commission is empowered, among other things, to (a) prevent unfair methods of competition and unfair or deceptive acts or practices in or affecting commerce; (b) seek monetary redress and other relief for conduct injurious to consumers; (c) prescribe rules defining with specificity acts or practices that are unfair or deceptive, and establishing requirements designed to prevent such acts or practices; (d) gather and compile information and conduct investigations relating to the organization, business, practices, and

management of entities engaged in commerce; and (e) make reports and legislative recommendations to Congress and the public.

Source: Federal Trade Commission (2022a)

The FTC is responsible for a wide range of activities that are designed to provide various protections to consumers. This includes efforts to provide compensation to those consumers that may have suffered a fiscal loss that was the direct result of disingenuous or outright illegal business practices. The FTC also establishes guidelines that determine what would constitute unfair or deceptive practices in a given industry, conducts investigations to determine if unfair business practices are present and furnish reports to Congress (and the public) that will be the basis for future legislative changes if deemed necessary. The FTC designates the following three broad categories as being the main focal point of responsibilities fulfilled by this federal agency:

1) Enforcement

The FTC enforces federal consumer protection laws that prevent fraud, deception and unfair business practices. The Commission also enforces federal antitrust laws that prohibit anticompetitive mergers and other business practices that could lead to higher prices, fewer choices, or less innovation.

Whether combating telemarketing fraud, Internet scams or price-fixing schemes, the FTC's mission is to protect consumers and promote competition.

The FTC administers a wide variety of laws and regulations, including the Federal Trade Commission Act, Telemarketing Sale Rule, Identity Theft Act, Fair Credit Reporting Act, and Clayton Act. In total, the Commission has enforcement or administrative responsibilities under more than 70 laws.

Source: Federal Trade Commission (2022b)

2) Policy

We work to advance government policies that protect consumers and promote competition. As part of its policy, advocacy, and research work, the agency:

- files advocacy letters
- files amicus briefs to aid in court deliberations
- gives Congressional testimony
- solicits and reviews public comments regarding rules, cases, and policies

- issues advisory opinions
- conducts workshops
- publishes reports that examine cutting-edge antitrust and consumer protection issues
- conducts studies pursuant to Section 6 of the Federal Trade Commission Act, 15 USC § 46

The FTC also works with competition and consumer protection agencies around the world to promote cooperation and sound policy approaches. The FTC has built strong relationships with its counterparts abroad, and helps countries around the world to develop and enhance their competition and consumer protection programs.

Source: Federal Trade Commission (2022c)

3) Advice and Guidance
Learn more about your rights as a consumer and how to spot and avoid scams. Find the resources you need to understand how consumer protection law impacts your business.

Source: Federal Trade Commission (2022d)

Ultimately, the FTC, in many ways, is focused on establishing a transparent and accountable playing field, so that consumers are able to transact within a market environment that is more equitable, for all parties, from an information standpoint especially. In the vein of establishing advice and guidance, the FTC has provided information on the agency's website and developed educational programs to provide relevant materials to consumers regarding the growth of the emergent field of Bitcoin. For example, the following broad warnings are provided at the FTC website for those who are potentially interested in cryptocurrency investments in an effort to help avoid industry scams designed to defraud consumers:

Only scammers demand payment in cryptocurrency. No legitimate business is going to demand you send cryptocurrency in advance – not to buy something, and not to protect your money. That's always a scam.

Only scammers will guarantee profits or big returns. Don't trust people who promise you can quickly and easily make money in the crypto markets.

Never mix online dating and investment advice. If you meet someone on a dating site or app, and they want to show you how to invest in crypto, or asks you to send them crypto, that's a scam.

Source: Federal Trade Commission (2022e)

The FTC also holds educational events, such as the one held on June 25, 2018, at DePaul University, that was entitled "Decrypting Cryptocurrency Scams" (Federal Trade Commission 2018), and which sought to provide the following informative guidance:

> As consumer interest in cryptocurrencies like bitcoin has grown, scammers have reportedly become more active in this area. Reported scams include deceptive investment and business opportunities, bait-and-switch schemes, and deceptively marketed mining machines. The FTC has continued its efforts to educate consumers about cryptocurrencies and hold fraudsters accountable.
>
> The half-day event brought together consumer groups, law enforcement, research organizations, and the private sector to explore how scammers are exploiting public interest in cryptocurrencies such as bitcoin and Litecoin and to discuss ways to empower and protect consumers.
>
> *Source: Federal Trade Commission (2018, paragraphs 1–3)*

Should the industry's influence expand further into the U.S. economy, government entities, such as the FTC, will be continuously responsible for efforts to devise diverse means designed to protect consumers who may be interested in delving into fiscal opportunities that involve cryptocurrency, such as Bitcoin. This is especially important as the rise of cryptocurrency usage in society has resulted in a corresponding increase in fiscal losses, which are often based on online scams involving this industry (Fletcher, 2022). Relatedly, recent reports have indicated that cryptocurrency scams have increasingly been on the rise as fraudsters are targeting the public at an increasing rate, as evidenced in part by the following:

> From January 1, 2021 through March 31, 2022, people reported to the FTC that $417 million in cryptocurrency was lost to fraud originating on social media. $273 million of these losses were to fraud categorized as investment related, followed by romance scams ($69 million), and business imposters ($35 million).
>
> *Source: Fletcher (2022)*

Here, the rise in cryptocurrency scams facilitated through social media has become a growing concern for the FTC, who is charged with the responsibility to assist in the protection of consumers by monitoring markets. The rise of social media's role in cryptocurrency fraud is going to be an area of concern that will require government intervention to limit, or preferably eliminate, the ability of this type of fraud to exist in the market. In this, there may be some measure of cooperation on behalf of federal agencies that can contribute to this goal, and information sharing may serve as a critical first step in such efforts. The educational efforts on behalf of the FTC also extend to include other law-enforcement entities, as reflected by the Consumer Sentinel Network that is maintained by the agency (https://www.ftc.gov/enforcement/consumer-sentinel-network). The Consumer Sentinel Network is available without cost to any law-enforcement entity at the national, state, and local levels of government, and this online investigative tool provides access to a database of reports, submitted to the FTC, associated with potential scams meant to defraud consumers through a diverse array of topical means (Federal Trade Commission, 2022f). The idea behind this educational effort is to reduce the ability of fraudsters to succeed by sharing pertinent information with all levels of law enforcement, in the hopes that doing so will help with preventing future fraud-related harm to consumers. Consequently, this effort on behalf of the FTC runs counter to the somewhat antiquated, traditional silo model of bureaucracy and is more representative of interagency behavior that reflects a cooperative response to the cryptocurrency industry.

The FTC has implemented a broad and diverse educational campaign that is designed to disseminate pertinent information to a wide array of system actors in the hopes of preventing cryptocurrency related fraud. However, at present, there is generally a lesser presence on behalf of the FTC that is geared toward enforcement of the cryptocurrency industry in relation to the mandated duties of the agency. In general, the FTC is empowered to pursue enforcement functions in accordance with its mandated duties, which provides an opportunity for the agency to actively engage in protecting consumers against various forms of fraud, corruption, and unfair business practices. Among the over 70 statutes that are enforced by the FTC, thus far there is very little evidence that cryptocurrency is yet a primary focus of this agency. For example, by clicking on the "industry" tab at the statutes section of the FTC website, there are 28 main areas of interest, none of which include any variations of cryptocurrency (Federal Trade Commission, 2022g). Similarly, while using the broader "search" function at the statutes section, terms such as "cryptocurrency" and "Bitcoin" result in limited results being found (Federal Trade Commission, 2022g). This is an area that is deserved of further attention on behalf of the agency itself, and relatedly by those investigating the FTC to determine its role in the cryptocurrency industry in the years to come.

The Department of the Treasury and Cryptocurrency: Financial Crimes and Enforcement Network (FinCEN)

As noted previously, the Necessary and Proper Clause of the Constitution empowered the U.S. Congress to create the Department of the Treasury, which was mandated to fulfill very important functions associated with maintaining a strong economy and protecting against threats to the financial system. This is indicated by the mission statement at the website for the U.S. Department of the Treasury:

> The U.S. Department of the Treasury's mission is to maintain a strong economy and create economic and job opportunities by promoting the conditions that enable economic growth and stability at home and abroad, strengthen national security by combating threats and protecting the integrity of the financial system, and manage the U.S. Government's finances and resources effectively.
>
> *Source: U.S. Department of the Treasury (2022)*

By extension, Congress also drafted legislation that would create the U.S. Mint (responsible for furnishing fiat coinage) and the Bureau of Engraving and Printing (responsible for furnishing fiat paper money), which would play an important role as these two bureaus would fall under the organizational umbrella of the Department of the Treasury. Here, it will be prudent to introduce the particulars associated with another key bureau within the Department of the Treasury, which has a direct role in addressing specific criminality concerns that may stem from the cryptocurrency industry: Financial Crimes and Enforcement Network (FinCEN). The mission statement of this bureaucratic entity is as follows:

> The mission of the Financial Crimes Enforcement Network is to safeguard the financial system from illicit use, combat money laundering and its related crimes including terrorism, and promote national security through the strategic use of financial authorities and the collection, analysis, and dissemination of financial intelligence.
>
> *Source: FinCEN (2022a)*

FinCEN is a bureau operating within the Department of the Treasury that "carries out its mission by receiving and maintaining financial transactions data; analyzing and disseminating that data for law-enforcement purposes; and building global cooperation with counterpart organizations in other countries and with international bodies" (FinCEN, 2022b, paragraph 2). Here, the focus of FinCEN's responsibility is broader than many other U.S. bureaucratic entities, due in part because of having to address the global reach associated with the cryptocurrency industry that, due to its digital nature, easily traverses nations' borders, creating a more elusive dynamic, from a regulatory standpoint, that to some degree may be insufficiently addressed through lone jurisdictional efforts. Domestically, FinCEN plays a primary role in the implementation of the previously

242 Government Regulatory Efforts of the Cryptocurrency Industry

mentioned Bank Secrecy Act of 1970 (and subsequent amended legislative updates, such as Title III of the 2001 Patriot Act). Calvery (2013, p. 3) observes that the primary function of FinCEN is "in administering the BSA is to ensure the integrity and transparency of the U.S. financial system so that money laundering and terrorist financing can be prevented and, where it does occur, be detected or follow up action." To expound further on the mandated duties issued by Congress per key legislative acts, the FinCEN bureau is focused on the following:

> FinCEN exercises regulatory functions primarily under the Currency and Financial Transactions Reporting Act of 1970, as amended by Title III of the USA PATRIOT Act of 2001 and other legislation, which legislative framework is commonly referred to as the "Bank Secrecy Act" (BSA). The BSA is the nation's first and most comprehensive Federal anti-money laundering and counter-terrorism financing (AML/CFT) statute. In brief, the BSA authorizes the Secretary of the Treasury to issue regulations requiring banks and other financial institutions to take a number of precautions against financial crime, including the establishment of AML programs and the filing of reports that have been determined to have a high degree of usefulness in criminal, tax, and regulatory investigations and proceedings, and certain intelligence and counter-terrorism matters. The Secretary of the Treasury has delegated to the Director of FinCEN the authority to implement, administer, and enforce compliance with the BSA and associated regulations.
>
> *Source: FinCEN (2022b)*

As an enforcement arm of the Department of the Treasury, FinCEN's mandate requires preventive actions that are focused on addressing the causal link between finances and a wide scope of criminal acts, which may serve to threaten various aspects of U.S. security. Relatedly, the emergence of cryptocurrency such as Bitcoin has caused FinCEN to begin to focus its administrative attention on how this industry may be used in anti-money laundering and counter-terrorism financing (AML/CFT). FinCEN's responsibility as it relates to AML/CFT in the context of cryptocurrency will be expanded on here to provide further evidence of the important role that cyclically flexible adjustments to policy initiatives plays in regulating this industry to help prevent acts of criminality. Prior to the creation of cryptocurrency, the domain of FinCEN was generally focused on areas such as ensuring that fiat currency was not used in efforts to commit a wide range of criminality in association with AML/CFT. As cryptocurrency, such as Bitcoin, has slowly permeated the fringes of the U.S. economic system, government entities such as FinCEN have been required to consider the implication of this proliferation in the context of mandated duties assigned by Congress.

The recent growth of virtual currency, which includes types of cryptocurrencies, such as Bitcoin, has yielded newly emergent concerns for government entities, such as FinCEN, in ensuring its ability to meet the technological challenges presented by this industry within the context of its mandated duties. This includes concerns associated with preventing the usage of virtual currencies to facilitate a wide range of criminal acts, such as funding terrorism and money laundering. Goldman et al. (2017, p. 12) notes that "virtual currencies may be appealing to terrorist groups for the same reason they appeal to legitimate actors. VCs are mainly distinguished by their global reach, often a decentralized structure, varying degrees of anonymity, rapid transactions, and minimal costs." Thus far, terrorists' usage of virtual currency is presently an occurrence that is "fairly recent" and considered to be "episodic and not widespread," with the understanding that the more familiar the world becomes within this form of currency the more possible that criminality may be committed with such (Goldman et al., 2017, p. 13). Virtual currency has an appeal to those seeking to commit illegal acts associated with money laundering and terrorism on the basis that: 1) clients maintain a level of pseudo-anonymity, 2) there is a decentralized dynamic lacking in administrators actively logging information regarding clients, 3) virtual currency is user friendly and relatively inexpensive, 4) virtual currency has a globalized reach that is available to anyone with a mobile device (cell phone, computer, etc.) that connects to the Internet, 5) cryptocurrency such as Bitcoin utilizes blockchain, which ensures relative security for users, and 6) cryptocurrency transactions are irreversible (Abboushi, 2017, p.15). Similarly, Calvery (2013) observes that those intent on committing illegal acts may attempt to use virtual currency to facilitate such because this:

- Enables the user to remain relatively anonymous.
- Is relatively simple for the user to navigate.
- May have low fees.
- Is accessible across the globe with a simple Internet connection.
- Can be used both to store value and make international transfers of value.
- Does not typically have transaction limits.
- Is generally secure.
- Features irrevocable transactions.
- Depending on the system, may have been created with the intent (and added features) to facilitate money laundering.

244 Government Regulatory Efforts of the Cryptocurrency Industry

- If it is decentralized, has no administrator to maintain information on users and report suspicious activity to governmental authorities.
- Can exploit weaknesses in the anti-money laundering/counter-terrorist financing (AML/CFT) regimes of various jurisdictions, including international disparities in, and a general lack of, regulations needed to effectively support the prevention and detection of money laundering and terrorist financing.

Source: Calvery (2013, p. 1)

Abboushi (2017, p.15) notes that such qualities "may appeal to parties tempted to use the system for illicit purposes especially when coupled with the fact that anti-money laundering (AML) and counter terrorist financing (CFT) laws in different jurisdictions across the globe are weak and have varying degrees of rigor, consistency and enforcement." Calvery (2013, p. 3) expands on this notion by noting that "because any financial institution, payment system, or medium of exchange has the potential to be exploited for money laundering, fighting such illicit use requires consistent regulation across the financial system." Calvery (2013, p. 3) explains that "virtual currency is not different from other financial products and services in this regard." Calvery (2013, p. 3) notes that because of this "what is important is that financial institutions that deal in virtual currency put effective AML/CFT controls in place to harden themselves from becoming the targets of illicit actors that would exploit any identified vulnerabilities." Calvery (2013, p. 4) reports that on "March 18, 2013, FinCEN supplemented its money services business regulations with interpretive guidance designed to clarify the applicability of the regulations implementing the BSA to persons creating, obtaining, distributing, exchanging, accepting, or transmitting virtual currencies." Calvery (2013, p. 4) further explains that "FinCEN's guidance explains that administrators or exchangers of virtual currencies must register with FinCEN, and institute certain recordkeeping, reporting and AML program control measures, unless an exception to these requirements applies." Calvery (2013, p. 4) closes by noting that "the guidance also explains that those who use virtual currencies exclusively for common personal transactions like buying goods or services online are users, not subject to regulatory requirements under the BSA." Essentially, FinCEN extended the requirements associated with transparency that are inherent within the BSA, and subsequent legislative amendments to the cryptocurrency industry, by attaching such guidelines to the exchange services that transact in virtual currency.

This effort on behalf of FinCEN appropriately highlights the previous discussions regarding the fact that federal entities often pursue achieving mandated responsibilities by co-opting applicable aspects of preexisting legislative actions. Ultimately, FinCEN has within its operational purview means by which to apply the BSA and the U.S. Patriot Act of 2001, which together serve as legislative efforts providing coordinating parameters focused on establishing reporting dynamics as part of the broader effort to prevent criminality facilitated through cryptocurrency. As such, it is important to provide further descriptive information regarding the role of Department of the Treasury in the fulfillment of BSA related duties. In relation, the Office of the Comptroller of the Currency (2013) is a yet another bureau, within the layered labyrinth operating under the organizational umbrella of the Department of the Treasury, that provides the following descriptive information regarding the broad guidelines established by the BSA:

> Under the Bank Secrecy Act (BSA), financial institutions are required to assist U.S. government agencies in detecting and preventing money laundering, and: Keep records of cash purchases of negotiable instruments; File reports of cash transactions exceeding $10,000 (daily aggregate amount); and Report suspicious activity that might signal criminal activity (e.g., money laundering, tax evasion).
>
> *Source: Office of the Comptroller of the Currency (2013)*

The Office of the Comptroller of the Currency (2013) adds that "an amendment to the BSA incorporates provisions of the USA Patriot Act, which requires every bank to adopt a customer identification program as part of its BSA compliance program." Here, the BSA and Patriot Act are legislative designs focused on ensuring reporting methods are congruent to prevent a wide range of criminal acts by providing the following statutory guidance:

> Section 326 of the USA PATRIOT Act amended the BSA to require financial institutions, including broker-dealers, to establish written customer identification programs (CIP). FinCEN's implementing rule requires a broker-dealer's CIP to include, at a minimum, procedures for: obtaining customer identifying information from each customer prior to account opening; verifying the identity of each customer, to the extent reasonable and practicable, within a reasonable time before or after account opening; making and maintaining a record of information obtained relating to identity verification; determining within a reasonable time after account opening or earlier whether a customer appears on any list of known or suspected terrorist organizations designated by Treasury; and providing each customer with adequate notice, prior to opening an account, that information is being requested to verify the customer's identity.
>
> *Source: U.S. Securities and Exchange Commission (2022d)*

In the modern era, the aforementioned guidelines associated with the BSA have been extended to include a wider variety of non-banking entities that may be involved in transmitting convertible currencies. The efforts on behalf of FinCEN to ensure reporting requirements associated with the BSA is one that involve defining money service businesses (MSBs) and participants (user, administrator, and exchanger) that may be involved in transactions involving convertible currency, which are transmitting through such third-party venues. This includes the following guidelines, which are geared toward expanding the traditional scope of the BSA from banking institutions to include non-banking institutions in the following context:

FinCEN's rules define certain businesses or individuals as money services businesses (MSBs) depending on the nature of their financial activities. MSBs have registration requirements and a range of anti-money laundering, recordkeeping, and reporting responsibilities under FinCEN's regulations. The guidance considers the use of virtual currencies from the perspective of several categories within FinCEN's definition of MSBs.

Source: FinCEN (2013a)

In the release entitled "Am I an MSB?" FinCEN (2013b) provides further definitional parameters to include a wide range of services provided (i.e. money orders, traveler's checks, money transmission, check cashing, currency exchange, currency dealing, prepaid access) by non-banking financial institutions that would qualify as money service businesses (MSBs), which would require the entity to report information in accordance with the BSA. Relatedly, the following information highlights activity thresholds regarding money transmitters and fiscal entities that falls outside definitional parameters associated with defining an MSBs:

No activity threshold applies to the definition of money transmitter. Thus, a person who engages as a business in the transfer of funds is an MSB as a money transmitter, regardless of the amount of money transmission activity.

Notwithstanding the previous discussion, the term "money services business" does not include:

A bank, as that term is defined in 31 CFR 1010.100(d) (formerly 31 CFR 103.11(c)), or A person registered with, and regulated or examined by, the Securities and Exchange Commission or the Commodity Futures Trading Commission.

Source: FinCEN (2022c)

Additionally, FinCEN extended BSA requirements associated with reporting information to include specific groups engaged in exchange services that transact with various forms of convertible virtual currency, in which the following information and guidance was provided:

This guidance refers to the participants in generic virtual currency arrangements, using the terms "user," "exchanger," and "administrator." A user is a person that obtains virtual currency to purchase goods or services. An exchanger is a person engaged as a business in the exchange of virtual currency for real currency, funds, or other virtual currency. An administrator is a person engaged as a business in issuing (putting into circulation) a virtual currency, and who has the authority to redeem (to withdraw from circulation) such virtual currency.

Users of Virtual Currency: A user who obtains convertible virtual currency and uses it to purchase real or virtual goods or services is not an MSB under FinCEN's regulations. Such activity, in and of itself, does not fit within the definition of "money transmission services" and therefore is not subject to FinCEN's registration, reporting, and recordkeeping regulations for MSBs.Administrators and Exchangers of Virtual Currency

An administrator or exchanger that (1) accepts and transmits a convertible virtual currency or (2) buys or sells convertible virtual currency for any reason is a money transmitter under FinCEN's regulations, unless a limitation to or exemption from the definition applies to the person. FinCEN's regulations define the term "money transmitter" as a person that provides money transmission services, or any other person engaged in the transfer of funds. The term "money transmission services" means "the acceptance of currency, funds, or other value that substitutes for currency from one person and the transmission of currency, funds, or other value that substitutes for currency to another location or person by any means."

The definition of a money transmitter does not differentiate between real currencies and convertible virtual currencies. Accepting and transmitting anything of value that substitutes for currency makes a person a money transmitter under the regulations implementing the BSA. FinCEN has reviewed different activities involving virtual currency and has made determinations regarding the appropriate regulatory treatment of administrators and exchangers under three scenarios: brokers and dealers of e-currencies and e-precious metals; centralized convertible virtual currencies; and de-centralized convertible virtual currencies.

Source: FinCEN (2013c)

248 Government Regulatory Efforts of the Cryptocurrency Industry

FinCEN indicates that a money transmitter working within an MSB, by definition, can enact transfers in fiat currency or convertible virtual currencies (such as types of cryptocurrencies like Bitcoin). In relation, FinCEN provides definitions for three categories of participants that may generally be involved in facilitating cryptocurrency transactions: user, exchanger, and administrator. A user that obtains and transacts in any form of convertible virtual currency would not be defined as a money service business, indicating that an individual engaged in such practices would fall outside the FinCEN statutory requirements in conjuncture with the BSA associated with registration, reporting, and recordkeeping. However, the acceptance and transmittance of "anything of value" that can be converted into fiat currency would qualify the administrator or exchanger as a money transmitter, which would require adhering to FinCEN's guidance associated with the BSA. Here, regulatory guidelines for MSBs associated with the BSA would be enforced by FinCEN for administrators and exchangers involved in transacting in convertible virtual currency. In this sense, FinCEN would monitor the behavior of actors operating within the money service business such as administrators and exchangers by requiring that those engaged in the business side of transacting in all forms of convertible currency—be it fiat or non-fiat cryptocurrency—would be required to obtain information about their clients in the same manner that banks are required to do so in accordance with the BSA. As such, exchange services dealing in convertible cryptocurrency such as Bitcoin would be required to ascertain personal information to identify the clients that are utilizing this type of MSB. The application of the BSA in the context of MSBs is representative of an attempt by government to thwart those seeking to use anonymity typical of cryptocurrency that is established through its internal, decentralized blockchain process in order to commit a wide range of criminal acts (i.e. money laundering, funding of terrorism, etc.). Without an overarching legislative effort on behalf of Congress to create a whole-of-government approach to addressing the field of cryptocurrency, bureaucratic entities such as FinCEN must continuously seek to apply regulatory guidance based on the potential applicability of existing policy such as the Bank Secrecy Act.

With the understanding that domestic efforts to thwart illegalities committed with virtual currencies may be more comprehensively effective with international cooperation, U.S. government entities such as FinCEN are still responsible for enacting means by which to effort to mitigate criminal acts facilitated with the likes of cryptocurrency. The usage of cryptocurrency as a means by which to bypass requirements regarding AML/CFT (anti-money laundering/combating the financing of terrorism) is recognized on behalf of FinCEN, which helps to ensure that it is better able to prevent such as doing so falls within the mandated purview of this bureau within the Department of the Treasury. This includes FinCEN efforts to institute the aforementioned rules associated with Customer Identification Programs (CIP) in relation to the legislative efforts such as the Bank Secrecy Act (BSA). Here, FinCEN is responsible for applying existing statutory guidelines (i.e. BSA of 1970, Patriot Act of 2001, etc.) to regulate money service business that facilitate cryptocurrency exchanges. Doing so provides a major means for FinCEN to reduce the appeal of using cryptocurrency exchanges associated with anonymity, which would otherwise be an attractive quality for those seeking to use this service to facilitate a wide array of criminal acts involving money laundering or terrorism. Here, FinCEN targets cryptocurrency exchanges facilitated through qualifying MSBs in the same manner that the bureau works to ensure that banks are required to eliminate anonymity in transactions of a certain value threshold to help prevent criminality performed with fiat currency. In this sense, FinCEN focuses on ensuring that money service businesses that facilitate convertible virtual currency exchanges conduct transactions in a manner that is transparent and accountable, by making efforts to remove the anonymity aspects attributed to cryptocurrency, which may appeal to those intent on applying such to commit criminal endeavors. Ultimately, FinCEN initiatives fulfill aspects associated with enacting educational guidance and enforcements measures that are options within the scope of potential action available to a given agency. In this sense, there is a measure of congruence regarding the ability of each agency to operate within its own bureaucratic sphere, in that pursuit of goal achievement in accordance with respective mandates may include an action approach to address the field of cryptocurrency that is reflective of a combination of education and enforcement measures.

State-Level Government and the Cryptocurrency Industry

The federal-government policy efforts have largely lagged behind the growth of the emergent cryptocurrency industry, which has slowly, but steadily, begun to proliferate elements of U.S. society and is increasingly viewed as a more accepted means by which to transact in many economic scenarios. Without a broad, unifying legislative effort on behalf of Congress to explicitly provide direct guidance for addressing cryptocurrency, a whole-of-government approach to this industry is presently yet to be fulfilled. Additionally, federal entities' internal efforts have oft taken a singularly cautious approach to regulating the industry, which includes a combination of introductory policy guidelines regarding enforcement, coupled with a wide range of educational efforts focused on disseminating

250 Government Regulatory Efforts of the Cryptocurrency Industry

information to system actors regarding cryptocurrency. Generally, federal agencies opt to regulate the industry by defining cryptocurrency in relation to the mandated duties assigned by Congress. Any number of corresponding bureaucratic entities will often apply preexisting legislative efforts that may provide some measure of blanket justification for action in a given area of public policy. This includes examples such as FinCEN, which extended aspects of the BSA associated with reporting requirements to non-banking entities qualifying as MSBs involved in the facilitation of transactions involving cryptocurrency. In relation, aspects of the Patriot Act, such as section 326, requiring documentation of written Customer Identification Programs (CIP), that have been incorporated into the activities by agencies such as FinCEN provide a more robust means by which to ensure that AML/CFT efforts are not circumvented by those attempting to commit criminality based on the relative anonymity provided by cryptocurrency, such as Bitcoin. In this sense, elements of original legislation and subsequent amendments are co-opted into efforts by a bureau such as FinCEN to address growing concerns associated with the cryptocurrency industry, such as those associated with its potential usage in acts of criminality.

On the federal level, agency actions to address the growing cryptocurrency industry are largely piecemeal and incremental in nature. Broadly speaking, this has largely created a fragmented approach, in which policymaking and its subsequent implementation is oft generated on behalf of the federal agencies acting of their own volition in determining how to go about addressing the cryptocurrency industry as it relates to the duties to be performed by each respective bureaucratic entity. Until there are significant and plentiful legislative efforts on behalf of Congress, broadly designed to precisely provide direct guidelines in a whole-of-government approach, a fragmented and incremental policy path is followed internally by individualized agencies serving as the de facto method to the federal government's overarching policymaking efforts to address the field of cryptocurrency. As stated previously, the U.S. has a federal system, in which state and local levels of government also have some measure of agency in determining how to go about addressing areas of public policy, such as cryptocurrency. In general, actions mandated by Congressional legislation would provide a template for broad governmental responses in a field of public policy to be followed at the national, state, and local levels of the U.S. federal system. Relatedly, the state may choose to follow the federal guidelines without alteration, exceed minimum federal standards, or even challenge the constitutionality of the law by bringing a case to the Supreme Court. Without clear, broadly directed federal legislation, the lower levels of government are afforded discretionary powers to enact policy designs that are reflective of localized preferences to address an area of interest within that given jurisdiction. In accordance with the spirit of the tenth amendment, the states are permitted discretion that allows flexible policymaking at the localized levels. This constitutionally granted discretionary power relates directly to the idea of lower levels of government serving as policy laboratories, in which trial and error in this regard can provide information regarding successful, or unsuccessful, endeavors that are capable of later guiding public-sector decision making within other jurisdictions including at the federal level. Relatedly, representatives operating daily within the lower levels of government may have keener insight derived from logistical advantages than those in office that must consider federal perspectives in Washington, D.C. when it comes to the process of identifying localized preferences regarding how the public sector should craft policy responses to address a given topic of interest. In the modern era, a good example of this dynamic in practice is illustrated by the development of state and local policy efforts designed to address the emergent field of cryptocurrency, which has grown slowly over the past decade, especially as it relates to the ability of Bitcoin to penetrate the U.S. economy. The gradual encroachment of cryptocurrency such as Bitcoin into larger aspects of U.S. society, including the economy, obviously requires some measure of governmental efforts capable of addressing any identified problems that may be caused by this process.

Thus far, within the context of the U.S. federal system, there have also been several unique policy efforts at the lower levels of government designed to address various situational and contextual aspects associated with virtual currency dynamics occurring within that respective jurisdiction. This includes at the state levels of government, in which legislatures enacted new laws and various bureaucratic entities developed policy to provide regulatory guidance for the cryptocurrency industry. For example, state entities such as the Department of Financial Resources (DFR) in New York developed a unique initiative that sought to establish the requirement for a license (BitLicense) for those sellers of Bitcoin, which would create some measure of protections for consumers and institutionalize means for law enforcement to better regulate this form of cryptocurrency. In addition, there have been additional unique initiatives within other states that sought to be on the forefront of policymaking regarding cryptocurrency, such as Bitcoin, including California, Texas, and Wyoming. The following discussion will provide evidence of policy initiatives that were enacted by state agencies and will also introduce legislative efforts on behalf of select state legislatures that sought to address various aspects of the cryptocurrency industry.

New York

The state of New York developed an innovative policy action through the New York Department of Financial Resources (NYDFS: https://www.dfs.ny.gov/), which provided a unique approach to regulating the cryptocurrency industry. Here, the NYDFS sought to provide specific regulatory guidance focused on virtual currency-based transactional dynamics, creating a policy environment more proactively protective of system actors that may be involved in corresponding activities associated with cryptocurrency such as Bitcoin. According to the New York Department of Financial Resources (2019, paragraph 1), "in June 2015, DFS issued its virtual currency regulation, 23 NYCRR Part 200, under the New York Financial Services Law." This groundbreaking effort in 2015 was designed to regulate the cryptocurrency industry in accordance with 23 NY Comp Codes Rules and Regs § 200.3 that addressed licensing requirements for virtual currency, which is current through Register Vol. 44, No. 38, September 21, 2022:

> (a) License required. No Person shall, without a license obtained from the superintendent as provided in this Part, engage in any Virtual Currency Business Activity. Licensees are not authorized to exercise fiduciary powers, as defined under Section 100 of the Banking Law.
> (b) Unlicensed agents prohibited. Each Licensee is prohibited from conducting any Virtual Currency Business Activity through an agent or agency arrangement when the agent is not a Licensee.
> (c) Exemption from licensing requirements. The following Persons are exempt from the licensing requirements otherwise applicable under this Part:
>
> > (1) Persons that are chartered under the New York Banking Law and are approved by the superintendent to engage in Virtual Currency Business Activity; and (2) merchants and consumers that utilize Virtual Currency solely for the purchase or sale of goods or services or for investment purposes.
> > *Source: New York State (2015a)*

Furthermore, the NYDFS issued information in section 200.5 that established clear guidelines focused on the costs associated with obtaining a BitLicense:

> As part of an application for licensing under this Part, each applicant must submit an initial application fee, in the amount of five thousand dollars, to cover the cost of processing the application, reviewing application materials, and investigating the financial condition and responsibility,

financial and business experience, and character and general fitness of the applicant. If the application is denied or withdrawn, such fee shall not be refunded. Each Licensee may be required to pay fees to the Department to process additional applications related to the license.

Source: New York State (2015b)

According to Benjamin M. Lawsky (then Superintendent of Financial Services), this regulatory guidance would lead to the following first step in the licensing process:

New York State Department of Financial Services (NYDFS) granted a charter under the New York Banking Law to itBit Trust Company, LLC – a commercial Bitcoin exchange. ItBit, which is based in New York City, is the first virtual currency company to receive a charter from NYDFS.

Source: Lawsky (2015)

Lawsky (2015) continues by expanding on the rationale in which this initiative was undertaken on behalf of the NYDFS, which decidedly took a judiciously proactive approach that was reflective of the precautionary principle in practice:

We have sought to move quickly but carefully to put in place rules of the road to protect consumers and provide greater regulatory certainty for virtual currency entrepreneurs. The technology behind Bitcoin and other virtual currencies could ultimately hold real promise and it is critical that we set up appropriate rules of the road to help safeguard customer funds. Indeed, we believe that regulation will ultimately be important to the long-term health and development of the virtual currency industry.

Source: Lawsky (2015, paragraph 2)

The New York Department of Financial Services (NYDFS) provided further illustrative information regarding the registration effects of issuing said licensing over a five-year period since the program was initiated in 2015:

.....under that "BitLicense" regulation or the limited purpose trust company provisions of the New York Banking Law, DFS has granted 25 virtual currency licenses and charters to ensure that New Yorkers have a well-regulated way to access the virtual currency marketplace and that New York remains at the center of technological innovation and forward-looking regulation.

Source: New York Department of Financial Resources
(2019, paragraph 1)

254 Government Regulatory Efforts of the Cryptocurrency Industry

Relatedly, this systemic regulatory measure developed by the state of New York included provisions further establishing industry requirements associated with books and records (200.12), reports and financial disclosures (200.14), anti-money laundering programs (200.15), and consumer protection (200.19). These requirements introduce greater levels of transparency and accountability for those involved in various transactional events involving cryptocurrency, such as Bitcoin, within the state of New York. This includes the regulatory guidance establishing reporting requirements in accordance with anti-money laundering programs that institutionalized a customer identification program in which a licensed entity would make reasonable efforts to obtain requisite participant information associated with each account. To some, this regulatory regime may mitigate the preferred levels of anonymity involved in cryptocurrency transactions and may also integrate an unwelcome cost for obtaining a license for those wishing to become involved in the business side of this dynamic. In this sense, the BitLicense in New York is a policy effort that may be looked at unfavorably by industry professionals who prefer a regulatory environment that is more reflective of technocratic ideals such as those associated with permissionless innovation. Here, many of the appealing aspects associated with cryptocurrency, such as being able to transact in relative anonymity and without potentially cost-prohibitive entry fees for businesses, may create an unwelcome burden on private-sector entities that would otherwise be interested in becoming fiscally involved in this industry. Ultimately, the BitLicense serves as an attempt by the state of New York to regulate the cryptocurrency industry by creating enforceable rules that directly affect system actors involved in a static point in Bitcoin's dynamic progression through its economic lifecycle. In doing so, the NYDFS, in this instance, integrated components that more closely reflect the precautionary principle as the state opted to pursue a cautiously proactive policy path designed to protect consumers, as opposed to leaving the industry without regulatory guidance at this stage of its development.

As is often the case with policymaking, the initial efforts on behalf on the NYDFS in 2015 to institute BitLicensing as a means to regulate the cryptocurrency industry and to promote consumer protection was subject to later addendums. This includes that, according to a DFS press release in 2018, Maria T. Vullo (who served as the Financial Services Superintendent from 2016–2019) indicated that Gemini Trust Company LLC and Paxos Trust Company LLC had been authorized to furnish stablecoin (a price-stable cryptocurrency) valued in U.S. dollars (New York Department of Financial Resources, 2018, paragraph 1). In doing so, the DFS indicated the following:

> As part of the approval of these new products, DFS has established required conditions to ensure that each trust company maintains robust policies and procedures to address risks and apply New York's strong

standards and regulations regarding anti-money laundering, anti-fraud, and consumer protection measures.

Source: New York Department of Financial Resources (2018)

Relatedly, in June of 2022 the NYDFS would later amend 23 NYCRR Part 200 in order to provide further guidance as to the dynamics involved in issuing U.S. dollar-backed stablecoins (New York Department of Financial Resources, 2022). Here, the DFS is actively engaging in policymaking to address the continuously shifting nature of the cryptocurrency industry. The state of New York additionally actively monitored the regulatory environment regarding the dynamic role of cryptocurrency in society and, as expected in a democratic system, was able to begin to develop a flexible policy response to changes within the industry associated with the emergence of variant forms in stablecoin. On this account, stablecoin is a more recent development in the lifecycle of cryptocurrency that seeks to avoid volatility in value, which often affects manifestations such as Bitcoin by pursuing steadying activities associated with tying the worth to more stable fiscal assets external to the industry, such as U.S. dollars, Euros, or gold. Instead of applying a rationale rigidly rooted in permissionless innovation, in this instance the DFS policy choices generally affords greater credence to prudent application of the precautionary principle. Overall, the state of New York was proactive in this policy effort designed to address the growing cryptocurrency industry by instituting BitLicenscing requirements and in providing initial statutory recognition for the emergence of stablecoins, which together provide some measure of structural guidance to industry participants operating within the state's jurisdictional purview.

California and Texas

In the U.S federal system, the national government is expected to continuously enact any number of official designs to address an area of policy that is perceived by system actors to be in need of public-sector intervention. This includes instances in which federal statutory efforts provide guidance to the lower levels of government, creating some measure of cohesiveness in how an area of public policy is addressed in an official capacity. However, in cases in which the federal government provides little-to-no mandated actions, via legislation by Congress, the lower levels of government are entitled to address policymaking as seen fit within that locality. In some cases, the policy efforts at the lower levels of government deemed promising may later provide a template for use by other states or even by the federal government. For example, the New York state's BitLicense was a targeted policy effort that sought to regulate a specific action point within the cryptocurrency industry through the issuance of rules meant to provide

256 Government Regulatory Efforts of the Cryptocurrency Industry

standardized guidance for those businesses directly involved in facilitating exchange dynamics in that jurisdiction's economic marketplace. As such, the policy efforts in the state of New York that proactively created a regulatory regime over specific aspects associated with the cryptocurrency industry could provide a template for other states to attempt to adopt. Relatedly, California was recently unsuccessful in establishing a similar policy initiative when, on September 23, 2022, Governor Gavin Newsom vetoed a bill entitled the Digital Financial Assets Law that had been approved by the state legislature (California State Legislature, 2022). Among the many components inherent within the proposed Digital Financial Assets Law, such as provisions to establish industry requirements associated with stablecoin, the intended initiative sought to include regulatory licensing guidelines based on the following:

> ....on and after January 1, 2025, prohibit a person from engaging in digital financial asset business activity, or holding itself out as being able to engage in digital financial asset business activity, with or on behalf of a resident unless any of certain criteria are met, including the person is licensed with the Department of Financial Protection and Innovation, as prescribed. The bill would define "digital financial asset" to mean a digital representation of value that is used as a medium of exchange, unit of account, or store of value, and that is not legal tender, whether or not denominated in legal tender, except as specified.
>
> *Source: California State Legislature (2022)*

Whereas the policy effort in New York was enacted by the Department of Financial Services (DFS), the unsuccessful effort to pass a policy initiative was done on behalf of the California state legislature that sought to empower the California Department of Financial Protection and Innovation (DFPI: https://dfpi.ca.gov/) to oversee proposed regulatory means associated with crypto licensing. Here, the effort to create cryptocurrency licensing was initiated by different government entities in New York and California, in which only the former was successful in the attempt.

Despite the unsuccessful effort to pass the Digital Financial Assets Law in 2022, the state of California was still among the first movers in creating a uniquely significant policy initiative associated with the cryptocurrency industry. This includes that California is credited with taking an early first legislative step in 2014, which has had the potential to create a greater opportunity for cryptocurrency, such as Bitcoin, to be used to transact more widely within the economy of that state. In 2014, then Governor Jerry Brown signed into law "AB-129 Lawful Money: Alternative Currency," which specifically repealed section 107 of California State law, paving the way for the usage of non-fiat, virtual currency in that state. Prior to that time, California Corporations Code (2018), Sec. 107 indicated the following: "No corporation, social purpose corporation, association, or individual shall issue or put in circulation, as money, anything but the lawful money of the United States." When introduced, Assembly Bill 129 was intended as "an act to repeal Section 107 of the Corporations Code, relating to business associations." (California State Legislature, 2014, paragraph 1). After successfully traversing through California's Congress, Governor Jerry Brown signed this bill into law on June 28, 2014. In doing so, AB-129 would effectively change the conceptualization of money within the state of California, establishing an opportunity for a wide range of alternate, non-fiat currencies, including cryptocurrencies, to become financial options with the state's economic system. This initiative is summed up in the Senate Floor Analysis by Farouk (2014):

> This bill makes clarifying changes to current law to ensure that various forms of alternative currency such as digital currency, points, coupons, or other objects of monetary value do not violate the law when those methods are used for the purchase of goods and services or the transmission of payments. Modern methods of payment have expanded beyond the typical cash or credit card transactions. Bitcoin, a digital currency (also called cryptocurrency), has gained massive media attention recently as the number of businesses has expanded to accept Bitcoins for payment. Long before the introduction of digital currencies, various businesses have created points models that reward consumers with points for completion of various tasks such as spending a certain dollar amount, or even by purchasing points with dollars. These point systems effectively operate as currency allowing the consumers to buy a retail item or pay for some type of service. Many communities across the United States and in California have created "community currencies" that are created by members of a community in conjunction with merchants who agree to accept the alternative currency. These "community currencies" are created for a variety of reasons, some of which include encouraging consumers to shop at small businesses within the community or increasing neighborhood cohesiveness. "Community currency" has also become a form of political protest as some communities that use such currency do so in protest of United States monetary policies, or large financial institutions.
>
> *Source: Farouk (2014)*

Prior to passing AB-129, legally it was impermissible for alternative currencies to circulate for use in the economy. In addition to utilizing fiat U.S.

currency, AB-129 sought to open the California economy to a wider array of payment options by essentially authorizing alternate forms of non-fiat money for use within the state. This includes that AB-129 sought to permit cryptocurrency such as Bitcoin to be used as money within the state of California. The legislative effort by California was a pioneering design that created a statutory template for review by other state governments, and even the U.S. Congress, should the field of cryptocurrency continue to grow, warranting further consideration in this regard. Additionally, AB-129 would pave the way for other policy initiatives in the state of California that sought to create greater clarity regarding the regulation of the cryptocurrency industry. This includes that, in 2022, Governor Gavin Newsom Signed Executive Order N-9-22, which sought to initiate the process to create regulatory guidance associated with the cryptocurrency industry and to broadly consider the potential usage of blockchain technology to be applied in the performance of official state duties (https://www.gov.ca.gov/wp-content/uploads/2022/05/5.4.22-Blockchain-EO-N-9-22-signed.pdf).

The U.S. federal system is often rife with policymaking initiatives designed to address a given topic that are vastly different in scope from state to state. For example, this dynamic is evidenced across a wide range of policy areas such as the fact that, despite failing to be legalized by the federal government as of 2022, 37 states, plus the District of Columbia, have legalized marijuana for medical purposes. In relation, as of 2022, 19 states, plus the District of Columbia, have approved recreational use marijuana. Similarly, states may develop policy means that are intended to address the very scope and nature of money itself that is available for wide fiscal usage with that jurisdiction. As California sought to integrate cryptocurrency into the fold of legally accepted forms of money, states like Texas took a different approach by choosing to avoid permitting cryptocurrency to act as money in any official capacity. On this account, the Texas Department of Banking (2014) indicated that:

On April 3, 2014, Texas Banking Commissioner Charles G. Cooper issued Supervisory Memorandum 1037, Regulatory Treatment of Virtual Currencies under the Texas Money Services Act. The memorandum was issued to provide clarity and regulatory certainty for businesses and individuals engaged in the rapidly growing area of virtual currencies.

For purposes of money transmission and currency exchange, the Texas Money Services Act, codified in Texas Finance Code Chapter 151, provides narrow definitions of money and currency. Cryptocurrencies do not fit the statutory definitions of either currency or money, and consequently do not by themselves trigger the licensing requirements of the Act.

Source: Cooper (2014, paragraphs 1–2)

The original memo from 2014 (and the subsequent revised version in 2019) provided insight regarding how cryptocurrency would officially be addressed within the state of Texas. This includes providing definitional parameters for several terms and policymaking guidance as to how cryptocurrency, such as Bitcoin, would be addressed from a governmental standpoint within the state of Texas. Among the important ideas in the memo that would provide governmental guidance to those residing in the state was the fact that cryptocurrency such as Bitcoin would not be defined as money or treated as such in an official capacity. Texas Banking Commissioner Charles G. Cooper indicated that "at this point a cryptocurrency like Bitcoin is best viewed like a speculative investment, not as money. However, as this innovative technology develops, the Department will continue to evaluate whether the nature of cryptocurrencies and the potential harm to the public warrant additional action" (Cooper, 2014, paragraph 3). Cooper (2019, p. 3) would later expand on this notion by noting that:

> Cryptocurrency is not currency as that word is defined in the Money Services Act. A unit of cryptocurrency is also not a claim. It does not entitle its owner to anything and creates no duties or obligations in a person who gives, sells, or transfers it. There is no entity that must honor the value of a cryptocurrency or exchange any given unit of a cryptocurrency for sovereign currency. For comparison, under federal law U.S. coin and paper currency must be honored for payment of all debts, public charges, taxes, and dues, and the U.S. Treasury Department must redeem it for "lawful money." But the owner of a unit of a cryptocurrency has no right or guaranteed ability to convert that unit to sovereign currency.
>
> *Source: Cooper (2019)*

If cryptocurrency fails to be classified as fiat currency by government, then its inability to officially achieve monetary status can have a wide range of effects on its capacity to be utilized as a medium of exchange in the economy. Falling short of an overly hostile approach that would outright ban all forms of cryptocurrency from its jurisdiction, Texas is still far less accommodating than California on this matter, whose initiative sought to bring this industry one step closer to legitimacy within that state's economy by classifying types such as Bitcoin as permissible for use as money.

In sum, the state of California and the state of Texas took vastly different approaches in addressing cryptocurrency in which the former chose to treat such as viable money and the latter termed such as speculative investment. As noted in earlier chapters, treating something as money will

260 Government Regulatory Efforts of the Cryptocurrency Industry

determine how society views this item(s) and correspondingly will help to shape decision making from a policymaking standpoint. The decision of each respective states' governments in providing definitional parameters for cryptocurrency would directly affect its usage by the public and regulatory focus by the whole of government with each's jurisdiction. The differentiating approaches by California and Texas as to whether the use of cryptocurrency is permissible as money or not is able to affect how that industry fairs within each's jurisdictional boundaries to some extent. Although cryptocurrency has a global reach, allowing anyone with access to the device connected to the Internet to become transactional, there is still some measure of acceptance required on behalf of consumers, vendors, and government that will affect the ability of this industry to become more entrenched within the economy. Achieving official consent for use as money by a state government will provide a greater opportunity for cryptocurrency to play an increased role in the localized economy, but this dynamic will also require corresponding efforts on behalf of the public sector from a regulatory standpoint. An increased societal acceptance by a wider assortment of system actors will create a greater opportunity for cryptocurrency to proliferate the economy at each of the respective levels of government within the U.S. federal system. In relation, the choices made at each of the levels of government reflects a certain measure of interconnectivity that contributes to the nation's broader economic system. The expansion or contraction of the usage of cryptocurrencies, such as Bitcoin, will be affected to some degree by the societal perception of the viability of this industry within the U.S. economic structure at each of the levels of governance. Therefore, official actions taken on behalf of states like California and Texas may respectively contribute to enhancing or diminishing societal acceptance of cryptocurrency as a viable means by which to engage in various economic activities.

Wyoming

As noted previously, federal agencies such as the IRS, SEC, and CFTC have different mandated responsibilities assigned to them on behalf of Congress. As such, each agency may go about developing internal policy means intended to address the cryptocurrency industry in a manner that is tailored specifically to the Congressionally mandated responsibilities of that agency. For example, the IRS will go about developing policy that is focused on the understanding that cryptocurrency is defined as property. Similarly, the SEC will develop policy based on defining cryptocurrency as a security, and the CFTC will develop policy based on defining cryptocurrency as a commodity. Additionally, in the absence of a clearly defined Congressional policy path that would allow for bureaucratic responses to be facilitated in a whole-of-government approach, it is not uncommon that federal agencies are left to apply preexisting legislation that may provide some measure of applicability to efforts to regulate the cryptocurrency industry. As federal agencies may be left to their own volition to develop regulatory guidance to address cryptocurrency such as Bitcoin, so too may state legislatures and bureaucracies seek to enact official means capable of filling the policy gap left by Congressional inaction. Without broad federal legislation efforts on behalf of Congress that directly serves to provide unifying regulatory guidance dictating actions regarding the field of cryptocurrency, states such as Wyoming are left to their own devices to do so to some degree. In addition, in some cases states may enact policies that seemingly contradict federal preferences in a given field, including processes associated with defining cryptocurrency. Wolfson (2018, paragraph 4) explains that while the SEC and CFTC continue to pursue defining cryptocurrencies as securities or commodities, respectively, Wyoming is among the first states in the U.S. that "is taking action by laying down the law at a state level" in a manner that is reflective of a unique approach to this policy task. Wolfson (2018, paragraph 5) explains that Wyoming has led the way as the being the U.S. state that initially enacted policy (i.e. Wyoming House Bill 70) that would "define cryptocurrencies as an entirely new asset class". HB70 was one of several bills that were signed into law by the Governor of Wyoming in 2018 that are deserved of further discussion in order to further illustrate the regulatory environment in that state, which has steadily become more favorable to the cryptocurrency industry.

The state of Wyoming began to make a concerted policy effort that was designed to create a regulatory environment that would be appealing to the cryptocurrency industry in several key aspects. State Representative Tyler Lindholm (2018) discussed this dynamic by noting that, since 2018, key legislative efforts in Wyoming were being designed with the idea of "opening up a regulatory gate and ensuring that there is essentially a sandbox for these developers to play in." Previously, the cryptocurrency industry was largely disinterested in establishing a significant presence in the state due to the fact that "the Wyoming money transmitter's act was being used to essentially to regulate Bitcoin and other digital currencies so the large exchanges would not operate in the state of Wyoming" (Lindholm, 2018). Lindholm (2018) also touted that HB70 enacted groundbreaking policy that would positively affect the cryptocurrency industry in Wyoming, in that it "identified utility tokens as a new asset class and by doing so we're the first legislative body in the world to do so." As it relates to Initial Coin Offerings (ICOs), which is a means by which emergent cryptocurrencies publicly raise capital from investors, Wyoming was attempting to develop policy that would allow for this state to remain "out in front of the SEC and hopefully be a good example for them." Lindholm (2018) also noted that Wyoming has enacted legislation that would exempt virtual currencies from being subjected to property taxes, which in addition to having no income tax and no corporate tax would make this state highly appealing to the cryptocurrency industry. Lindholm (2018) expanded further on the fact that Wyoming is a high energy producer that pursues a diverse approach (i.e. coal, natural gas, hydro). In relation, Lindholm (2018) explains that Wyoming using only 10 percent of its energy production for use within the state makes for an attractive locale, because access to plentiful energy sources is an essential requirement for the cryptocurrency industry to function in the context of mining production. For a favorable policy environment to begin to be cultivated, several legislative designs were enacted within the state of Wyoming since 2018, which are further highlighted below.

In 2018, Governor Mead signed into law several bills passed by the Wyoming state legislature, and these statutes sought to allow cryptocurrency to flourish in an environment that was more friendly to the industry from a policy standpoint. The links to each of those laws and a summative discussion of the essential areas of policy that would promote an attractive regulatory environment for the cryptocurrency industry are provided:

House Bill 70: https://wyoleg.gov/2018/Digest/HB0070.pdf
(Wyoming State Legislature, 2018a)
House Bill 19: https://www.wyoleg.gov/Legislation/2018/HB0019
(Wyoming State Legislature, 2018b)
House Bill 101: https://www.wyoleg.gov/Legislation/2018/HB0101
(Wyoming State Legislature, 2018c)
House Bill 126: https://www.wyoleg.gov/Legislation/2018/HB0126
(Wyoming State Legislature, 2018d)
Senate File 0111: https://www.wyoleg.gov/Legislation/2018/SF0111
(Wyoming State Legislature, 2018e)

For example, Governor Matt Mead signed HB70 bill into law in 2018, which provided the following specific guidelines that would apply to the cryptocurrency industry within that state:

AN ACT relating to securities; providing that a person who develops, sells or facilitates the exchange of an open blockchain token is not subject to specified securities and money transmission laws; providing specified verification authority to the secretary of state and banking commissioner; making conforming amendments; and providing for an effective date.

Source: Wyoming State Legislature (2018a)

In passing HB70, the cryptocurrency industry, operating within the jurisdictional boundaries of Wyoming, was exempted from strict regulatory guidelines associated with securities and money transmission laws. Similarly, HB19 sought to create a regulatory environment that was welcoming to all those associated with virtual currencies by providing exemptions from the Wyoming Money Transmitters Act. Additionally, there were a wide range of bills signed into law in 2018 that also contributed to making a favorable regulatory environment in Wyoming, including HB101 (providing provisions to permit the use of blockchain for electronic document storage purposes by corporations), HB126 (providing greater ease to forming LLCs and subsidiary LLCs), and SF0111 (exempting the virtual currency industry from being subject to property tax). The trend toward official legislative mandates that are favorable toward the cryptocurrency industry in Wyoming has continued along this policy arc for the time being. For example, the Wyoming Utility Token Act of 2020 and the updated amendment from 2022 broadly addressed virtual currencies by indicated that "open blockchain tokens classified as intangible personal property" (a legal concept regarding ownership of nonmaterial articles such as copyrights and patents) so that cryptocurrency such as Bitcoin would be taxable accordingly (Wyoming State Legislature, 2020 and 2022). Each Wyoming legislative effort, in their own way, is contributing to creating a regulatory environment that would be favorable to cryptocurrency while further establishing governing parameters for the industry. In doing so, the state of Wyoming is slowly establishing itself as a potentially attractive destination to the cryptocurrency industry, in not only the U.S. but also the world.

In addition to the favorable regulatory environment that has become increasingly institutionalized in Wyoming, this state has within its borders another highly attractive attribute to those operating within the cryptocurrency industry, in that there is access to plentiful and diverse sources of energy. In relation, approximately 90 percent of the energy that is produced in Wyoming can be retained for usage to help power the cryptocurrency industry within its own jurisdictional borders or can be made exportable to other states. Relatedly, the abundance of energy is derived from a diverse range of sources, including coal, natural gas, and hydro power. Wind power is another source of natural energy that is overly abundant in Wyoming that could prove appealing to support mining dynamics involved in the cryptocurrency industry. By continuing to pass favorable laws that are focused on making the state more appealing, from a regulatory standpoint, to those involved in cryptocurrency mining and transaction processes, Wyoming is becoming a "beacon" to the industry in the U.S. with the understanding that there is still room for improvement regarding developing legislation to stimulate the use of alternate energy to provide power to the industry in the state (Moffit, 2021, p. 12). Moffit (2021, p. 3) notes that instead of utilizing "excess natural gas" it is possible that a shift in Wyoming to channeling "overgenerated wind" to power cryptocurrency mining could serve to "redistribute the global hashrate, incentivize Bitcoin miners to move their operations to Wyoming, and stimulate job growth as a result." It is plausible that the Wyoming state government developing public policy, combined with similarly focused federal legislative designs, could provide a legal foundation capable of promoting wind power as one of many essential means by which to provide energy to the cryptocurrency mining industry (Moffit, 2021). This would require some measure of coordinated efforts at the federal and state levels of government to ensure that the necessary infrastructure is in place to create a viable means to provide this type of renewable energy to Wyoming and other states, to transition the workforce in the energy industry to be able to accommodate the provision of wind power, and to develop public policy designed to provide a legal foundation by which to promote the advancement of wind power (Moffit, 2021). This may prove difficult initially in Wyoming, since this state is a primary source of coal production in the United States and the state legislature has developed laws designed to protect the coal industry instead of allowing for alternate energy to develop in a similar fashion (Moffit, 2021). Because Wyoming's public-policy efforts are presently less focused on "providing economic benefits for companies that reduce their carbon footprint," the state has room to improve regarding institutionalizing usage of alternative sources of renewable energy, such as wind, that could be beneficial in providing power for the cryptocurrency industry (Moffit, 2021, p. 6). Ultimately, there would need to be a concerted effort by government and the energy industry alike to provide a means by which to allow for greater input of alternative sources such as wind power to, at the very least, add to the existing fossil fuel industry used to provide energy for cryptocurrency mining and beyond. For this to occur, the state government would need to pursue a policy path that is supportive of generating wind power, and justifying this could in part be accomplished under the policy umbrella of ensuring that Wyoming is open to the cryptocurrency industry to establish a significant presence there. Being a coal-producing state that allows for greater wind power production would not necessarily require overly expedient or rational-comprehensive action that supplants the former with the later. Instead, maintaining the coal industry in the immediate future, while establishing wind power as an increasingly viable option, would provide a greater measure of diversity in energy means that are available within the state for use by the cryptocurrency industry. In addition to a greater capacity to produce energy, the diverse approach would provide greater levels of power to either export to surrounding states or to use in supporting the cryptocurrency industry should relocation to

Wyoming be an increasingly attractive prospect. Should this occur, Wyoming could be viewed with increasing its viability to become an even more attractive home to the cryptocurrency industry. If Wyoming is to continue pursuit of a regulatory environment that is welcoming to the cryptocurrency industry, then it will be important to continue to enact legislation capable of changing various conditions across a broad array of policy areas (i.e. energy, taxation, etc.) so that the state has a lasting broader appeal. It is often the case that state governments serve as "policy laboratories" by which efforts within that localized jurisdiction may provide insight to other state governments or the federal government regarding crafting legislation on the same topic(s). Wyoming's continued efforts to open up the state to the cryptocurrency industry by crafting policy that creates a favorable regulatory environment can result in identifying standards of successes, or highlighting failures, that could serve to provide a template for which other state governments, or the federal government, may later utilize.

Closing Remarks

Although a unified global effort in the future may potentially have great merit in contributing to increased levels of policy solidarity for regulating the cryptocurrency industry at the international level, this is not to imply that any such efforts should be at the expense of relinquishing all sovereign choice on the matter. This is especially important to note given the global reach of cryptocurrency and the general lack of congruency in policy efforts to presently address this industry from among the international community. Therefore, nations such as the U.S. will benefit from domestically developing a regulatory approach to address cryptocurrency in which responsive policy efforts are capable of reflecting situational and contextual factors within a given jurisdictional purview. As such, this chapter has been focused primarily on a selection of official actions taken on behalf of the U.S. government operating within the federal system, which have thus far begun to play an initial role in developing policy responses to the emergent cryptocurrency industry. At present, the U.S. political system lacks a broadly composed, unifying legislative structural path on behalf of Congress, which would completely encompass all aspects of the cryptocurrency industry and would be applicable at each of the levels of government. In relation, the U.S. regulatory environment for cryptocurrency, such as Bitcoin, has largely reflected a fragmented and incremental approach to policymaking in which federal agencies and various entities at the lower levels of government have largely been free to pursue the development of official means in accordance with mandated powers. Thus far, the U.S. policy approach has been relatively accommodating to the industry by attempting

266 Government Regulatory Efforts of the Cryptocurrency Industry

to place cryptocurrency inside the "existing legal labyrinth" (Xie, 2019, p. 457) and by avoiding being overly restrictive in scope and nature when crafting regulatory guidance. In general, federal bureaucratic entities are often left to cope with cryptocurrency concerns, in accordance with the expected fulfillment of assigned duties, by applying existing legislative actions that may be deemed applicable to address aspects associated with this industry. This includes examples such as FinCEN's application of the Bank Secrecy Act of 1970 and iterations of the Patriot Act that provide updated statutory structure regarding AMT/CFL regulatory guidelines. Relatedly, it is also common that decision makers in federal agencies have opted to define the concept of virtual currencies, and all corresponding variants that fall under its conceptual umbrella, in the context of the assigned duties that the entity is responsible for fulfilling in accordance with the creation mandate from Congress. This includes the IRS (property tax), SEC (securities), and CFTC (commodities), which all define examples of cryptocurrency in a manner that allows for each respective agency to develop internal measures geared to the performance of its expected functions. In doing so, each bureaucratic entity is able to provide a combination of policy directives and educational information intended to help guide the behavior of system actors as it relates to the field of cryptocurrency.

The presence of situational and contextual differences at the lower levels of government in the U.S. federal system can impact the motivation of decision makers present there who ultimately will play a role in determining public-policy outcomes regarding regulatory responses to the cryptocurrency industry. This is evidenced in part by states taking different policy approaches in an effort to address the emergent cryptocurrency industry. The lower levels of government in the U.S. political system can serve as policy laboratories, and this dynamic in action is well-represented by the vast array of official efforts within several states that have been enacted in order to address various aspects of the cryptocurrency industry. In this regard, many aspects of the cryptocurrency industry are able to be addressed differently within each state in accordance with the powers granted to that level of government via the tenth amendment of the U.S. Constitution. In that, the tenth amendment indicates that powers not expressly granted to the federal government are thusly reserved for the states, permitting this level of government to employ discretionary powers to act accordingly as deemed necessary. Thus far, there have been uniquely variant efforts at the state level of government in which legislatures and bureaucratic entities each apply discretionary powers to craft policy responses to address the broad field of virtual currency within that jurisdiction. This includes the stark differences in establishing legal parameters for specific aspects of the industry as evidenced by California's efforts to permit virtual currencies such as cryptocurrency to be accepted for use as money, which contrasts with Texas's policy initiatives that views cryptocurrency not as money but as a speculative investment. Each state's definition and official treatment of cryptocurrency will correspondingly affect the wider range of localized policymaking efforts that will further address other aspects of this industry within that respective jurisdiction. Similarly, the states of New York and Wyoming have taken largely divergent approaches to policymaking that have shaped the structural capacity of the regulatory environment for the cryptocurrency industry within each localized sphere of influence. In this instance, New York leaned toward regulatory efforts more reflective of an application of the precautionary principle by creating a preemptively restrictive BitLicense requirement for the cryptocurrency industry within its jurisdiction. On the other hand, Wyoming's efforts to enact means that are strategically accommodating was reflective of a modestly adapted policy path focused on yielding a regulatory environment more accepting of the cryptocurrency industry across a wide range of interconnected topical areas (i.e. taxation, money transmission, etc.). Although reflective of different policy outcomes in scope and nature, neither New York nor Wyoming opted to leave cryptocurrency completely unregulated, as would have been preferred by advocates of technocratically derived rationales. Instead, both states chose to flexibly apply the precautionary principle to meet situational and contextual local interests in which each respective policy effort yielded varied degrees of influence in the cryptocurrency industry. This provides further credence to the possibility for a more nuanced assessment of permission to affect decision making, so that the regulatory environment maintains the ability to enact policy proactively and reactively as deemed necessary.

In the future, the U.S. Congress may opt to further develop legislation that can more directly provide statutory guidelines serving as a policy anchor capable of comprehensively producing greater clarity at each of the levels of government regarding expected action to address various aspects of the cryptocurrency industry. Until that time, the incremental policy approach to cryptocurrency that is presently employed will tacitly maintain a relatively fragmented regulatory environment within the U.S. federal system. Unlike technocratically oriented approaches to policymaking, which reflect preferences to circumvent traditional democratic participation, creating a permissive regulatory environment that is highly protective of the technology industry, it is important that efforts are made to provide opportunities for interested parties to engage in meaningful discourse actively and routinely through multiple points of access present within the communicative structure as expected in the U.S. deliberative system. In doing so, the democratic expectations of government transparency, flexibility, and accountability are maintained by allowing for responsive action to be developed based on an open assessment of the situational and contextual cues related to a given area of public policy. In the modern era, the policy efforts on behalf of the U.S. government to address potential problems derived from technology are expected to be reflective of a fluid and flexible approach that is also appropriately measured in scope due to the highly mercurial nature of innovations themselves. This is especially important in circumstances involving government decision making intended to address an emergent field, such as cryptocurrency, that still involves a vast array of unknowns regarding identifying potential problems and a range of applicable solutions. As the cryptocurrency industry is still very much in the early stages of development, the U.S. government must avoid automatically ceding decision-making authority to technocratic preferences that are dismissive of the precautionary principle that, if judiciously applied, would allow for flexible regulatory responses as needed. In this sense, the U.S. government is better served by endeavoring to maintain the expected levels of flexibility that will allow for officially generated responses if there is agreement among system actors that policy action is needed to address aspects associated with the rapidly changing field of cryptocurrency. Overall, the regulatory environment should avoid being excessively permissive or overly restrictive, as exclusively committing to either extreme policy path would fall short of providing a responsibly balanced approach to government decision making to address the field of technology. In this, being excessively permissive of the technology industry by ceding decision-making authority to technology experts and only considering policy action in cases in which it has been proven that technology caused harm to society would fall short of expectations associated with participatory dynamics and government responsiveness in a deliberative democracy. A policy environment that reflects permissionless innovation would reduce, or worse yet eliminate, the expected participatory opportunities for system actors to engage in meaningful dialogue that are expected to help dictate responsive government actions in American democracy. In doing so, technology is protected at the expense of democracy, which may not only yield policy efforts that are incongruent with system needs but that is also capable of degrading the levels of trust held by citizens in the validity of democratic processes and resulting outcomes. Also, a policy path should avoid being overly restrictive and creating a regulatory environment that actively inhibits the technology industry too comprehensively, because this potentially may unnecessarily stymie the natural growth of innovation to a point where it is diminished significantly, or worse, driven to technological extinction. Here, responsible government action can be achieved through modest application of the precautionary principle, which may allow for some measure of industry freedom while still

Government Regulatory Efforts of the Cryptocurrency Industry **269**

empowering government decision making to be flexible as needed, should a perceived need to act arise. At this stage of the cryptocurrency industry's development, the prominent policy path in the present political system is largely reflective of a balanced approach, allowing decision makers at each of the levels of government in the federal system some measure of discretion to adopt regulatory guidelines based on a dynamic assessment of the situational and contextual cues present within the American democracy. Ultimately, it is the responsibility of the U.S. government to pursue a policy path that can bring non-fiat virtual currency, such as cryptocurrency, into the statutory fold, as this industry cannot be permitted to permeate broader society without clear, concise, and current regulatory guidance.

References

Abboushi, S. (2017). Global Virtual Currency – Brief Overview. *Journal of Applied Business and Economics*, 19(6).

Boxerman, S. J & Schwerin, M. F. (2017). Its Bark is Worse Than Its Bit(E). *Criminal Justice*, 31(4), 10–15.

Brandeis, L. (1932). Supreme Court Justice Dissenting Opinion: New State Ice Co v. Liebmann. https://www.law.cornell.edu/supremecourt/text/285/262

California State Legislature. (2014). Assembly Bill No. 129. https://leginfo.legislature.ca.gov/faces/billTextClient.xhtml?bill_id=201320140AB129

California State Legislature. (2022). AB-2269 Digital financial asset businesses: regulation. https://leginfo.legislature.ca.gov/faces/billTextClient.xhtml?bill_id=202120220AB2269

California Public Law (2018). California Corporations Code, Sec. 107. https://california.public.law/codes/ca_corp_code_section_107

Calvery, J. (2013). Silk Road – Potential Risks, Threats, and Promises of Virtual Currencies. Testimony, Senate Homeland Security and Governmental Affairs Committee Hearing.

Cambridge Centre for Alternative Finance (2021). Bitcoin Mining Map. https://ccaf.io/cbeci/mining_map

Cooper, C. G. (2014). Texas Banking Commissioner Issues Supervisory Memorandum on Virtual Currency. Texas Department of Banking. https://www.dob.texas.gov/sites/default/files/files/news/press-releases/2014/04-03-14pr.pdf

Cooper, C. G. (2019). Banking Commissioner: Supervisory Memorandum – 1037. Texas Department of Banking. https://www.dob.texas.gov/public/uploads/files/consumer-information/sm1037.pdf

Executive Order on Ensuring Responsible Development of Digital Assets (2022). President Joseph R. Biden, Jr., the U.S. White House. https://www.whitehouse.gov/briefing-room/presidential-actions/2022/03/09/executive-order-on-ensuring-responsible-development-of-digital-assets/

Farouk, M. (2014). Assembly Floor Analysis. https://leginfo.legislature.ca.gov/faces/billAnalysisClient.xhtml?bill_id=201320140AB129

Federal Trade Commission. (2018). Decrypting Cryptocurrency Scams. https://www.ftc.gov/news-events/events/2018/06/decrypting-cryptocurrency-scams

270 Government Regulatory Efforts of the Cryptocurrency Industry

Federal Trade Commission. (2022a). Federal Trade Commission Act. https://www. ftc.gov/legal-library/browse/statutes/federal-trade-commission-act

Federal Trade Commission. (2022b). Federal Trade Commission: Enforcement. https://www.ftc.gov/enforcement

Federal Trade Commission. (2022c). Federal Trade Commission: Policy. https:// www.ftc.gov/policy

Federal Trade Commission. (2022d). Federal Trade Commission: Advice and Guidance. https://consumer.ftc.gov/

Federal Trade Commission. (2022e). What to Know About Cryptocurrency and Scams. https://consumer.ftc.gov/articles/what-know-about-cryptocurrency-and-scams

Federal Trade Commission. (2022f). Consumer Sentinel Network. https://www.ftc. gov/enforcement/consumer-sentinel-network

Federal Trade Commission. (2022g). Legal Library: Statutes. https://www.ftc.gov/ legal-library/browse/statutes?search=Bitcoin

FinCEN. (2013a). FinCEN Issues Guidance on Virtual Currencies and Regulatory Responsibilities. https://www.fincen.gov/news/news-releases/fincen-issues-guidance-virtual-currencies-and-regulatory-responsibilities

FinCEN. (2013b). Am I an MSB? https://www.fincen.gov/am-i-msb

FinCEN. (2013c). Application of FinCEN's Regulations to Persons Administering, Exchanging, or Using Virtual Currencies. https://www.fincen.gov/ resources/statutes-regulations/guidance/application-fincens-regulations-persons-administering

FinCEN. (2022a). Mission. https://www.fincen.gov/about/mission

FinCEN. (2022b). What We Do. https://www.fincen.gov/what-we-do

FinCEN (2022c). Money Services Business Definition. https://www.fincen.gov/ money-services-business-definition

Fletcher, E. (2022). Reports Show Scammers Cashing in on Crypto Craze. https://www.ftc.gov/news-events/data-visualizations/data-spotlight/2022/06/ reports-show-scammers-cashing-crypto-craze#crypto6

Goldman, Z., Maruyama, E., Rosenberg, E., Saravalle, E., & Soloman-Strauss, J. (2017). Terrorist Use of Virtual Currencies: Containing the Potential Threat. *Energy, Economics and Security*. Center for a New American Security. https:// www.lawandsecurity.org/wp-content/uploads/2017/05/CLSCNASReport-TerroristFinancing-Final.pdf

Hertig, A. & Leech, O. (2021). "What Does Hashrate Mean and Why Does It Matter? Miners must compete using their machines to solve a difficult mathematical problem." CoinDesk.com, September 14. https://www.coindesk. com/tech/2021/02/05/what-does-hashrate-mean-and-why-does-it-matter/

Kim, T. (2015). The Predecessors of Bitcoin and Their Implications for the Prospect of Virtual Currencies. *PLoS ONE, 10*(4), 1–18. https://doi.org/10.1371/journal. pone.0123071

Lawsky, B. M. (2015). NYDFS Grants First Charter To a New York Virtual Currency Company Bitcoin Exchange "itBit"– Based in New York City – Receives License Under New York Banking Law. May 7. https://www.dfs. ny.gov/reports_and_publications/press_releases/pr1505071

Lee, J., Long, A., McRae, M., Steiner, J., & Handler, S. G. (2015). Bitcoin Basics: A Primer on Virtual Currencies. *Business Law International, 16*(1), 21–48.

Government Regulatory Efforts of the Cryptocurrency Industry **271**

Lindholm, T. (2018). Power Lunch: Wyoming passes blockchain bills to lure crypto business. https://www.cnbc.com/video/2018/03/12/wyoming-passes-blockchain-bills-to-lure-crypto-business.html

IRS (2014). Notice 2014-21. March 25. http://www.irs.gov/pub/irs-drop/n-14-21.pdf

IRS (2019). Revenue Ruling 2019-24. https://www.irs.gov/pub/irs-drop/rr-19-24.pdf

IRS. (2022). The Agency, its Mission and Statutory Authority. https://www.irs.gov/about-irs/the-agency-its-mission-and-statutory-authority

Maidan, L. (2022). Kazakhstan's electricity and internet shutdown took bitcoin miners offline. The cofounder of a mining operation says it's time to explore other options, including satellite internet and alternative countries. *Business Insider.* https://www.msn.com/en-us/money/markets/kazakhstan-s-electricity-and-internet-shutdown-took-bitcoin-miners-offline-the-cofounder-of-a-mining-operation-says-it-s-time-to-explore-other-options-including-satellite-internet-and-alternative-countries/ar-AASLNku?ocid=uxbndlbing

Marinova, P. (2018). SEC Appoints New Crypto Chief to Oversee Digital Assets and ICOs. *Fortune.com*, 1.

Moffit, T. (2021). Beyond Boom and Bust: An emerging clean energy economy in Wyoming. *UC San Diego: Climate Science and Policy.* https://escholarship.org/uc/item/0zp872rt

Naheem, M. A. (2018). Regulating virtual currencies – the challenges of applying fiat currency laws to digital technology services. *Journal of Financial Crime, 25*, 562–575.

New York Department of Financial Resources. (2018). DFS Continues to Foster Responsible Growth in New York's FinTech Industry with New Virtual Currency Product Approvals. https://www.dfs.ny.gov/reports_and_publications/press_releases/pr1809101

New York Department of Financial Resources. (2019). Guidance Regarding Adoption or Listing of Virtual Currencies. https://www.dfs.ny.gov/industry_guidance/industry_letters/il20200624_adoption_listing_vc

New York Department of Financial Resources. (2022). Guidance on the Issuance of U.S. Dollar-Backed Stablecoins. https://www.dfs.ny.gov/industry_guidance/industry_letters/il20220608_issuance_stablecoins

New York State (2015a). New York Codes, Rules and Regulations Title 23 – FINANCIAL SERVICES Chapter I – Regulations of the Superintendent of Financial Services Part 200 – VIRTUAL CURRENCIES Section 200.3 – License. https://regulations.justia.com/states/new-york/title-23/chapter-i/part-200/section-200-3/#:~:text=Universal percent20Citation percent3A percent2023 percent20NY percent20Comp percent20Codes percent20Rules percent20and, Part percent2C percent20engage percent20in percent20any percent20Virtual percent20Currency percent20Business percent20Activity

New York State (2015b). New York Codes, Rules and Regulations: Title 23 – FINANCIAL SERVICES, Chapter I – Regulations of the Superintendent of Financial Services Part 200 – VIRTUAL CURRENCIES Section 200.5 – Application fees. https://regulations.justia.com/states/new-york/title-23/chapter-i/part-200/section-200-5/

Office of the Comptroller of the Currency. (2013). Suspicious Activity Reports (SAR). https://www.occ.treas.gov/topics/supervision-and-examination/

bank-operations/financial-crime/suspicious-activity-reports/index-suspicious-activity-reports.html#:~:text=Under%20the%20Bank%20Secrecy%20Act%20%28BSA%29%2C%20financial%20institutions,signal%20criminal%20activity%20%28e.g.%2C%20money%20laundering%2C%20tax%20evasion%29.

Parveen, R. & Alajmi, A. (2019). An Overview of Bitcoin's Legal and Technical Challenges. *Journal of Legal, Ethical and Regulatory Issues*, 22(S1), 1–8.

Rauchs, M. (2021). New data reveals timeline of China's bitcoin mining exodus. Cambridge Centre for Alternative Finance (CCAF). https://www.jbs.cam.ac.uk/insight/2021/new-data-reveals-timeline-of-chinas-bitcoin-mining-exodus/

Sergeenkov, A. (2021). China Crypto Bans: A Complete History. Coindesk. September 29. https://www.coindesk.com/learn/china-crypto-bans-a-complete-history/

Sigalos, M. (2022). Kazakhstan's deadly protests hit bitcoin, as the world's second-biggest mining hub shuts down. *CNBC*. https://www.cnbc.com/2022/01/06/kazakhstan-bitcoin-mining-shuts-down-amid-fatal-protests.html

Stoll, C., Klaaßen, L., & Gallersdörfer, U. (2019). The Carbon Footprint of Bitcoin. *Joule*, 3(7), 1647–1661. https://doi-org.libproxy.troy.edu/10.1016/j.joule.2019.05.012

Tu, K. V. & Meredith, M. W. (2015). Rethinking Virtual Currency Regulation in the Bitcoin Age. *Washington Law Review*, 90(1), 271–348.

U.S. Commodity Futures Trading Commission (2023). Customer Advisory: Use Caution When Buying Digital Coins or Tokens. https://www.cftc.gov/LearnAndProtect/AdvisoriesAndArticles/caution_of_digital_currencies.html

U.S. Congress. (2021). Infrastructure Investment and Jobs Act (H.R.3684). https://www.congress.gov/bill/117th-congress/house-bill/3684/text

U.S. Department of the Treasury. (2022). Role of the Treasury. https://home.treasury.gov/about/general-information/role-of-the-treasury

U.S. Securities and Exchange Commission. (2022a). What We Do? https://www.sec.gov/about/what-we-do

U.S. Securities and Exchange Commission. (2022b). Investor Alert: Bitcoin and Other Virtual Currency-Related Investments. https://www.sec.gov/oiea/investor-alerts-bulletins/investoralertsia_bitcoin.html

U.S. Securities and Exchange Commission. (2022c). Spotlight on Initial Coin Offerings (ICOs). https://www.sec.gov/ICO

U.S. Securities and Exchange Commission. (2022d). Customer Identification Programs. https://www.sec.gov/about/offices/ocie/amlmfsourcetool

Virga, J. M. (2015). International Criminals and Their Virtual Currencies: The Need for an International Effort in Regulating Virtual Currencies and Combating Cyber Crime. *Brazilian Journal of International Law*, 12(2), 512–527.

Volpicelli, G. M. (2022). As Kazakhstan Descends Into Chaos, Crypto Miners Are at a Loss. *Wired*. https://www.wired.com/story/kazakhstan-cryptocurrency-mining-unrest-energy/

Wolfson, R. (2018). U.S. State Of Wyoming Defines Cryptocurrency 'Utility Tokens' As New Asset Class. *Forbes*. March 13. https://www.forbes.com/sites/rachelwolfson/2018/03/13/u-s-state-of-wyoming-defines-cryptocurrency-utility-tokens-as-new-asset-class/?sh=3ec02d504816

Wyoming State Legislature. (2018a). H.B. No. 0070 Open blockchain tokens-exemptions. https://wyoleg.gov/2018/Digest/HB0070.pdf

Wyoming State Legislature. (2018b). HB0019 – Wyoming Money Transmitter Act-virtual currency exemption. https://www.wyoleg.gov/Legislation/2018/HB0019

Wyoming State Legislature. (2018c). HB0101 – Electronic corporate records. https://www.wyoleg.gov/Legislation/2018/HB0101

Wyoming State Legislature. (2018d). HB0126 – Limited liability companies-series. https://www.wyoleg.gov/Legislation/2018/HB0126

Wyoming State Legislature. (2018e). SF0111 – Property taxation-digital currencies. https://www.wyoleg.gov/Legislation/2018/SF0111

Wyoming State Legislature. (2020 and 2022). Wyoming Utility Token Act of 2020: Title 34- Property, Conveyances and Security Transactions, Chapter 29, Digital Assets. https://law.justia.com/codes/wyoming/2020/title-34/chapter-29/section-34-29-106/ and https://law.justia.com/codes/wyoming/2022/title-34/chapter-29/section-34-29-106/

Xie, R. (2019). Why China Had to Ban Cryptocurrency but the U.S. Did Not: Comparative Analysis of Regulations on Crypto-Markets between the U.S. and China. *Washington University Global Studies Law Review*, 18(2), 457–492.

INDEX

Abboushi, S. 244
accountability 3, 17, 109, 185;
     deliberative democracy 24,
     25, 33; E-Government and
     E-Governance 38, 39, 40, 45,
     66, 68, 73; narrative analysis
     and permissionless innovation
     124, 136; regulation of
     cryptocurrency industry 232,
     254, 268
ACP *see* Affordable Connectivity
     Program (ACP)
Affordable Connectivity Program
     (ACP) 61
Agrawal, S. 38
AML/CFT (anti-money laundering and
     counter-terrorism financing)
     242, 244, 248, 250, 266
Anderson, J. E. 8
Angel, J. J. 191
anti-money laundering and counter-
     terrorism financing (AML/
     CFT) *see* AML/CFT (anti-
     money laundering and counter-
     terrorism financing)
Arstein, S. R. 23
Asencio, H. 45, 63, 64

Baber, W. F. 11
Baby Boomers 56

Bank Secrecy Act (BSA), 1970 222,
     242, 245–249, 250
banks 152, 153, 159, 173, 180, 234,
     242, 248, 249; central-bank
     issued digital currencies 167;
     compared with Bitcoin 182; *see
     also* Bank Secrecy Act (BSA),
     1970; fiat currency; financial
     institutions; money, concept of
Bannister, F. 36–37
barriers: artificial 121; to entry
     121; logistical 46, 123; to
     participation 47, 125; physical
     47; to technocracy 18
Bartless, R. V. 11
Beiró, M. G. 173
BEP *see* Bureau of Engraving and
     Printing (BEP)
bidding process 51, 52, 76
Biden, Joe 225
Bill of Rights 154
Bitcoin 148, 218; acceptance levels
     169, 184, 185, 189, 193,
     194; anonymity, limited 180;
     benefits to users 174–175, 181,
     182, 183, 197; and blockchain
     technology 214; in comparable
     U.S. dollars 169, 184–185,
     186, 190, 191, 196, 207;
     comparison with traditional

276 Index

banking industry 182; concept 171; costs reduction 180, 182; counting as money, whether 166, 188–194; creation (2009) 213, 230; credit cards compared 183; decentralization 168, 174, 176, 181; defining 215, 233–234; definitional parameters 168; development 209, 232; difficulty in counterfeiting 177; digital wallets 188; double-spending, preventing 174; example of convertible virtual currency 150; expansion or contraction of usage 260; first transaction in a block 170; flexibility provided by 181; functionality 189, 190, 197; global proliferation 180, 213; growing role in economy 170, 209, 221, 224; inflation resistant 191; initial funding of fiat currency required 182; integrity of 178, 179; intentional digital duplication 178–179; irreversibility of transactions 183; lack of stability 191–192; medium of exchange 189, 194; mining of 174, 175, 177, 179, 217, 218; non-fiat virtual currency 172; non-legal tender 172, 184; not dependent on conventional means to establish trust 180–181; numbers in circulation 175; operational status 169; origins 169–171; outside of government involvement 199; peer-to-peer network 170, 171, 181, 215; Ponzi scheme 222, 234, 236; possible threats to security 177–180; potential growth as a viable means of exchange 204–205; potential role in the stock market 184–187; proof-of-work 170, 217; pros and cons 166, 180–184; protections against inflation rate fluctuations 180; retention of savings benefit 183; scalability 187–188; standing within the cryptocurrency industry 168–169; status compared with fiat currency 185; theft of 177–178; transaction fees 183–184, 195, 196; transactions in denominations previously unavailable 182; trust issues 192, 197–198; unit of account, seen as 172; verification process 174; viability of 185, 189, 192, 198; volatility of transaction fees 184; volatility of value 184, 224–225; white paper 170, 194; *see also* blockchain technology; cryptocurrency; cryptocurrency industry, regulation of; virtual currency, non-fiat

BitLicense, New York 223, 251–256, 267

blockchain technology 166, 173; and Bitcoin industry 214; confirmation lags 176, 179; counterfeiting, protection against 207; design 179; distributed ledger, recording on 167, 173, 174; double-spending 170, 175–180; and energy consumption 217; hash (standardized identifier) 174; "irreversible mathematic algorithm," as 174; open blockchain tokens, Wyoming 263; original and new protocol 231; private key, suggested usage of 173; public ledger 174; security of 171–180, 217; transaction malleability, susceptibility to 177; validation/verification process 175, 176, 177, 179, 217, 230; virtual ledger as a blockchain 173; *see also* Bitcoin; cryptocurrency; cryptocurrency industry, regulation of

Böhme, R. 175

Bottorff, C. 184

Bouncken, R. B. 191

Boxerman, S. J. 173, 180, 211

Brandeis, L. 223–224

broadband 60; Affordable Connectivity Program (ACP) 61; and

digital divide 54, 55; Division of Broadband and Digital Equity, North Carolina 53; Emergency Broadband Benefit Program (EBB Program) 61; *see also* digital divide; ICTs (information and communication technology)

Brown, Jerry 256–257

BTC.com (Bitcoin mining pool) 218

budgeting 44, 66, 73, 82

Bureau of Engraving and Printing (BEP) 160, 223, 241

Cable, S. 56

California: Assembly Bill 129 (AB-129) 257–258; cryptocurrency industry, regulation of 251, 256–258, 259, 260, 266–267; cryptocurrency seen as viable money 259; Department of Financial Protection and Innovation (DFPI) 256; Digital Financial Assets Law bill, vetoing of 256; Executive Order N-9-22 258; State Legislature 256, 257

California Corporations Code 257

Calvery, J. 242, 243–244

Cambridge Bitcoin Electricity Consumption Index (CBECI) 218

Cambridge Centre for Alternative Finance (CCAF) 218

Centeno, M. A. 1, 4, 6

Central Intelligence Agency (CIA) 219

CFTC *see* Commodity Futures Trading Commission (CFTC)

China 218

Ciaian, P. 175

citizen engagement 77; availability of participatory means 22; choices 47; citizen–government interactions 25; deliberative mini-publics 81–82; diminishing 50; discursive events 47; E-Government and E-Governance 21–22, 24, 25, 29, 38, 41, 43–46, 49, 50, 55, 59, 67–68, 74, 76, 81–82; E-Participation 64; exchanging of ideas 45; facilitating 64, 68;

increasing 47, 55, 56; lacking 23; ladder of 23; lobbying, for value-based preferences 45; networked interactions 45; opportunities for 21–22, 24, 25, 29, 38, 47, 49, 55, 59, 67–68, 76, 82, 110, 135, 139, 181; public policy 4–5, 19; public sector, engagement with 45, 52, 53, 76, 78; Web 1.0 technologies 70; Web 2.0 technologies 68, 78; *see also* dialogue, opportunities for; preferences

Cohen, J. 20, 21–22

Coinage Act (1792) 159, 160

Coinbase Global, Inc. (COIN) 186–187, 224

Commodity Futures Trading Commission (CFTC) 149, 210, 213, 222, 232, 260, 261, 266

communication: asynchronous 46–47; civic 42; democratic 63; direct 71; dynamics 26, 37, 43, 78, 80; facilitating 42, 78, 81; framework 33; global 96; informal 26; innovations, communication-based 78; interactive capacity 39; Internet-based 53, 68; limited 78; networks (*see* communication networks); one-way 37, 39, 71; processes 80; radio 59; structures/structural capacity 32, 39, 44, 46, 47; synchronous 47; technology-based 78; tools 80; two-way 39, 79, 81; unsolicited 234; voice 54; *see also* communication networks; Communications Act (1934); communicative structures

communication networks 25, 26, 27, 46

Communications Act (1934) 59, 60

communicative structures 20–22, 77, 110, 128; deliberative democracy 19, 22, 26, 82, 109

Congress 154–162, 203, 250, 258, 265; and Bitcoin/cryptocurrency 156, 157–158, 161, 199, 213, 216, 224;

278 Index

constitutional authority 163; decision-makers in 155–156; and Department of the Treasury 241; legislative mandate and agency actions 15–16, 158–159, 185, 210, 211, 219–224, 225, 232, 260; policymaking 156–157; powers of 154–155, 157, 158, 199

Connolly, R. 36–37

Constitution of the United States 151, 154–162; articles 154–155, 157; cryptocurrency contradicting 207; Framers 155, 199, 208; Necessary and Proper Clause 154–157, 160, 161, 199, 240–241; tenth amendment 221, 266

Consumer Sentinel Network 240

Cooper, C. G. 258, 259

counterfeiting, protection against 207, 208

CPUs (central processing units), power of 170, 171, 174, 177, 187, 188, 196, 198; collective power of networked CPUs 195

credit-card companies 152, 153, 184

credit cards 182, 195; compared with Bitcoin 183, 194

crowdsourcing 68, 81

cryptocurrency 166–202; acceptance by system actors 143, 144, 169, 184, 185, 189, 192, 193; administrators 248; anonymity, limited 167, 180; attractions for vendors 183, 184, 195; Bitcoin's standing within industry 168–169; compared with fiat currency 168; competition 217; concept 166; confirmation lags 176, 179; costs reduction 180; creating a crypto account 153; criminality, risk of 188, 196, 243; cryptography, use of 167, 168; decentralization 45, 153, 157, 167, 168, 172–176, 180–183, 187, 206, 208, 210, 215, 217, 233, 243, 244, 248; definitional parameters for 260; development 163; digitally counterfeiting 177;

distributed ledger, recording on 167, 173; double-spending 167, 175–180; embezzlement 178; exchangers 248; exchanges 177, 215, 224, 249; failing to be classified as fiat currency 166, 259; fiat 167; fraud 173, 177–179, 195, 196, 198, 233–240, 255; hashrate 217–218; independence from central authority 167; key systemic features 167–168; longitudinal process 173, 184, 185, 187; medium of exchange 189, 194; mining industry 217, 218; natural growth of industry 209; newness of 209; proliferation of 163, 212; purchasing or exchanging 153; regulation of (*see* cryptocurrency industry, regulation of); state-sanctioned 163; threat to fiat money 168; timestamping 171, 172, 195; uniqueness 176; usage within the U.S. economy 209; users of 248; verification process 172; *see also* Bitcoin; blockchain technology; virtual currency, non-fiat

cryptocurrency industry, regulation of 203–273; Commodity Futures Trading Commission (CFTC) 210, 213, 222, 232, 260; and energy consumption 216–219; executive orders 225; federal government, U.S. 224–249; Federal Trade Commission (FTC) 210, 226, 236–240; Financial Crimes and Enforcement Network (FinCEN) 210, 223, 240–249, 266; fragmentation 156, 221; government agencies 225; guidance 203; Infrastructure Investment and Jobs Act (2021) 225; Internal Revenue Service 209–210, 222, 226–232, 260, 266; and permissionless innovation/precautionary principle 204, 209, 254, 255; policymaking 86, 204, 231–232; present U.S. regulatory

environment 206; Security and Exchange Commission (SEC) 210, 232–236, 260, 266; state-level government 249–265
crypto-stock 186
currency: fiat (*see* fiat currency); modern-era 147–151; virtual (*see* virtual currency, non-fiat); *see also* Bitcoin; blockchain technology; cryptocurrency; money, concept of
Currency and Financial Transactions Reporting Act (1970) 242
Customer Identification Programs (CIP) 249, 250

Dafoe, A. 101–102
Dahl, R. 10
Daj, A. 167
decentralization (Bitcoin/cryptocurrency/virtual currency) 153, 157, 167, 168, 172–176, 180–183, 187; Bitcoin 168, 174, 176, 181; regulation of cryptocurrency industry 206, 208, 210, 215, 217, 233, 243, 244, 248
decision-making processes 64; and Congress 155–156; internal 15; permissionless innovation and precautionary principle 122, 127, 129, 136, 156; public sector 1–3, 5–7, 9, 10, 14, 47, 49, 69, 90, 94, 106, 108, 110, 199, 251; in technocracy 2, 4, 7–9, 11, 15–17, 19, 30, 31, 33, 34; technological determinism 87, 93, 94, 96, 108; *see also* policymaking; permissionless innovation and precautionary principle; public sector; technocracy and expert/specialized knowledge
DeJesus, T. 183
deliberative democracy 13, 18–27, 29–34, 46, 51–52, 74, 76, 83, 104, 106, 107, 109, 115; accountability 24, 26, 33, 39, 66, 68, 73; associated expectations of 3, 7, 30–33, 34, 38, 39, 44, 45, 47, 49, 58, 65, 68, 74, 77, 79, 81, 82, 88,

93–95, 101, 108, 110, 113, 124–125, 127–128, 130, 131, 135–136, 162; availability of participatory means 22, 24, 25; communicative structures for engagement 19, 22, 26, 82, 109; complex interactions 63; "conscious democratic steering" 127; cyclicity 24, 25, 26, 39, 73; deliberative politics 25; digital divide, effect on 55, 56, 58; discourse/deliberations expected 7, 12, 19–23, 29, 30, 32, 68, 93; discourse-theoretical methodology 20; discursive events 5, 7, 11, 20–27, 31–34, 43–49, 52, 53, 55, 58, 64, 65, 68, 74, 75, 77, 78, 80, 87, 93, 94, 96, 108–111, 113, 125, 130, 131, 135; E-Governance/E-Government, role of 38, 41–43, 61, 65; feedback loops 22, 65; functions of E-Governance 43; institutionalizing of expectations 33, 39, 68, 74, 77, 110; integrity of 31, 57, 109; legitimacy of 22–24, 109; opportunities for citizens to engage 21–22, 24, 25, 29, 38, 49, 55, 59, 67, 68, 76, 82, 110, 135, 139, 181; permissionless innovation and precautionary principle 114, 119, 136, 139; policymaking 10, 17–19, 33, 48, 69, 101, 113, 117; political system, U.S. 18, 20, 21; process of deliberation 19; and public sector 21, 24, 34, 38, 42, 49, 82, 108, 129, 130; range of expectations relating to 19–20, 101; and regulation of cryptocurrency industry 162; responsiveness/responsible government 31, 46, 93, 101, 108, 109, 119, 120, 135, 140, 205, 221, 268; system openness 23, 30; technological determinism, role 111, 113, 114; technology industry, potential role for narrative analysis 131–136; threat of technocracy to expectations 9,

280 Index

18, 19, 29, 30–31; traditional, in the United States 4–6, 30–32; transparency 24, 33, 39, 66, 68, 73; *see also* citizen engagement; dialogue, opportunities for; discursive events; E-Governance; E-Government; permissionless innovation and precautionary principle

Department of Education 66

Department of Homeland Security (DHS) 219, 223

Department of Housing and Urban Development 66

Department of Justice 178, 198

Department of the Treasury 160, 222, 226, 240–241; and Congress 160–161; "greenbacks" created by 160; mission statement 241; on virtual currency 148, 149, 158, 159; *see also* Financial Crimes and Enforcement Network (FinCEN)

DFS *see* New York Department of Financial Resources (NYDFS)

dialogue, opportunities for 4, 136, 186, 268; deliberative democracy 20, 25; E-Government and E-Governance 38, 69, 79–80; in a technocracy 12, 17

digital currency 148, 151, 163, 167, 173, 176, 257; *see also* cryptocurrency; cryptocurrency industry, regulation of; fiat currency; money, concept of; virtual currency, non-fiat

digital divide 45, 53–61; defining 53; and digital literacy training 54; effect on deliberative democracy 55, 56, 58; and individual choice 57; potential to affect technology-based inequity 55; and public sector 53, 56, 58, 65; requirement to use the Internet 54; scope of 57; service delivery 67; technological haves vs. technological have-nots 54, 57; those affected by 57–58; usability and accessibility concerns 53–54

digital signatures 170

digital wallets 188, 198

discursive events 5, 7, 11, 20–27, 31–34; citizen engagement 47; cognitive/psychocultural obstacles limiting government 96; collaborative nature 74; cyclical 110; digital events and E-Government/E-Governance 43–49, 50, 52, 53, 55, 58, 64, 65–66, 68–69, 74, 75, 77, 81; facilitating 25, 26, 32, 46, 77, 78, 80; formalized 23, 32; ICTs-facilitated 44–45, 74; and permissionless innovation/precautionary principle 113, 125, 130, 131, 135; public-sector-generated 21, 48; technological determinism 87, 93, 94, 96, 108–111; Web 2.0 technologies creating 75

District of Columbia 258

Dobeck, M. F. 142, 144

Dotson, T. 91, 96, 123–124

double-spending dilemma, cryptocurrency 175–180; Bitcoin 176, 178–179; compared with digital fiat currency 175–176; criminality 188; defining 176; duplicate double spending 177; preventing/mitigating against 167, 170, 171, 174, 176, 180, 188, 196

EBB *see* Emergency Broadband Benefit Program (EBB Program)

E-clogging 50

E-Democracy 64

E-Governance: application of information gathered 44; asynchronous means of facilitating activities 46–47; chat rooms 47; citizen engagement 47; complementary to E-Government 42, 43; decision-making (*see* policymaking); E-Government initiatives originally outpacing 70; functions 42–43; implementation 62; information dissemination 73; integration of ICTs into the communicative

Index **281**

structure 77; interactive nature of 65, 68, 74; interrelation with E-Government 73; levels of acceptance for 48–49; longitudinal process 31, 33, 38, 48, 49, 51–52, 74, 76; network structures 46; practical concerns 49–61; privacy and security concerns 53; public sector responsibilities, fulfilling 42–43; scope and nature of 48; synchronous communication 47; technological means used to facilitate 65–72; usage of ICTs 43, 45, 47–49, 53, 55, 69, 77; Web 2.0 technologies 45, 62–72; *see also* E-Government; ICTs (information and communication technology); public sector; technological means

E-Government: citizen engagement 38, 41, 49, 55, 59, 67–68, 74, 76, 82; complementary to E-Governance 42, 43; decision-making (*see* policymaking); defining 36; digital divide 53–61; functions 42–43; implementation 62; information dissemination 44, 65–66, 67, 72; information overload 52; initiatives originally outpacing those of E-Governance 70; interrelation with E-Governance 73; longitudinal process 38, 39, 49, 51–52, 66, 72, 74; origin of 36–37; phases 40, 41; practical concerns 49–61; privacy and security concerns 53; public sector responsibilities, fulfilling 42–43; public support for 48; retaining some traditional transactions, need for 67, 75; service delivery 73–74; stages of process 40, 41, 71; task-oriented 46; technological means used to facilitate 65–72; transactional nature of 42; usage of ICTs 37, 39, 41, 43, 53, 55, 66, 69, 70; Web 1.0 technologies 62–63, 65–66, 67; *see also* citizen

engagement; E-Governance; ICTs (information and communication technology); public sector; technological means

Elastic Clause *see* Necessary and Proper Clause

elections 20, 43

elites 1, 2, 7, 9, 198; rise of "technically skilled counter-elites" 11

Elliott, E. 142, 144

Emergency Broadband Benefit Program (EBB Program) 61

energy: blockchain validation process 217; and cryptocurrency production 216–219; electricity 217; fossil fuels 217; hydro power 263; natural gas 263, 264; renewable energy 217; wind power 264; in Wyoming 263, 264

E-Participation 64

e-perceptions 52

Ethereum 217

expert knowledge, role in technocracy *see* technocracy and expert/specialized knowledge

Farouk, M. 257

FCC *see* Federal Communications Commission (FCC)

Federal Bureau of Investigations (FBI) 219

Federal Communications Act (1934) 134

Federal Communications Commission (FCC) 59, 60, 61

federal system, U.S.: Congressional legislative mandate 15–16, 219–224; E-Government and E-Governance 66, 72; regulation of cryptocurrency industry 216, 250, 255, 258, 260, 266

Federal Trade Commission (FTC): advice and guidance 238; consumer protection 239, 240; and cryptocurrency regulation 210, 226, 236–240; "Decrypting Cryptocurrency Scams" 239; educational

282 Index

campaign 240; enforcement by 237; Federal Trade Commission Act (1914) 236–237; guidelines 237; policy 237–240
fiat currency 147, 160, 161, 163, 208, 242; alternative forms 148; Bitcoin not qualified as 166, 175; characteristics of money 194; coins and paper money 147, 149, 160; collapse of 168; compared with cryptocurrency 168; competing with Bitcoin 203; counterfeiting 178; creation 167, 199, 207; criminality 178, 249; cryptocurrency a threat to 168; cryptocurrency convertible to 163; cryptocurrency failing to be classified as 166, 259; digital 148, 175–176; electronically transacted versions 163; evolutionary societal events affecting 158; exchange rates, costs 182; exchanging 152; as a form of money 151; funding 182; government-sanctioned 150; and inflation 182; initial funding required, for cryptocurrency transactions 182; legal tender 147, 163; and non-fiat virtual currency 153; stability 151, 181; status compared with Bitcoin 185; tangible 178; traditional 168, 192, 232; transfers in 248; U.S. 184, 185, 189, 190; *see also* cryptocurrency; cryptocurrency industry, regulation of; money, concept of; virtual currency, non-fiat
Financial Crimes and Enforcement Network (FinCEN) 210, 240–249, 266; application of the BSA 266; within Department of the Treasury 223, 226, 241–242; enforcement by 242; guidance 244; mandate 242; rules and regulations 246, 247; statutory requirements 248; on virtual currency 149
financial institutions 242, 244, 245; established 185, 186; large 257;

non-banking 246; traditional 152–153, 178, 181, 182, 183; *see also* banks; credit-card companies
FinCEN *see* Financial Crimes and Enforcement Network (FinCEN)
Finger, M. 51
Fischer, F. 2, 3, 8
Fletcher, E. 239
Foundry (Bitcoin mining pool) 218
Fountain, J. 89
fraud, cryptocurrency 173, 177–179, 195, 196, 198, 236–240, 255; investment schemes 233, 234, 235; scams 238
FTC *see* Federal Trade Commission (FTC)
FTX case 178, 192

Galbraith, J. K. and J. K. 143
Gallersdörfer, U. 217
Gauvin, L. 173
Gen Xers 56
Gibson, R. 57
Goldman, Z. 243
Greiling, D. 38
guerilla marketing 186

Haber, S. 172
Halachmi, A. 38
Hamilton, A. 158
Hammond, A. S. 55
Haque, S. 37, 38
Harwick, C. 175
hashrate 217–218
Hauer, T. 89
Hertig, A. 217
House of Representatives 154
Howland, J. S. 54
Hughes, T. P. 89, 102, 105
hyperinflation 168

ICOs *see* Initial Coin Offerings (ICOs)
ICTs (information and communication technology) 36–38, 74; acceptance 73; application on behalf of government 55; and citizen engagement 41, 47; collective power of networked CPUs 195; computational power 187; consistent access to

54; CPU power 170, 171, 174, 177, 187, 188, 195, 196, 198; defining 62; development 36, 38–39, 73; digitally facilitating governmental activities 47; discursive events facilitated by 44–45; early-stage 70, 71; integration into communication structures 43, 44, 47, 62, 76; leveraging of 41, 42, 43, 67, 81, 173; role in modern-era American democracy 62–72; usage by E-Government and E-Governance 37, 39, 41, 43, 45, 47–49, 53, 55, 66, 70; Web 1.0 and Web 2.0 technologies 62–72; *see also* broadband; digital divide; E-Governance; E-Government; technological determinism; technological means; technology industry

inflation 152, 180; resistance to 191; supply-oriented 182, 191, 197, 207; *see also* hyperinflation

information 11, 44, 169, 205, 232, 233, 235, 251, 252; access to 38; accurate 50; Bitcoin 169, 185, 188, 231; descriptive 88, 164, 245; digital publication 50; and disinformation 50, 52; dissemination 27, 37–39, 41–44, 49, 62, 63, 65–67, 70–73, 74, 125, 249–250; educational 234, 236, 266; E-Government and E-Governance-based dissemination 41–44, 46, 48–50, 52; elitism 9; exchange of 52, 63, 82; expanding on 88, 114, 233; gathering of 44, 230, 236; government 37, 43, 44, 63, 65–66, 73, 74; guiding decision-making 12; illustrative 225, 253; introductory 86; and learning 27; online 41, 46, 52, 238; overload 50, 52, 76, 81; participant 254; permeability of 45; personal 192, 248; posting on social media 80; published 76; records 245; reporting 225, 246, 247; requests for 62, 245; sharing 41, 62, 63, 219, 240;

technical 171; transaction 152, 185; voting 43

information and communication technologies *see* ICTs (information and communication technology)

Infrastructure Investment and Jobs Act (2021) 60–61; Sec. 80603 225

Initial Coin Offerings (ICOs) 235, 261

innovation arbitrage 121–122

innovation migration 122–123

innovations 45, 73, 89; citizen expectations 62; communication-based 63, 78; dangers of over-investment in 56; in decision-making 89; and digital currencies 148; emerging 33, 63, 64, 67, 72; ingrained in U.S. society 90; Internet technologies 37, 39, 72; lack of access to 58; liberties of innovators and permissionless innovation 127; proliferation of 99, 107, 129, 130; public sector, applicable for use in 72, 75; regulation lagging behind 204, 213; societal change 95, 96; and technological determinism 89–93, 95, 97–98, 117; timestamping 171, 172; Web 1.0 technologies 71; Web 2.0 technologies 62, 64, 72; *see also* digital divide; E-Governance; E-Government; ICTs (information and communication technology); permissionless innovation and precautionary principle; Web 1.0 technologies; Web 2.0 technologies

institutionalization 7, 15, 159, 193, 198; application of ICTs 69; of deliberative democracy expectations 33, 39, 68, 74, 77, 110, 139; E-Government and E-Governance 38, 59, 60, 65, 73; and permissionless innovation/precautionary principle 118, 127, 138–139; redundancy 219; standard 10; state-level government and cryptocurrency industry 251,

254, 263, 264; technocracy and deliberative democracy 9, 18, 25, 26; and technological determinism 97, 101, 109, 110; transparency 45
Internal Revenue Service (IRS), U.S.: on cryptocurrency/virtual currency 149–150, 156, 167; E-Government and E-Governance 66; imposter scams 134; Internal Revenue Code 227; IRS notice 2014–21, Question (Q) and Answer (A) layout 227–230; IRS Revenue Ruling 2019–24 230–231; mission 226–227; permissionless innovation applied by 232; and regulation of cryptocurrency industry 209–210, 222, 226–232, 260, 266; statutory authority 227–232
Internet: adoption in the 1990s 37, 72, 73; citizens connected to 37; development 36; Internet-based communication 53, 68; leveraging of 43, 67; power of 39, 41; quality of 55; reducing barriers to entry 121; requirement to use 54; scams 237; see also E-Governance; E-Government; ICTs (information and communication technology)
IRS see Internal Revenue Service (IRS), U.S.

Johnson, R. W. 147
Jorgensen, D. J. 56
Joyce, P. G. 147

Kancs, d'A 175
Kazakhstan 218
Kim, T. 215
Klaaßen, L. 217
Kraus, S. 191

ladder of citizen engagement 23
Lansky, J. 147, 167
Lawsky, B. M. 253
Lee, R. D. (Jr) 147
Leech, O. 217

legal tender 147–151, 163, 168, 184
Leonard, K. 184
Lerer, M. 167, 173
Lindholm, Tyler 261, 262
longitudinal process 14, 31, 220; cryptocurrency 173, 184, 185, 187; cyclically longitudinal 33, 66; deliberative democracy 21–23, 27; E-Government and E-Governance 31, 33, 38, 48, 49, 51–52, 72, 74, 76; money, concept of 142, 145, 150–151; permissionless innovation/precautionary principle 118, 132; regulation of cryptocurrency industry 191–193, 221; technological determinism 89, 99, 100, 102, 103

McCabe, D. 191
McNiven, J. D. 37, 42
Marche, S. 37, 42
Marinova, P. 213
Mead, Matt 262
medium of exchange 142, 144–147, 152, 162; cryptocurrency 189, 194
Menger, C. 143
Miles, I. 36, 38
Millennials 56
Mises, L. V. 145–146; *The Theory of Money and Credit* 145
Mittal, M. 38
Moffit, T. 263–264
money, concept of 141–165; attribution of value 144; Bitcoin counting as money, whether 188–194; Bitcoin counting as, whether 207; definitions 141, 142; difficulty of duplicating/counterfeiting 142, 162; divisibility 142, 162, 173, 190; durability 142, 162, 173, 190; early money 143; forms, in a historical sense 143–144; fungible 173, 190; history 143, 144–145, 162; influence on public policy 141; legal tender 147–151, 163, 168, 184; longitudinal process 142, 145, 150–151; medium of exchange

142, 144–147, 152, 162, 189, 194; modern-era currency 147–151; network effects 192; origins of money 143, 144–145; portability 162, 173, 190; "real money" 147, 149; scarcity 190; socially constructed 144, 145; stability 142, 151, 162; stand-alone value 189; store of value 142, 145, 151; switching costs 192; tangible 141, 144, 148, 178, 189; transfer of money 144; trust in money 144; unit of account 141, 142, 144, 193; universally accepted fiscal worth 142; and U.S. Constitution/Congress 154–162; *see also* cryptocurrency; cryptocurrency industry, regulation of; fiat currency; virtual currency, non-fiat
money service businesses (MSBs) 246–249, 250
money transmitters 247–248
Moon, M. J. 39–40, 41
MSBs *see* money service businesses (MSBs)
Mt. Gox case 177, 192, 224

Naheem, M. A. 174
Nakamoto, S. 170, 171, 173, 194
narrative analysis: permissionless innovation 123–131, 137–138; precautionary principle 131–136, 137–138; "stable-feeling counter-narratives" 132; technological determinism 95–98
National Institute of Standards and Technology 62
Necessary and Proper Clause 154–157, 160, 161, 199, 240–241
New State Ice Co v. Liebmann 223–224
New York: Banking Law 252; cryptocurrency industry, regulation of 223, 252–256; licensing requirements for cryptocurrency 223, 252–253, 254; NYSE Bitcoin Index 185; NYSE Global Index Feed (GIF) 185; *see also* BitLicense, New

York; New York City Council; New York Department of Financial Resources (NYDFS); New York Stock Exchange (NYSE)
New York City Council 82
New York Department of Financial Resources (NYDFS) 251–256
New York Stock Exchange (NYSE) 185, 186
Newsom, Gavin 256, 258
Ngai, K. 168, 191
non-fiat virtual currency *see* virtual currency, non-fiat
Norris, D. F. 37
North Carolina, Division of Broadband and Digital Equity 53
NYDFS *see* New York Department of Financial Resources (NYDFS)
NYSE Bitcoin Index 185
NYSE Global Index Feed (GIF) 185

Office of Investor Education and Advocacy 233
Office of the Comptroller of the Currency 245

Parino, F. 173
participatory budgeting 82
Pathrannarakul, P. 37, 38
Patriot Act (2001) 242, 245, 250, 266
peer-to-peer network, virtual currency 170–172, 181, 195, 233; Bitcoin 170, 171, 181, 215; network 170
permissionless innovation and precautionary principle 113–140, 232; balanced argument, need for 114, 125, 129, 133; case for limited government intervention 117–131, 136; and cryptocurrency 205; decision-making processes 122, 127, 129, 136, 156; defining the precautionary principle 115; degree of freedom for the technology industry 115–116; degree of regulation, perspectives on 97, 115, 116, 117, 128–129; deliberative democracy expectations

127–128, 135–136; discursive events 113, 125, 130, 131, 135; longitudinal process 118, 132; narrative analysis 123–136, 137–138; normative and nomological aspect of permissionless innovation 123–124, 134; opportunities for dialogue, affecting 268; opposing perceptions of preferred role of government in regulating 86, 114–117, 129, 137, 204, 208, 209; policymaking 115, 120, 123, 161, 212, 231; potential role of precautionary principle in policymaking 131–136; preferences 124, 127, 129; public policy 115, 117–119, 121, 124–126, 128–131, 133, 135; rationale for permissionless innovation 115–116, 118–120, 121, 123, 125–127, 129, 137, 204; rationale for precautionary principle 132–136, 137; reactionary vs. preemptive approach to regulating technology industry 119–121, 133, 138; and regulation of cryptocurrency industry 204, 209, 254, 255; responsiveness and the precautionary principle 117; risk assessment 127–128, 129; and technological determinism 88, 97; theory 124; undermining unquestioned acceptability of permissionless innovation 132, 133–134; value-laden arguments 132–134, 137

Peters, G. W. 142, 150

"policy laboratory," governments acting as 224, 265, 266

policymaking 3, 19, 92, 204; anti-trust laws 125; ceding to technology experts 7, 30, 268; by Congress 156–157; cryptocurrency industry, regulation of 86, 204, 231–232; E-Government and E-Governance 43–45, 47, 48, 50, 55, 64, 67, 73,

74, 76, 79, 81; expertise and specialization, role of 1–12, 16–20, 28–31, 33, 48, 69, 87, 88, 101, 113, 117; flexibility 115; fragmented 156, 221; government agenda aligning with public preferences 79; innovations as driving force 89; permissionless innovation 115, 120, 123–131, 161; "policy laboratory," governments acting as (see "policy laboratory," governments acting as); and potential dangers of technocracy 16–17; precautionary principle 131–136, 161; public sector 1–3, 5–7, 9, 10, 14–16, 33, 47, 49, 67, 69, 90, 94, 106, 108, 115, 117, 161, 199, 251; technological determinism 94, 98–106, 111; whole-of-government approach to 13–14, 17, 220; see also decision-making processes; deliberative democracy; dialogue, opportunities for; public policy; public sector; technocracy and expert/specialized knowledge

political system, U.S. 1; decline in trust 3–4, 136; deliberative democracy 18, 20, 21; E-Government and E-Governance 43, 59, 68, 78; money, concept of 162; permissionless innovation 113, 118, 124, 129, 139; regulation of cryptocurrency industry 226, 265, 266; technocracy, potential role in 12–16; technological determinism 95, 99, 101, 108, 110, 111

polling, deliberative 82

polycentric networks of government 26

Poolin (Bitcoin mining pool) 218

precautionary principle see permissionless innovation and precautionary principle

preferences 3, 5, 48, 129, 161, 261, 267; competing 19, 21, 23, 31, 34; debates over 23; experiential 115; localized 220, 251;

permissionless innovation and precautionary principle 124, 127, 129; policy/political 4, 7, 21, 22, 26, 27, 32, 43, 44, 50, 58, 79–81, 110, 114, 115, 204; public sector 21, 26, 74, 82; societal 12, 21, 74, 80, 103, 193; system 23, 34; of technocrats 7, 9, 13, 14, 20, 95, 124, 268; technological determinism 95–98; value-based 45

private sector 138, 148, 239, 254; citizen-state-private sector interaction 44; E-Government and E-Governance 51, 53, 70, 71, 72, 76, 80, 81; technological determinism 87, 91, 94, 101, 108; *see also* public sector

privatization 51–53, 76

public choice theory 14, 28

public policy 29, 86, 136; Bitcoin production 218; and democratic procedures/dialogue 4–6, 20, 28, 33, 97, 139; development 12, 26, 92, 117–118, 140, 203; environment, changes in 26; factual evidence 52; ICTs, contribution of 81; integration of technocracy into 8; and money/cryptocurrency 141, 155, 158, 161, 187, 199, 203, 210; participatory procedures, derived from 4–5, 19; and permissionless innovation/precautionary principle 115, 117–118, 119, 121, 124–126, 128–131, 133, 135; and role of experts/ specialized knowledge 4, 8, 12, 18–19, 20, 27, 87; stages of process 12; standard operating procedures during creation of 8; technocratization of policy process 8; technology-based 132; and U.S. regulation of cryptocurrency 216, 218, 219, 250, 255, 264, 266; Wyoming 264; *see also* deliberative democracy; policymaking

public sector 4, 27, 44, 50, 57, 77, 81, 87, 159, 260; application

of technology/contribution of ICTs to 24, 32, 37, 39, 45, 48, 51, 54, 58, 62–65, 71–72, 77–78, 80, 91; association with E-Government/E-Governance 36–45, 56, 58, 61, 63, 64, 67, 69, 75, 76, 79; citizen engagement with 45, 52, 53, 76, 78; decision-making processes 1–3, 5–7, 9, 10, 14, 47, 49, 69, 90, 94, 106, 108, 110, 199, 251; and deliberative democracy 21, 24, 34, 38, 42, 49, 82, 108, 129, 130; and digital divide 53, 56, 58, 65; duties/responsibilities 10, 25, 26, 38, 42, 46, 49, 51, 61, 76, 77, 79, 125, 138, 219; fiscal capacity/policy 71, 82, 160; inefficiency and ineffectiveness 13, 79; innovations applicable for use in 72, 75; interactive designs 72; intervention by 198, 255; and money/cryptocurrency 205, 214, 221; organizational goals 48, 66; performance of duties 39, 43, 80, 101; and permissionless innovation/ precautionary principle 138; policymaking 1–3, 5–7, 9, 10, 14–16, 33, 47, 49, 67, 69, 90, 94, 106, 108, 110, 115, 117, 161, 199, 251; preemptive action by 120; preferences 21, 26, 74, 82; public-sector-generated discursive events 21; reciprocity 71; responsiveness 221; and technocracy 3, 5–6, 7, 15, 17, 30, 39; and technological determinism 101; technological means, turning to 51; trust in 6, 52, 55; Web 2.0 usage 77–78; *see also* private sector; technocracy and expert/ specialized knowledge

Qian, H. 44

Rachfal, C. L. 54
Rajcaniova, M. 175
Rauchs, M. 218
Reddick, C. G. 37

288 Index

Regression Theorem 145
responsiveness/responsible government
46, 93; deliberative democracy
31, 46, 93, 101, 108, 109,
119, 120, 135, 140, 205,
221, 268; E-Government
and E-Governance 67; and
permissionless innovation/
precautionary principle 119,
135, 137, 140; regulation of
cryptocurrency industry 205,
221, 268–269; technological
determinism 108, 109
Richter, C. 191
Roberts, N. 19
Rogers, E. M. 53
Rose, R. 48
Russian Federation 218

Sánchez-Torres, J. 36, 38
scalability, Bitcoin 187–188
scams: cryptocurrency 239–240;
Internet 237; IRS imposter 134;
online 237, 239; potential 240;
romance 239; spotting 238
Schnurer, E. B. 99
Schwerin, M. F. 173, 180, 211
Security and Exchange Commission
(SEC): capital formation,
facilitating 233; consumer
protection 185; and
cryptocurrency regulation 210,
226, 232–236, 245, 260–262,
266; fair, orderly and efficient
markets, maintaining 233;
Investment Adviser Public
Disclosure (IAPD) website
235; investor alerts 233–234;
mandate 234; Office of Investor
Education and Advocacy 233;
protection of investors 233;
SEC vs. Shavers 222; on virtual
currency 156
Senate 154
Senate Floor Analysis 257
service delivery: cost effective 66; and
E-Government/E-Governance
39, 41, 43, 46, 63, 65–67, 83;
integrated 40; privatization
of 76; public processes 51;
traditional 52
Sethi, P. 38, 42

Smith, D.L. 45, 45, 47
Smith, M. L. 89, 90
Smith, M. R. 89
social constructivism 103, 107
social media 32, 50, 64, 68, 81; and
regulation of cryptocurrency
industry 236, 239–240; and
Web 2.0 technologies 79, 80
specialized knowledge, role in
technocracy see technocracy
and expert/specialized
knowledge
Sprecher, M. 36, 38
stablecoin (price-stable
cryptocurrency), New York
254–255
standard operating procedure (SOP) 8
state-level government and
cryptocurrency industry:
California 256–258, 259, 260;
New York 252–256; Texas
258–260; Wyoming 260–265
stock market: Bitcoin, potential role
in 184–187, 197; crypto-stock
186; New York Stock Exchange
(NYSE) 185, 186
Stoll, C. 217
Stornetta, W. S. 172
Supplemental Nutrition Assistance
Program (SNAP) 66
Supreme Court 220

technical know-how 40, 48, 53, 58, 71
technocracy and expert/specialized
knowledge 1–19; absence of
"cohesiveness of technocrats"
10; accumulation of knowledge
1, 2, 28; achieving status of
an expert 10; authoritarian
nature of technocracy 4; averse
to/lacking faith in role of
politics in democracy 9–10,
20; and bureaucracy 15–16;
case by case basis, role for 14;
compared with experts in law
11; conflict between experts
11; control, degrees of 2, 6;
critiques/dangers of exclusively
relying on 4, 6–12, 18, 27–30;
deferring to experts 2, 5, 7–8,
14, 16; elites 1, 2, 7, 9, 11,
198; institutionalization 7, 15;

Index **289**

justification by technocrats 1–6, 8, 18–19, 87; levels of influence 88; methodological objectivity 4; non-experts, calling for diminished role 2, 8; as one among several tools, suggestions for 12, 14; policy analysis 3; policymaking 1–12, 16–20, 28–31, 87, 88; political dialogue, unfavorable to 4, 5; potential role for in American democracy 12–18; precedence of rationality over the political 10–11; preferences of technocrats 7, 9, 13, 14, 20, 95, 124, 268; and public sector 3, 5–6, 7, 15, 17, 30, 39; role of technocrat, defining 1–2; self-interest 14–15; separateness of technocrats from local political context 3; as standard, technocrats' arguments for 2, 7, 10, 136; supplementary role, argument for 7, 8, 14, 16, 33–34; technocratization of policy process 8; threat to expectations of deliberative democracy 9, 18, 19, 29, 30–31; trust in political systems, decline in 3–4; usefulness associated with 5, 13, 14, 29; world view 2; *see also* public policy; public sector; technological means

technological determinism 86–112, 208; concept 88, 102; continuum approach of 100–105, 110–111; critiques 98–109, 113; cultural stature, in the U.S. 90; decision making, application during 94, 98–106, 111; defining 88–95; discursive events, limited role in relation to 87, 93, 94, 96, 108–111, 113–114; embeddedness of technology in society 92, 97; entrenchment of 92, 96, 97, 98; foundational concept 87–88; government, role of 96; hard or soft interpretations of role of technology 102, 103; human element, neglecting 106–107;

and innovations 89–93, 95, 97–98, 117; limitations of 99–101; minimal regulation, belief in 97; narrative constructs 95–98; and permissionless innovation/ precautionary principle 88, 97; preferences 95–98; protecting technological development, belief in 91–92, 94, 96, 98, 109–110; rationale of advocates for 89–92, 94–95; relationship between technology and society 102–105, 107, 108; role in deliberative democracy 111, 113, 114; and social constructivism 103, 107; societal change, technocrats' belief in 88–109; technological momentum 105–106, 110–111; theory 111; undermining unquestioned acceptability of 132; values behind 96; *see also* innovations; permissionless innovation and precautionary principle; technocracy and expert/specialized knowledge; technological continuum; technological means; technology industry

technological means 47, 49, 51, 52; advancements in 76; blockchain technology 168; cautions relating to 49, 51, 52, 61; entrenchment of 71; facilitating interactions/citizen engagement 43, 44, 51; first-generation 78; integration of 27, 55, 78; proliferation, as a longitudinal process 39; *see also* E-Governance; E-Government; ICTs (information and communication technology); technology industry

technological momentum 105–106, 110–111

technology industry 92, 98, 267; degree of freedom for 115–116; opposing perceptions of preferred role of government in regulating 114–117; political environment protective of 93, 94, 103, 104–105, 107,

109–110; potential role of precautionary principle and narrative analysis 131–136; proof of technology-based harm 121; protectionist approach, rationale for 92, 94, 95, 109, 116, 120, 128; reactionary vs. preemptive approach to regulating 119–121, 133, 138; self-regulation 115, 120; *see also* E-Governance; E-Government; ICTs (information and communication technology); technological determinism; technological means

Temporary Assistance for Needy Families (TANF) 66

Texas: cryptocurrency industry, regulation of 251, 258–260, 267; cryptocurrency seen as speculative investment 259, 267; Department of Banking 258; Supervisory Memorandum 1037, Regulatory Treatment of Virtual Currencies 258

Texas Finance Code Chapter 151 258

Texas Money Services Act 258, 259

theory: discourse-theoretical methodology 20; permissionless innovation 124; public choice 14, 28; technological determinism 111; value of money 145, 146

timestamping 171, 172, 195

tokenism 23

transaction fees, virtual currency 153, 175; Bitcoin 183–184, 195, 196; credit-card companies, compared with 184

transparency 109, 185; cryptocurrency industry, regulation of 232, 242, 244, 254, 267; deliberative democracy 24, 25, 33; E-Government and E-Governance 38, 45, 68; narrative analysis and permissionless innovation 124, 136

Trotta, A. 20–21, 22, 25, 37, 56–57, 62

trust: in political systems, decline in 3–4, 136; in the public sector 5, 6, 52, 55; restoring 5

United States: Bitcoin production 218; Constitution/Congress 154–162; courts 220, 222, 234; deliberative democracy (*see* deliberative democracy); Department of Education 66; Department of Financial Protection and Innovation (DFPI), California 256; Department of Homeland Security (DHS) 219, 223; Department of Housing and Urban Development 66; Department of Justice 178; Department of the Treasury (*see* Department of the Treasury); dynamic nature of policymaking in 212–213; federal agencies 211; Federal Communications Commission (FCC) 59–60; federal government and cryptocurrency industry 224–249; federal system (*see* federal system, U.S.); Federal Trade Commission 210, 226, 236–240; fiat currency 184, 185, 189, 190; Financial Crimes and Enforcement Network (FinCEN) (*see* Financial Crimes and Enforcement Network (FinCEN)); Internal Revenue Service (IRS) (*see* Internal Revenue Service (IRS), U.S.); Mint 159, 160; New York Department of Financial Resources (NYDFS) 251–256; non-fiat virtual currency, legal tender issues 147–151, 168; political system (*see* political system, U.S.); regulatory environment 210–219; Security and Exchange Commission (SEC) (*see* Security and Exchange Commission (SEC)); stock exchanges 224; U.S. Mint 241

universal service 59–60

Index **291**

unlicensed sellers, cryptocurrency 235
unsolicited offers, cryptocurrency 234

Van Dijik, J. A. G. M. 53
ViaBTC (Bitcoin mining pool) 218
Virga, J. M. 147, 150, 152
virtual currency, non-fiat 141, 148,
163, 211, 223, 244, 246, 251;
attractions for the unbanked
153; benefits of use 152–153;
and Bitcoin 208; in California
256–257, 266–267; and
concept of money 148, 149,
266; concerns regarding 150,
152, 153, 156, 157, 163, 178,
187, 188, 195, 199, 204, 207,
215, 220, 232, 233, 241, 243,
250, 266; constitutional threats
150, 157–158; convertibility
149, 150, 151, 163, 247, 248,
249; counterfeiting, protection
against 207, 208; criminality
243; cryptocurrency as a form
of 152, 154, 155, 157, 269;
defining 149; definitional
parameters 150, 151, 229,
260; electronically transacted
versions 163; equivalent value
in real currency 149–150;
exchange of 230, 247;
exemptions from tax 262;
fair market value 228, 229;
fiscal relevancy 150; generic
247; growth of 163, 243,
258; guerilla marketing 186;
illegalities 248; increasing
opportunity to utilize 150–151;
instability 151; leveraging of
153; licensing requirements
252, 253; manifestations of
154; medium of exchange 152,
194; micropayments, facilitating
152, 153; mimicking money
150; mining of 229, 230;
not counting as legal tender
147–151, 168, 172, 184; peer-
to-peer 170–172, 181, 195,
233; prevention of criminal acts
243; pros and cons 151–153,
154, 156; regulation issues
151, 152, 153, 163, 213, 214,
263; replaceability 151; rise

of 215; statutory regulation
269; and taxation 228,
229, 230, 262; and terrorist
groups 215, 243; as threat
to Congress 161; transaction
fees 153, 175, 183, 184,
195, 196; types 161; and the
"unbanked"/"underbanked"
152; used in place of fiat money
151; users of 247; Virtual
Currency Business Activity 252;
see also Bitcoin; cryptocurrency;
cryptocurrency industry,
regulation of; fiat currency
voting 15, 43, 44, 74; records 66, 73
Vullo, M. T. 254

Web 1.0 technologies: citizen
engagement 70; decision-
making 69; facilitating
E-Government activities 62,
75; "first movers" 70; ICTs'
usage of 70; information
dissemination 65–66, 67, 72;
initial stage of development 62–
63, 71–72; limitations of 63,
78; proliferation of 62, 63, 67,
70, 72; *see also* E-Government;
information
Web 2.0 technologies 62–72; citizen
engagement 68, 78; decision-
making 69; defining 63;
development 64, 73; discursive
events, creating 75; enhanced
levels of interaction 63–64;
expansion of 72; facilitating
E-Governance activities 62, 71;
ICT-associated 45; interactions,
greater level of 78–79;
interactive nature of 65, 68,
72; proliferation of 72; public-
sector usage 77–78; usage of
79–80; *see also* E-Governance;
ICTs (information and
communication technology)
West, D. M. 40–41
whole-of-government approach,
policy-making 13–14, 17;
cryptocurrency industry,
regulation of 220, 221, 224,
248, 249, 261; and digital
divide 56, 67

292 Index

Wickman, F. 2
Wolfson, R. 232, 261
World Wide Web 71; creation of 36; *see also* Web 1.0 technologies; Web 2.0 technologies
Wyoming: coal production 263, 264; cryptocurrency industry, regulation of 251, 260–265; energy sources 262, 263, 264; House Bill 19 (HB19) 262, 263; House Bill 70 (HB70) 261, 262, 263; House Bill 101 (HB101) 262, 263; House Bill 126 (HB126) 262, 263; hydro power 263; Money Transmitters Act 263; natural gas 263, 264; policy actions to benefit cryptocurrency industry 223, 224; public policy 264; Senate File 0111 (SF 0111)) 262, 263; State Legislature 262, 263, 264; Utility Token Act 263; wind power 264

Xu, H. 45, 63, 64

Printed in the United States
by Baker & Taylor Publisher Services